Alexander Hamilton:
The True and Romantic Story
of America's Greatest Statesman

—⁓—

Special Collector's Edition

Gertrude Franklin Atherton

Library House Books
www.libraryhousebooks.com
Paramount, CA

Library of Congress Cataloging-in-Publication
Alexander Hamilton: The True and Romantic Story
of America's Greatest Statesman
by Gertrude Franklin Atherton
Special Library Edition
ISBN: 978-1-936828-59-3 (Softcover)

First Collector's Edition 2018

CONTENTS

—⟋⟋⟍—

EXPLANATION

—⚏—

It was my original intention to write a biography of Alexander Hamilton in a more flexible manner than is customary with that method of reintroducing the dead to the living, but without impinging upon the territory of fiction. But after a visit to the British and Danish West Indies in search of the truth regarding his birth and ancestry, and after a wider acquaintance with the generally romantic character of his life, to say nothing of the personality of this most endearing and extraordinary of all our public men, the instinct of the novelist proved too strong; I no sooner had pen in hand than I found myself working in the familiar medium, although preserving the historical sequence. But, after all, what is a character novel but a dramatized biography? We strive to make our creations as real to the world as they are to us. Why, then, not throw the graces of fiction over the sharp hard facts that historians have laboriously gathered? At all events, this infinitely various story of Hamilton appealed too strongly to my imagination to be frowned aside, so here, for better or worse, is the result. Nevertheless, and although the method may cause the book to read like fiction, I am conscientious in asserting that almost every important incident here related of his American career is founded on documentary or published facts or upon family tradition; the few that are not have their roots among the probabilities, and suggested themselves. As for the West Indian part, although I was obliged to work upon the bare skeleton I unearthed in the old Common Records and Church Registers, still the fact remains that I did find the skeleton, which I have emphasized as far as is artistically possible. No date is given nor deed referred to that cannot be found by other visitors to the Islands. Moreover, I made a careful study of these Islands as they were in the time of Hamilton and his maternal ancestors, that I might be enabled to exercise one of the leading principles of the novelist, which is to create character not only out of certain well-known facts of heredity, but out of understood conditions. In this case I had, in addition, an extensive knowledge of Hamilton's

2

character to work backward from, as well as his estimate of the friends of his youth and of his mother. Therefore I feel confident that I have held my romancing propensity well within the horizon of the probabilities; at all events, I have depicted nothing which in any way interferes with the veracity of history. However, having unburdened my imagination, I shall, in the course of a year or two, write the biography I first had in mind. No writer, indeed, could assume a more delightful task than to chronicle, in any form, Hamilton's stupendous services to this country and his infinite variety.

G.F.A.

NEVIS

In the eighteenth century Nevis was known as The Mother of the English Leeward Caribbees. A Captain-General ruled the group in the name of the King, but if he died suddenly, his itinerant duties devolved upon the Governor of Nevis until the crown heard of its loss and made choice of another to fill that high and valued office. She had a Council and a House of Assembly, modelled in miniature upon the Houses of Peers and Commons; and was further distinguished as possessing the only court in the English Antilles where pirates could be tried. The Council was made up of ten members appointed by the Captain-General, but commanded by "its own particular and private Governor." The freeholders of the Island chose twenty-four of their number to represent them in the House of Assembly; and the few chronicles of that day agree in asserting that Nevis during her hundred proud years of supremacy was governed brilliantly and well. But the careful administration of good laws contributed in part only to the celebrity of an Island which to-day, still British as she is, serves but as a pedestal for the greatest of American statesmen. In these old days she was a queen as well as a mother. Her planters were men of immense wealth and lived the life of grandees. Their cane-fields covered the mountain on all its sides and subsidiary peaks, rising to the very fringe of the cold forest on the cone of a volcano long since extinct. The "Great Houses," built invariably upon an eminence that commanded a view of the neighbouring islands.—St. Christopher, Antigua, Montserrat,—were built of blocks of stone so square and solid and with a masonry so perfect that one views their ruins in amazement to-day. They withstood hurricanes, earthquakes, floods, and tidal waves. They were impregnable fortresses against rioting negroes and spasmodically aggressive Frenchmen. They even survived the abolition of slavery, and the old gay life went on for many years. English people, bored or in search of health, came for the brilliant winter, delighted with the hospitality of the planters, and to renew their vitality in the famous climate and sulphur baths, which, of all her possessions, Time has spared to Nevis. And then, having weathered all the ills to which even a West Indian Island can be subject, she succumbed—to the price of sugar. Her great families drifted away one by one. Her estates were given over to the agent for a time, finally to the mongoose. The magnificent stone mansions, left without even a caretaker, yielded helplessly to the diseases of age, and the first hurricane entering unbarred windows carried their roofs to the sea. In Charles Town, the capital since the submergence of James Town in 1680, are the remains of large town houses and fine old stone walls, which one can hardly see from the roadstead, so thick are the royal palms and the cocoanut trees among the ruins, wriggling their slender bodies through every crevice and flaunting their glittering luxuriance above every broken wall.

But in the days when the maternal grandparents of Alexander Hamilton looked down a trifle upon those who dwelt on other isles, Nevis recked of future insignificance as little as a beauty dreams of age. In the previous century England, after the mortification of the Royalists by Cromwell, had sent to Nevis Hamiltons, Herberts, Russells, and many another refugee from her historic houses. With what money they took with them they founded the great estates of the eighteenth century, and their sons sent their own children to Europe to become accomplished men and women. Government House was a miniature court, as gay and splendid as its offices were busy with the commerce of the world. The Governor and his lady drove about the Island in a carriage of state, with outriders and postilions in livery. When the Captain-General came he outshone his proud second by the gorgeousness of his uniform only, and both dignitaries were little more imposing than the planters themselves. It is true that the men, despite their fine clothes and powdered perukes, preferred a horse's back to the motion of a lumbering coach, but during the winter season their wives and daughters, in the shining stuffs, the pointed bodices, the elaborate head-dress of Europe, visited Government House and their neighbours with all the formality of London or Bath. After the first of March the planters wore white linen; the turbaned black women were busy among the stones of the rivers with voluminous wardrobes of cambric and lawn.

Several estates belonged to certain offshoots of the ducal house of Hamilton, and in the second decade of the eighteenth century Walter

5

Hamilton was Captain-General of the English Leeward Caribbees and "Ordinary of the Same." After him came Archibald Hamilton, who was, perhaps, of all the Hamiltons the most royal in his hospitality. Moreover, he was a person of energy and ambition, for it is on record that he paid a visit to Boston, fleeing from the great drought which visited Nevis in 1737. Then there were William Leslie Hamilton, who practised at the bar in London for several years, but returned to hold official position on Nevis, and his brother Andrew, both sons of Dr. William Hamilton, who spent the greater part of his life on St. Christopher. There were also Hugh Hamilton, Charles, Gustavus, and William Vaughn Hamilton, all planters, most of them Members of Council or of the Assembly.

And even in those remote and isolated days, Hamiltons and Washingtons were associated. The most popular name in our annals appears frequently in the Common Records of Nevis, and there is no doubt that when our first President's American ancestor fled before Cromwell to Virginia, a brother took ship for the English Caribbees.

From a distance Nevis looks like a solitary peak in mid-ocean, her base sweeping out on either side. But behind the great central cone— rising three thousand two hundred feet—are five or six lesser peaks, between which are dense tropical gorges and mountain streams. In the old days, where the slopes were not vivid with the light green of the cane-field, there were the cool and sombre groves of the cocoanut tree, mango, orange, and guava.

Even when Nevis is wholly visible there is always a white cloud above her head. As night falls it becomes evident that this soft aggravation of her beauty is but a night robe hung on high. It is at about seven in the evening that she begins to draw down her garment of mist, but she is long in perfecting that nocturnal toilette. Lonely and neglected, she still is a beauty, exacting and fastidious. The cloud is tortured into many shapes before it meets her taste. She snatches it off, redisposes it, dons and takes it off again, wraps it about her with yet more enchanting folds, until by nine o'clock it sweeps the sea; and Nevis, the proudest island of the Caribbees, has secluded herself from those cynical old neighbours who no longer bend the knee.

BOOK I
RACHAEL LEVINE

—୨ୠ—

I

Nevis gave of her bounty to none more generously than to John and Mary Fawcett. In 1685 the revocation of the Edict of Nantes had sent the Huguenots swarming to America and the West Indies. Faucette was but a boy when the Tropics gave him shelter, and learning was hard to get; except in the matter of carving Caribs. But he acquired the science of medicine somehow, and settled on Nevis, remodelled his name, and became a British subject. Brilliant and able, he was not long accumulating a fortune; there were swamps near Charles Town that bred fever, and the planters lived as high and suffered as acutely as the English squires of the same period. His wife brought him money, and in 1714 they received a joint legacy from Captain Frank Keynall; whether a relative of hers or a patient of his, the Records do not tell.

Mary Fawcett was some twenty years younger than her husband, a high-spirited creature, with much intelligence, and a will which in later years John Fawcett found himself unable to control. But before that period, when to the disparity in time were added the irritabilities of age in the man and the imperiousness of maturity in the woman, they were happy in their children, in their rising fortunes, and, for a while, in one another.

For twenty-eight years they lived the life of the Island. They built a Great House on their estate at Gingerland, a slope of the Island which faces Antigua, and they had their mansion in town for use when the Captain-General was abiding on Nevis. While Mary Fawcett was bringing up and marrying her children, managing the household affairs of a large estate, and receiving and returning the visits of the other grandees of the Island, to say nothing of playing her important part in all social functions, life went well enough. Her children, far away from the swamps of Charles Town, throve in the trade winds which temper the sun of Nevis and make it an isle of delight. When they were not studying with their governesses, there were groves and gorges to play in, ponies to ride, and monkeys and land crabs to hunt. Later came the gay life of the Capital, the routs at Government House, frequent even when the Chief was elsewhere, the balls at neighbouring estates, the picnics in the cool high forests, or where more tropical trees and tree ferns grew thick, the constant meeting with distinguished strangers, and the visits to other islands.

The young Fawcetts married early. One went with her husband, Peter Lytton, to the island of St. Croix. The Danish Government, upon obtaining possession of this fertile island, in 1733, immediately issued an invitation to the planters of the Leeward Caribbees to immigrate, tempting many who were dissatisfied with the British Government or wished for larger estates than they could acquire on their own populous islands. Members of the Lytton, Mitchell, and Stevens families of St. Christopher were among the first to respond to the liberal offer of the Danish Government. The two sons of James Lytton, Peter and James, grew up on St. Croix, Danish by law, British in habit and speech; and both married women of Nevis. Peter was the first to wed, and his marriage to young Mary Fawcett was the last to be celebrated in the Great House at Gingerland.

When Peter Lytton and his wife sailed away, as other sons and other daughters had sailed before, to return to Nevis rarely,—for those were the days of travel unveneered,—John and Mary Fawcett were left alone: their youngest daughter, she who afterward became the wife of Thomas Mitchell of St. Croix, was at school in England.

By this time Dr. Fawcett had given up his practice and was living on his income. He took great interest in his cane-fields and mills, and in the culture of limes and pine-apples; but in spite of his outdoor life his temper soured and he became irritable and exacting. Gout settled in him as a permanent reminder of the high fortunes of his middle years, and when the Gallic excitability of his temperament, aggravated by a half-century of hot weather, was stung to fiercer expression by the twinges of his disease, he was an abominable companion for a woman twenty years closer to youth.

In the solitudes of the large house Mary Fawcett found life unendurable. Still handsome, naturally gay of temper, and a brilliant figure in society, she frequently deserted her elderly husband for weeks at a time. The day came when he peremptorily forbade her to leave the place without him. For a time she submitted, for although a woman of uncommon independence of spirit, it was not until 1740 that she broke free of traditions and astonished the island of Nevis. She shut herself up with her books and needlework, attended to her house and domestic negroes with the precision of long habit, saw her friends when she could, and endured the exactions of her husband with only an occasional but mighty outburst.

It was in these unhappy conditions that Rachael Fawcett was born.

II

The last affliction the Fawcetts expected was another child. This little girl came an unwelcome guest to a mother who hated the father, and to Dr. Fawcett, not only because he had outgrown all liking for crying babies, but because, as in his excited disturbance he admitted to his wife, his fortune was reduced by speculations in London, and he had no desire to turn to in his old age and support another child. Then Mary Fawcett made up her definite mind: she announced her intention to leave her husband while it was yet possible to save her property for herself and the child to whom she soon became passionately attached. Dr. Fawcett laughed and shut himself up in a wing where the sounds of baby distress could not reach him; and it is doubtful if his glance ever lingered on the lovely face of his youngest born. Thus came into the world under the most painful conditions one of the unhappiest women that has lived. It was her splendid destiny to become the mother of the greatest American of his centuries, but this she died too soon to know, and she accomplished her part with an immediate bitterness of lot which was remorselessly ordained, no doubt, by the great Law of Compensation.

There were no divorce laws on the Islands in the eighteenth century, not even an act for separate maintenance; but Mary Fawcett was a woman of resource. It took her four years to accomplish her purpose, but she got rid of Dr. Fawcett by making him more than anxious to be rid of her. The Captain-General, William Matthew, was her staunch friend and admirer, and espoused her cause to the extent of issuing a writ of supplicavit for a separate maintenance. Dr. Fawcett gradually yielded to pressure, separated her property from his, that it might pass

9

under her personal and absolute control, and settled on her the sum of fifty-three pounds, four shillings annually, as a full satisfaction for all her dower or third part of his estate.

Mistress Fawcett was no longer a woman of consequence, for even her personal income was curtailed by the great drought of 1737, and Nevis, complaisant to the gallantry of the age, was scandalized at the novelty of a public separation. But she was free, and she was the woman to feel that freedom to her finger tips; she could live a life with no will in it but her own, and she could bring up her little girl in an atmosphere of peace and affection. She moved to an estate she owned on St. Christopher and never saw John Fawcett again. He died a few years later, leaving his diminished property to his children. Rachael's share was the house in Charles Town.

The spot on which Rachael spent her childhood and brief youth was one of the most picturesque on the mountain range of St. Christopher. Facing the sea, the house stood on a lofty eminence, in the very shadow of Mount Misery. Immediately behind the house were the high peaks of the range, hardly less in pride than the cone of the great volcano. The house was built on a ledge, but one could step from the terrace above into an abrupt ravine, wrenched into its tortuous shape by earthquake and flood, but dark for centuries with the immovable shades of a virgin tropical forest. The Great House, with its spacious open galleries and verandahs, was surrounded with stone terraces, overflowing with the intense red and orange of the hybiscus and croton bush, the golden browns and softer yellows of less ambitious plants, the sensuous tints of the orchid, the high and glittering beauties of the palm and cocoanut. The slopes to the coast were covered with cane-fields, their bright young greens sharp against the dark blue of the sea. The ledge on which the house was built terminated suddenly in front, but extended on the left along a line of cliff above a chasm, until it sloped to the road. On this flat eminence was an avenue of royal palms, which, with the dense wood on the hill above it, was to mariners one of the most familiar landmarks of the Island of "St. Kitts." From her verandah Mary Fawcett could see, far down to the right, a large village of negro huts, only the thatched African roofs visible among the long leaves of the cocoanut palms with which the blacks invariably surround their dwellings. Beyond was Brimstone Hill with its impregnable fortress. And on the left, far out at sea, her purple heights and palm-fringed shores deepening the exquisite blue of the Caribbean by day, a white ever changing spirit in the twilight, and no more vestige of her under the stars than had she sunk whence she came—Nevis. Mary Fawcett never set foot on her again, but she learned to sit and study her with a whimsical affection which was one of the few liberties she allowed her imagination. But if the unhappiest years of her life had been spent there, so had her fairest. She had loved her brilliant husband in her youth, and all the social triumphs of a handsome and fortunate young woman had been hers. In the deep calm which now intervened between the two mental hurricanes of her life, she sometimes wondered if she had exaggerated her past afflictions; and before she died she knew how insignificant the tragedy of her own life had been.

Although Rachael was born when her parents were past their prime, the vitality that was in her was concentrated and strong. It was not enough to give her a long life, but while it lasted she was a magnificent creature, and the end was abrupt; there was no slow decay. During her childhood she lived in the open air, for except in the cold nights of a brief winter only the jalousies were closed; and on that high shelf even the late summer and early autumn were not insufferable. Exhausted as the trade winds become, they give what little strength is in them to the heights of their favourite isles, and during the rest of the year they are so constant, even when storms rage in the North Atlantic, that Nevis and St. Christopher never feel the full force of the sun, and the winter nights are cold.

Rachael was four years old when her parents separated, and grew to womanhood remembering nothing of her father and seeing little of her kin, scattered far and wide. Her one unmarried sister, upon her return from England, went almost immediately to visit Mrs. Lytton, and married Thomas Mitchell, one of the wealthiest planters of St. Croix. Mary Fawcett's children had not approved her course, for they remembered their father as the most indulgent and charming of men, whose frequent tempers were quickly forgotten; and year by year she became more wholly devoted to the girl who clung to her with a passionate and uncritical affection.

Clever and accomplished herself, and quick with ambition for her best beloved child, she employed the most cultivated tutors on the

Island to instruct her in English, Latin, and French. Before Rachael was ten years old, Mistress Fawcett had the satisfaction to discover that the little girl possessed a distinguished mind, and took to hard study, and to *les graces*, as naturally as she rode a pony over the hills or shot the reef in her boat.

For several years the women of St. Christopher held aloof, but many of the planters who had been guests at the Great House in Gingerland called on Mistress Fawcett at once, and proffered advice and service. Of these William Hamilton and Archibald Hamn became her staunch and intimate friends. Mr. Hamn's estate adjoined hers, and his overlooker relieved her of much care. Dr. James Hamilton, who had died in the year preceding her formal separation, had been a close friend of her husband and herself, and his brother hastened with assurance of his wish to serve her. He was one of the eminent men of the Island, a planter and a member of Council; also, a "doctor of physic." He carried Rachael safely through her childhood complaints and the darkest of her days; and if his was the hand which opened the gates between herself and history, who shall say in the light of the glorified result that its master should not sleep in peace?

In time his wife called, and his children and stepchildren brought a new experience into the life of Rachael. She had been permitted to gambol occasionally with the "pic'nees" of her mother's maids, but since her fourth year had not spoken to a white child until little Catherine Hamilton came to visit her one morning and brought Christiana Huggins of Nevis. Mistress Huggins had known Mary Fawcett too well to call with Mistress Hamilton, but sent Christiana as a peace offering. Mary's first disposition was to pack the child off while Mistress Hamilton was offering her embarrassed explanations; but Rachael clung to her new treasure with such shrieks of protest that her mother, disconcerted by this vigour of opposition to her will, permitted the intruder to remain.

The wives of other planters followed Mistress Hamilton, for in that soft voluptuous climate, where the rush and fret of great cities are but a witch's tale, disapproval dies early. They would have called long since had they not been a trifle in awe of Nevis, more, perhaps, of Mistress Fawcett's sharp tongue, then indolent. But when Mistress Hamilton suddenly reminded them that they were Christians, and that Dr. Fawcett was dead, they put on their London gowns, ordered out their coaches, and called. Mary Fawcett received them with a courteous indifference. Her resentment had died long since, and they seemed to her, with their coaches and brocades and powdered locks, but the ghosts of the Nevis of her youth. Her child, her estate, and her few tried friends absorbed her. For the sake of her daughter's future, she ordered out her ancient coach and made the round of the Island once a year. The ladies of St. Kitts were as moderately punctilious.

And so the life of Rachael Fawcett for sixteen years passed uneventfully enough. Her spirits were often very high, for she inherited the Gallic buoyancy of her father as well as the brilliant qualities of his mind. In the serious depths of her nature were strong passions and a tendency to melancholy, the result no doubt of the unhappy conditions of her birth. But her mother managed so to occupy her eager ambitious mind with hard study that the girl had little acquaintance with herself. Her English studies were almost as varied as a boy's, and in addition to her accomplishments in the ancient and modern languages, she painted, and sang, played the harp and guitar. Mary Fawcett, for reasons of her own, never let her forget that she was the most educated girl on the Islands.

"I never was one to lie on a sofa all day and fan myself, while my children sat on the floor with their blacks, and munched sugar-cane, or bread and sling," she would remark superfluously. "All my daughters are a credit to their husbands; but I mean that you shall be the most brilliant woman in the Antilles."

The immediate consequences of Rachael's superior education were two: her girl friends ceased to interest her, and ambitions developed in her strong imaginative brain. In those days women so rarely distinguished themselves individually that it is doubtful if Rachael had ever heard of the phenomenon, and the sum of her worldly aspirations was a wealthy and intellectual husband who would take her to live and to shine at foreign courts. Her nature was too sweet and her mind too serious for egoism or the pettier vanities, but she hardly could help being conscious of the energy of her brain; and if she had passed through childhood in ignorance of her beauty, she barely had entered her teens when her happy indifference was dispelled; for the young planters besieged her gates.

13

Girls mature very early in the tropics, and at fourteen Rachael Fawcett was the unresponsive toast from Basseterre to Sandy Point. Her height was considerable, and she had the round supple figure of a girl who has lived the out-door life in moderation; full of strength and grace, and no exaggeration of muscle. She had a fine mane of reddish fair hair, a pair of sparkling eager gray eyes which could go black with passion or even excited interest, a long nose so sensitively cut that she could express any mood she chose with her nostrils, which expanded quite alarmingly when she flew into a temper, and a full well-cut mouth. Her skin had the whiteness and transparency peculiar to the women of St. Kitts and Nevis; her head and brow were nobly modelled, and the former she carried high to the day of her death. It was set so far back on her shoulders and on a line so straight that it would look haughty in her coffin. What wonder that the young planters besieged her gates, that her aspirations soared high, that Mary Fawcett dreamed of a great destiny for this worshipped child of her old age? As for the young planters, they never got beyond the gates, for a dragon stood there. Mistress Fawcett had no mind to run the risk of early entanglements. When Rachael was old enough she would be provided with a distinguished husband from afar, selected by the experienced judgement of a woman of the world.

But Mary Fawcett, still hot-headed and impulsive in her second half-century, was more prone to err in crises than her daughter. In spite of the deeper passions of her nature, Rachael, except when under the lash of strong excitement, had a certain clearness of insight and deliberation of judgement which her mother lacked to her last day.

III

Rachael had just eaten the last of her sixteenth birthday sweets when, at a ball at Government House, she met John Michael Levine. It was her début; she was the fairest creature in the room, and, in the idiom of Dr. Hamilton, the men besieged her as were she Brimstone Hill in possession of the French. The Governor and the Captain General had asked her to dance, and even the women smiled indulgently, disarmed by so much innocent loveliness.

Levine, albeit a Dane, and as colourless as most of his countrymen, was her determined suitor before the night was half over. It may be that he was merely dazzled by the regal position to which the young men had elevated her, and that his cold blood quickened at the thought of possessing what all men desired, but he was as immediate and persistent in his suit as any excitable creole in the room. But Rachael gave him scant attention that night. She may have been intellectual, but she was also a girl, and it was her first ball. She was dazzled and happy, delighted with her conquests, oblivious to the depths of her nature.

The next day Levine, strong in the possession of a letter from Mr. Peter Lytton,—for a fortnight forgotten,—presented himself at Mistress Fawcett's door, and was admitted. The first call was brief and perfunctory, but he came the next day and the next. Rachael, surprised, but little interested, and longing for her next ball, strummed the harp at her mother's command and received his compliments with indifference. A week after his first call Mary Fawcett drove into town and spent an hour with the Governor. He told her that Levine had brought him a personal letter from the Governor of St. Croix, and that he was wealthy and well born. He was also, in his Excellency's opinion, a distinguished match even for the most beautiful and accomplished girl on the Island. Peter Lytton had mentioned in his letter that Levine purposed buying an estate on St. Croix and settling down to the life of a planter. On the following day Levine told her that already he was half a West Indian, so fascinated was he with the life and the climate, but that if she would favour his suit he would take Rachael to Copenhagen as often as she wished for the life of the world.

Mary Fawcett made up her mind that he should marry Rachael, and it seemed to her that no mother had ever come to a wiser decision. Her health was failing, and it was her passionate wish not only to leave her child encircled by the protection of a devoted husband, but to realize the high ambitions she had cherished from the hour she foresaw that Rachael was to be an exceptional woman.

Levine had not seen Rachael on the morning when he asked for her hand, and he called two days later to press his suit and receive his answer. Mistress Fawcett told him that she had made up her own mind and would perform that office for Rachael at once, but thought it best that he should absent himself until the work was complete. Levine, promised an answer on the morrow, took himself off, and Mary Fawcett sent for her daughter.

Rachael entered the library with a piece of needlework in her hand.

Her mind was not on her books these days, for she had gone to another ball; but her hands had been too well brought up to idle, however her brain might dream. Mary Fawcett by this time wore a large cap with a frill, and her face, always determined and self-willed, was growing austere with years and much pain: she suffered frightfully at times with rheumatism, and her apprehension of the moment when it should attack her heart reconciled her to the prospect of brief partings from her daughter. Her eyes still burned with the fires of an indiminishable courage however; she read the yellow pages of her many books as rapidly as in her youth, and if there was a speck of dust on her mahogany floors, polished with orange juice, she saw it. Her negroes adored her but trembled when she raised her voice, and Rachael never had disobeyed her. She expected some dissatisfaction, possibly a temper, but no opposition.

Rachael smiled confidently and sat down. She wore one of the thin white linens, which, like the other women of the Islands, she put aside for heavier stuffs on state occasions only, and her hair had tumbled from its high comb and fallen upon her shoulders. Mary Fawcett sighed as she looked at her. She was too young to marry, and had it not been for the haunting terror of leaving her alone in the world, the Dane, well circumstanced as he was, would have been repulsed with contumely.

"Rachael," said her mother, gently, "put down your tapestry. I have something to say to you, something of great import."

Rachael dropped her work and met her mother's eyes. They were hard with will and definite purpose. In an instant she divined what was coming, and stood up. Her face could not turn any whiter, but her eyes were black at once, and her nostrils spread.

"It cannot be possible that you wish me to marry that man— Levine," she stammered. "I do not know how I can think of such a thing—but I do—it seems to me I see it in your eyes."

"Yes," said her mother, with some uneasiness. "I do; and my reasons are good—"

"I won't listen to them!" shrieked Rachael. "I won't marry him! His whiteness makes me sick! I know he is not a good man! I feel it! I never could be happy with him! I never could love him!"

Mary Fawcett looked at her aghast, and, for a moment, without answering; she saw her own will asserting itself, heard it on those piercing notes, and she knew that it sprang from stronger and more tragic foundations than had ever existed in her own nature; but believing herself to be right, she determined to prevail.

"What do you know about men, my darling?" she said soothingly. "You have been dreaming romantic dreams, and young Levine does not resemble the hero. That is all. Women readjust themselves marvellously quick. When you are married to him, and he is your tender and devoted husband, you will forget your prince—who, no doubt, is dark and quite splendid. But we never meet our princes, my dear, and romantic love is only one of the things we live for—and for that we live but a little while. Levine is all that I could wish for you. He is wealthy, aristocratic, and chivalrously devoted."

Her long speech had given her daughter time to cool, but Rachael remained standing, and stared defiantly into the eyes which had relaxed somewhat with anxious surprise.

"I *feel* that he is not a good man," she repeated sullenly, "and I hate him. I should die if he touched me. I have not danced with him. His hands are so white and soft, and his eyes never change, and his mouth reminds me of a shark's."

"Levine is a remarkably handsome man," exclaimed Mistress Fawcett, indignantly. "You have trained your imagination to some purpose, it seems. Forget your poets when he comes to-morrow, and look at him impartially. And cannot he give you all that you so much desire, my ambitious little daughter? Do you no longer want to go to Europe? to court? to be *grande dame* and converse with princes?"

"Oh, yes," said Rachael. "I want that as much as ever; but I want to love the man. I want to be happy."

"Well, *do* love him," exclaimed her mother with energy. "Your father was twenty years older than myself, and a Frenchman, but I made up my mind to love him, and I did—for a good many years."

"You had to leave him in the end. Do you wish me to do the same?"

"You will do nothing of the kind. There never was but one John Fawcett."

"I don't love this Levine, and I never shall love him. I don't believe at all that that kind of feeling can be created by the brain, that it responds to nothing but the will. I shall not love that way. I may be ignorant, but I know that."

17

"You have read too much Shakespeare! Doubtless you imagine yourself one of his heroines—Juliet? Rosalind?"

"I have never imagined myself anybody but Rachael Fawcett. I *cannot* imagine myself Rachael Levine. But I know something of myself—I have read and thought enough for that. I could love someone—but not this bleached repulsive Dane. Why will you not let me wait? It is my right. No, you need not curl your lip—I am *not* a little girl. I may be sixteen. I may be without experience in the world, but you have been almost my only companion, and until just now I have talked with middle-aged men only, and much with them. I had no real childhood. You have educated my brain far beyond my years. To-day I feel twenty, and it seems to me that I see far down into myself—much deeper than you do. I tell you that if I marry this man, I shall be the most hopeless wretch on earth."

Mary Fawcett was puzzled and distressed, but she did not waver for a moment. The cleverest of girls could not know what was best for herself, and the mother who permitted her daughter to take her life into her own hands was a poor creature indeed.

"Listen, my dear child," she said tenderly, "you have always trusted in me, believed me. I *know* that this is a wise and promising marriage for you. And—" she hesitated, but it was time to play her trump. "You know that my health is not good, but you do not know how bad it is. Dr. Hamilton says that the rheumatism may fly to my heart at any moment, and I *must* see you married—"

She had ejaculated the last words; Rachael had shrieked, and flung herself upon her, her excitement at this sudden and cruel revelation bursting out in screams and sobs and a torrent of tears. Her mother had seen her excited and in brief ungovernable tempers, but she never had suspected that she was capable of such passion as this; and, much disturbed, she led her off to bed, and sent for her advisers, Archibald Hamn and Dr. Hamilton.

IV

Mr. Hamn responded at once to the widow's call, his adjacence giving him the advantage of Dr. Hamilton, of whom he was a trifle jealous. He was an old bachelor and had proposed to Mistress Fawcett— a captivating woman till her last hour—twice a year since her husband's death. But matrimony had been a bitter medicine for Mary after her imagination had ceased to sweeten it, and her invariable answer to her several suitors was the disquieting assertion that if ever she was so rash as to take another husband, she certainly should kill him. Archibald was not the man to conquer her prejudices, although she loved the sterling in him and attached him to her by every hook of friendship. He was a dark nervous little man, spare as most West Indians, used a deal of snuff, and had a habit of pushing back his wig with a jerking forearm when in heated controversy with Dr. Hamilton, or expounding matrimony to the widow.

Dr. Hamilton, for whose arrival Mr. Hamn was kept waiting,—Mistress Fawcett tarried until her daughter fell asleep,—was a large square man, albeit lean, and only less nervous than the widow's suitor. His white locks were worn in a queue, a few escaping to soften his big powerful face. Both men wore white linen, but Dr. Hamilton was rarely seen without his riding-boots, his advent, except in Mistress Fawcett's house, heralded by the clanking of spurs. Mary would have none of his spurs on her mahogany floors, and the doctor never yet had been able to dodge the darkey who stood guard at her doorstep.

The two men exchanged mild surmises as to the cause of the summons; but as similar summons occurred when newly wedded blacks were pounding each other's heads, provoked thereto by the galling chain of decency, or an obeah doctor had tied a sinister warning to Mistress Fawcett's knocker, neither of the gentlemen anticipated serious work. When Mary Fawcett entered the long room, however, both forgot the dignity of their years and position, and ran forward.

Dr. Hamilton lifted her as if she had been a palm leaf, and laid her on the sofa. He despatched Mr. Hamn for a glass of Spanish port, and forbade her to speak until he gave permission.

But Mary Fawcett made brief concessions to the weakness of the flesh.
She drank the wine, then sat up and told her story.

"Oh, Mary," said Dr. Hamilton, sadly, "why do you ask our advice? Your ear may listen, but never your mind. If it were a matter of business, we might even be allowed to act for you; but in a domestic—"

"What?" cried Mistress Fawcett; "have I not asked your advice a thousand times about Rachael, and have I not always taken it?"

19

"I recall many of the conversations, but I doubt if you could recall the advice. However, if you want it this time, I will give it to you. Don't force the girl to marry against her will—assuredly not if the man is repulsive to her. For all your brains you are a baby about men and women. Rachael knows more by instinct. She is an extraordinary girl, and should be allowed time to make her own choice. If you are afraid of death, leave her to me. I will legally adopt her now, if you choose—"

"Yes, and should you die suddenly, your wife would think Rachael one too many, what with your brood and the Edwardses to boot." Mistress Fawcett was nettled by his jibe at the limit of her wisdom. "I shall leave her with a husband. To that I have made up my mind. What have you to say, Archibald?"

This was an advantage which Mr. Hamn never failed to seize; he always agreed with the widow; Dr. Hamilton never did. Moreover, he was sincerely convinced that—save, perhaps, in matters of money—Mary Fawcett could not err.

"I like the appearance of this Dane," he said, reassuringly, "and his little country has a valiant history. This young man is quite prince-like in his bearing, and his extreme fairness is but one more evidence of his high breeding—"

"He looks like a shark's belly," interrupted Dr. Hamilton, "I don't wonder he sickens Rachael. I have nothing against him but his appearance, but if he came after Kitty I'd throw him out by the seat of his breeches."

"He never looked at Kitty, at Government House, nor at Mistress Montgomerie's," cried Mary. "You are jealous, Will, because Rachael has carried off the foreign prize."

Dr. Hamilton laughed, then added seriously, "I am too fond of the girl to forbear to give my advice. Let her choose her own husband. If you dare to cut out her future, as if it were one of her new frocks, you have more courage than I. She has more in her than twenty women. Let her alone for the next five years, then she will have no one to answer to but herself. Otherwise, my lady, you may find yourself holding your breath in a hurricane track, with no refuge from the storm you've whipped up but five feet underneath. If you won't give her to me, there are her sisters. They are all wealthy—"

"They are years older than Rachael and would not understand her at all."

"I can't see why they should not understand her as well as a strange man."

"He will be her husband, madly in love with her."

"Levine will never be madly in love with anybody. Besides, it would not matter to Rachael if her sisters did not understand her; she has too strong a brain not to be independent of the ordinary female nonsense; moreover, she has a fine disposition and her own property. But if her husband did not understand her,—in other words, if their tastes proved as opposite as their temperaments,—it would make a vast deal of difference. Sisters can be got rid of, but husbands—well, you know the difficulties."

"I will think over all you have said," replied Mary, with sudden humility; she had great respect for the doctor. "But don't you say a word to Rachael."

"I'm far too much afraid of you for that. But I wish that Will were home or Andrew old enough. I'd set one of them on to cut this Dane out. Well, I must go; send for me whenever you are in need of advice," and with a parting laugh he strode out of the house and roared to the darkey to come and fasten his spurs.

Archibald Hamn, who foresaw possibilities in the widow's loneliness, and who judged men entirely by their manners, remained to assure Mistress Fawcett of the wisdom of her choice, and to offer his services as mediator. Mary laughed and sent him home. She wrote to Levine not to call until she bade him, and for several days pondered deeply upon her daughter's opposition and Dr. Hamilton's advice. The first result of this perturbing distrust in her own wisdom was a violent attack of rheumatism in the region of her heart; and while she believed herself to be dying, she wrung from her distracted daughter a promise to marry Levine. She recovered from the attack, but concluded that, the promise being won, it would be folly to give it back. Moreover, the desire to see her daughter married had been aggravated by her brush with death, and after another interview with Levine, in which he promised all that the fondest mother could demand, she opened her chests of fine linen.

Rachael submitted. She dared not excite her mother. Her imagination, always vivid though it was, refused to picture the end she dreaded; and she never saw Levine alone. His descriptions of life in

21

Copenhagen interested her, and when her mother expatiated upon the glittering destiny which awaited her, ambition and pride responded, although precisely as they had done in her day dreams. She found herself visioning Copenhagen, jewels, brocades, and courtiers; but she realized only when she withdrew to St. Kitts, that Levine had not entered the dream, even to pass and bend the knee. Often she laughed aloud in merriment. As the wedding-day approached, she lost her breath more than once, and her skin chilled. During the last few days before the ceremony she understood for the first time that it was inevitable. But time—it was now three months since the needlewomen were set at the trousseau—and her unconscious acceptance of the horrid fact had trimmed her spirit to philosophy, altered the habit of her mind. She saw her mother radiant, received the personal congratulations of every family on the Island. Her sisters came from St. Croix, and made much of the little girl who was beginning life so brilliantly; beautiful silks and laces had come from New York, and Levine had given her jewels, which she tried on her maid every day because she thought the mustee's tawny skin enhanced their lustre. She was but a child in spite of her intellect. Her union with the Dane came to appear as one of the laws of life, and she finished by accepting it as one accepted an earthquake or a hurricane. Moreover, she was profoundly innocent.

V

Mary Fawcett accompanied the Levines to Copenhagen, but returned to St. Christopher by a ship which left Denmark a month later, being one of those women who picture their terrestrial affairs in a state of dissolution while deprived of their vigilance. She vowed that the North had killed her rheumatism, and turned an absent ear to Rachael's appeal to tarry until Levine was ready to return to St. Croix. She remained long enough in Denmark, however, to see her daughter presented at court, and installed with all the magnificence that an ambitious mother could desire. There was not a misgiving in her mind, for Rachael, if somewhat inanimate, could not be unhappy with an uxorious husband and the world at her feet; and although for some time after her marriage she had behaved like a naughty child caught in a trap, and been a sore trial to her mother and Mr. Levine, since her arrival in Copenhagen she had deported herself most becomingly and indulged in

22

no more tantrums. Levine had conducted himself admirably during his trying honeymoon. Upon his arrival in Copenhagen he had littered his wife's boudoir with valuable gifts, and exhibited the beauty he had won with a pride very gratifying to his mother-in-law. In six months he was to sail for his estates on St. Croix, and pay an immediate visit to St. Kitts, whence Mistress Fawcett would return with her daughter for a sojourn of several months. She returned to her silent home the envy of many Island mothers.

Rachael wrote by every ship, and Mary Fawcett pondered over these letters, at first with perplexity, finally with a deep uneasiness. Her daughter described life in Denmark, the court and society, her new gowns and jewels, her visits to country houses, the celebrities she met. But her letters were literary and impersonal, nor was there in them a trace of her old energy of mind and vivacity of spirit. She never mentioned Levine's name, nor made an intimate allusion to herself.

"Can she no longer love me?" thought Mary Fawcett at last and in terror; "this child that I have loved more than the husband of my youth and all the other children I have borne? It cannot be that she is unhappy. She would tell me so in a wild outburst—indeed she would have run home to me long since. Levine will never control her. Heaven knows what would have happened if I had not gone on that wedding-journey. But she settled down so sweetly, and I made sure she would have loved him by this. It is the only thing to do if you have to live with one of the pests. Perhaps that is it—she has given him all her love and has none left for me." And at this she felt so lonely and bitter that she almost accepted Archibald Hamn when he called an hour later. But in the excitement of his risen hopes his wig fell on the floor, and she took offence at his yellow and sparsely settled scalp.

There were few gleams of humour left in life for Mary Fawcett. Rachael's letters ceased abruptly. Her mother dared not sail for Denmark, lest she pass the Levines on their way to St. Croix. She managed to exist through two distracted months, then received a note from her daughter, Mrs. Mitchell.

"Rachael is Here," it ran, "but refuses to see Us. I do not know what to think. I drove over as soon as I heard of Their arrival. Levine received Me and was as Courteous and Polished as ever, but Rachael had a *Headache* and did not come out. Mary and I have been there Twice since, and with the *same* result. Levine assured us that he had begged her to see her Sisters, but that She is in a very *low* and *melancholy* state, owing doubtless to her Condition. He seemed much *concerned*, but More, I could not help thinking, because he feared to lose an Heir than from any *love* for my little Sister. Peter and Mary agree with Me, that *You had best come here* if You can."

Mary Fawcett, whatever her foibles, had never failed to spring upright under the stiffest blows of her life. Ignoring her physical pains, which had been aggravated by the mental terrors of the last two months, and sternly commanding the agony in her heart to be silent, she despatched a note at once to Dr. Hamilton,—Archibald Hamn was in Barbados,—asking him to charter a schooner, if no ship were leaving that day for the Danish Islands, and accompany her to St. Croix. He sent her word that they could sail on the following morning if the wind were favourable, and the black women packed her boxes and carried them on their heads to Basseterre.

That evening, as Mary Fawcett was slowly walking down the avenue, leaning heavily on her cane, too wretched to rest or sleep, a ship flying the German colours sailed past. She wondered if it had stopped at St. Croix, then forgot it in the terrible speculations which her will strove to hold apart from her nerves.

Wearied in body, she returned to the house and sat by the window of her room, striving to compose her mind for sleep. She was forcing herself to jot down instructions for her housekeeper, whom she had taught to read, when she heard a chaise and a pair of galloping horses enter the avenue. A moment later, Dr. Hamilton's voice was roaring for a slave to come and hold his horses. Then it lowered abruptly and did not cease.

Mary Fawcett knew that Rachael had come to her, and without her husband. For a moment she had a confused idea that the earth was rocking, and congratulated herself that the house was too high for a tidal wave to reach. Then Dr. Hamilton entered with Rachael in his arms and laid her on the bed. He left at once, saying that he would return in the morning. Mary Fawcett had not risen, and her chair faced the bed. Rachael lay staring at her mother until Mary found her voice and begged her to speak. She knew that her hunger must wait until she had stood at the bar and received her sentence.

Rachael told her mother the story of her married life from the day she had been left alone with John Levine,—a story of unimaginable horrors. Like many cold men to whom the pleasures of the world are, nevertheless, easy, Levine was a voluptuary and cruel. Had his child been safely born, there would have been no measure in his brutality. Rachael had watched for her opportunity, and one night when he had been at a state function in Christianstadt, too secure in her apparent apathy to lock her door, she had bribed a servant to drive her to Frederikstadt, and boarded the ship her maid had ascertained was about to leave. She knew that he would not follow her, for there was one person on earth he feared, and that was Mary Fawcett. He would not have returned to St. Croix, had his investments been less heavy; but on his estates he was lord, and had no mind that his mother-in-law should set foot on them while he had slaves to hold his gates.

Mary Fawcett listened to the horrid story, at first with a sort of frantic wonder, for of the evil of life she had known nothing; then her clear mind grasped it, her stoicism gave way, and she shrieked and raved in such agony of soul that she had no fear of hell thereafter. Rachael had to rise from the bed and minister to her, and the terrified blacks ran screaming about the place, believing that their mistress had been cursed.

She grew calm in time, but her face was puckered like an old apple, and her eyes had lost their brilliancy for ever. And it was days before she realized that her limbs still ached.

Rachael never opened her lips on the subject again. She went back to bed and clung to her mother and Dr. Hamilton until her child was born. Then for three months she recognized no one, and Dr. Hamilton, with all his skill, did not venture to say whether or not her mind would live again.

The child was a boy, and as blond as its father. Mary Fawcett stood its presence in the house for a month, then packed it off to St. Croix. She received a curt acknowledgment from Levine, and an intimation that she had saved herself much trouble. As for Rachael, he would have her back when he saw fit. She wrote an appeal to the Captain-General and he sent her word that the Danes would never bombard Brimstone Hill, and there was no other way by which Levine could get her daughter while one of her friends ruled the Leeward Caribbees.

Many thoughts flitted through the brain of Mary Fawcett during that long vigil. Her mind for the first time dwelt with kindness, almost with softness, on the memory of her husband. Beside this awful Dane his shadow was god-like. He had been high-minded and a gentleman in his worst tantrums, and there was no taint of viciousness in him. A doubt grew in her brain, grew to such disquieting proportions that she sometimes deserted Rachael abruptly and went out to fatigue herself in the avenue. Had she done wrong to leave him alone in his old age, to bear, undiverted, the burden of a disease whose torments she now could fully appreciate, to die alone in that great house with only his slaves to tend him? It had seemed to her when she left him that human nature could stand no more, and that she was justified; but she was an old woman now and knew that all things can be endured. When that picture of his desolate last years and lonely death had remorselessly shaped itself in her imagination, and she realized that it would hang there until her hands were folded, she suffered one more hour of agony and abasement, then caught at the stoicism of her nature, accepted her new dole, and returned to her daughter.

VI

Rachael's mind struggled past its eclipse, but her recovery was very slow. Even after she recognized her mother and Dr. Hamilton, she sat for months staring at Nevis, neither opening a book nor looking round upon the life about her. But she was only eighteen, and her body grew strong and vital again. Gradually it forced its energies into her brain, released her spirit from its apathy, buried memory under the fresher impressions of time. A year from the day of her return, if there were deep and subtle changes in her face and carriage, which added ten years to her appearance, she was more beautiful to experienced eyes than when she had flowered for the humming-birds. She took up her studies where she had dropped them, a little of her old buoyancy revived; and if her girlishness was buried with ideals and ambitions, her intellect was clear and strong and her character more finely balanced. She flew into no more rages, boxed her attendants' ears at rarer intervals, and the deliberation which had seemed an anomaly in her character before, became a dominant trait, and rarely was conquered by impulse. When it worked alone her mother laid down her weapons, edged as they still were, and when impulse flew to its back, Mary Fawcett took refuge in oblivion. But she made no complaint, for she and her daughter were more united than when the young girl had seemed more fit to be her grandchild.

The Governor of St. Christopher had written a letter to his friend, the Governor of St. Croix, which had caused that estimable functionary to forbid Levine the door of Government House. Levine could not endure social ostracism. He left St. Croix immediately, and took his son Peter with him. To this child Rachael never referred, and her mother doubted if she remembered anything associated with its impending birth. Perhaps she believed it dead. At all events, she made no sign. Except that she was called Mistress Levine, there was nothing in her outer life to remind her that for two years the markers in her favourite books had not been shifted. She had studied music and painting with the best masters in Copenhagen, and in the chests which were forwarded by her sisters from St. Croix, there were many new books. She refused to return to society, and filled her time without its aid; for not only did she have the ample resources of her mind, her mother, the frequent companionship of Dr. Hamilton and four or five other men of his age and attainments, but she returned to the out-door life with enthusiasm. On her spirit was an immovable shadow, in her mind an indelible stain, but she had strong common sense and a still stronger will. An experience which would have embittered a less complete nature, or sent a lighter woman to the gallantries of society, gave new force and energy to her character, even while saddening it. To the past she never willingly gave a thought; neither was she for a moment unconscious of its ghost.

VII

Two years passed. Rachael was twenty, a beautiful and stately creature, more discussed and less seen than any woman on the islands of Nevis and St. Christopher. Occasionally Christiana Huggins paid her a visit, or Catherine Hamilton rode over for the day; but although Christiana at least, loved her to the end, both were conscious of her superiority of mind and experience, and the old intimacy was not resumed.

Dr. Hamilton had used all his influence in the Council to promote a special bill of divorce, for he wanted Rachael to be free to marry again. He had no faith in the permanent resources of the intellect for a young and seductive woman, and he understood Rachael very thoroughly. The calm might be long, but unless Levine died or could be legally disposed of, she would give the Islands a heavier shock than when the innovation of Mary Fawcett had set them gabbling. Against the conservatism of his colleagues, however, he could make no headway, and both the Governor and Captain-General disapproved of a measure which England had never sanctioned.

But Dr. Hamilton and her mother were more disturbed at the failure of the bill than Rachael. Time had lifted the shadow of her husband from the race, but, never having loved, even a little, her imagination modelled no pleasing features upon the ugly skull of matrimony. It is true that she sometimes thought of herself as a singularly lonely being, and allowed her mind to picture love and its companionships. As time dimmed another picture she caught herself meditating upon woman's chief inheritance, and moving among the shadows of the future toward that larger and vitalizing part of herself which every woman fancies is on earth in search of her. When she returned from these wanderings she sternly reminded herself that her name was Levine, and that no woman after such an escape had the right to expect more. She finally compelled herself to admit that her avoidance of society was due to prudence as well as to her stern devotion to intellect, then studied harder than ever.

But it is a poor fate that waits upon the gathering together of many people.

VIII

Rachael was riding home one afternoon from Basseterre, where she had been purchasing summer lawns and cambrics. It was March, and the winter sun had begun to use its summer fuel; but the trades blew softly, and there was much shade on the road above the sea. There was one long stretch, however, where not a tree grew, and Rachael drew rein for a moment before leaving the avenue of tamarinds which had rustled above her head for a mile or more. Although it was a hot scene that lay before her, it was that which, when away from home, for some reason best known to her memory, had always been first to rise. The wide pale-gray road rose gradually for a long distance, dipped, and rose again. On either side were cane-fields, their tender greens sharp against the deep hard blue of the sea on the left, rising to cocoanut groves and the dark heights of the mountains above the road. Far away, close to the sea, was Brimstone Hill, that huge isolated rock so near in shape to the crater of Mount Misery. Its fortifications showed their teeth against the faded sky, and St. Christopher slept easily while tentative conquerors approached, looked hard at this Gibraltar of the West Indies, and sailed away.

But there scarcely was a sail on the sea to-day. Its blue rose and fell, in that vast unbroken harmony which quickens the West Indian at times into an intolerable sense of his isolation. Rachael recalled how she had stared at it in childish resentment, wondering if a mainland really lay beyond, if Europe were a myth. She did not care if she never set foot on a ship again, and her ambitions were in the grave with her desire for a wealthy and intellectual husband.

On the long road, rising gray and hot between the bright green cane-fields, horsemen approached, and a number of slave women moved slowly: women with erect rigid backs balancing large baskets or stacks of cane on their heads, the body below the waist revolving with a pivotal motion which suggests an anatomy peculiar to the tropics. They had a dash of red about them somewhere, and their turbans were white. Rachael's imagination never gave her St. Kitts without its slave women, the "pic'nees" clinging to their hips as they bore their burdens on the road or bent over the stones in the river. They belonged to its landscape, with the palms and the cane-fields, the hot gray roads, and the great jewel of the sea.

Rachael left the avenue and rode onward. One of the horsemen took off his Spanish sombrero and waved it. She recognized Dr. Hamilton and shook her whip at him. He and his companion spurred their horses, and a moment later Rachael and James Hamilton had met.

"An unexpected pleasure for me, this sudden descent of my young kinsman," said the doctor, "but a great one, for he brings me news of all in Scotland, and he saw Will the day before he sailed."

"It is too hot to stand here talking," said Rachael. "Come home with me to a glass of Spanish port, and cake perhaps."

The doctor was on his way to a consultation, but he ordered his relative to go and pay his respects to Mistress Fawcett, and rode on whistling. The two he had recklessly left to their own devices exchanged platitudes, and covertly examined each other with quick admiration.

There are dark Scots, and Hamilton was one of them. Although tall and slight, he was knit with a close and peculiar elegance, which made him look his best on a horse and in white linen. His face was burnt to the hue of brick-dust by the first quick assault of the tropic sun, but it was a thin face, well shaped, in spite of prominent cheek bones, and set with the features of long breeding; and it was mobile, fiery, impetuous, and very intelligent: ancestral coarseness had been polished fine long since.

They left the road and mounted toward the dark avenue of the Fawcett estate, Rachael wondering if her mother would be irritated at the informality of the stranger's first call; he should have arrived in state with Dr. Hamilton at the hour of five. Perhaps it was to postpone the moment of explanation that she permitted her horse to walk, even after they had reached the level of the avenue, and finally to crop the grass while she and Hamilton dismounted and sat down in a heavy grove of tamarinds on the slope of the hill.

"I'm just twenty-one and have my own way to make," he was telling her. "There are three before me, so I couldn't afford the army, and as I've a fancy for foreign lands, I've come out here to be a merchant. I have so many kinsmen in this part of the world, and they've all succeeded so well, I thought they'd be able to advise me how best to turn over the few guineas I have. My cousin, the doctor, has taken me in hand, and if I have any business capacity I shall soon find it out. But I ached for the army, and failing that, I'd have liked being a scholar—as I know you are, by your eyes."

His Scotch accent was not unlike that of the West Indians, particularly of the Barbadians; but his voice, although it retained the huskiness of the wet North, had, somewhere in its depths, a peculiar metallic quality which startled Rachael every time it rang out, and was the last of all memories to linger, when memories were crumbling in a brain that could stand no more.

How it happened, Rachael spent the saner hours of the morrow attempting to explain, but they sat under the tamarinds until the sun went down, and Nevis began to robe for the night. Once they paused in their desultory talk and listened to the lovely chorus of a West Indian evening, that low incessant ringing of a million tiny bells. The bells hung in the throats of nothing more picturesque than grasshoppers, serpents, lizards, and frogs so small as to be almost invisible, but they rang with a harmony that the inherited practice of centuries had given them. And beyond was the monotonous accompaniment of the sea on the rocks. Hamilton lived to be an old man, and he never left the West Indies; but sometimes, at long and longer intervals, he found himself listening to that Lilliputian orchestra, his attention attracted to it, possibly, by a stranger; and then he remembered this night, and the woman for whom he would have sacrificed earth and immortality had he been lord of them.

Heaven knows what they talked about. While it was light they stared out at the blue sea or down on the rippling cane-fields, not daring to exchange more than a casual and hasty glance. Both knew that they should have separated the moment they met, but neither had the impulse nor the intention to leave the shade of the wood; and when the brief twilight fell and the moon rose, there still was Nevis, and after her the many craft to divert their gaze. Hamilton was honourable and shy, and Rachael was a woman of uncommon strength of character and had been brought up by a woman of austere virtue. These causes held them apart for a time, but one might as well have attempted to block two comets rushing at each other in the same orbit. The magnetism of the Inevitable embraced them and knit their inner selves together, even while they sat decorously apart. Rachael had taken off her hat at once, and even after it grew dark in their arbour, Hamilton fancied he could see the gleam of her hair. Her eyes were startled and brilliant, and her nostrils quivered uneasily, but she defined none of the sensations that possessed her but the overwhelming recrudescence of her youth. It had seemed to her that it flamed from its ashes before Dr. Hamilton finished his formal words of introduction, and all its forgotten hopes and impulses, timidity and vagueness, surged through her brain during those hours beside the stranger, submerging the memory of Levine. Indeed, she felt even younger than before maturity so suddenly had been thrust upon her; for in those old days she had been almost as severely intellectual as yesterday, and when she had dreamed of the future, it had been with the soberness of an overtaxed brain. But to-day even the world seemed young again. She fancied she could hear the unquiet pulses of the Island, so long grown old, and Nevis had never looked so fair. She hardly was conscious of her womanhood, only of that possessing sense of happiness in youth. As for Hamilton, he had never felt otherwise than young, although he was a college-bred man, something of a scholar, and he had seen more or less of the world since his boyhood. But the intensity and ardour of his nature had received no check, neither were they halfway on their course; and he had never loved. It had seemed to him that the Island opened and a witch came out, and in those confused hours he hardly knew whether she were good or bad, his ideal woman or his ideal devil; but he loved her. He was as pale as his sunburn would permit him to be, and his hands were clasped tightly about his knees, when relief came in the shape of Mary Fawcett.

Her daughter's horse had gone home and taken the stranger with him, and Mistress Fawcett, with quick suspicion, new as it was, started at once down the avenue. Rachael heard the familiar tapping of her mother's stick, hastily adjusted her hat, and managed to reach the road with Hamilton before her mother turned its bend.

Mary Fawcett understood and shivered with terror. She was far from being her imperious self as her daughter presented the stranger and remarked that he was a cousin of Dr. Hamilton, characteristically refraining from apology or explanation.

"Well," she said, "the doctor will doubtless bring you to call some day. I will send your horse to you. Say good evening to the stranger, Rachael, and come home." She was one of the most hospitable women in the Caribbees, and this was the kinsman of her best friend, but she longed for power to exile him out of St. Kitts that night.

Hamilton lifted his hat, and Rachael followed her mother. She was cold and frightened, and Levine's white malignant face circled about her.

Her mother requested her support, and she almost carried the light figure to the house. Mistress Fawcett sent a slave after Hamilton's horse, then went to her room and wrote a note to Dr. Hamilton, asking him to call on the following day and to come alone. The two women did not meet again that night.

But there is little privacy in the houses of St. Kitts and Nevis. Either the upper part of almost every room is built of ornamental lattice-work, or the walls are set with numerous jalousies, that can be closed when a draught is undesirable but conduct the slightest sound. Rachael's room adjoined her mother's. She knew that the older woman was as uneasily awake as herself, though from vastly different manifestations of the same cause. At four o'clock, when the guinea fowl were screeching like demons, and had awakened the roosters and the dogs to swell the infernal chorus of a West Indian morning, Rachael sat up in bed and laughed noiselessly.

"What a night!" she thought. "And for what? A man who companioned me for four hours as no other man had ever done? and who made me feel as if the world had turned to fire and light? It may have been but a mood of my own, it is so long since I have talked with a man near to my own age—and he is so near!—and yet so real a man.... No one could call him handsome, for he looks like a flayed Carib, and I have met some of the handsomest men in Europe and not given them a thought. Yet this man kept me beside him for four hours, and has me awake a whole night because he is not with me. Has the discipline of these last years, then, gone for nothing? Am I but an excitable West Indian after all, and shall I have corded hands before I am twenty-five? It was a mistake to shut myself away from danger. Had I been constantly meeting the young men of the Island and all strangers who have come here during the last two years, I should not be wild for this one—even if he has something in him unlike other men—and lie awake all night like the silly women who dream everlastingly of the lover to come. I am a fool."

She lit her candle and went into her mother's room. Mary Fawcett was sitting up in bed, her white hair hanging out of her nightcap. It seemed to her that the end of the world had come, and she cursed human nature and the governors of the Island.

"I know what has kept you awake," said Rachael, "but do not fear. It was but a passing madness—God smite those guinea fowl! I have lived the life of a nun, and it is an unnatural life for a young woman. Yesterday I learned that I have not the temperament of the scholar, the recluse— that is all. I should have guessed it sooner—then I should not have been fascinated by this brilliant Scot. It was my mind that flew eagerly to companionship—that was all. The hours were pleasant. I would not regret them but for the deep uneasiness they have caused you. To-day I shall enter the world again. There are many clever and accomplished young men on St. Kitts. I will meet and talk to them all. We will entertain them here. There is a ball at Government House to-night, another at Mistress Irwin's on Wednesday week. I promise you that I will be as gay and as universal as a girl in her first season, and this man shall see no more of me than any other man."

Her mother watched her keenly as she delivered her long tirade. Her face was deeply flushed. The arm that held the candle was tense, and her hair fell about her splendid form like a cloud of light. Had Hamilton seen anything so fair in Europe? What part would he play in this scheme of catholicity?

"You will meet this man if you go abroad," she replied. "Better stay here and forbid him the gates."

"And think about him till I leap on my horse and ride to meet him? A fevered imagination will make a god of a Tom Noddy. If I see him daily—with others—he will seem as commonplace as all men."

Mary Fawcett did not speak for some moments. Then she said: "Hark ye, Rachael. I interfered once and brought such damnable misery upon you that I dare not—almost—(she remembered her note to Dr. Hamilton) interfere again. This time you shall use your own judgement, something you have taught me to respect. Whatever the result, I will be to the end what I always have been, the best friend you have. You are very strong. You have had an awful experience, and it has made a woman of thirty of you. You are no silly little fool, rushing blindly into the arms of the first man whose eyes are black enough. You have been brought up to look upon light women with horror. In your darkest days you never sought to console yourself as weaker women do. Therefore, in spite of what I saw in both your faces yesterday, I hope."

"Yes—and give yourself no more uneasiness. Could *I* look upon the love of man with favour? Not unless I were to be born again, and my memory as dead as my body."

"If you love, you will be born again; and if this man overmasters your imagination, your memory might quite as well be dead. One of the three or four things in my life that I have to be thankful for is that I never had to pass through that ordeal. You are far dearer to me than I ever was to myself, and if you are called upon to go through that wretched experience, whose consequences never finish, and I with so little time left in which to stand by and protect you—" She changed abruptly. "Promise me that you will do nothing unconsidered, that you will not behave like the ordinary Francesca—for whom I have always had the most unmitigated contempt. The hour. The man. The fall. The wail: 'The earth rocked, the stars fell. I knew not what I did!' You have deliberation and judgement. Use them now—and do not ramble alone in the gorge with this handsome Scot—for he is a fine man; I would I could deny it. I felt his charm, although he did not open his mouth."

Rachael's eyes flashed. "Ah! did you?" she cried. "Well, but what of that? Are not our creoles a handsome race, and have not all but a few been educated in England? Yes, I will promise you—if you think all this is serious enough to require a promise."

"But you care so little for the world. You would be sacrificing so much less than other women—nevertheless it would make you wretched and humiliate just as much; do not forget that. I almost am tempted to wish that you had a lighter nature—that you would flirt with love and brush it away, while the world was merely amused at a suspected gallantry. But *you*—you would love for a lifetime, and you would end by living with him openly. There is no compromise in you."

"Surely we have become more serious than an afternoon's talk with an interesting stranger should warrant. I am full of a sudden longing for the world, and who knows but I shall become so wedded to it that I would yield it for no man? Besides, do I not live to make you happy, to reward as best I can your unselfish devotion? If ever I could love any man more than I love you, then that love would be overwhelming indeed. But although I can imagine myself forgetting the world in such a love, I cannot picture you on the sacrificial altar."

IX

Rachael was asleep when Dr. Hamilton called. Mistress Fawcett received him in the library, which was at the extreme end of the long house. He laughed so heartily at her fears that he almost dispelled them. Whatever he anticipated in Rachael's future, he had no mind to apprehend danger in every man who interested her.

"For God's sake, Mary," he exclaimed, "let the girl have a flirtation without making a tragedy of it. She is quite right. The world is what she wants. If ever there was a woman whom Nature did not intend for a nun it is Rachael Levine. Let her carry out her plan, and in a week she will be

35

the belle of the Island, and my poor cousin will be consoling himself with some indignant beauty only a shade less fair. I'll engage to marry him off at once, if that will bring sleep to your pillow, but I can't send him away as you propose. I am not King George, nor yet the Captain-General. Nor have I any argument by which to persuade him to go. I have given him too much encouragement to stay. I'll keep him away from routs as long as I can—but remember that he is young, uncommonly good-looking, and a stranger: the girls will not let me keep him in hiding for long. Now let the girl alone. Let her think you've forgotten my new kinsman and your fears. I don't know any way to manage women but to let them manage themselves. Bob Edwards failed with Catherine. I have succeeded. Take a leaf out of my book. Rachael is not going through life without a stupendous love affair. She was marked out for it, specially moulded and equipped by old Mother Nature. Resign yourself to it, and go out and put up your hands against the next tidal wave if you want an illustration of what interference with Rachael would amount to. I wish Levine would die, or we could get a divorce law through on this Island. But the entire Council falls on the table with horror every time I suggest it. Don't worry till the time comes. I'll fill my house with all the pretty girls on St. Kitts and Nevis, and marry this hero of romance as soon as I can."

Rachael went to the ball at Government House that night, glittering in a gown of brocade she had worn at the court of Denmark: Levine had sent her trunks to Peter Lytton's, but not her jewels. She was the most splendid creature in the rooms, and there was no talk of anyone else. But before the night was a third over she realized that the attention she would receive during this her second dazzling descent upon society would differ widely from her first. The young men bowed before her in deep appreciation of her beauty, then passed on to the girls of that light-hearted band to which she no longer belonged. She was a woman with a tragic history and a living husband; she had a reputation for severe intellectuality, and her eyes, the very carriage of her body, expressed a stern aloofness from the small and common exteriorities of life. The Governor, the members of Council, of the Assembly, of the bench and bar, and the clergy, flocked about her, delighted at her return to the world, but she was the belle of the matrons, and not a young man asked her to dance.

She shrugged her shoulders when she saw how it was to be.

"Can they guess that I am younger than they are?" she thought. "And would I have them? Would I share that secret with any in the world—but one? Do I want to dance—to *dance*—Good God! And talk nonsense and the gossip of the Island with these youths when I have naught to say but that my soul has grown wings and that the cold lamp in my breast has blown out, and lit again with the flame that keeps the world alive? Even if I think it best never to see him again, he has given me that, and I am young at last."

When she returned home, as the guinea fowl were at their raucous matins, she was able to tell her mother that the Scot had not attended the ball, and Mary Fawcett knew that Dr. Hamilton had managed to detain him.

But a fortnight later they met again at the house of Dr. George Irwin, an intimate friend of the Hamiltons.

The Irwin's house in Basseterre was on the north side of the Park, which was surrounded by other fine dwellings and several public buildings. The broad verandahs almost overhung the enclosure, with its great banyan tree, the royal palms about the fountain, the close avenues, the flaming hedges of croton and hybiscus, and the traveller's palm and tree ferns brought from the mountains. When a ball was given at one of the houses about this Park on a moonlight night, there was much scheming to avoid the watchful eyes of lawful guardians.

It was inevitable that Hamilton should attend this ball, for the Irwins and his relatives were in and out of each other's houses all day and half the night. By this time, however, he had met nearly every girl on St. Kitts, and his cousin had ridden out that afternoon to assure Mistress Fawcett that the danger weakened daily.

But for an hour, he did not leave Rachael's side that night. The beauties of St. Christopher—and they were many, with their porcelain-like complexions and distinguished features—went through all their graceful creole paces in vain. That he was recklessly in love with Rachael Levine was manifest to all who chose to look, and as undaunted by her intellect and history as any man of his cousin's mature coterie. As for Rachael, although she distributed her favours impartially for a while, her mobile face betrayed to Dr. Hamilton that mind and body were steeped in that tremulous content which possesses a woman when close to an undeclared lover in a public place; the man, and Life and her own emotions unmortalized, the very future bounded by the gala walls, the music, the lights, and the perfume of flowers. These walls were hung with branches of orange trees loaded with fruit, and with ferns and orchids brought fresh from the mountains. A band of blacks played on their native instruments the fashionable dances of the day with a weird and barbaric effect, and occasionally sang a wailing accompaniment in voices of indescribable softness. There was light from fifty candles, and the eternal breeze lifted and dispersed the heavy perfume of the flowers. Hamilton had been in many ball-rooms, but never in one like this. He abstained from the madeiras and ports which were passed about at brief intervals by the swinging coloured women in their gay frocks and white turbans; but he was intoxicated, nevertheless, and more than once on the point of leaving the house. The unreality of it all held him more than weakness, for in some things James Hamilton was strong enough. The weakness in him was down at the roots of his character, and he was neither a feathercock nor a flasher. He had no intention of making love to Rachael until he saw his future more clearly than he did to-night. During the fortnight that had passed since he met her, he had thought of little else, and to-night he wanted nothing else, but impulsive and passionate as he was, he came of a race of hard-headed Scots. He had no mind for a love affair of tragic seriousness, even while his quickened imagination pictured the end.

He deliberately left her side after a time and joined a group of men who were smoking in the court. After an hour of politics his brain had less blood in it, and when he found himself standing beside Rachael on the verandah he suggested that they follow other guests into the Park. He gave Rachael his arm in the courtly fashion of the day, and they walked about the open paths and talked of the negroes singing in the cane-fields, and the squalid poverty of the North, as if their hearts were as calm as they are to-day. People turned often to look at them, commenting according to the mixing of their essences, but all concurring in praise of so much beauty. Hamilton's sunburn had passed the acute stage, leaving him merely brown, and his black silk small clothes and lace ruffles, his white silk stockings and pumps, were vastly becoming. His hair, lightly powdered, was tied with a white ribbon, but although he carried himself proudly, there was no manifest in his bearing that the vanities consumed much of his thought. He was gallanted like a young blood of the period, and so were the young men of St. Kitts. Rachael wore a heavy gold-coloured satin, baring the neck, and a stiff and pointed stomacher, her hair held high with a diamond comb. Her fairness was dazzling in the night-light, and it was such a light as Hamilton never had seen before: for in the Tropics the moon is golden, and the stars are crystal. The palm leaves, high on their slender shafts, glittered like polished dark-green metal, and the downpour was so dazzling that more than once the stranger shaded his eyes with his hand. Had it not been for the soft babble of many voices, the silence would have been intense, until the ear was tuned to the low tinkle of the night bells, for the sea was calm.

Once, as if in explanation for words unspoken, he commented nervously on the sensation of unreality with which these tropic scenes inspired him, and Rachael, who longed to withdraw her hand from his arm, told him of an entertainment peculiar to the Islands, a torchlight hunt for land-crabs, which once a year travel down from the mountains to the sea, to bathe and shed their shells. Words hastened. Before she drew breath she had arranged a hunt for the night of the 10th of April, and received his promise to be one of her guests. They were not so happy as they had been within doors, for the world seemed wider. But their inner selves pressed so hard toward each other that finally they were driven to certain egotisms as a relief.

"I think little of the future," she said, after a direct question, "for that means looking beyond my mother's death, and that is the one fact I have not the courage to face. But of course I know that it holds nothing for me. A ball occasionally, and the conversation of clever men who admire me but care for some one else, books the rest of the week, and life alone on a shelf of the mountain. The thought that I shall one day be old does not console me as it may console men, for with women the heart never grows old. The body withers, and the heart in its awful eternal youth has the less to separate and protect it from the world that has no use for it. Then the body dies and is put away, but the heart is greedily consumed to feed the great pulses of the world that lives faster every year. We give, and give, and give."

"And are only happy in giving," said Hamilton, quickly. "But if men preserve the balance of the world by taking all that women give them, at

39

least the best of us find our happiness in the gifts of one woman, and a woman so besought dare not assert that her heart is empty. I understand—and no one more clearly than I do to-night—that if she give too much, she may curse her heart and look out bitterly upon the manifold interests that could suppress it for weeks and months—if life were full enough. Is yours? What would you sacrifice if you came to me?"

He asked the question calmly, for there were people on every side of them, but he asked it on an uncontrollable impulse, nevertheless; he had vowed to himself that he would wait a month.

His natural repose was greater than hers, for she had the excitable nerves of the Tropics. He felt her arm quiver before she dropped her hand from his arm. But she replied almost as calmly: "Nothing after my mother's death. Absolutely nothing. When a woman suffers as I have done, and her future is ruined in any case, the world counts for very little with her, unless it always has counted for more than anything else. We grow the more cynical and contemptuous as we witness the foolish gallantries of women who have so much to lose. I am not hard. I am very soft about many things, and since you came I am become the very tragedy of youth; but I have no respect for the world as I have seen it. For many people in the world I have a great deal, but not for the substance out of which Society has built itself. One never loses one's real friends, no matter what one does. Every circumstance of my life has isolated me from this structure called society, forced me to make my own laws. I may never be happy, because my capacity for happiness is too great, but in my own case there is no alternative worth considering. This is the substance of what I have thought since we met, but you are not to speak to me of it again while my mother lives."

"I do not promise you that—but this: that I will do much thinking before I speak again."

X

But although they parted with formal courtesy, it was several nights before either slept. Rachael went home to her bed and lay down, because she feared to agitate her mother, but her disposition was to go out and walk the circuit of the Island, and she rose as soon as she dared, and climbed to the highest crest behind the house. It was cold there, and the

40

wind was keen. She sat for hours and stared out at Nevis, who was rolling up her mists, indifferent to the torment of mortals.

During the past fortnight she had conceived a certain stern calm, partly in self-defence, due in part to love for her mother. But since she had left Hamilton, last night, there had been moments when she had felt alone in the Universe with him, exalted to such heights of human passion that she had imagined herself about to become the mother of a new race. Her genius, which in a later day might have taken the form of mental creation, concentrated in a supreme capacity for idealized human passion, and its blind impulse was a reproduction of itself in another being.

Were she and Hamilton but the victims of a mighty ego roaming the Universe in search of a medium for human expression? Were they but helpless sacrifices, consummately equipped, that the result of their union might be consummately great? Who shall affirm or deny? The very commonplaces of life are components of its eternal mystery. We know absolutely nothing. But we have these facts: that a century and a half ago, on a tropical island, where, even to common beings, quick and intense love must seem the most natural thing in the world, this man and woman met; that the woman, herself born in unhappy conditions, but beautiful, intellectual, with a character developed far beyond her years and isolated home by the cruel sufferings of an early marriage, reared by a woman whose independence and energy had triumphed over the narrow laws of the Island of her birth, given her courage to snap her fingers at society—we know that this woman, inevitably remarkable, met and loved a stranger from the North, so generously endowed that he alone of all the active and individual men who surrounded her won her heart; and that the result of their union was one of the stupendous intellects of the world's history.

Did any great genius ever come into the world after commonplace pre-natal conditions? Was a maker of history ever born amidst the pleasant harmonies of a satisfied domesticity? Of a mother who was less than remarkable, although she may have escaped being great? Did a woman with no wildness in her blood ever inform a brain with electric fire? The students of history know that while many mothers of great men have been virtuous, none have been commonplace, and few have been happy. And lest the moralists of my day and country be more prone

41

to outraged virtue, in reading this story, than were the easy-going folk who surrounded it, let me hasten to remind them that it all happened close upon a hundred and fifty years ago, and that the man and woman who gave them the brain to which they owe the great structure that has made their country phenomenal among nations, are dust on isles four hundred miles apart.

A century and a half ago women indulged in little introspective analysis. They thought on broad lines, and honestly understood the strength of their emotions. Moreover, although Mary Wollstonecraft was unborn and "Émile" unwritten, Individualism was germinating; and what soil so quickening as the Tropics? Nevertheless, to admit was not to lay the question, and Rachael passed through many hours of torment before hers was settled. She was not unhappy, for the intoxication lingered, and behind the methodical ticking of her reason, stood, calmly awaiting its time, that sense of the Inevitable which has saved so many brains from madness. She slept little and rested less, but that sentinel in her brain prevented the frantic hopelessness which would have possessed her had she felt herself strong enough to command James Hamilton to leave the Island.

She met him several times before the night of her entertainment, and there were moments when she was filled with terror, for he did not whisper a reference to the conversation in the Park. Had he thought better of it? Would he go? Would he conquer himself? Was it but a passing madness? When these doubts tormented her she was driven to such a state of jealous fury that she forgot every scruple, and longed only for the bond which would bind him fast; then reminded herself that she should be grateful, and endeavoured to be. But one day when he lifted her to her horse, he kissed her wrist, and again the intoxication of love went to her head, and this time it remained there. Once they met up in the hills, where they had been asked with others to take a dish of tea with Mistress Montgomerie. They sat alone for an hour on one of the terraces above the house, laughing and chattering like children, then rode down the hills through the cane-fields together. Again, they met in the Park, and sat under the banyan tree, discussing the great books they had read, all of Europe they knew. For a time neither cared to finish that brief period of exquisite happiness and doubt, where imagination rules, and the world is unreal and wholly sweet, and they its first to love.

The wrenching stage of doubt had passed for Hamilton, but he thought on the future with profound disquiet. He would have the woman wholly or not at all, after Mary Fawcett's death; he knew from Dr. Hamilton that it would occur before the year was out. He had no taste for intrigue. He wanted a home, and the woman he would have rejoiced to marry was the woman he expected to love and live with for the rest of his life. Once or twice the overwhelming sense of responsibility, the certainty of children, whom he could not legalize, the possible ruin of his worldly interests, as well as his deep and sincere love for the woman, drove him almost to the bows of a homeward-bound vessel. But the sure knowledge that he should return kept him doggedly on St. Christopher. He even had ceased to explain his infatuation to himself by such excuse as was given him by her beauty, her grace, her strong yet charming brain. He loved her, and he would have her if the skies fell.

It is doubtful if he understood the full force of the attraction between them. The real energy and deliberation, the unswerving purpose in her magnetized the weakness at the roots of his ardent, impulsive, but unstable character. Moreover, in spite of the superlative passion which he had aroused in her, she lacked the animal magnetism which was his in abundance. Her oneness was a magnet for his gregariousness and concentrated it upon herself. That positive quality in him overwhelmed and intoxicated her; and in intellect he was far more brilliant and far less profound than herself. His wit and mental nimbleness stung and pricked the serene layers which she had carefully superimposed in her own mind to such activities as mingled playfully with his lighter moods or stimulated him in more intellectual hours. While the future was yet unbroken and imagination remodelled the face of the world, there were moments when both were exalted with a sense of completeness, and terrified, when apart, with a hint of dissolution into unrelated particles.

When a man and woman arrive at that stage of reasoning and feeling, it were idle for their chronicler to moralize; her part is but to tell the story.

XI

Mary Fawcett encouraged her daughter's social activity, and as Hamilton's name entered the rapid accounts of revels and routs in the most casual manner, she endeavoured to persuade herself that the madness had passed with a languid afternoon. She was a woman of the world, but the one experience that develops deepest insight had passed her by, and there were shades and moods of the master passion over which her sharp eyes roved without a shock.

As she was too feeble to sit up after nine o'clock, she refused to open her doors for the crab hunt, but gave Rachael the key of a little villa on the crest of a peak behind the house, and told her to keep her friends all night if she chose.

This pavilion, designed for the hotter weeks of the hurricane season, but seldom used by the Fawcetts, was a small stone building, with two bedrooms and a living room, a swimming bath, and several huts for servants. The outbuildings were dilapidated, but the house after an airing and scrubbing was as fit for entertainment as any on St. Kitts. The furniture in the Tropics is of cane, and there are no carpets or hangings to invite destruction. Even the mattresses are often but plaited thongs of leather, covered with strong linen, and stretched until they are hard as wood. All Mary Fawcett's furniture was of mahogany, the only wood impervious to the boring of the West Indian worm. This tiny house on the mountain needed but a day's work to clean it, and another to transform it into an arbour of the forest. The walls of the rooms were covered with ferns, orchids, and croton leaves. Gold and silver candelabra had been carried up from the house, and they would hold half a hundred candles.

All day the strong black women climbed the gorge and hill, their hips swinging, baskets of wine, trays of delicate edibles, pyramids of linen, balanced as lightly on their heads as were they no more in weight and size than the turban beneath; their arms hanging, their soft voices scolding the "pic'nees" who stumbled after them.

Toward evening, Rachael and Kitty Hamilton walked down the mountain together, and lingered in the heavy beauty of the gorge. The ferns grew high above their heads, and palms of many shapes. The dark machineel with its deadly fruit, the trailing vines on the tamarind trees, the monkeys leaping, chattering with terror, through flaming hybiscus and masses of orchid, the white volcanic rock, the long torn leaves of the banana tree, the abrupt declines, crimson with wild strawberries, the loud boom of the sunset gun from Brimstone Hill—Rachael never forgot a detail of that last walk with her old friend. Hers was not the nature for intimate friendships, but Catherine Hamilton had been one of her first remembered playmates, her bridesmaid, and had hastened to companion her when she emerged from the darkness of her married life. But Catherine was an austere girl, of no great mental liveliness, and the friendship, although sincere, was not rooted in the sympathies and affections. She believed Rachael to be the most remarkable woman in the world, and had never dared to contradict her, although she lowered her fine head to no one else. But female virtue, as they expressed it in the eighteenth century, stood higher in her estimation than all the gifts of mind and soul which had been lavished upon Rachael Levine, and she was the first to desert her when the final step was taken. But on this evening there was no barrier, and she talked of her future with the man she was to marry. She was happy and somewhat sentimental. Rachael sighed and set her lips. All her girlhood friends were either married or about to be—except Christiana, who had not a care in her little world. Why were sorrow and disgrace for her alone? What have I done, she thought, that I seem to be accursed? I have wronged no one, and I am more gifted than any of these friends of mine. Not one of them has studied so severely, and learned as much as I. Not one of them can command the homage of such men as I. And yet I alone am singled out, first, for the most hideous fate which can attack a woman, then to live apart from all good men and women with a man I cannot marry, and who may break my heart. I wish that I had not been born, and I would not be dead for all the peace that is in the most silent depths of the Universe.

At ten o'clock, that night, the hills were red with the torches of as gay a company as ever had assembled on the Island. The Governor and Dr. Hamilton were keen sportsmen, and nothing delighted them more than to chase infuriated land-crabs down the side of a mountain. There were some twenty men in the party, and most of them followed their distinguished elders through brush and rocky passes. Occasionally, a sudden yell of pain mingled with the shouts of mirth, for land-crabs have their methods of revenge. The three or four girls whom Rachael had induced to attend this masculine frolic, kept to the high refuge of the villa, attended by cavaliers who dared not hint that maiden charms were less than land-crabs.

Hamilton and Rachael sat on the steps of the terrace, or paced up and down, watching the scene. Just beyond their crest was the frowning mass of Mount Misery. The crystal flood poured down from above, and the moon was rising over the distant hills. The sea had the look of infinity. There might be ships at anchor before Basseterre or Sandy Point, but the shoulders of the mountain hid them; and below, the world looked as if the passions of Hell had let loose—the torches flared and crackled, and the trees took on hideous shapes. Once a battalion of the pale venomous-looking crabs rattled across the terrace, and Rachael, who was masculine in naught but her intellect, screamed and flung herself into Hamilton's arms. A moment later she laughed, but their conversation ceased then to be impersonal. It may be said here, that if Hamilton failed in other walks of life, it was not from want of resolution where women were concerned. And he was tired of philandering.

The hunters returned, slaves carrying the slaughtered crabs in baskets. There were many hands to shell the victims, and in less than half an hour Mary Fawcett's cook sent in a huge and steaming dish. Then there were mulled wines and port, cherry brandy and liqueurs to refresh the weary, and sweets for the women. A livelier party never sat down to table; and Hamilton, who was placed between two chattering girls, was a man of the world, young as he was, and betrayed neither impatience nor ennui. Rachael sat at the head of the table, between the Governor and Dr. Hamilton. Her face, usually as white as porcelain, was pink in the cheeks; her eyes sparkled, her nostrils fluttered with triumph. She looked so exultant that more than one wondered if she were intoxicated with her own beauty; but Dr. Hamilton understood, and his supper lost its relish. Some time since he had concluded that where Mary Fawcett failed he could not hope to succeed, but he had done his duty and lectured his cousin. He understood human nature from its heights to its dregs, however, and promised Hamilton his unaltered friendship, even while in the flood of remonstrance. He was a philosopher, who invariably held out his hand to the Inevitable, with a shrug of his shoulders, but he loved Rachael, and wished that the ship that brought Levine to the Islands had encountered a hurricane.

The guests started for home at one o'clock, few taking the same path. The tired slaves went down to their huts. Rachael remained on the mountain, and Hamilton returned to her.

XII

It was a month later that Rachael, returning after a long ride with Hamilton, found her mother just descended from the family coach.

"Is it possible that you have been to pay visits?" she asked, as she hastened to support the feeble old woman up the steps.

"No, I have been to Basseterre with Archibald Hamn."

"Not to St. Peter's, I hope."

"Oh, my dear, I do not feel in the mood to jest. I went to court to secure the future of my three dear slaves, Rebecca, Flora, and Esther."

Rachael placed her mother on one of the verandah chairs and dropped upon another.

"Why have you done that?" she asked faintly. "Surely—"

"There are several things I fully realize, and one is that each attack leaves me with less vitality to resist the next. These girls are the daughters of my dear old Rebecca, who was as much to me as a black ever can be to a white, and that is saying a good deal. I have just signed a deed of trust before the Registrar—to Archibald. They are still mine for the rest of my life, yours for your lifetime, or as long as you live here; then they go to Archibald or his heirs. I want you to promise me that they shall never go beyond this Island or Nevis."

"I promise." Rachael had covered her face with her hand.

"I believe you kept the last promise you made me. It is not in your character to break your word, however you may see fit to take the law into your own hands."

"I kept it."

"And you will live with him openly after my death. I have appreciated your attempt to spare me."

"Ah, you *do* know me."

"Some things may escape my tired old eyes, but I love you too well not to have seen for a month past that you were as happy as a bride. I shall say no more—save for a few moments with James Hamilton. I am old and ill and helpless. You are young and indomitable. If I were as vigorous and self-willed as when I left your father, I could not control you now. I shall leave you independent. Will Hamilton, Archibald, and a few others will stand by you; but alas! you will, in the course of nature, outlive them all, and have no friend in the world but Hamilton— although I shall write an appeal to your sisters to be sent to them after

47

my death. But oh, how I wish, how I wish, that you could marry this man."

Mary Fawcett was attacked that night by the last harsh rigours of her disease and all its complications. Until she died, a week later, Rachael, except for the hour that Hamilton sat alone beside the bed of the stricken woman, did not leave her mother. The immortal happiness of the last month was forgotten. She was prostrate, literally on her knees with grief and remorse, for she believed that her mother's discovery had hastened the end.

"No, it is not so," said Mary Fawcett, one day. "My time has come to die. Will Hamilton will assure you of that, and I have watched the space between myself and death diminish day by day, for six months past. I have known that I should die before the year was out. It is true that I die in sorrow and with a miserable sense of failure, for you have been my best-beloved, my idol, and I leave you terribly placed in life and with little hope of betterment. But for you I have no reproach. You have given me love for love, and duty for duty. Life has treated you brutally; what has come now was, I suppose, inevitable. Human nature when it is strong enough is stronger than moral law. I grieve for you, but I die without grievance against you. Remember that. And Hamilton? He is honourable, and he loves you utterly—but is he strong? I wish I knew. His emotions and his active brain give him so much apparent force—but underneath? I wish I knew."

Rachael was grateful for her mother's unselfish assurance, but she was not to be consoled. The passions in her nature, released from other thrall, manifested themselves in a grief so profound, and at times so violent, that only her strong frame saved her from illness. For two weeks after Mary Fawcett's death she refused to see James Hamilton; but by that time he felt at liberty to assert his rights, and her finely poised mind recovered its balance under his solace and argument. Her life was his, and to punish him assuaged nothing of her sorrow. He had decided, after consultation with his cousin, to take her to Nevis, not only to seclude her from the scandalized society she knew best, but that he might better divert her mind, in new scenes, from her heavy affliction. Hamilton had already embarked in his business enterprise, but he had bought and manned a sail-boat, which would carry him to and from St. Kitts daily. In the dead calms of summer there was little business doing.

"I attempted no sophistry with my cousin," said Hamilton, "and for that reason I think I have put the final corking-pin into our friendship. Right or wrong we are going to live together for the rest of our lives, because I will have no other woman, and you will have no other man; and we will live together publicly, not only because neither of us has the patience for scheming and deceit, but because passion is not our only motive for union. There is gallantry on every side of us, and doubtless we alone shall be made to suffer; for the world loves to be fooled, it hates the crudeness of truth. But we have each other, and nothing else matters."

And to Rachael nothing else mattered, for her mother was dead, and she loved Hamilton with an increasing passion that was long in culminating.

XIII

They sailed over to Nevis, accompanied by a dozen slaves, and took possession of Rachael's house in Main Street. It stood at the very end of the town, beyond the point where the street ceased and the road round the Island began. The high wall of the garden surrounded a grove of palms and cocoanut trees. Only sojourners from England had occupied the big comfortable house, and it was in good repair.

When the acute stage of her grief had passed, it was idle for Rachael to deny to Hamilton that she was happy. And at that time she had not a care in the world, nor had he. Their combined incomes made them as careless of money as any planter on the Island. Every ship from England brought them books and music, and Hamilton was not only the impassioned lover but the tenderest and most patient of husbands. Coaches dashed by and the occupants cast up eyes and hands. The gay life of Nevis pulsed unheeded about the high walls, whose gates were always locked. The kinsman of the leading families of the Island and the most beautiful daughter of old John and Mary Fawcett were a constant and agitating theme, but two people lived their life of secluded and poignant happiness, and took Nevis or St. Kitts into little account.

BOOK II

ALEXANDER HAMILTON:
HIS YOUTH IN THE WEST INDIES
AND IN THE COLONIES OF NORTH AMERICA

—◦◦◦—

I

I should have been glad to find an old Almanac of Nevis which contained a description of its 11th of January, 1757. But one January is much like another in the Leeward Islands, and he who has been there can easily imagine the day on which Alexander Hamilton was born. The sky was a deeper blue than in summer, for the sun was resting after the terrific labours of Autumn, and there was a prick in the trade winds which stimulated the blood by day and chilled it a trifle at night. The slave women moved more briskly, followed by a trotting brood of "pic'nees," one or more clinging to their hips, all bewailing the rigours of winter. Down in the river where they pounded the clothes on the stones, they vowed they would carry the next linen to the sulphur springs, for the very marrow in their bones was cold. In the Great Houses there were no fires, but doors and windows were closed early and opened late, and blankets were on every bed. The thermometer may have stood at 72°.

Nevis herself was like a green jewel casket, after the autumn rains. Oranges and sweet limes were yellow in her orchards, the long-leaved banana trees were swelling with bunches of fruit, the guavas were ready for cream and the boiling. The wine was in the cocoanut, the royal palms had shed their faded summer leaves and glittered like burnished metal. The gorgeous masses of the croton bush had drawn fresh colour from the rain. In the woods and in the long avenues which wound up the mountain to the Great House of every estate, the air was almost cold; but out under the ten o'clock sun, even a West Indian could keep warm, and the negroes sang as they reaped the cane. The sea near the shore was like green sunlight, but some yards out it deepened into that intense hot blue which is the final excess of West Indian colouring. The spray flew high over the reef between Nevis and St. Kitts, glittering like the salt ponds on the desolate end of the larger island, the roar of the breakers audible in the room where the child who was to be called Alexander Hamilton was born.

Rachael rose to a ceaseless demand upon her attention for which she was grateful during the long days of Hamilton's absence. Alexander turned out to be the most restless and monarchical of youngsters and preferred his mother to his black attendants. She ruled him with a firm hand, however, for she had no mind to lessen her pleasure in him, and although she could not keep him quiet, she prevented the blacks from spoiling him.

During the hurricane months Hamilton yielded to her nervous fears, as he had done in the preceding year, and crossed to St. Kitts but seldom. As a matter of fact, hurricanes of the first degree, are rare in the West Indies, the average to each island being one in a century. But from the 25th of August, when all the Caribbean world prostrates itself in church while prayers for deliverance from the awful visitation are read, to the 25th of October, when the grateful or the survivors join in thanksgiving, every wind alarms the nervous, and every round woolly cloud must contain the white squall. Rachael knew that Nevis boats had turned over when minor squalls dashed down the Narrows between the extreme points of the Islands, and that they were most to be dreaded in the hurricane season. Hamilton's inclination was to spare in every possible way the woman who had sacrificed so much for him, and he asked little urging to idle his days in the cool library with his charming wife and son. Therefore his business suffered, for his partners took advantage of his negligence; and the decay of their fortunes began when Rachael, despite the angry protests of Archibald Hamn, sold her property on St. Kitts and gave Hamilton the money. He withdrew from the firm which had treated him inconsiderately, and set up a business for himself. For a few years he was hopeful, although more than once obliged to borrow money from his wife. She gave freely, for she had been brought up in the careless plenty of the Islands. Mary Fawcett, admirable manager as she was, had been lavish with money, particularly when her favourite child was in question; and Rachael's imagination had never worked toward the fact that money could roll down hill and not roll up again. She was long in discovering that the man she loved and admired

51

was a failure in the uninteresting world of business. He was a brilliant and charming companion, read in the best literatures of the world, a thoughtful and adoring husband. It availed Archibald Hamn nothing to rage or Dr. Hamilton to remonstrate. Rachael gradually learned that Hamilton was not as strong as herself, but the maternal instinct, so fully aroused by her child, impelled her to fill out his nature with hers, while denying nothing to the man who did all he could to make her happy.

In the third year Hamilton gave up his sail-boat, and had himself rowed across the Narrows, where the overlooker of a salt estate he had bought awaited him with a horse. Once he would have thought nothing of walking the eight miles to Basseterre, but the Tropics, while they sharpen the nerves, caress unceasingly the indolence of man. During the hurricane season he crossed as often as he thought necessary, for with expert oarsmen there was little danger, even from squalls, and the distance was quickly covered.

Gradually Rachael's position was accepted. Nothing could alter the fact that she was the daughter of Dr. and Mary Fawcett, and Hamilton was of the best blood in the Kingdom. She was spoken of generally as Mistress Hamilton, and old friends of her parents began to greet her pleasantly as she drove about the Island with her beautiful child. In time they called, and from that it was but another step to invite, as a matter of course, the young Hamiltons to their entertainments. After all, Rachael was not the first woman in tropical Great Britain to love a man she could not marry, and it was fatiguing to ask the everlasting question of whether the honesty of a public irregular alliance were not counterbalanced by its dangerous example. It was a day of loose morals, the first fruit of the vast scientific movement of the century, whose last was the French Revolution. Moreover, the James Hamiltons were delightful people, and life on the Islands was a trifle monotonous at times; they brought into Nevis society fresh and unusual personalities, spiced with a salient variety. Hamilton might almost be said to have been born an astute man of the world. He opened his doors with an accomplished hospitality to the most intelligent and cultivated people of the Island, ignoring those who based their social pretensions on rank and wealth alone. In consequence he and his wife became the leaders of a small and exclusive set, who appreciated their good fortune. Dr. Hamilton and a few other Kittifonians were constant visitors in this hospitable mansion. Christiana Huggins, who had taken a bold stand from the first, carried her father there one day in triumph, and that austere parent laid down his arms. All seemed well, and the crumbling of the foundations made no sound.

And Alexander? He was an excitable and ingenious imp, who saved himself from many a spanking by his sparkling mind and entrancing sweetness of temper. He might fly at his little slaves and beat them, and to his white playmates he never yielded a point; but they loved him, for he was generous and honest, and the happiest little mortal on the Island. He could get into as towering a rage as old John Fawcett, but he was immediately amenable to the tenderness of his parents.

When he was four years old he was sent to a small school, which happened to be kept by a Jewess. In spite of his precocity his parents had no wish to force a mind which, although delightful to them in its saucy quickness, aroused no ambitious hopes; they sent him to school merely that there might be less opportunity to spoil him at home. His new experience was of a brief duration.

Hamilton on a Sunday was reading to Rachael in the library. Alexander shoved a chair to the table and climbed with some difficulty, for he was very small, to an elevated position among the last reviews of Europe. He demanded the attention of his parents, and, clasping his hands behind his back, began to recite rapidly in an unknown tongue. The day was very hot, and he wore nothing but a white apron. His little pink feet were bare on the mahogany, and his fair curls fell over a flushed and earnest face, which at all times was too thin and alert to be angelic or cherubic. Hamilton and Rachael, wondering whom he fancied himself imitating, preserved for a moment a respectful silence, then, overcome by his solemn countenance and the fluency of his outlandish utterance, burst into one of those peals of sudden laughter which seem to strike the most sensitive chord in young children. Alexander shrieked in wrath and terror, and made as if to fling himself on his mother's bosom, then planted his feet with an air of stubborn defiance, and went on with his recital. Hamilton listened a moment longer, then left the house abruptly. He returned in wrath.

"That woman has taught him the Decalogue in Hebrew!" he exclaimed. "'Tis a wonder his brains are not addled. He will sail boats in the swimming-bath and make shell houses in the garden for the next three years. We'll have no more of school."

II

Alexander Hamilton had several escapes from imminent peril when he was a boy, and the first occurred in the month of December, 1761. Hamilton had gone to St. Croix on business, and Rachael and the child spent the fortnight of his absence with Christiana Huggins. Rachael was accustomed to Hamilton's absences, but Nevis was in a very unhealthy condition, through lack of wind and rains during the preceding autumn. The sea had looked like a metal floor for months, the Island was parched and dry, the swamps on the lowlands were pestiferous. Many negroes had died in Charles Town, and many more were ill. The obeah doctors, with their absurd concoctions and practices, were openly defying the physicians of repute, for the terrified blacks believed that the English had prayed once too often that the hurricane should be stayed, and that he sulked where none might feel his faintest breath. Therefore they cursed the white doctor as futile, and flung his physic from the windows.

Rachael was glad to escape to the heights with Alexander. There it was almost as cool as it should be in December, and she could watch for her husband's sloop. He had gone with the first light wind, and there was enough to bring him home, although with heavy sail. She forgot the muttering negroes and the sickness below. Her servants had been instructed to nurse and nourish where assistance was needed, and up here there was nothing to do but wander with her friend and child through the gay beauty of the terraced garden, or climb the stone steps to the cold quiet depths of the forest.

At the end of a fortnight there was no sign of her husband's sloop, but the wind was strengthening, and she decided to return home and make ready for him. During the long drive she passed negroes in large numbers, either walking toward Charles Town or standing in muttering groups by the roadside. At one time the driveway was so thick with them that her coach could not pass until the postilion laid about him with his whip.

"This is very odd," she said to her nurse. "I have never seen anything like this before."

"Me no t'ink he nothin'. All go tee tick—oh, dis pic'nee no keep till one minit. Me no t'ink about he'n de road."

She lifted the child between her face and her mistress's eyes, and Rachael saw that her hand trembled. "Can the negroes be rising?" she wondered; and for a moment she was faint with terror, and prayed for Hamilton's return.

But she was heroic by nature, and quickly recovered her poise. When she arrived at home she sent the nurse to Charles Town on an errand, then went directly to her bedroom, which was disconnected from the other rooms, and called her three devoted maids, Rebecca, Flora, and Esther. They came running at the sound of her voice, and she saw at once that they were terrified and ready to cling to her garments.

"What is the matter?" she demanded. "Tell me at once."

"Me no know fo' sure," said Rebecca, "but me t'ink, t'ink, till me yell in me tleep. Somethin' ter'ble go to happen. Me feel he in de air. All de daddys, all de buddys, 'peak, 'peak, togedder all de time, an' look so bad—an' de oby doctors put de curse ebberywheres. Me fine befo' de gate dis mornin' one pudden', de mud an' oil an' horsehair, but me no touch he. Me ask all de sissys me know, what comes, but he no 'peak. He run out he tongue, and once he smack me ear. Oh, Mistress, take us back to Sinkitts."

"But do you *know* nothing?"

They shook their heads, but stared at her hopefully, for they believed implicitly in her power to adjust all things.

"And my other slaves? Do you think they are faithful to me?"

"All in de town all de time. Me ask ebbery he tell me what comes, and he say 'nothin,' but I no believe he."

"And has the Governor taken no notice?"

"De Gobbenor lord and all de noble Buckras go yis'day to Sinkitts. Take de militia for one gran' parade in Bassetarr. Is de birfday to-morrow de Gobbenor lord de Sinkitts. Up in de Great Houses no hear nothin', an' all quiet on 'states till yes'day. Now comin' to town an' look so bad, so bad!"

"Very well, then, the Governor and the militia must come back. Rebecca, you are the most sensible as well as the weakest in the arms. You will stay here to-night, and you will not falter for a moment. As soon as it is dark Flora and Esther will row me across the channel, and I will send the Buckra's agent on a fast horse with a note to the Governor. If the other house servants return, you will tell them that I am ill and that Flora and Esther are nursing me. You will lock the gates, and open them to no one unless your Buckra should return. Do you understand?"

The slave rolled her eyes, but nodded. She might have defied the Captain-General, but not one of the Fawcetts.

There were two hours before dark. Rachael was conscious of every nerve in her body, and paced up and down the long line of rooms which terminated in the library, until Alexander's legs were worn out trotting after her, and he fell asleep on the floor. Twice she went to the roof to look for Hamilton's sloop, but saw not a sail on the sea; and the streets of Charles Town were packed with negroes. England sent no soldiers to protect her Islands, and every free male between boyhood and old age was forced by law to join the militia. It was doubtful if there were a dozen muscular white men on Nevis that night, for the birthday of a Governor was a fête of hilarities. Unless the militia returned that night, the blacks, if they really were plotting vengeance, and she knew their superstitions, would have burned every house and cane-field before morning.

The brief twilight passed. The mist rolled down from the heights of Nevis. Rachael, with Alexander in her arms, and followed by her maids, stole along the shore through the thick cocoanut groves, meeting no one. They were far from the town's centre, and all the blacks on the Island seemed to be gathered there. The boat was beached, and it took the combined efforts of the three women to launch it. When they pushed off, the roar of the breakers and the heavy mist covered their flight. But there was another danger, and the very physical strength of the slaves departed before it. They had rowed their mistress about the roadstead before St. Kitts a hundred times, but the close proximity of the reef so terrified them that Rachael was obliged to take the oars; while Flora caught Alexander in so convulsive an embrace that he awoke and protested with all the vigour of his lungs. His mother's voice, to which he was peculiarly susceptible, hushed him, and he held back his own, although the gasping bosom on which he rested did not tend to soothe a nervous child. But there were other ways of expressing outraged feelings, and he kicked like a little steer.

Rachael herself was not too sure of her knowledge of the dangerous channel, although she had crossed it many times with Hamilton; and the mist was floating across to St. Kitts. The hollow boom of the reef seemed so close that she expected to hear teeth in the boat every moment, and she knew that far and wide the narrows bristled. She wondered if her hair were turning white, and her straining nerves quivered for a moment with a feminine regret; for she knew the power of her beauty over Hamilton. But her arms kept their strength. Life had taught her to endure more than a half-hour of mortal anxiety.

She reached the shore in safety, and Esther recovered her muscle and agreed to run to the overlooker's house and send him, on his fleetest horse, with her mistress's note to the Governor of Nevis. When the others reached the house, a mile from the Narrows, the man had gone; and Rachael could do no more. The overlookers wife mulled wine, and the maids were soon asleep. Alexander refused to go to bed, and Rachael, who was not in a disciplinary mood, led him out into the open to watch for the boats of the Governor and his militia. There was no moon; they could cross and land near Hamilton's house and overpower, without discharging a gun, the negroes packed in Charles Town. If the Governor were prompt, the blacks, even had they dispersed to fire the estates, would not have time for havoc; and she knew the tendency of the negro to procrastinate. They did not expect the Governor until late on the following day; they could drink all night and light their torches at dawn when Nevis was heavy in her last sleep. Nevertheless, Rachael watched the Island anxiously.

Fortunately, Alexander possessed an inquiring mind, and she was obliged to answer so many questions that the strain was relieved. They walked amidst a wild and dismal scene. The hills were sterile and black. The salt ponds, sunken far below the level of the sea, from lack of rain, glittered white, but they were set with aloes and manchineel, and there were low and muddy flats to be avoided. It was a new aspect of nature to the child who had lived his four years amid the gay luxuriance of tropic verdure, and he was mightily interested. Nevertheless, it was a long hour before the overlooker returned with word that the Governor was on his way to Nevis with the militia of both Islands—for St. Kitts was quiet, its negroes having taken the drouth philosophically—and that her husband was with them. He had arrived at Basseterre as the boats were leaving; as a member of the Governor's staff, he had no choice. He had sent her word, however, not to return to Nevis that night; and Rachael and

Alexander went down to the extreme point of the Island and sat there through a cold night of bitter anxiety. With the dawn Hamilton came for them.

The negroes, surprised and overwhelmed, had surrendered without resistance, and before they had left the town. They confessed that their intention had been to murder every white on the Island, seize the ammunition which was stored on the estates, and fire upon the militia as it passed, on the following day. The ringleaders and obeah doctors were either publicly executed or punished with such cruelty that the other malcontents were too cowed to plan another rebellion; and the abundant rains of the following autumn restored their faith in the white man.

III

When Alexander was five years old, James arrived, an object of much interest to his elder brother, but a child of ordinary parts to most beholders. He came during the last days of domestic tranquillity; for it was but a few weeks later that Hamilton was obliged to announce to Rachael that his fortunes, long tottering, had collapsed to their rotten foundations. It was some time before she could accommodate her understanding to the fact that there was nothing left, for even Levine had not dared to lose his money, far less her own; and had she ever given the subject of wealth a thought, she would have assumed that it had roots in certain families which no adverse circumstance could deplace. She had overheard high words between Archibald Hamn and her husband in the library, but Hamilton's casual explanations had satisfied her, and she had always disliked Archibald as a possible stepfather. Dr. Hamilton had frequently looked grave after a conversation with his kinsman, but Rachael was too unpractical to attribute his heavier moods to anything but his advancing years.

When Hamilton made her understand that they were penniless, and that his only means of supporting her was to accept an offer from Peter Lytton to take charge of a cattle estate on St. Croix, Rachael's controlling sensation was dismay that this man whom she had idolized and idealized, who was the forgiven cause of her remarkable son's illegitimacy, was a failure in his competition with other men. Money would come somehow, it always had; but Hamilton dethroned, shoved out of the ranks of planters and merchants, reduced to the status of one of his own overlookers, almost was a new and strange being, and she dared not bid forth her hiding thoughts.

Fortunately the details of moving made life impersonal and commonplace. The three slaves whose future had been the last concern but one of Mary Fawcett, were sent, wailing, to Archibald Hamn. Two of the others were retained to wait upon the children, the rest sold with the old mahogany furniture and the library. The Hamiltons set sail for St. Croix on a day in late April. The sympathy of their friends had been expressed in more than one offer of a lucrative position, but Hamilton was intensely proud, and too mortified at his failure to remain obscure among a people who had been delighted to accept his princely and exclusive hospitality. On St. Croix he was almost unknown.

They made the voyage in thirty-two hours, but as the slaves were ill, after the invariable habit of their colour, Rachael had little respite from her baby, or Hamilton from Alexander, whose restless legs and enterprising mind kept him in constant motion; and the day began at five o'clock. There was no opportunity for conversation, and Hamilton was grateful to the miserable mustees. He had the tact to let his wife readjust herself to her damaged idols without weak excuses and a pleading which would have distressed her further, but he was glad to be spared intimate conversation with her.

As they sailed into the bright green waters before Frederikstadt, the sun blazed down upon the white town on the white plain with a vicious energy which Rachael had never seen on Nevis during the hottest and most silent months of the year. She closed her eyes and longed for the cool shallows of the harbour, and even Alexander ceased to watch the flying fish dart like silver blades over the water, and was glad to be stowed comfortably into one of the little deck-houses. As for the slaves, weakened by illness, they wept and refused to gather themselves together.

But Rachael's soul, which had felt faint for many days, rose triumphant in the face of this last affliction. Like all West Indians, she hated extreme heat, and during those months on her own Islands when the trades hibernated, rarely left the house. She remembered little of St. Croix. Her imagination had disassociated itself from all connected with it, but now it burst into hideous activity and pictured interminable years

59

of scorching heat and blinding glare. For a moment she descended to the verge of hysteria, from which she struggled with so mighty an effort that it vitalized her spirit for the ordeal of her new life; and when Hamilton, cursing himself, came to assist her to land, she was able to remark that she recalled the beauty of Christianstadt, and to anathematize her sea-green maids.

The trail of Spain is over all the islands, and on St. Croix has left its picturesque mark in the heavy arcades which front the houses in the towns. Behind these arcades one can pass from street to street with brief egress into the awful downpour of the sun, and they give to both towns an effect of architectural beauty. At that time palms and cocoanuts grew in profusion along the streets of Frederikstadt and in the gardens, tempering the glare of the sun on the coral.

Peter Lytton's coach awaited the Hamiltons, and at six o'clock they started for their new home. The long driveway across the Island was set with royal palms, beyond which rolled vast fields of cane. St. Croix was approaching the height of her prosperity, and almost every inch of her fertile acres was under cultivation. They rolled up and over every hill, the heavy stone houses, with their negro hamlets and mills, rising like half-submerged islands, unless they crowned a height. The roads swarmed with Africans, who bowed profoundly to the strangers in the fine coach, grinning an amiable welcome. Surrounded by so generous a suggestion of hospitality and plenty, with the sun low in the west, the spirits of the travellers rose, and Rachael thought with more composure upon the morrow's encounter with her elder sisters. She knew them very slightly, their husbands less. When her connection with Hamilton began, correspondence between them had ceased; but like others they had accepted the relation, and for the last three years Hamilton had been a welcome guest at their houses when business took him to St. Croix. Mrs. Lytton had been the first to whom he had confided his impending failure, and she, remembering her mother's last letter and profoundly pitying the young sister who seemed marked for misfortune, had persuaded her husband to offer Hamilton the management of his grazing estates on the eastern end of the Island. She wrote to Rachael, assuring her of welcome, and reminding her that her story was unknown on St. Croix, that she would be accepted without question as Hamilton's wife and their sister. But Rachael knew that the truth would come out as soon as they had attracted the attention of their neighbours, and she had seen enough of the world to be sure that what people tolerated in the wealthy they censured in the unimportant. To depend upon her sisters' protection instead of her own lifelong distinction, galled her proud spirit. For the first time she understood how powerless Hamilton was to protect her. The glamour of that first year when nothing mattered was gone for ever. She had two children, one of them uncommon, and they were to encounter life without name or property. True, Levine might die, or Hamilton make some brilliant coup, but she felt little of the buoyancy of hope as they left the cane-fields and drove among the dark hills to their new home.

The house and outbuildings were on a high eminence, surrounded on three sides by hills. Below was a lagoon, which was separated from the sea by a deep interval of tidal mud set thick with mangroves. The outlet through this swamp was so narrow that a shark which had found its way in when young had grown too large to return whence he came, and was the solitary and discontented inhabitant of the lagoon. The next morning Rachael, rising early and walking on the terrace with Alexander, was horrified to observe him warming his white belly in the sun. On three sides of the lagoon was a thick grove of manchineels, hung with their deadly apples; here and there a palm, which drooped as if in discord with its neighbours. It was an uncheerful place for a woman with terror and tumult in her soul, but the house was large and had been made comfortable by her brother-in-laws' slaves.

Mrs. Lytton and Mrs. Mitchell drove over for the eleven o'clock breakfast. They were very kind, but they were many years older than the youngest of their family, proudly conscious of their virtue, uncomprehending of the emotions which had nearly wrenched Rachael's soul from her body more than once. Moreover, Mrs. Mitchell was the physical image of Mary Fawcett without the inheritance of so much as the old lady's temper; and there were moments, as she sat chattering amiably with Alexander, with whom she immediately fell in love, when Rachael could have flown at and throttled her because she was not her mother. Mrs. Lytton was delicate and nervous, but more reserved, and Rachael liked her better. Nevertheless, she was heartily glad to be rid of both of them, and reflected with satisfaction that she was to live on the most isolated part of the Island. She had begged them to ask no one to call, and for months she saw little of anybody except her family.

Her household duties were many, and she was forced at once to alter her lifelong relation to domestic economics. Hamilton's salary was six hundred pieces of eight, and for a time the keeping of accounts and the plans for daily disposal of the small income furnished almost the only subjects of conversation between her husband and herself. His duties kept him on horseback during all but the intolerable hours of the day, and until their new life had become a commonplace they were fortunate in seeing little of each other.

Alexander long since had upset his father's purpose to defer the opening of his mind until the age of seven. He had taught himself the rudiments of education by such ceaseless questioning of both his parents that they were glad to set him a daily task and keep him at it as long as possible. In this new home he had few resources besides his little books and his mother, who gave him all her leisure. There were no white playmates, and he was not allowed to go near the lagoon, lest the shark get him or he eat of forbidden fruit. Just after his sixth birthday, however, several changes occurred in his life: Peter Lytton sent him a pony, his father killed the shark and gave him a boat, and he made the acquaintance of the Rev. Hugh Knox.

This man, who was to play so important a part in the life of Alexander Hamilton, was himself a personality. At this time but little over thirty, he had, some years since, come to the West Indies with a classical library and a determination to rescue the planters from that hell which awaits those who drowse through life in a clime where it is always summer when it is not simply and blazingly West Indian. He soon threw the mantle of charity over the patient planters, and became the boon companion of many; but he made converts and was mightily proud of them. His was the zeal of the converted. When he arrived in the United States, in 1753, young, fresh from college, enthusiastic, and handsome, he found favour at once in the eyes of the Rev. Dr. Rogers of Middletown on the Delaware, to whom he had brought a letter of introduction. Through the influence of this eminent divine, he obtained a school and many friends. The big witty Irishman was a welcome guest at the popular tavern, and was not long establishing himself as the leader of its hilarities. He was a peculiarly good mimic, and on Saturday nights his boon companions fell into the habit of demanding his impersonation of some character locally famous. One night he essayed a reproduction of Dr. Rogers, then one of the most celebrated men of his cloth. Knox rehearsed the sermon of the previous Sunday, not only with all the divine's peculiarity of gesture and inflection, but almost word for word; for his memory was remarkable. At the start his listeners applauded violently, then subsided into the respectful silence they were wont to accord Dr. Rogers; at the finish they stole out without a word. As for Knox, he sat alone, overwhelmed with the powerful sermon he had repeated, and by remorse for his own attempted levity. His emotional Celtic nature was deeply impressed. A few days later he disappeared, and was not heard of again until, some months after, Dr. Rogers learned that he was the guest of the Rev. Aaron Burr at Newark, and studying for the church. He was ordained in due course, converted his old companions, then set sail for St. Croix.

Hamilton met him at Peter Lytton's, talked with him the day through, and carried him home to dinner. After that he became little less than an inmate of the household; a room was furnished for him, and when he did not occupy it, he rode over several times a week. His books littered every table and shelf.

Alexander was his idol, and he was the first to see that the boy was something more than brilliant. Hamilton had accepted his son's cleverness as a matter of course, and Rachael, having a keen contempt for fatuous mothers, hardly had dared admit to herself that her son was to other boys as a star to pebbles. When Knox, who had undertaken his education at once, assured her that he must distinguish himself if he lived, probably in letters, life felt almost fresh again, although she regretted his handicap the more bitterly. As for Knox, his patience was inexhaustible. Alexander would have everything resolved into its elements, and was merciless in his demand for information, no matter what the thermometer. He had no playmates until he was nine, and by that time he had much else to sober him. Of the ordinary pleasures of childhood he had scant knowledge.

Rachael wondered at the invariable sunniness of his nature,—save when he flew into a rage,—for under the buoyancy of her own had always been a certain melancholy. Before his birth she had gone to the extremes of happiness and grief, her normal relation to life almost forgotten. But the sharpened nerves of the child manifested themselves in acute sensibilities and an extraordinary precocity of intellect, never in morbid or irritable moods. He was excitable, and had a high and sometimes furious temper, but even his habit of study never extinguished his gay and lively spirits. On the other hand, beneath the surface sparkle of his mind was a British ruggedness and tenacity, and a stubborn oneness of purpose, whatever might be the object, with which no lighter mood interfered. All this Rachael lived long enough to discover and find compensation in, and as she mastered the duties of her new life she companioned the boy more and more. James was a good but uninteresting baby, who made few demands upon her, and was satisfied with his nurse. She never pretended to herself that she loved him as she did Alexander, for aside from the personality of her first-born, he was the symbol and manifest of her deepest living.

Although Rachael was monotonously conscious of the iron that had impaled her soul, she was not quite unhappy at this time, and she never ceased to love Hamilton. Whatever his lacks and failures, nothing could destroy his fascination as a man. His love for her, although tranquillized by time, was still strong enough to keep alive his desire' to please her, and he thought of her as his wife always. He felt the change in her, and his soul rebelled bitterly at the destruction of his pedestal and halo, and all that fiction had meant to both of them; but he respected her reserve, and the subject never came up between them. He knew that she never would love any one else, that she still loved him passionately, despite the shattered ideal of him; and he consoled himself with the reflection that even in giving him less than her entire store, she gave him, merely by being herself, more than he had thought to find in any woman. His courteous attentions to her had never relaxed, and in time the old companionship was resumed; they read and discussed as in their other home; but this their little circle was widened by two, Alexander and Hugh Knox. The uninterrupted intimacy of their first years was not to be resumed.

They saw little of the society of St. Croix. In 1763 Christiana Huggins, visiting the Peter Lyttons, married her host's brother, James, and settled on the Island. She drove occasionally to the lonely estate in the east, but she had a succession of children and little time for old duties. Rachael exchanged calls at long intervals with her sisters and their intimate friends, the Yards, Lillies, Crugers, Stevens, Langs, and Goodchilds, but she had been too great a lady to strive now for social position, practically dependent as she was on the charity of her relatives.

IV

In the third year of their life on St. Croix, Rachael discovered that Peter Lytton was dissatisfied with Hamilton, and retained him to his own detriment, out of sympathy for herself and her children. From that time she had few tranquil moments. It was as if, like the timid in the hurricane season, she sat constantly with ears strained for that first loud roar in the east. She realized then that the sort of upheaval which shatters one's economic life is but the precursor of other upheavals, and she thought on the unknown future until her strong soul was faint again.

Hamilton was one of those men whose gifts are ruined by their impulses, in whom the cultivation of sober judgement is interrupted by the excesses of a too sanguine temperament. He was honourable, and always willing to admit his mistakes, but years and repeated failure did little toward balancing his faults and virtues. In time he wore out the patience of even those who loved and admired him. His wife remained his one loyal and unswerving friend, but her part in his life was near its finish. The day came when Peter Lytton, exasperated once too often, after an ill-considered sale of valuable stock, let fly his temper, and further acceptance of his favour was out of the question. Hamilton, after a scene with his wife, in which his agony and remorse quickened all the finest passions in her own nature, sailed for the Island of St. Vincent, in the hope of finding employment with one of his former business connections. He had no choice but to leave his wife and children dependent upon her relatives until he could send for them; and a week later Rachael was forced to move to Peter Lytton's.

Her brother-in-law's house was very large. She was given an upstairs wing of it and treated with much consideration, but this final ignominy broke her haughty spirit, and she lost interest in herself. She was thankful that her children were not to grow up in want, that Alexander was able to continue his studies with Hugh Knox. He was beyond her now in everything but French, in which they read and talked together daily. She also discussed constantly with him those heroes of history distinguished not only for great achievements, but for sternest honour. She dreamed of his future greatness, and sometimes of her part in it. But her inner life was swathed like a mummy.

To Alexander the change would have been welcome had he understood his mother less. But the ordinary bright boy of nine is acute and observing, and this boy of Rachael's, with his extraordinary intuitions, his unboyish brain, his sympathetic and profound affection for his mother, felt with her and criticised his father severely. To him failure was incomprehensible, then, as later, for self-confidence and indomitability were parts of his equipment; and that a man of his father's age and experience, to say nothing of his education and intellect, should so fail in the common relation of life, and break the heart and pride of the uncommonest of women, filled him with a deep disappointment, which, no doubt, was the first step toward the early loss of certain illusions.

Otherwise his life was vastly improved. He soon became intimate with boys of neighbouring estates, Edward and Thomas Stevens, and Benjamin Yard, and for a time they all studied together under Hugh Knox. At first there was discord, for Alexander would have led a host of cherubims or had naught to do with them, and these boys were clever and spirited. There were rights of word and fist in the lee of Mr. Lytton's barn, where interference was unlikely; but the three succumbed speedily, not alone to the powerful magnetism in little Hamilton's mind, and to his active fists, but because he invariably excited passionate attachment, unless he encountered jealous hate. When his popularity with these boys was established they adored the very blaze of his temper, and when he formed them into a soldier company and marched them up and down the palm avenue for a morning at a time, they never murmured, although they were like to die of the heat and unaccustomed exertion. Neddy Stevens, who resembled him somewhat in face, was the closest of these boyhood friends.

Alexander was a great favourite with Mr. Lytton, who took him to ride every morning; Mrs. Lytton preferred James, who was a comfortable child to nurse; but Mrs. Mitchell was the declared slave of her lively nephew, and sent her coach for him on Saturday mornings. As for Hugh Knox, he never ceased to whittle at the boy's ambition and point it toward a great place in modern letters. Had he been born with less sound sense and a less watchful mother, it is appalling to think what a brat he would have been; but as it was, the spoiling but fostered a self-confidence which was half the battle in after years.

Hamilton never returned. His letters to his wife spoke always of the happiness of their final reunion, of belief in the future. His brothers had sent him money, and he hoped they would help him to recover his fortunes. But two years passed and he was still existing on a small salary, his hopes and his impassioned tenderness were stereotyped. Rachael's experience with Hamilton had developed her insight. She knew that man requires woman to look after her own fuel. If she cannot, he may carry through life the perfume of a sentiment, and a tender regret, but it grows easy and more easy to live without her. It was a long while before she forced her penetrating vision round to the certainty that she never should see Hamilton again, and then she realized how strong hope had been, that her interest in herself was not dead, that her love must remain quick through interminable years of monotony and humiliation. For a time she was so alive that she went close to killing herself, but she fought it out as she had fought through other desperate crises, and wrenched herself free of her youth, to live for the time when her son's genius should lift him so high among the immortals that his birth would matter as little as her own hours of agony. But the strength that carried her triumphantly through that battle was fed by the last of her vitality, and it was not long before she knew that she must die.

Alexander knew it first. The change in his mother was so sudden, the earthen hue of her white skin, the dimming of her splendid eyes, spoke so unmistakably of some strange collapse of the vital forces, that it seemed to the boy who worshipped her as if all the noises of the Universe were shrieking his anguish. At the same time he fought for an impassive exterior, then bolted from the house and rode across the Island for a doctor. The man came, prescribed for a megrim, and Alexander did not call him again; nor did he mention his mother's condition to the rest of the family. She was in the habit of remaining in her rooms for weeks at a time, and she had her own attendants. Mrs. Lytton was an invalid, and Peter Lytton, while ready to give of his bounty to his wife's sister, had too little in common with Rachael to seek her companionship. Alexander felt the presence of death too surely to hope, and was determined to have his mother to himself during the time that remained. He confided in Hugh Knox, then barely left the apartments.

Just before her collapse Rachael was still a beautiful woman. She was only thirty-two when she died. Her face, except when she forced her brain to activity, was sad and worn, but the mobile beauty of the features was unimpaired, and her eyes were luminous, even at their darkest. Her head was always proudly erect, and nature had given her a grace and a dash which survived broken fortunes and the death of her coquetry. No doubt this is the impression of her which Alexander carried through life, for those last two months passed to the sound of falling ruins, on which he was too sensible to dwell when they had gone into the control of his will.

After she had admitted to Alexander that she understood her condition, they seldom alluded to the subject, although their conversation was as rarely impersonal. The house stood high, and Rachael's windows commanded one of the most charming views on the Island. Below was the green valley, with the turbaned women moving among the cane, then the long white road with its splendid setting of royal palms, winding past a hill with groves of palms, marble fountains and statues, terraces covered with hibiscus and orchid, and another Great House on its summit. Far to the right, through an opening in the hills, was a glimpse of the sea.

Rachael lay on a couch in a little balcony during much of the soft winter day, and talked to Alexander of her mother and her youth, finally of his father, touching lightly on the almost forgotten episode with Levine. All that she did not say his creative brain divined, and when she told him what he had long suspected, that his mother's name was unknown to the Hamiltons of Grange, he accepted the fact as but one more obstacle to be overthrown in the battle with life which he had long known he was to fight unaided. To criticise his mother never occurred to him; her control of his heart and imagination was too absolute. His only regret was that she could not live until he was able to justify her. The audacity and boldness of his nature were stimulated by the prospect of this sharp battle with the world's most cherished convention, and he was fully aware of all that he owed to his mother. When he told her this she said:—

"I regret nothing, even though it has brought me to this. In the first place, it is not in me to do anything so futile. In the second place, I have been permitted to live in every part of my nature, and how many women can say that? In the third, you are in the world, and if I could live I should see you the honoured of all men. I die with regret because you need me for many years to come, and I have suffered so much that I never could suffer again. Remember always that you are to be a great man, not merely a successful one. Your mind and your will are capable of all things. Never try for the second best, and that means to put your immediate personal desire aside when it encounters one of the ideals of your time. Unless you identify yourself with the great principles of the world you will be a failure, because your mind is created in harmony with them, and if you use it for smaller purposes it will fail as surely as if it tried to lie or steal. Your passions are violent, and you have a blackness of hate in you which will ruin you or others according to the control you acquire over it; so be warned. But you never can fail through any of the ordinary defects of character. You are too bold and independent to lie, even if you had been born with any such disposition; you are honourable and tactful, and there is as little doubt of your fascination and your power over others. But remember—use all these great forces when your ambition is hottest, then you can stumble upon no second place. As for your heart, it will control your head sometimes, but your insatiable brain will accomplish so much that it can afford to lose occasionally; and the warmth of your nature will make you so many friends, that I draw from it more strength to die than from all your other gifts. Leave this Island as soon as you can. Ah, if I could give you but a few thousands to force the first doors!"

She died on the 25th of February, 1768. Her condition had been known for some days, and her sisters had shed many tears, aghast and deeply impressed at the tragic fate of this youngest, strangest, and most gifted of their father's children. Unconsciously they had expected her to do something extraordinary, and it was yet too soon to realize that she had. His aunts had announced far and wide that Alexander was the brightest boy on the Island, but that a nation lay folded in his saucy audacious brain they hardly could be expected to know.

V

The Great House of Peter Lytton was hung with white from top to bottom, and every piece of furniture looked as if the cold wing of death had touched it. A white satin gown, which had come from London for Rachael six years before,—just too late, for she never went to a ball again,—was taken from her mahogany press and wrapped about her wasted body. Her magnificent hair was put out of sight in a cap of blond lace.

The fashionable world of St. Croix, which had seen little of Rachael in life, came to the ceremonious exit of her body. They sat along the four sides of the large drawing-room, looking like a black dado against the white walls, and the Rev. Cecil Wray Goodchild, the pastor of the larger number of that sombre flock, sonorously read the prayers for the dead. Hugh Knox felt that his was the right to perform that ceremony; but he was a Presbyterian, and Peter Lytton was not one of his converts. He was there, however, and so were several Danes, whose colourless faces and heads completed the symbolization encircling the coffin. People of Nevis, St. Christopher, and St. Croix were there, the sisters born of the same mother, a kinsman of Hamilton's, himself named James Hamilton, these bleached people of the North, whose faces, virtuous as they were, would have seemed to the dead woman to shed the malignant aura of Levine's,—and the boy for whom the sacrificial body had been laid on the altar. He paid his debt in wretchedness then and there, and stood by the black pall which covered his mother, feeling a hundred years older than the brother who sat demurely on Mrs. Lytton's agitated lap.

When Mr. Goodchild closed his book, the slave women entered with silver pitchers containing mulled wines, porter mixed with sugar and spice, madeira, and port wine. Heaped high on silver salvers were pastries and "dyer bread," wrapped in white paper sealed with black wax. The guests refreshed themselves deeply, then followed the coffin, which was borne on the shoulders of the dead woman's brothers and their closest friends, across the valley to the private burying-ground of the Lyttons. Old James Lytton was placed beside her in the following year, and ten years later a child of Christiana Huggins, the wife of his son. The cane grows above their graves to-day.

VI

Alexander went home with Mrs. Mitchell, and it was long before he returned to Peter Lytton's. His favourite aunt was delighted to get him, and her husband, for whom Alexander had no love, was shortly to sail on one of his frequent voyages.

Mrs. Mitchell had a winter home in Christianstadt, for she loved the gay life of the little capital, and her large house, on the corner of King and Strand streets, was opened almost as often as Government House. This pile, with its imposing façade, represented to her the fulfilment of worldly ambitions and splendour. There was nothing to compare with it on Nevis or St. Kitts, nor yet on St. Thomas; and her imagination or memory gave her nothing in Europe to rival it. When Government House was closed she felt as if the world were eating bread and cheese. The Danes were not only the easiest and most generous of rulers, but they entertained with a royal contempt of pieces of eight, and their adopted children had neither the excuse nor the desire to return to their native isles.

Christianstadt, although rising straight from the harbour, has the picturesque effect of a high mountain-village. As the road across the Island finds its termination in King Street, the perceptible decline and the surrounding hills, curving in a crescent to the unseen shore a mile away, create the illusion. On the left the town straggles away in an irregular quarter for the poor, set thick with groves of cocoanut and palm. On the right, and parallel with the main road, is Company Street, and above is the mountain studded with great white stone houses, softened by the lofty roofs of the royal palm. All along King Street the massive houses stand close together, each with its arcade and its curious outside staircase of stone which leads to an upper balcony where one may catch the breeze and watch the leisures of tropic life. Almost every house has a court opening into a yard surrounded by the overhanging balconies of three sides of the building; and here the guinea fowl screech their matins, the roosters crow all night, there is always a negro asleep under a cocoanut tree, and a flame of colour from potted plants.

Down by the sea is the red fort, built on a bluff, and commanding a harbour beautiful to look upon, with its wooded island, its sharp high points, its sombre swamps covered with lacing mangroves, but locked from all the world but that which can come in sailing ships, by the coral reef on which so many craft have gone to pieces.

From Alexander's high window in Thomas Mitchell's house, he could see the lively Park behind the Fort; the boats sail over from the blue peaks of St. Thomas and St. John, the long white line of the sounding reef. Above the walls of Government House was the high bold curve of the mountain with its dazzling façades, its glitter of green. In the King Street of that day gentlemen in knee breeches and lace shirts, their hair in a powdered queue, were as familiar objects as turbaned blacks and Danes in uniform. After riding over their plantations "to hear the cane grow," they almost invariably brought up in town to talk over prospects with the merchants, or to meet each other at some more jovial resort. Sometimes they came clattering down the long road in a coach and four, postilions shouting at the pic'nees in the road, swerving, and halting so suddenly in some courtyard, that only a planter, accustomed to this emotional method of travel, could keep his seat. Ordinarily he preferred his horse, perhaps because it told no tales.

Thomas Mitchell had made his large fortune in the traffic of slaves, and was on terms of doubtful courtesy with Peter Lytton, who disapproved the industry. Blacks were by no means his only source of revenue; he had one of the two large general stores of the Island—the other was Nicholas Cruger's—and plantations of cane, whose yield in sugar, molasses, and rum never failed him. He was not a pleasing man in his family, and did not extend the hospitality of its roof to Alexander with a spontaneous warmth. His own children were married, and he did not look back upon the era of mischievous boys with sufficient enthusiasm to prompt him to adopt another. He yielded to his wife's voluble supplications because domestic harmony was necessary to his content, and Mistress Mitchell had her ways of upsetting it. Alexander was immediately too busy with his studies to pay attention to the indifferent grace with which Mr. Mitchell accepted his lot, and, fortunately, this industrious merchant was much away from home. Hugh Knox, as the surest means of diverting the boy from his grief, put him at his books the day after he arrived in Christianstadt. His own house was on Company Street, near the woods out of which the town seemed to spring; and in his cool library he gathered his boys daily, and crammed their brains with Latin and mathematics. The boys had met at Peter Lytton's before, but Knox easily persuaded them to the new arrangement, which was as grateful to him—he was newly married—as to Alexander. When the lessons were over he gave his favourite pupil a book and an easy-chair, or made experiments in chemistry with him until it was cool enough to ride or row. In the evening Alexander had his

72

difficult lessons to prepare, and when he tumbled into bed at midnight he was too healthy not to sleep soundly. He spent two days of every week with his friend Ned Stevens, on a plantation where there were lively people and many horses. Gradually the heaviness of his grief sank of its weight, the buoyancy and vivacity of his mind were released, the eager sparkle returned to his eyes. He did not cease to regret his mother, nor passionately to worship her memory; but he was young, the future was an unresting magnet to his ambitious mind, devoted friends did their utmost, and his fine strong brain, eager for novelty and knowledge, opened to new impressions, closed with inherent philosophy to what was beyond recall. So passed Rachael Levine.

A year later his second trial befell him. Ned Stevens, the adored, set sail for New York to complete his education at King's College. Alexander strained his eyes after the sails of the ship for an hour, then burst unceremoniously into the presence of Hugh Knox.

"Tell me quick," he exclaimed; "how can I make two thousand pieces of eight? I must go to college. Why didn't my uncles send me with Neddy? He had no wish to go. He swore all day yesterday at the prospect of six years of hard work and no more excuses for laziness. I am wild to go. Why could it not have been I?"

"That's a curious way the world has, and you'll be too big a philosopher in a few years to ask questions like that. If you want the truth, I've wrangled with Peter Lytton,—it's no use appealing to Tom Mitchell,—but he's a bit close, as you know, when it actually comes to putting his hand in his pocket. He didn't send any of his own sons to New York or England, and never could see why anyone else did. Schooling, of course, and he always had a tutor and a governess out from England; but what the devil does a planter want of a college education? I argued that I couldn't for the life of me see the makings of a planter in you, but that by fishing industriously among your intellects I'd found a certain amount of respectable talent, and I thought it needed more training than I could give it; that I was nearing the end of my rope, in fact. Then he asked me what a little fellow like you would do with a college education after you got it, for he couldn't stand the idea of you trying to earn your living in a foreign city, where there was ice and snow on the ground in winter; and when I suggested that you might stay on in the college and teach, if you were afraid of being run over or frozen to

73

death in the street, he said there was no choice between a miserable teacher's life and a planter's, and he'd leave you enough land to start you in life. I cursed like a planter, and left the house. But he loves you, and if you plead with him he might give way."

"I'd do anything else under heaven that was reasonable to get to New York but ask any man for money. Peter Lytton knows that I want learning more than all the other boys on this island; and if I'm little, I've broken in most of his colts and have never hesitated to fight. He finds his pathos in his purse. Why can't I make two thousand pieces of eight?"

"You'd be so long at it, poor child, that it would be too late to enter college; for there's a long apprenticeship to serve before you get a salary. But you must go. I've thought, thought about it, and I'll think more." He almost wished he had not married; but as he had no other cause to regret his venture, even his interest in young Hamilton did not urge him to deprive his little family of the luxuries so necessary in the West Indies. Economy on his salary would mean a small house instead of large rooms where one could forget the heat; curtailment of the voluminous linen wardrobes so soon demolished on the stones of the river; surrender of coach and horses. He trusted to a moment of sudden insight on the part of Peter Lytton, assisted by his own eloquent argument; and his belief in Alexander's destiny never wavered. Once he approached Mrs. Mitchell, for he knew she had money of her own; but, as he had expected, she went into immediate hysterics at the suggestion to part with her idol, and he hastily retreated.

Alexander turned over every scheme of making money his fertile brain conceived, and went so far as to ask his aunt to send him to New York, where he could work in one of the West Indian houses, and attend college by some special arrangement. He, too, retreated before Mrs. Mitchell's agitation, but during the summer another cause drove him to work, and without immediate reference to the wider education.

Mr. Mitchell was laid up with the gout and spent the summer on his plantation. His slaves fled at the sound of his voice, his wife wept incessantly at this the heaviest of her life's trials, and it was not long before Alexander was made to feel his dependence so keenly by the irascible planter that he leaped on his horse one day and galloped five miles under the hot sun to Lytton's Fancy.

"I want to work," he announced, with his usual breathless

impetuosity when excited, bursting in upon Mr. Lytton, who was mopping his face after his siesta. "Put me at anything. I don't care what, except in Uncle Mitchell's store. I won't work for him."

Mr. Lytton laughed with some satisfaction. "So you two have come to loggerheads? Tom Mitchell, well, is insufferable. With gout in him he must bristle with every damnable trait in the human category. Come back and live with me," he added, in a sudden burst of sympathy, for the boy looked hot and tired and dejected; and his diminutive size appealed always to Peter Lytton, who was six feet two. "You're a fine little chap, but I doubt you're strong enough for hard work, and you love your books. Come here and read all day if you like. When you're grown I'll make you manager of all my estates. Gad! I'd be glad of an honest one! The last time I went to England, that devil, Tom Collins, drank every bottle of my best port, smashed my furniture, broke the wind of every horse I had, and kept open house for every scamp and loafer on the Island, or that came to port. How old are you—twelve? I'll turn everything over to you in three years. You've more sense now than any boy I ever saw. Three years hence, if you continue to improve, you'll be a man, and I'll be only too glad to put the whole thing in your hands."

Alexander struggled with an impulse to ask his uncle to send him to college, but not only did pride strike at the words, but he reflected with some cynicism that the affection he inspired invariably expressed itself in blatant selfishness, and that he might better appeal to the enemies he had made to send him from the Island. He shook his head.

"I'll remain idle no longer," he said. "I'm tired of eating bread that's given me. I'd rather eat yours than his, but I've made up my mind to work. What can you find for me now?"

"You are too obstinate to argue with in August. Cruger wants a reliable clerk. I heard him say so yesterday. He'll take you if I say the word, and give you a little something in the way of salary."

"I like Mr. Cruger," said Alexander, eagerly, "and so did my mother."

"He's a kind chap, but he'll work you to death, for he's always in a funk that Tom Mitchell'll get ahead of him. But you cannot do better. I have no house in town, but you can ride the distance between here and Christianstadt night and morning, if my estimable brother-in-law—whom may the gout convince of his sins—is too much for you."

But Alexander had no desire to return to the house where he had passed those last terrible weeks with his mother, and Mrs. Mitchell begged him on her knees to forgive the invalid, and sent him to the house in Christianstadt, where he would be alone until December; by that time, please God, Tom Mitchell would be on his way to Jamaica. But Alexander had little further trouble with that personage. Mr. Mitchell had his susceptibilities; he was charmed with a boy of twelve who was too proud to accept the charity of wealthy relatives and determined to make his living. Alexander entered Mr. Cruger's store in October. Mr. Mitchell did not leave the Island again until the following spring, and moved to town in November. He and Alexander discussed the prospects of rum, molasses, and sugar, the price of mahogany, of oats, cheese, bread, and flour, the various Island and American markets, until Mrs. Mitchell left the table. Her husband proudly told his acquaintance that his nephew, Alexander Hamilton, was destined to become the cleverest merchant in the Caribbees.

VII

But Alexander had small liking for his employment. He had as much affinity with the sordid routine of a general store and counting-house as Tom Mitchell had with the angels. But pride and ambition carried him through most of the distasteful experiences of his life. He would come short in nothing, and at that tender age, when his relatives were prepared to forgive his failures with good-humoured tact, he was willing to sacrifice even his books to clerical success. He soon discovered that he had that order of mind which concentrates without effort upon what ever demands its powers,—masters the detail of it with incredible swiftness. At first he was a general clerk, and attended to the loading and unloading of Mr. Cruger's sloops; after a time he was made bookkeeper; it was not long before he was in charge of the counting-house. He got back to his books in time—for business in the Islands finishes at four o'clock—and when he had learned all the Latin, Greek, Hebrew, and mathematics Hugh Knox could teach him, he spent his leisure hours with Pope, Plutarch, Shakespeare, Milton, Plato, and the few other English poets and works of Greek philosophers which Knox possessed, as well as several abridged histories of England and Europe. These interested him more than aught else, purely literary as his proclivities were supposed to be, and he read and reread them, and longed for some huge work in twenty volumes which should reveal Europe to his searching vision. But this was when he was fourteen, and had almost forgotten what the life of a mere boy was like. Shortly after he entered Mr. Cruger's store he wrote his famous letter to young Stevens. It will bear republication here, and its stilted tone, so different from the concise simplicity of his business letters, was no doubt designed to produce an effect on the mind of his more fortunate friend. He became a master of style, and before he was twenty; but there is small indication of the achievement in this letter, lovable as it is:—

ST. CROIX, November 11, 1769.

DEAR EDWARD, This serves to acknowledge the receipt of yours per Capt. Lowndes, which was delivered me yesterday The truth of Capt. Lightbowen and Lowndes' information is now verified by the presence of your father and sister, for whose safe arrival I pray, and that they may convey that satisfaction to your soul, that must naturally flow from the sight of absent friends in health; and shall for news this way, refer you to them.

As to what you say, respecting your soon having the happiness of seeing us all, I wish for an accomplishment of your hopes, provided they are concomitant with your welfare, otherwise not; though doubt whether I shall be present or not, for to confess my weakness, Ned, my ambition is prevalent, so that I contemn the grovelling condition of a clerk, or the like, to which my fortune condemns me, and would willingly risk my life, though not my character, to exalt my station. I am confident, Ned, that my youth excludes me from any hopes of immediate preferment, nor do I desire it; but I mean to prepare the way for futurity. I'm no philosopher, you see, and may be justly said to build castles in the air; my folly makes me ashamed, and beg you'll conceal it; yet, Neddy, we have seen such schemes successful, when the projector is constant. I shall conclude by saying I wish there was a war.

I am, Dear Edward, Yours

ALEX. HAMILTON.

P.S. I this moment received yours by William Smith, and pleased to see you give such close application to study.

He hoped that in time Mr. Cruger would find it necessary to send him to New York; but his employer found him too useful on St. Croix, and recognized his abilities, not to the extent of advancing his intellectual interests, but of taxing and developing his capacity for business and its heavy responsibilities. In the following year he placed him in temporary charge of his branch house, in Frederikstadt, and Alexander never wished for war so desperately as when he stood under the arcade on Bay Street and stared out at the shallow green roadstead and the inimitable ocean beyond. Frederikstadt was a hamlet compared to Christianstadt, and unredeemed—the arcades excepting—by any of the capital's architectural or natural beauty. Alexander believed it to be the hottest, dullest, and most depressing spot on either hemisphere. The merchants and other residents were astonished that Nicolas Cruger should send a lad of thirteen to represent him in matters which involved large sums of money, but they recognized young Hamilton's ability even while they stared with some rudeness at the small figure in white linen, and the keen but very boyish face. When they passed him under the arcades, and asked him what ship he expected to heave in sight, he was tempted to say a man-of-war, but had no mind to reveal himself to the indifferent. He read from sundown until midnight or later, by the light of two long candles protected from draughts and insects by curving glass chimneys. Mosquitoes tormented him and cockroaches as long as his hand ran over the table; occasionally a land-crab rattled across the room, or a centipede appeared on the open page. But he was accustomed to these embellishments of tropic life, and although he anathematized them and the heat, he went on with his studies. It was about this time that he began to indulge in literary composition; and although less gifted boys than Alexander Hamilton struggle through this phase of mental development as their body runs the gamut of juvenile complaints, still it may be that had not his enormous energies been demanded in their entirety by a country in the terrible straits of rebirth, or had he dwelt on earth twenty years longer, he would have realized the ambitions of his mother and Hugh Knox, and become one of the greatest literary forces the world has had. But although this exercise of his restless faculties gave him pleasure, it was far from satisfying him, even then. He wanted the knowledge that was locked up in vast libraries far beyond that blinding stretch of sea, and he wanted action, and a sight of and a part in the great world. Meanwhile, he read every book he could find on the Island, made no mistakes in Mr. Cruger's counting-house, and stood dreaming under the arcade for hours at a time, muttering his thoughts, his mobile features expressing the ceaseless action of his brain.

Sometime during the previous year Peter Levine had returned to St. Croix for his health, and he remained with relatives for some time. He and Alexander met occasionally and were friendly. As he was a decent little chap our hero forgave him his paternity, although he never could quite assimilate the fact that he was his mother's child.

Alexander returned, after six months of Frederikstadt, to the East End of the Island. A few months later, Mr. Cruger, whose health had failed, went to New York for an extended sojourn, leaving the entire responsibility of the business in young Hamilton's hands. Men of all ages were forced to obey and be guided by a boy in the last weeks of his fourteenth year, and there were many manifestations of jealous ill-will. Some loved, others hated him, but few submitted gracefully to a leadership which lowered their self-esteem. For the first time Alexander learned that even a mercantile life can be interesting. He exercised all the resources of his inborn tact with those who had loved and those who did not hate him, and won them to a grateful acceptance of a mastership which was far more considerate and sympathetic than anything they had known. As for his enemies, he let them see the implacable quality of his temper, mortified them by an incessant exposure of their failings, struck aside their clumsy attempts to humiliate him with the keen blade of a wit that sent them skulking. Finally they submitted, but they cursed him, and willingly would have wrung his neck and flung him into the bay. As for Hamilton, there was no compromise in him, even then, where his enemies were concerned. He enjoyed their futile wrath, and would not have lifted his finger to flash it into liking.

Only once the tropical passions of his inheritance conquered his desire to dominate through the forces of his will alone. One of the oldest employees, a man named Cutter, had shown jealousy of young Hamilton from the first, and a few days after Mr. Cruger's departure began to manifest signs of open rebellion. He did his work ill, or not at all, absented himself from the store for two days, and returned to his post without excuse, squaring his shoulders about the place and sneering his contempt of youthful cocks of the walk. Alexander struggled to maintain a self-control which he felt to be strictly compatible with the dignity of his position, although his gorge rose so high that it threatened to choke him. The climax came when he gave Cutter a peremptory order, and the man took out a cigar, lit it, and laughed in his face. For the next few moments Alexander had a confused impression that he was in hell, struggling his way through the roar and confusion of his nether quarters. When he was himself again he was in the arms of his chief assistant, and Mr. Cutter bled profusely on the floor. He was informed later that he had "gone straight over the counter with a face like a hurricane" and assaulted his refractory hireling with such incredible rapidity of scientific fist that the man, who was twice his size, had succumbed from astonishment and an almost supernatural terror. Alexander, who was ashamed of himself, apologized at once, but gave the man his choice of treating him with proper respect or leaving the store. Cutter answered respectfully that he would remain; and he gave no further trouble.

"You'll get your head blown off one of these days," said Hugh Knox to Alexander, on a Sunday, as they sat in the library over two long glasses of "Miss Blyden," a fashionable drink made of sugar, rum, and the juice of the prickly pear, which had been buried in the divine's garden for the requisite number of months. "These Creoles are hot, even when they're only Danes. It's not pleasant for those clerks, for it isn't as if you had the look of the man you are. You look even younger than your age, and for a man of thirty to say 'Yes, sir' to a brat like you chokes him, and no wonder. I believe if there was a war this minute, you'd rouse the Island and lead it to battle without a misgiving or an apology. Well, don't let your triumphs lead to love of this business. I happen to know that Cruger means to make a partner of you in a few years, for he thinks the like of you never dropped into a merchant's counting-house; but never forget that your exalted destiny is to be a great man of letters, a historian, belike. You're taking to history, I notice, and you're getting a fine vocabulary of your own."

"I'd like to know what I'll write the history of if I'm to rot in this God-forsaken place. Caribs? Puling rows between French and English? I'd as well be up on Grange with my mother if it wasn't for you and your books. I want the education of a collegian. I want to study and read everything there is to be studied and read. I've made out a list of books to send for, when I've money enough, as long as you are. It's pinned on the wall of my room."

"And I suppose you've never a qualm but that head of yours will hold it all. You've a grand opinion of yourself, Alec."

"That's a cutting thing for you to say to me, sir," cried Alexander, springing to his feet. "I thought you loved me. If you think I'm a fool, I'll not waste more of your time."

"A West Indian temper beats the conceit out of the Irish. You'll control yours when you're older, for there's nothing you won't do when you put your mind to it, and you'll see the need for not making a fool of yourself too often. But as for its present liking for exercise—it's a long way the liveliest thing on St. Croix. However, you've forgiven me; I know that by the twinkle in your eye, so I'll tell you that your brain will hold all you care to put into it, and that you'll have made another list as long as King Street before you're five years older. Meanwhile, I've some books on theology and ethics you haven't had a dash at yet, and you can't read my other old books too often. Each time you'll find something new. Sitting up till midnight won't hurt you, but don't forget to say your prayers."

Knox, long since, had laid siege to Alexander's susceptible and ardent mind with the lively batteries of his religious enthusiasms. His favourite pupil was edifyingly regular in attendance at church, and said his prayers with much fervour. The burden of his petitions was deliverance from St. Croix.

When this deliverance was effected by a thunderbolt from heaven, his saving sense of humour and the agitated springs of his sympathy forbade a purely personal application. But twenty years later he might have reflected upon the opportune cause of his departure from St. Croix as one of the ironies of the world's history; for an Island was devastated, men were ruined, scores were killed, that one man might reach his proper sphere of usefulness.

VIII

Early in August, 1772, Mr. Cruger sent him on a business tour to several of the neighbouring Islands, including the great *entrepôt* of the West Indies,—St. Thomas. Despite the season, the prospect of no wind for days at a time, or winds in which no craft could live, Alexander trembled with delight at the idea of visiting the bustling brilliant versatile town of Charlotte Amalie, in whose harbour there were sometimes one hundred and eighty ships, where one might meet in a day men of every clime, and whose beauty was as famous as her wealth and importance. How often Alexander had stared at the blue line of the hills above her! Forty miles away, within the range of his vision, was a bit of the great world, the very pivot of maritime trade, and one cause and another had prevented him from so much as putting his foot on a sloop whose sails were spread.

As soon as the details of his tour were settled he rode out to the plantations to take leave of his relatives. Mrs. Mitchell, who barred the hurricane windows every time, the wind rose between July and November, and sat with the barometer in her hand when the palms began to bend, wept a torrent and implored him to abstain from the madness of going to sea at that time of the year. Her distress was so acute and real that Alexander, who loved her, forgot his exultation and would have renounced the trip, had he not given his word to Mr. Cruger.

"I'll be careful, and I'll ride out the day after I return," he said, arranging his aunt on the sofa with her smelling-bottle, an office he had performed many times. "You know the first wind of the hurricane is a delight to the sailor, and we never shall be far from land. I'm in command, and I'll promise you to make for shore at the first sign of danger. Then I shall be as safe as here."

His aunt sighed for fully a minute. "If I only could believe that you would be careful about anything. But you are quite a big boy now, almost sixteen, and ought to be old enough to take care of yourself."

"If I could persuade you that I am not quite a failure at keeping the breath in my body we both should be happier. However, I vow not to set sail from any island if a hurricane is forming, and to make for port every time the wind freshens."

"Listen for that terrible roar in the southeast, and take my barometer—Heaven knows what barometers are made for; there are not three on the Island. I shall drive in to church every Sunday and besiege Heaven with my supplications."

"Well, spare me a breeze or I shall pray for a hurricane."

He did not see Mrs. Lytton or James, but Mr. Lytton had scant apprehension of hurricanes, and was only concerned lest his nephew roll about in the trough of the sea under an August sun for weeks at a time. "That's when a man doesn't repent of his sins; he knows there is nothing worse to come," he said. "I'd rather have a hurricane," and Alexander nodded. Mr. Lytton counted out a small bag of pieces of eight and told the boy to buy his aunt a silk gown in Charlotte Amalie. "I've noticed that if it's all one colour you're not so sure to have it accepted with a sigh of resignation," he said. "But be careful of plaids and stripes." And Alexander, with deeper misgivings than Mrs. Mitchell had inspired, accepted the commission and rode away.

He set sail on the following day, and made his tour of the lesser islands under a fair breeze. Late in the month he entered the harbour of St. Thomas, and was delighted to find at least fifty ships in port, despite the season. It was an unusually busy year, and he had dared to hope for crowded waters and streets; exquisite as Charlotte Amalie might be to look upon, he wanted something more than a lovely casket.

The town is set on three conical foot-hills, which bulge at equal distances against an almost perpendicular mountain, the tip, it is said, of a range whose foundations are four miles below. The three sections of the town sweep from base to pointed apex with a symmetry so perfect, their houses are so light and airy of architecture, so brilliant and varied of colour, that they suggest having been called into being by the stroke of a magician's wand to gratify the whim of an Eastern potentate. Surely, they are a vast seraglio, a triple collection of pleasure houses where captive maidens are content and nautch girls dance with feet like larks. Business, commerce, one cannot associate with this enchanting vista; nor cockroaches as long as one's foot, scorpions, tarantulas, and rats.

When Alexander was in the town he found that the houses were of stone, and that one long street on the level connected the three divisions. Flights of steps, hewn out of the solid rock of that black and barren range, led to the little palaces that crowned the cones, and there were palms, cocoanuts, and tamarind trees to soften the brilliancy of façade and roof. Above the town was Blackbeard's Castle; and Bluebeard's so high on the right that its guns could have levelled the city in an hour. Although not a hundred years old, and built by the Danes, both these frowning towers were museums of piratical tradition, and travellers returned to Europe with imaginations expanded.

The long street interested Alexander's practical mind more than legends or architecture. Huge stone buildings—warehouses, stores, exchange- and counting-houses—extended from the street to the edge of the water, where ships were unloaded and loaded from doors at the rear. Men of every nation and costume moved in that street; and for a day Mr. Cruger's business was in abeyance, while the boy from the quiet Island of St. Croix leaned against one of the heavy tamarind trees at the foot of the first hill, and watched the restless crowd of Europeans, Asiatics, Cubans, Puerto Ricans, North and South Americans. There were as many national costumes as there were rival flags in the harbour. There was the British admiral in his regimentals and powdered queue, the Chinaman in his blouse and pigtail, the Frenchman with his earrings, villanous Malays, solemn merchants from Boston, and negroes trundling barrows of Spanish dollars. But it was the extraordinary assortment of faces and the violent contrasts of temperament and character they revealed which interested Alexander more than aught else. With all his reading he had not imagined so great a variety of types; his mental pictures had been the unconscious reflection of British, Danish, or African. Beyond these he had come in contact with nothing more striking than sailors from the neighbouring Islands, who had suggested little besides the advisability of placing an extra guard over the money boxes whilst they were in port. Most of these men who surged before him were merchants of the first rank or the representatives of others as important,—captains of large ships and their mates. The last sauntered and cursed the heat, which was infernal; but the merchants moved rapidly from one business house to another, or talked in groups, under the tamarind trees, of the great interests which brought them to the Indies. Upon the inherent characteristics which their faces expressed were superimposed the different seals of those acquired,—shrewdness, suspicion, a hawk-like alertness, the greed of acquisition. Alexander, with something like terror of the future, reflected that there was not one of these men he cared to know. He knew there were far greater cities than the busy little *entrepôt* of the West Indies, but he rightly doubted if he ever should see again so cosmopolitan a mob, a more picked assortment of representative types. Not one looked as if he remembered his wife and children, his creed, or the art and letters of his land. They were a sweating, cursing, voluble, intriguing, greedy lot, picturesque to look upon, profitable to study, calculated to rouse in a boy of intellectual passions a fury of final resentment against the meannesses of commercial life. Alexander jerked

84

his shoulders with disgust and moved slowly down the street. After he had reflected that great countries involved great ideas, and that there was no place for either political or moral ideals in an isolated and purely commercial town like little Charlotte Amalie, he recovered his poise, and lent himself to his surroundings again with considerable philosophy.

He had almost crossed the foot of the third hill when he turned abruptly into a large store, unlike any he had seen. It was full of women, splendid creatures, who were bargaining with merchants' clerks for the bales of fine stuffs which had been opened for the display of samples to the wholesale buyers from other Islands. These women purchased the exiled stuffs to sell to the ladies of the capital, and this was the only retail trade known to the St. Thomas of that day. Alexander bethought himself of his uncle's commission, and precipitately bought from the open bale nearest the door, then, from the next, a present for Mrs. Mitchell. Mrs. Lytton, who was an invalid and fifty-eight, received, a fortnight later, a dress pattern of rose-coloured silk, and Mrs. Mitchell, who aspired to be a leader of fashion, one of elderly brown. But Alexander was more interested in the sellers than in the possible dissatisfaction of his aunts. The women of his acquaintance were fair and fragile, and the Africans of St. Croix were particularly hideous, being still of parent stock. But these creatures were tawny and magnificent, with the most superb figures, the most remarkable swing, that ever a man had looked upon; and glorious eyes, sparkling with deviltry. On their heads the white linen was wound to a high point and surmounted by an immense hat, caught up at one side with a flower. They wore for clothing a double skirt of coloured linen, and a white fichu, open in a point to the waist and leaving their gold-coloured arms quite bare. They moved constantly, if only from one foot to the other. Occasionally their eyes flashed sparks, and they flew at each other's throats, screeching like guinea fowl, but in a moment they were laughing good-naturedly again, and chattering in voices of a remarkable soft sweetness. Several of them noticed Alexander, for his beauty had grown with his years. His eyes were large and gray and dark, like his mother's, but sparkled with ardour and merriment. His mouth was chiselled from a delicate fulness to a curving line; firm even then, but always humorous, except when some fresh experience with the

85

ingenuous self-interest of man deepened the humour to cynicism. The nose was long, sharply cut, hard, strong in the nostrils, the head massive, the brow full above the eyes, and the whole of a boyish and sunburned fairness. He could fetch a smile that gave his face a sweet and dazzling beauty. His figure was so supple and well knit, so proud in its bearing, that no woman then or later ever found fault with its inconsiderable inches; and his hands and feet were beautiful. His adoring aunt attended to his wardrobe, and he wore to-day, as usual, white linen knee-breeches, black silk stockings, a lawn shirt much beruffled with lace. His appearance pleased these gorgeous birds of plumage, and one of them snatched him suddenly from the floor and gave him a resounding smack. Alexander, much embarrassed, but not wholly displeased, retreated hurriedly, and asked an Englishman who they were and whence they came.

"They are literally the pick of Martinique, Cuba, Puerto Rico, and the other Islands celebrated for beautiful women. Of course they've all got a touch of the tar brush in them, but the French or the Spanish blood makes them glorious for a few years, and during those few they come here and make hay. Some come at certain seasons only, others perch here till they change in a night from houri to hag. This daylight trade gives them a *raison d'être*, but wait till after dark. God! this is a hell hole; but by moonlight or torchlight this street is one of the sights of the earth. The magnificent beauty of the women, enhanced by silken stuffs of every colour, the varied and often picturesque attire of the men, all half mad with drink—well, if you want to sleep, you'd better get a room high up."

"Mine is up one hundred and seventeen steps. I am but afraid I may not see all there is to see."

But before the week was half out he had tired of St. Thomas by day and by night. The picture was too one-sided, too heavily daubed with colour. It made a palette of the imagination, sticky and crude. He began to desire the green plantations of St. Croix, and more than ever he longed for the snow-fields of the north. Two days of hard work concluded Mr. Cruger's business, and on the thirtieth of the month he weighed anchor, in company with many others, and set sail for St. Croix. He started under a fair breeze, but a mile out the wind dropped, and he was until midnight making the harbour of Christianstadt When they were utterly becalmed the sun seemed to focus his hell upon the little sloop. It rolled sickeningly in the oily wrinkled waters, and Alexander put his Pope in his pocket. The sea had a curious swell, and he wondered if an earthquake were imminent. The sea was not quite herself when her foundations were preparing to shake. Earth-quakes had never concerned him, but as the boat drifted past the reef into the harbour of Christianstadt at midnight, he was assailed by a fit of terror so sudden and unaccountable that he could recall but one sensation in his life that approached it: shortly after he arrived on the Island he had stolen down to the lagoon one night, fascinated by the creeping mist, the scowling manchineels, the talk of its sinister inhabitant, and was enjoying mightily his new feeling of creeping terror, when the silence was broken by a heavy swish, and he saw the white belly of the shark not three feet from him. He had scampered up the hill to his mother's skirts as fast as his legs could carry him, nor visited the lagoon again until the shark was mouldering on its bed. To-night a mist, almost imperceptible except on the dark line of coast, changed the beauty of the moonbeams to a livid light that gave the bay the horrid pallor of a corpse. The masses of coral rock in the shallow waters looked leprous, the surface was so glassy that it fell in splinters from the oars of the boat that towed them to shore. There was not a sound from the reef, not a sound from the land. The slender lacing mangroves in the swamp looked like upright serpents, black and petrified, and the Fort on the high bluff might have been a sarcophagus full of dead men but for the challenge of the sentry.

Alexander began to whistle, then climbed down into the boat and took an oar. When he had his feet on land he walked up King Street more hastily than was his habit in the month of August. But here, although the town might have been a necropolis, so quiet was it, it had not put on a death mask. There was no mist here; the beautiful coral houses gleamed under the moonbeams as if turned to marble, and Alexander forgot the horror of the waters and paused to note, as he had done many times before, the curious Alpine contrast of these pure white masses against the green and burnished arches of tropic trees. Then he passed through the swimming-bath to his bed, and a half-hour later slept as soundly as if the terrible forces of the Caribbean world were safe in leash.

87

IX

When he awoke, at seven o'clock, he heard a dull low roar in the southeast, which arrested his attention at once as a sound quite dissimilar from the boom of the reef. As he crossed Strand Street to Mr. Cruger's store, an hour later, he noticed that a strong wind blew from the same direction and that the atmosphere was a sickly yellow. For a moment, he thought of the hurricane which he had passed his life expecting, but he had a head full of business and soon forgot both roar and wind. He was immediately immersed in a long and precise statement of his trip, writing from notes and memory, muttering to himself, utterly oblivious to the opening of the windows or the salutations of the clerks. Mr. Cruger arrived after the late breakfast. He looked worried, but shook Alexander's hand heartily, and thanked heaven, with some fervour, that he had returned the night before. They retired to the private office on the court, and Mr. Cruger listened with interest to young Hamilton's account of his trip, although it was evident that his mind felt the strain of another matter. He said abruptly:—

"The barometer was down two-tenths when I visited the Fort at a quarter to eleven. I'd give a good deal to know where it is now."

Alexander remembered his aunt's barometer, which he had hung in his room before sailing, and volunteered to go over and look at it.

"Do," exclaimed Mr. Cruger; "and see if the wind's shifted."

As Alexander crossed Strand Street to the side door of Mr. Mitchell's house he encountered the strongest wind he had ever known, and black clouds were racing back and forth as if lost and distracted. He returned to tell Mr. Cruger that the barometer stood at 30.03.

"And the wind hasn't shifted?" demanded Mr. Cruger. "That means we'll be in the direct path of a hurricane before the day is half out, unless things change for the better. If the barometer falls four-tenths"—he spread out his hands expressively. "Of course we have many scares. Unless we hear two double guns from the Fort, there will be no real cause for alarm; but when you hear that, get on your horse as quick as you can and ride to warn the planters. The Lyttons and Stevens and Mitchells will do for you. I'll send out three of the other boys."

They returned to accounts. Mr. Cruger expressed his gratification repeatedly and forgot the storm, although the wind was roaring up King Street and rattling the jalousies until flap after flap hung on a broken hinge. Suddenly both sprang to their feet, books and notes tumbling to the floor. Booming through the steady roar of the wind was the quick thunder of cannon, four guns fired in rapid succession.

As Alexander darted through the store, the clerks were tumbling over each other to secure the hurricane windows; for until the last minute, uneasy as they were, they had persuaded themselves that St. Croix was in but for the lashing of a hurricane's tail, and had bet St. Kitts against Monserrat as flattening in the path of the storm. The hurricane windows were of solid wood, clamped with iron. It took four men to close them against the wind.

Alexander was almost flung across Strand Street. Shingles were flying, the air was salt with spray skimmed by the wind from the surface of waves which were leaping high above the Fort, rain was beginning to fall. Mr. Mitchell's stables were in the rear of his house. Every negro had fled to the cellar. Alexander unearthed four and ordered them to close the hurricane windows. He had saddled many a horse, and he urged his into Strand Street but a few moments later. Here he had to face the wind until he could reach the corner and turn into King, and even the horse staggered and gasped as if the breath had been driven out of him. He reared back against the wall, and Alexander was obliged to dismount and drag him up the street, panting for breath himself, although his back was to the wind and he kept his head down. The din was terrific. Cannon balls might have been rattling against the stones of every house, and to this was added a roar from the reef as were all the sounds of the Caribbean Sea gathered there. Alexander would have pulled his hat down over his ears, for the noise was maddening, but it had flown over the top of a house as he left the store. He was a quarter of an hour covering the few yards which lay between the stable and the corner, and when he reached the open funnel of King Street he was nearly swept off his feet. Fortunately the horse loved him, and, terrified as it was, permitted him to mount; and then it seemed to Alexander, as they flew up King Street to the open country, that they were in a fork of the wind, which tugged and twisted at his neck while it carried them on. He flattened himself to the horse, but kept his eyes open and saw other messengers, as dauntless as himself, tearing in various directions to warn the planters, many of whom had grown callous to the cry of "Wolf."

The horse fled along the magnificent avenue of royal palms which connected the east and west ends of the Island. They were bending and creaking horribly, the masses of foliage on the summits cowering away from the storm, wrapping themselves about in a curiously pitiful manner; the long blade-like leaves seemed striving each to protect the other. Through the ever-increasing roar of the storm, above the creaking of the trees, the pounding of the rain on the earth, and on the young cane, Alexander heard a continuous piercing note, pitched upon one monotonous key, like the rattle of a girl's castinets he had heard on St. Thomas. His brain, indifferent now to the din, was as active as ever, and he soon made out this particular noise to be the rattle of millions of seeds in the dry pods of the "shaggy-shaggy," or "giant," a common Island tree, which had not a leaf at this season, nothing but countless pods as dry as parchment and filled with seeds as large as peas. Not for a second did this castinet accompaniment to the stupendous bass of the storm cease, and Alexander, whose imagination, like every other sense in him, was quickening preternaturally, could fancy himself surrounded by the orchestra of hell, the colossal instruments of the infernal regions performed upon by infuriate Titans. He was not conscious of fear, although he knew that his life was not worth a second's purchase, but he felt a wild exhilaration, a magnificent sense of defiance of the most powerful element that can be turned loose on this planet; his nostrils quivered with delight; his soul at certain moments, when his practical faculty was uncalled upon, felt as if high in the roaring space with the Berserkers of the storm.

Suddenly his horse, in spite of the wall of wind at his back, stood on his hind legs, then swerved so fiercely that his rider was all but unseated. A palm had literally leaped from the earth, sprawled across the road not a foot in front of the horse. The terrified brute tore across the cane-field, and Alexander made no attempt to stop him, for, although the rain was now falling as if the sea had come in on the high back of the wind, he believed himself to be on the Stevens plantation. The negro village was not yet deserted, and he rode to the west side of the mill and shouted his warning to the blacks crouching there. On every estate was a great bell, hung in an open stone belfry, and never to be rung except to give warning of riot, flood, fire, or hurricane. One of the blacks obeyed Alexander's peremptory command to ring this bell, and, as it was under the lee of the mill, reached it in a moment. As

Alexander urged his horse out into the storm again, he heard the rapid agitated clang of the bell mingle discordantly with the bass of the wind and the piercing rattle of the giant's castinets. He rode on through the cane-field, although if the horse stumbled and injured itself, he would have to lie on his face till the storm was over. But there was a greater danger in the avenue; he was close enough to see and hear tree after tree go down, or their necks wrenched and the great green heads rush through the air with a roar of their own, their long glittering leaves extended before them as if in supplication.

The Lytton plantation was next on his way, and Alexander rode straight for the house, as the mills and village lay far to the left. The hurricane shutters on the sides encountering the storm were already closed, and he rode round to the west, where he saw his uncle's anxious face at a drawing-room window. Mr. Lytton flung himself across the sash in an attempt to lift the boy from his horse into the room, and when Alexander shouted that he was on his way to the Mitchell estate, expostulated as well as he could without breaking his throat. He begged him to rest half an hour at least, but when informed that the Fort for the first time within the memory of man had fired its double warning, he ran to fasten his hurricane windows more securely, and despatch a slave to warn his blacks; their huts never would survive the direct attack of a hurricane. He was horrified to think of his favourite exposed to a fury, which, clever and intrepid as he was, he had small chance of outwitting; but at least he had that one chance, and Mrs. Mitchell was alone.

Alexander passed through one other estate before he reached Mr. Mitchell's, terrifying those he warned almost as much by his wild and ragged appearance—his long hair drove straight before him, and his thin shirt was in sodden ribbons—as by his news that a first-class hurricane was upon them. At last he was in the cane-fields of his destination, and the horse, as if in communication with that ardent brain so close to his own, suddenly accelerated his already mercurial pace, until it seemed to Alexander that he gathered up his legs and darted like an inflated swallow straight through crashing avenues and flying huts to the stable door. Fortunately this solid building opened to the west, and Alexander was but a few moments stalling and feeding the animal who had saved two necks by his clever feet that day. He was sorry so poorly to reward him as to close and bar the door, but he feared that he might forget to attend to it when the hurricane veered, and in all the fury of approaching climax was pouring out of the west.

The house was only an eighth of a mile away, but Alexander was half an hour reaching it. He had to travel on his knees, sometimes on his stomach, until he reached the western wall, keeping his arm pressed close against his eyes; his sense of humour, not to be extinguished by a hurricane, rebelling at the ignoble pass to which his pride had come. When he reached the north wall he rose, thinking he could cling to the projections, but he was still facing the storm; he flung himself prostrate again to avoid being lifted off his feet and sailing with the rubbish of Mr. Mitchell's plantation. As he reached the corner the wind gave him a vicious flip, which landed him almost at the foot of the steps, but he was comparatively safe, and he sat down to recover his breath. He could afford a few moments' rest, for the heavy wooden windows facing the east, north, and south, were closed. Here he was sheltered in a way. The only two good words that can be said for a hurricane are that it gives sufficient warning of its approach, and that it blows from one point of the compass at a time. Alexander sat there panting and watched the wild battle in mid-air of shingles, fences, thatched roofs, and tree-tops; listened to the artillery of the storm, which, with a stone building to break its steady roar, sounded as if a hundred cannon were bombarding the walls and rattling here and there on their carriages meanwhile; listened to crash after crash of tree and wall, the terrified bowlings and bellowings of beasts, the shrieking and grinding of trees, the piercing monotone of the dry seeds in their cases of parchment, the groans and prayers of the negroes in the cellar behind him. He turned his head and looked through the windows of the great apartment, which, although above ground, was supposed to be safest in a hurricane. All but the western blinds being closed, the cellar was almost dark, but Alexander knew that it was packed: doubtless every African on the estate was there; he could see, for some distance back, row after row of rolling eyes and hanging tongues. Some knelt on the shoulders of others to get the air. Alexander shuddered. The sight reminded him of his uncle's slave-ships, where the blacks came, chained together, standing in the hold, so closely packed that if one died he could not fall, nor the others protect themselves from the poisons of a corpse, which pressed hard against the living for twenty hours perhaps, before it was unchained and flung to

92

the sharks. Alexander went close to one of the windows and shouted to them not to forget to secure the western blinds when the lull came, then ran up the steps and vaulted through an open window. It was a few minutes before he found his aunt, and it must be recorded that on his way to the front of the house he looked under two beds and into four wardrobes. He came upon her in the drawing-room, valiantly struggling with a hurricane window. Her hair was dishevelled, and her eyes bulged with horror, but even as Alexander came to the rescue, she shoved the bar into place. Then she threw herself into his arms and fainted. He had but time to fling water on her face, when a loud rattle from another window sent him bounding to it, and for ten minutes he struggled to fasten the blind soundly again, while it seemed to him that a hundred malignant fingers were tugging at its edge. He had no sooner secured it, than his aunt's voice at his ear begged him to try every window on three sides of the house, and he went rapidly from one to the other, finding most of them in need of attention—long disuse had weakened both staples and hooks. His aunt trotted after him, thumping every window, and reminding him that if one went, and the wind burst in, the roof would be off and the torrents upon them before they could reach the cellar.

Fortunately for those who fought the storm, the temperature had fallen with the barometer, and these two dared not relax their vigilance for a moment. Every negro had deserted to the lower region. Alexander was unable to change his wet clothes or to refresh himself with so much as a banana, but there was not a second's time to think of hunger or discomfort. More than once that sense of wild exultation in fighting a mighty element possessed him. His own weak hands and a woman's weaker against one of the Titanic hurricanes of the world's history, with a prospect of winning the fight, was a sight to move comfortable gods to paean or laughter, according to their spiritual development.

But during much of that terrible day and night Alexander's brain was obliged to work on device after device to strengthen those battered boards which alone protected the house from destruction, its inmates, perhaps, from death. A tamarind tree came down on a corner of the roof with a crash; and when Mrs. Mitchell and Alexander reached the room, which was in a wing, the rain was struggling past the heavy mass through a hole in the roof. They closed up the room, as well as the jalousies of the inner walls, but as they returned to the windows they heard the rain fighting to pass the branches, and knew that if the wind snatched the tree, the deluge would come in.

Mrs. Mitchell neither fainted again nor exhibited other sign of fear. While that hurricane lasted she was all Mary Fawcett; and Alexander, meeting her eyes now and again, or catching sight of her as she darted forward at the first rattle of a shutter, recalled his mother's many anecdotes of his redoubtable grandmother, and wondered if that valiant old soul had flown down the storm to the relief of the fortress.

Toward evening that sudden lull came which means that at last the besieged are in the very centre of the hurricane, and will have respite while the monster is swinging his tail to the west. Alexander and Mrs. Mitchell, after opening the windows on the east side of the house, and securing those opening to the west, went to the pantry and made a substantial meal without sitting or selecting. To his last day Alexander could not remember what he ate that night, although he recalled the candle in the long chimney, the constant craning of his aunt's head, the incessant racing of the rats along the beams. He went to his room and took a cold bath, which with the food and suspended excitement quite refreshed him; put on dry clothes, nailed a board against the hole in the roof, then sat down with Mrs. Mitchell in the western gallery to await the hurricane's return.

"We have three windows where we had one before," remarked Mrs. Mitchell; "and the hinges of that door are rusty. God knows! If you had not come, the roof would have gone long before this."

"The silence is horrible," said Alexander.

It was, indeed, earsplitting. Not a sound arose from that devastated land. Birds and beasts must lie dead by the thousand; not a horseman ventured abroad; not a whisper came from the cellar, where two hundred Africans might be dead from fright or suffocation. Mrs. Mitchell had lit the candles, and there was something sinister and ironical in the steady flames. How long before they would leap and add the final horror to what must be a night of horrors? It was impossible to work in the dark, but every yellow point was a menace.

They had not long to endure the silence. This time the hurricane sent no criers before it. It burst out of the west with a fury so intensified that Alexander wondered if one stone in Frederikstadt were left upon another. It was evident that it had gathered its forces for a final assault, and its crashing and roaring, as it tore across the unhappy Island it had marked for destruction, was that of a gigantic wheel whirling ten thousand cannon, exploding, and lashing each other in mid-air. It seemed to Alexander that every ball they surely carried rattled on the roof, and the heavy stone structure vibrated for the first time. It was two hours before he and Mrs. Mitchell met again, for they worked at opposite ends of the long gallery; but in the third both rushed simultaneously to the door. It sprang back from its rusty fastenings, and they were but in time to seize the bar which passed through a staple in its middle, and pull it inward until it pressed hard against the jamb on the right. There was no other way to secure it, and for three hours Alexander and Mrs. Mitchell dragged at it alternately, while the other attended to the windows. By this time Alexander had ceased to wonder if he should see another morning, or much to care: the storm was so magnificent in its almighty power, its lungs of iron bellowed its purpose with such furious iteration, as if out of all patience with the mortals who defied it, that Alexander was almost inclined to apologize. More than once it took the house by the shoulders and shook it, and then a yell would come from below, a simultaneous note pitched in a key of common agony. Suddenly the house seemed to spring from its foundations, then sink back as if to collapse. Alexander called out that it had been uprooted and would go down the hill in another moment, but Mrs. Mitchell, who was at the bar, muttered, "An earthquake. I believe a hurricane shakes the very centre of the earth."

They feared that the foundations of the house had been loosened, and that the next blast would turn it over, but the house was one of the strongest in the Caribbees, built to withstand the worst that Nature could do, so long as man saw to its needs; and when the hurricane at last revolved its artillery away into the east, carrying with it that piercing rattle of the giant's castinets, which never for a moment had ceased to perform its part, roof and walls were firm. Mrs. Mitchell and Alexander sank where they had stood, and slept for twenty hours.

X

Alexander rode back to Christianstadt two days later, and again and again he drew a hard breath and closed his eyes. It was a sight to move any man, and the susceptible and tender nature of young

Hamilton bled for the tragedy of St. Croix. There was not a landmark, not a cane-field, to remind him that it was the beautiful Island on which he had spent the most of his remembering years. Although all of the Great Houses were standing, their mien and manner were so altered by the disappearance of their trees and outbuildings, and by the surrounding pulpy flats in place of the rippling acres of young cane, that they were unrecognizable. Here and there were masses of débris, walls and thatched roofs swept far from the village foundations; but as a rule there was but a board here or a bunch of dried leaves there, a battered utensil or a stool, to reward the wretched Africans who wandered about searching for the few things they had possessed before the storm. They looked hopeless and dull, as if their faculties had been stunned by the prolonged incessant noise of the hurricane.

Alexander was riding down what a week ago had been the most celebrated avenue in the Antilles. Where there were trees at all, they were headless, the long gray twisted trunks as repulsive as they had once been beautiful. The road was littered with many of the fallen; but others were far away in what had been the cane-fields, serpents and lizards sunning themselves on the dead roots. Even stone walls were down, and under them, sometimes, were men. Mills were in ruins; for no one had remained to keep bars in their staples. Tanks of last year's rum and treacle had been flung through the walls, and their odours mingled with the stench of decomposing men and cattle. The horrid rattle of the land-crab was almost the only sound in that desolate land. "The Garden of the Antilles" looked like a putrid swamp, and she had not a beauty on her.

Alexander turned at a cross-road into a path which led through the Grange estate to the private burying-ground of the Lyttons. These few moments taxed his courage more heavily than the ride with the hurricane had done, and more than once he opened his clenched teeth and half turned his horse's head. But he went on, and before long he had climbed to the end of his journey. The west wall of the little cemetery had been blown out, and the roof of old James Lytton's tomb lay with its débris. A tree, which evidently had been torn from the earth and flung from a distance, lay half in and half out of the enclosure. But his mother's headstone, which stood against the north wall, was undisturbed, although the mound above her was flat and sodden. The earth had been strong enough to hold her. Alexander remembered its awful air of finality as it opened to receive her, then closed over her. What he had feared was that the burying-ground, which stood on the crest of a hill, would have been uprooted and scattered over the cane-fields.

He rode on to Christianstadt. There the evidences of the hurricane were less appalling, for the houses, standing close together, had protected each other, and only two were unroofed; but everywhere the trees looked like twisted poles, the streets and gardens were full of rubbish, and down by the bay the shore was strewn with the wreckage of ships; the Park behind the Fort was thick with decaying fish, which the blacks were but just now sweeping out to the water.

After Alexander had ascertained that Mr. Mitchell's house was quite unharmed, although a neighbour had lost half a roof and been deluged in consequence, he walked out Company Street to see how it had fared with Hugh Knox. That worthy gentleman was treating his battered nerves with weak whiskey and water when he caught sight of Alexander through the library window. He gave a shout that drew an exasperated groan through the ceiling, flung open the door, and clasped his beloved pupil in his arms.

"I knew you were safe, because you are you, although I've been afraid to ask if you were dead or alive. Cruger sent out three others to warn the planters, and they've all been brought home, one dead, one maimed, one with chills and fever and as mad as a March hare. Good God! what a visitation! I'd rather have been on a moving bog in Ireland. You wouldn't have ridden out in that hurricane if I'd got you, not if I'd been forced to tie you up. Fancy your being here alive, and not even a cold in your head! But you've a grand destiny to work out, and the hurricane—which I believe was the Almighty in a temper—knew what it was about. Now tell me your experience. I'm panting to tell you mine. I've not had a soul to talk to since the hour it started. The Missis behaved like a Trojan while it lasted, then went to bed, and hasn't spoken to me since; and as for everyone else in Christianstadt—well, they've retired to calm their nerves in the only way,—prayer first and whiskey after."

Alexander took possession of his own easy-chair and looked gratefully around the room. The storm had not disturbed it, neither had a wench's duster. Since his mother's death he had loved this room with a more grateful affection than any mortal had inspired, well as he loved his aunt, Hugh Knox, and Neddy. But the room did not talk, and the men who had written the great books which made him indifferent to his island prison for days and weeks at a time, were dead, and their selfishness was buried with them.

Meanwhile Knox, forgetting his desire to hear the experience of his guest, was telling his own. It was sufficiently thrilling, but not to be compared with that of the planter's; and when he had finished, Alexander began with some pride to relate his impressions of the storm. He, too, had not talked for three days; his heart felt warm again; and in the familiar comfortable room, the terrible picture of the hurricane seemed to spring sharp and vivid from his memory; he had recalled it confusedly hitherto, and made no effort to live it again. Knox leaned forward eagerly, dropping his pipe; Alexander talked rapidly and brilliantly, finally springing to his feet, and concluding with an outburst so eloquent that his audience cowered and covered his face with his hands. For some moments Knox sat thinking, then he rose and pushed a small table in front of Alexander, littering it with pencils and paper, in his untidy fashion.

"My boy," he said, "you're still hot with your own eloquence. Before you cool off, I want you to write that down word for word as you told it to me. If it twisted my very vitals, it will give a similar pleasure to others. 'Twould be selfish to deny them. When it's done, I'll send it to Tiebout. Now I'll leave you, and if my niggers are still too demoralized to cook supper for you, I'll do it myself."

Alexander, whose brain, in truth, felt on fire, for every nerve had leapt to the recreating of that magnificent Force that had gathered an island into the hollow of its hand, crushed, and cast it back to the waters, dashed at the paper and wrote with even more splendour than he had spoken. When he had finished, he was still so excited that he rushed from the house and walked till the hideous sights and smells drove him home. He was quivering with the ecstasy of birth, and longed for another theme, and hours and days of hot creation. But he was to be spared the curse of the "artistic temperament."

XI

The description of the hurricane went to St. Christopher by sloop

98

two days later (there were no English papers on St. Croix), and was not heard from for two weeks. Meanwhile Alexander forgot it, as writers have a way of forgetting their infants of enthusiastic delivery. There was much to do on St. Croix. The negroes were put at once to rebuilding and repairing, and masters, as well as overlookers and agents, were behind them from morning till night. Mr. Mitchell had not returned, and Alexander was obliged to take charge of his estates. When he was not galloping from village to village and mill to mill, driving the sullen blacks before him, or routing them out of ruins and hollows, where they huddled in a demoralized stupor, he was consoling his aunt for the possible sacrifice of Mr. Mitchell to the storm. Alexander was quite confident that the hurricane had spared Tom Mitchell, whomsoever else it may have devoured, but his logic did not appeal to his aunt, who wept whenever he was there to offer his arm and shoulder. At other times she bustled about among her maids, who were sewing industriously for the afflicted.

Alexander was grateful for the heavy task Mr. Mitchell's absence imposed, for there was no business doing in Christianstadt, and his nerves were still vibrating to the storm he had fought and conquered. His rigorous self-control was gone, his suppressed energies and ambitions were quick and imperious, every vial of impatience and disgust was uncorked. As he rode through the hot sunlight or moved among the Africans, coaxing and commanding, getting more work out of them by his gay bright manner than the overlookers could extract with their whips, his brain was thumping with plans of delivery from a life which he hated so blackly that he would wrench himself free of it before the year was out if he had to ship as a common sailor for New York. It seemed to him that the vacancies in his brain ached. His imagination was hot with the future awaiting him beyond that cursed stretch of blinding water. For the first time he fully realized his great abilities, knew that he had in him the forces that make history. All the encouragement of his mother and Hugh Knox, the admiration and confidence of such men as Mr. Cruger, the spoiling of his relatives, and his easy conquest or equally flattering antagonism of the youth of the Island, had fostered his self-confidence without persuading him that he was necessarily a genius. Strong as his youthful ambitions had been, burning as his desire for more knowledge, much in his brain had been dormant, and a humorous philosophy, added to the sanguineness of youth and a deep affection for a few people, had enabled him to bear his lot with unbroken cheerfulness. But the clashing forces of the Universe had roused the sleeping giant in his brain and whirled his youth away. His only formulated ambition was to learn first all that schools could teach him, then lead great armies to battle. Until the day of his death his desire for military excitement and glory never left him, and at this time it was the destiny which heated his imagination. It seemed to him that the roar and rattle of the hurricane, in whose lead he had managed to maintain himself unharmed, were the loud prophecy of battle and conquest. At the same time, he knew that other faculties and demands of his brain must have their way, but he could only guess at their nature, and statesmanship was the one achievement that did not occur to him; the American colonies were his only hope, and there was no means by which he could know their wrongs and needs. Such news came seldom to the West Indies, and Knox retained little interest in the country where he had sojourned so short a while. And at this time their struggle hardly would have appealed to young Hamilton had he known of it. He was British by instinct and association, and he had never received so much as a scratch from the little-finger nail of the distant mother, whose long arm was rigid above her American subjects.

His deliverance was so quick and sudden that for a day or two he was almost as dazed as the Africans after the hurricane. One day Hugh Knox sent him out a copy of the St. Christopher newspaper which had published his description of the storm. With some pride in his first-born, he read it aloud to his aunt. Before he was halfway down the first column she was on the sofa with her smelling-salts, vowing she was more terrified than when she had expected to be killed every minute. When he had finished she upbraided him for torturing people unnecessarily, but remarked that he was even cleverer than she had thought him. The next morning she asked him to read it again; then read it herself. On the following day Hugh Knox rode out.

Alexander was at one of the mills. Knox told Mrs. Mitchell that he had sent a copy of the newspaper to the Governor of St. Croix, who had called upon him an hour later and insisted upon knowing the name of the writer. Knox not only had told him, but had expanded upon Alexander's abilities and ambitions to such an extent that the Governor at that moment was with Peter Lytton, endeavouring to persuade him to open his purse-strings and send the boy to college.

"He will not do all," added Knox, "and I rely upon you to do the rest. Between you, Alexander can get, first the education he wants now more than anything in life, then the chance to make a great reputation among men. If you keep him here you're no better than criminals, and that's all I have to say."

Mrs. Mitchell shuddered. "Do you think he really wants to go?" she asked.

"Do I think he wants to go!" roared Hugh Knox. "Do I think—Good God! Why he's been mad to go for five years. He'd have thought of nothing else if he hadn't a will like a bar of iron made for a hurricane door, and he'd have grown morbid about it if he hadn't been blest with a cheerful and a sanguine disposition. You adore him, and you couldn't see that!"

"He never said much about it," said Mrs. Mitchell, meekly; "but I think I can see now that you are right. It will make me ill to part with him, but he ought to go, and if Peter Lytton will pay half his expenses, I'll pay the other half, and keep him in pocket coin besides. Of course Tom won't give a penny, but I have something of my own, and he is welcome to it. Do have everything arranged before my husband's return. He is alive and well. I had a letter from him by the sloop that came from St. Kitts, and he'll be here by the next or the one after."

As soon as Knox had gone Mrs. Mitchell ordered her coach and drove to Lytton's Fancy. Her love for Alexander had struggled quite out of its fond selfishness, and she determined that go to New York he should and by the next ship. She found her brother-in-law meditating upon the arguments of the Governor, and had less difficulty in persuading him than she had anticipated.

"I'm sorry we haven't sent him before," he said finally. "For if two men like Walsterstorff and Knox think so highly of him, and if he can write like that,—it gave me the horrors,—he ought to have his chance, and this place is too small for him. I'll help you to keep him at college until he's got his education,—and it will take him less time than most boys to get it,—and then he'll be able to take care of himself. If he sails on Wednesday, there's no produce to send with him to sell; but I've silver, and so have you, and he can take enough to keep him until the

Island is well again. We'll do the thing properly, and he shan't worry for want of plenty."

When Alexander came home that evening he was informed that the world had turned round, and that he stood on its apex.

XII

The night before he sailed he rode out to the Grange estate. The wall of the cemetery had been repaired, James Lytton's slab was in its place, the tree had been removed, and he had rebuilt the mound above his mother as soon as the earth was firm again. There was no evidence of the hurricane here. The moon was out, and in her mellow bath the Island had the beauty of a desert. Alexander leaned his elbows on the wall and stared down at his mother's grave. He knew that he never should see it again. What he was about to do was for good and all. He would no more waste months returning to this remote Island than he would turn back from any of the goals of his future. And it mattered nothing to the dead woman there. If she had an immortal part, it would follow him, and she had suffered too much in life for her dust to resent neglect. But he passionately wished that she were alive and that she were sailing with him to his new world. He had ceased to repine her loss, much to miss her, but his sentiment for her was still the strongest in his life, and as a companion he had found no one to take her place. To-night he wanted to talk to her. He was bursting with hope and anticipation and the enthusiasm of the mere change, but he was close to melancholy.

Suddenly he bent his head. From the earth arose the golden music of a million tiny bells. They had hung rusty and warped since the hurricane, but to-night they rang again, and as sweetly as on the night, seventeen years ago, when their music filled the Universe, and two souls, whose destiny it was to bring a greater into the world, were flooded with a diviner music than that fairy melody. Alexander knew nothing of that meeting of his parents, when they were but a few years older than he was to-night, but the inherited echo of those hours when his own soul awaited its sentence may have stirred in his brain, for he stood there and dreamed of his mother and father as they had looked and thought when they had met and loved; and this he had never done before. The tireless little ringers filled his brain with their Lilliputian clamour, and his imagination gave him his parents in the splendour of their young beauty and passion. For the first time he forgave his father, and he had a deep moment of insight: one of the mysteries of life was bare before him. He was to have many of these cosmic moments, for although his practical brain relied always on hard work, never on inspiration, his divining faculty performed some marvellous feats, and saved him from much plodding; but he never had a moment of insight which left a profounder impression than this. He understood in a flash the weakness of the world, and his own. At first he was appalled, then he pitied, then he vibrated to the thrill of that exultation which had possessed his mother the night on the mountain when she made up her mind to outstay her guests. And then the future seemed to beckon more imperiously to the boy for whose sake she had remained, the radiant image of his parents melted in its crucible, and the world was flooded with a light which revealed more than the smoke of battlefields and the laurels of fulfilled ambition.

XIII

On the following day, as Alexander stood on the wharf with his tearful relatives and friends, Hugh Knox detached him from Mrs. Mitchell and led him aside.

"Alec," he said, "I've two pieces of parting advice for you, and I want you to put them into the pocket of your memory that's easiest to find. Get a tight rein on that temper of yours. It's improved in the last year, but there's room yet. That's the first piece. This is the second: keep your own counsel about the irregularity of your birth, unless someone asks you point-blank who has the right; if anyone else does, knock him down and tell him to go to hell with his impertinence. And never let it hit your courage in the vitals for a moment. You are not accountable; your mother was the finest woman I ever knew, and you've got the best blood of Britain in your veins, and not a relative in the world who's not of gentle blood. You're an aristocrat in body and brain, and you'll not find a purer in the American colonies. The lack of a priest at the right time can cause a good deal of suffering and trouble, but it can't muddy a pure stream; and many a lawful marriage has done that. So, mind you never bring your head down for a minute, nor persuade yourself that anyone has a better right to keep it up. It would be the death of you."

Alexander nodded, but did not reply. He was feeling very low, now that the hour for parting was come, for his affections were strong and tender, and they were all rooted in the Island he hated. He understood, however.

He was six weeks reaching Boston, for even the wind seemed to have had the life beaten out of it. He had a box of Knox's books, which he was to return by the Captain; and although he had read them before, he read them again, and wrote commentaries, and so kept his mind occupied for the greater part of the voyage. But an active brain, inexperienced in the world, and in no need of rest, is always bored at sea, and he grew sick of the sight of that interminable blue waste; of which he had seen too much all his life. When he had learned all there was to know about a ship, and read all his books, he burned for change of any sort. The change, when it came, was near to making an end of him: the ship caught fire, and they were a day and a night conquering the flames and preparing their philosophy to meet death; for the boats were unseaworthy. Alexander had all the excitement he wanted, for he fought the fire as hard as he had fought the hurricane, and he was delighted when the Captain gave him permission to turn in. This was his third touch-and-go with death.

He arrived in Boston late in October, and took passage immediately for New York. There had been no time to announce his coming, and he was obliged to find his own way to the house of Hercules Mulligan, a member of the West Indian firm, to whom Mr. Cruger had given him a warm letter of introduction. Mr. Mulligan, a good-natured Irishman, received him hospitably, and asked him to stop in his modest house until his plans were made. Alexander accepted the invitation, then started out in search of his friend, Ned Stevens, but paused frequently to observe the queer, straggling, yet imposing little city, the red splendour of the autumn foliage; above all, to enjoy the keen and frosty air. All his life he had longed for cold weather. He had anticipated it daily during his voyage, and, although he had never given way to the natural indolence of the Tropics, he had always been conscious of a languor to fight. But the moment the sharp air of the North had tingled his skin his very muscles seemed to harden, his blood to quicken, and even his brain to become more alert and eager. If he had been ambitious and studious in an average temperature of eighty-five degrees, what would happen when the thermometer dropped below zero? He smiled, but with much contentment. The vaster the capacity for study, the better; as for his ambitions, they could rest until he had finished his education. Now that his feet were fairly planted on the wide highway of the future, his impatience was taking its well-earned rest; he would allow no dreams to interfere with the packing of his brain.

It was late in the afternoon, and the fashionable world was promenading on lower Broadway and on the Battery by the Fort. It was the first time that Alexander had seen men in velvet coats, or women with hoopskirts and hair built up a foot, and he thought the city, with its quaint Dutch houses, its magnificent trees, and these brilliant northern birds, quite like a picture book. They looked high-bred and intelligent, these animated saunterers, and Alexander regarded the women with deep inquisitiveness. Women had interested him little, with the exception of his mother, who he took for granted *sui generis*. The sisters of his friends were white delicate creatures, languid and somewhat affected; and he had always felt older than either of his aunts. In consequence, he had meditated little upon the sex to which poets had formed a habit of writing sonnets, regarding them either as necessary appendages or creatures for use. But these alert, dashing, often handsome women, stirred him with a new gratitude to life. He longed for the day when he should have time to know them, and pictured them gracing the solid home-like houses on the Broadway, and in the fine grounds along the river front, where he strayed alter a time, having mistaken the way to King's College. He walked back through Wall Street, and his enthusiasm was beginning to ebb, he was feeling the first pangs of a lonely nostalgia, when he almost ran into Ned Stevens's arms. It was four years since they had met. Stevens had grown a foot and Alexander a few inches, but both were boyish in appearance still and recognized each other at once.

"When I can talk," exclaimed Stevens, "when I can get over my amazement—I thought at first it was my double, come to tell me something was wrong on the Island—I'll ask you to come to Fraunces' Tavern and have a tankard of ale. It's healthier than swizzle."

"That is an invitation, Neddy," cried Alexander, gaily. "Initiate me at once. I've but a day or two to play in, but I must have you for playfellow."

They dined at Fraunces' Tavern and sat there till nearly morning. Alexander had much to tell but more to hear, and before they parted at

Mr. Mulligan's door he knew all of the New World that young Stevens had patiently accumulated in four years. It was a stirring story, that account of the rising impatience of the British colonies, and Stevens told it with animation and brevity. Alexander became so interested that he forgot his personal mission, but he would not subscribe to his friend's opinion that the Colonials were in the right.

"Did I have the time, I should study the history of the colonies from the day they built their first fort," he said. "Your story is picturesque, but it does not convince me that they have all the right on their side. England—"

"England is a tyrannical old fool," young Stevens was beginning, heatedly, when a man behind arose and clapped a hand over his mouth.

"There are three British officers at the next table," he said. "We don't want any more rows. One too many, and God knows what next."

Stevens subsided, but Alexander's nostrils expanded. Even the mental atmosphere of this brilliant North was full of electricity.

The next day he presented to Dr. Rogers and Dr. Mason the letters which Hugh Knox had given him. He interested them at once, and when he asked their advice regarding the first step he should take toward entering college, they recommended Francis Barber's Grammar School, at Elizabethtown, New Jersey. Stevens had suggested the same institution, and so did other acquaintances he made during his brief stay in the city which was one day to be christened by angry politicians, "Hamiltonopolis." Early in the following week he crossed to New Jersey and rode through the forests to the village, with its quaint streets and handsome houses, "the Burial Yard Lot," beside the main thoroughfare of the proud little hamlet, and Mr. Barber's Grammar School at its upper end. Hamilton was accepted immediately, but where to lodge was a harassing question. The only rooms for hire were at the tavern, where permanent lodgement would be intolerable. When he presented a letter to Mr. Boudinot, which Mr. Cruger had given him, the problem was solved at once. Mr. Boudinot, one of the men of his time, had a spacious and elegant house, set amidst gardens, lawns, and forest trees; there were many spare bedrooms, and he invited Hamilton to become a member of his family. The invitation was given as a matter of course, and Hamilton accepted it as frankly. All the pupils who were far from home visited in the neighbourhood. Liberty Hall, on the Springfield turnpike, was finishing when Hamilton arrived. When the family was installed and he presented his letter to its owner, William Livingston, he received as pressing an invitation as Mr. Boudinot's, and divided his time between the two houses.

Mr. Boudinot was a large man, with a long nose and a kindly eye, who was deeply attached to his children. Susan was healthy, pretty, lively, and an ardent young patriot. The baby died, and Hamilton, having offered to sit up with the little body, entertained himself by writing an appropriate poem, which was long treasured by Mr. Boudinot.

At Liberty Hall life was even more interesting. William Livingston was one of the ablest lawyers, most independent thinkers, and ardent republicans of the unquiet times. Witty and fearless, he had for years made a target of kingly rule; his acid cut deep, doing much to weaken the wrong side and encourage the right. His wife was as uncompromising a patriot as himself; his son, Brockholst, and his sprightly cultivated daughters had grown up in an atmosphere of political discussion, and in constant association with the best intellects of the day. Sarah, the beauty, was engaged to John Jay, already a distinguished lawyer, notoriously patriotic and high-minded. He was a handsome man, with his dark hair brushed forward about his face, his nobility and classic repose of feature. Mr. Livingston wore his hair in a waving mass, as long as he had any. His nose was large and sharp, and he had a very disapproving eye. He took an immediate liking to young Hamilton, however, and his hospitality was frank and delightful. Brockholst and Alexander liked and admired each other in those days, although they were to become bitter enemies in the turbulent future. As for the lively bevy of women, protesting against their exile from New York, but amusing themselves, always, they adopted "the young West Indian." The delicate-looking boy, with his handsome sparkling face, his charming manners, and gay good humour captivated them at once; and he wrote to Mrs. Mitchell that he was become shockingly spoiled. When Mr. Livingston discovered that his brain and knowledge were extraordinary, he ceased at once to treat him as a fascinating boy, and introduced him to the men who were constantly entertained at his house: John Jay, James Duane, Dr. Witherspoon, President of Princeton; and members of the Morris, Schuyler, Ogden, Clinton, and Stockton families. The almost weekly conversation of these men contributed to the rapid maturing of Hamilton's mind. His recreation he found with the young women of the family, and their conversation was not always political. Sarah Livingston, beautiful, sweet, and clever, was pensively in love; but Kitty and Susan were not, and they were handsome and dashing. They were sufficiently older than Alexander to inspire him with the belief that he was in love with each in turn; and if he was constant to either, it was to Kitty, who was the first to reveal to him the fascination of her sex. But they did not interrupt the course of his studies; and in the dawn, when he repaired to the Burial Yard Lot to think out his difficult task for the day, not a living face haunted the tombstones.

And when winter came and he walked the vast black forests alone, the snow crunching under his feet, the blood racing in his body, a gun on his shoulder, lest he meet a panther, or skated till midnight under the stars, a crystal moon illuminating the dark woods on the river's edge, the frozen tide glittering the flattering homage of earth, he felt so alive and happy, so tingling and young and primeval, that had his fellow-inhabitants flown to the stars he would not have missed them. Until that northern winter embraced and hardened him, quickening mind and soul and body, crowding the future with realized dreams, he never had dared to imagine that life could be so fair and beautiful a thing.

On stormy winter nights, when he roasted chestnuts or popped corn in the great fireplace of Liberty Hall, under the tuition of all the Livingston girls, Sarah, Susan, Kitty, and Judith, he felt very sociable indeed; and if his ears, sometimes, were soundly boxed, he looked so penitent and meek that he was contritely rewarded with the kiss he had snatched.

The girls regarded him as a cross between a sweet and charming boy to be spoiled—one night, when he had a toothache, they all sat up with him—and a phenomenon of nature of which they stood a trifle in awe. But the last was when he was not present and they fell to discussing him. And with them, as with all women, he wore, because to the gay vivacity and polished manners of his Gallic inheritance he added the rugged sincerity of the best of Britons; and in the silences of his heart he was too sensible of the inferiority of the sex, out of which, first and last, he derived so much pleasure, not to be tender and considerate of it always.

Before the year of 1773 was out Mr. Barber pronounced him ready for college, and, his choice being Princeton, he presented himself to Dr. Witherspoon and demanded a special course which would permit him to finish several years sooner than if he graduated from class to class. He knew his capacity for conquering mental tasks, and having his own way to make in the world, had no mind to waste years and the substance of his relatives at college. Dr. Witherspoon, who had long been deeply interested in him, examined him privately and pronounced him equal to the heavy burden he had imposed upon himself, but feared that the board of trustees would not consent to so original a plan. They would not. Hamilton, nothing daunted, applied to King's College, and found no opposition there. He entered as a private student, attached to no particular class, and with the aid of a tutor began his customary annihilation of time. Besides entering upon a course of logic, ethics, mathematics, history, chronology, rhetoric, Hebrew, Greek, Latin, all the modern languages, and Belles Lettres, he found time to attend Dr. Clossy's lectures on anatomy, with his friend Stevens, who was studying medicine as a profession.

King's was a fine building facing the North River and surrounded by spacious grounds shaded by old sycamores and elms. There were many secluded corners for thought and study. A more favourite resort of Alexander's was Batteau Street, under whose great elms he formed the habit of strolling and muttering his lessons, to the concern of the passer-by. In his hours of leisure he rollicked with Stevens and his new friends, Nicolas Fish and Robert Troup. The last, a strong and splendid specimen of the young American collegian, had assumed at once the relation of big brother to the small West Indian, but was not long discovering that Hamilton could take care of himself; was flown at indeed by two agile fists upon one occasion, when protectiveness, in Alexander's measurement, rose to interference. But they formed a deep and lifelong friendship, and Troup, who was clever and alert, without brilliancy, soon learned to understand Hamilton, and was not long recognizing potentialities of usefulness to the American cause in his genius.

It was Troup who took him for his first sail up the Hudson, and except for the men who managed the boat, they went alone. Troup was a good listener, and for a time Hamilton chattered gaily as the boat sped up the river, jingling rhymes on the great palisades, which looked like the walls of some Brobdingnagian fortress, and upon the gorgeous masses of October colouring swarming over the perpendicular heights of Jersey and the slopes and bluffs of New York. It was a morning, and a piece of nature, to make the quicksilver in Hamilton race. The arch was blue, the tide was bluer, the smell of salt was in the keen and frosty air. Two boats with full white sails flew up the river. On either bank the primeval forest had burst in a night into scarlet and gold, pale yellow and crimson, bronze, pink, the flaming hues of the Tropics, and the delicate tints of hot-house roses. Hamilton had never seen such a riot of colour in the West Indies. They passed impenetrable thickets close to the water's edge, ravines, cliffs, irregular terraces on the hillside, gorges, solitary heights, all flaunting their charms like a vast booth which has but a day in which to sell its wares. They sped past the beautiful peninsula, then the lawns of Philipse Manor. Hamilton stepped suddenly to the bow of the boat and stood silent for a long while.

The stately but narrow end of the Hudson was behind; before him rolled a wide and ever widening majestic flood, curving among its hills and palisades, through the glory of its setting and the soft mists of distance, until the far mountains it clove trembled like a mirage. The eye of Hamilton's mind followed it farther and farther yet. It seemed to him that it cut the world in two. The sea he had had with him always, but it had been the great chasm between himself and life, and he had often hated it. This mighty river, haughty and calm in spite of the primeval savagery of its course, beat upon the gates of his soul, beat them down, filled him with a sense of grandeur which made him tremble. He had a vision of the vastness and magnificence of the New World, of the great lonely mountains in the North, with their countless lakes hidden in the immensity of a trackless forest, of other mountain ranges equally wild and lonely, cutting the monotony of plains and prairies, and valleys full of every delight. All that Hamilton had read or heard of the immense area beyond or surrounding the few cities and hamlets of the American colonies, flew to coherence, and he had a sudden appreciation of the stupendousness of this new untravelled world, understood that with its climate, fertility, and beauty, its large nucleus of civilization, its destiny must be as great as Europe's, nor much dissimilar, no matter what the variance of detail. The noblest river in the world seemed to lift its voice like a prophet, and the time came—after his visit to Boston—when Hamilton listened to it with a thrill of impatient pride and white-hot patriotism. But to-day he felt only the grandeur of life as he never had felt it before, felt his soul merge into this mighty unborn soul of a nation sleeping in the infinity, which the blue flood beneath him spoke of, almost imaged; with no premonition that his was the destiny to quicken that soul to its birth.

* * * * *

While on the ship, Alexander had written to his father, asking for news of him and telling of the change in his own fortunes. James Hamilton had replied at once, gratefully, but with melancholy; by this time he knew himself to be a failure, although he was now a planter in a small way. Alexander's letter, full of the hope and indomitable spirit of youth, interested as keenly as it saddened him. He recalled his own high courage and expectant youth, and wondered if this boy had stronger mettle than his own equipment. Then he remembered Rachael Levine and hoped. He lived to see hope fulfilled beyond any achievement of his imagination, although the correspondence, brisk for a time, gradually subsided. From Hugh Knox and Mrs. Mitchell Alexander heard constantly, and it is needless to state that his aunt kept him in linen which was the envy of his friends. His beruffled shirts and lace stocks were marvels, and if he was an exquisite in dress all his life, it certainly was not due to after-thought. Meanwhile, he lodged with the family of Hercules Mulligan, and wrote doggerel for their amusement in the evening. Troup relates that Hamilton presented him with a manuscript of fugitive poetry, written at this period. Mercifully, Troup lost it. Hamilton has been peculiarly fortunate in this respect. He lies more serenely in his grave than most great men.

When he was not studying, or joking, or rhyming, during those two short years of college life, he read: Cudworth's "Intellectual System," Hobbes's "Dialogues," Bacon's "Essays," Plutarch's "Morals," Cicero's "De Officiis," Montaigne's "Essays," Rousseau's "Émile," Demosthenes's "Orations," Aristotle's "Politics," Ralt's "Dictionary of Trade," and the "Lex Mercatoria."

He accomplished his mental feats by the—to him—simple practice of keeping one thing before his mind at a time, then relegating it uncompromisingly to the background; where, however, it was safe in the folds of his memory. What would have sprained most minds merely stimulated his, and never affected his spirits nor his health, highly as

111

nature had strung his nerves. He was putting five years college work into two, but the effect was an expansion and strengthening of the forces in his brain; they never weakened for an instant.

XIV

In the spring of 1774 Hamilton visited Boston during a short holiday. His glimpse of this city had been so brief that it had impressed his mind but as a thing of roofs and trees, a fantastic woodland amphitheatre, in whose depths men of large and solemn mien added daily to the sum of human discomfort. He returned to see the important city of Boston, but with no overwhelming desire to come in closer contact with its forbidding inhabitants. He quickly forgot the city in what those stern sour men had to tell him. For to them he owed that revelation of the tragic justice of the American cause which enabled him to begin with the pen his part in the Revolution, forcing the crisis, taking rank as a political philosopher when but a youth of seventeen; instead of bolting from his books to the battlefield at the first welcome call to arms. Up to this time he had adhered to his resolution to let nothing impede the progress of his education, to live strictly in the hour until the time came to leave the college for the world. Therefore, although he had heard the question of Colonies versus Crown argued week after week at Liberty Hall, and at the many New York houses where he dined of a Sunday with his friends, Stevens, Troup, and Fish, he had persistently refused to study the matter: there were older heads to settle it and there was only one age for a man's education. Moreover, he had grown up with a deep reverence for the British Constitution, and his strong aristocratic prejudices inclined him to all the aloofness of the true conservative. So while the patriots and royalists of King's were debating, ofttimes concluding in sequestered nooks, Hamilton remained "The young West Indian," an alien who cared for naught but book-learning, walking abstractedly under the great green shade of Batteau Street while Liberty Boys were shouting, and British soldiers swaggered with a sharp eye for aggression. This period of philosophic repose in the midst of electric fire darting from every point in turn and sometimes from all points at once, endured from the October of his arrival to its decent burial in Boston shortly after his seventeenth birthday.

Boston was sober and depressed, stonily awaiting the vengeance of the crown for her dramatic defiance in the matter of tea. Even in that rumbling interval, Hamilton learned, the Committee of Correspondence, which had directed the momentous act, had been unexcited and methodical, restraining the Mohawks day after day, hoping until the last moment that the Collector of Customs would clear the ships and send the tea whence it came. Hamilton heard the wrongs of the colonies discussed without any of the excitement or pyrotechnical brilliancy to which he had become accustomed. New York was not only the hot-bed of Toryism, but even such ardent Republicans as William Livingston, George Clinton, and John Jay were aristocrats, holding themselves fastidiously aloof from the rank and file that marched and yelled under the name of Sons of Liberty. To Hamilton the conflict had been spectacular rather than real, until he met and moved with these sombre, undemonstrative, superficially unpleasing men of Boston; then, almost in a flash, he realized that the colonies were struggling, not to be relieved of this tax or that, but for a principle; realized that three millions of people, a respectable majority honourable, industrious, and educated, were being treated like incapables, apprehensive of violence if they dared to protest for their rights under the British Constitution. Hamilton also learned that Boston was the conspicuous head and centre of resistance to the crown, that she had led the colonies in aggressiveness since the first Stamp Act of 1765 had shocked them from passive subjects into dangerous critics. He had letters which admitted him to clubs and homes, and he discussed but one subject during his visit. There were no velvet coats and lace ruffles here, except in the small group which formed the Governor's court. The men wore dun-coloured garments, and the women were not much livelier. It was, perhaps, as well that he did not see John Hancock, that ornamental head-piece of patriotic New England, or the harmony of the impression might have been disturbed; but, as it was, every time he saw these men together, whether sitting undemonstratively in Faneuil Hall while one of their number spoke, or in church, or in groups on Boston Common, it was as if he saw men of iron, not of flesh and blood. Every word they uttered seemed to have been weighed first, and it was impossible to consider such men giving their time and thought, making ready to offer up their lives, to any cause which should not merit the attention of all men.

Although Hamilton met many of them, they made no individual impression on him; he saw them only as a mighty brain, capable of solving a mighty question, and of a stern and bitter courage.

He returned to New York filled with an intense indignation against the country which he had believed too ancient and too firm in her highest principles to make a colossal mistake, and a hot sympathy for the colonists which was not long resolving itself into as burning a patriotism as any in the land. It was not in him to do anything by halves, it is doubtful if he ever realized the half-hearted tendency of the greater part of mankind. He studied the question from the first Stamp Act to the Tea Party. The day he was convinced, he ceased to be a West Indian. The time was not yet come to draw the sword in behalf of the country for which he conceived a romantic passion, which satisfied other wants of his soul, but he began at once on a course of reading which should be of use to her when she was free to avail herself of patriotic thinkers. He also joined the debating club of the college. His abrupt advent into this body, with his fiery eloquence and remarkable logic, was electrical. In a day he became the leader of the patriot students. There were many royalists in King's, and the president, Dr. Myles Cooper, was a famous old Tory. He looked upon this influential addition to the wrong side with deep disfavour, and when he discovered that the most caustic writer of Holt's Whig newspaper, who had carved him to the quick and broken his controversial lances again and again, was none other than his youngest and most revolutionary pupil, his wrath knew no bounds.

With the news of the order to close the port of Boston, the wave of indignation in the colonies rose so high that even the infatuated clergy wriggled. Philadelphia went so far as to toll her muffled bells for a day, and as for New York, then as now, the nerve-knot of the country, she exploded. The Sons of Liberty, who had reorganized after the final attempt of England to force tea on the colonies, paraded all day and most of the night, but were, as yet, more orderly than the masses, who stormed through the streets with lighted torches, shrieking and yelling and burning the king and his ministers in effigy.

The substantial citizens also felt that the time was come to prepare for the climax toward which their fortunes were hastening. That spiteful fist would be at their own skulls next, beyond a doubt. The result of a long and hot debate in the Exchange between the Sons of Liberty and the more conservative patriots was an agreement to call a Congress of the Colonies. The contest over the election of delegates was so bitter, however, the Committee of the Assembly, which was largely ministerial, claiming the right to nomination, that it was determined to submit the question to the people at large.

XV

In the early morning Hamilton still sauntered beneath the college trees or those of Batteau Street, pondering on his studies, and abstracting himself from the resting city, but in the evenings and during half the night he inhaled the hot breath of rebellion; and the flaring torches, the set angry faces, the constant shouting, the frightened pallor of the women at the windows of the great houses on the line of march, the constant brawls with British soldiers, stormed the curb he had put on his impatient spirit. He realized that the colonies were not yet prepared to fight, and he had no thought of doing anything rash, but it was his propensity to do a thing at once if it were to be done at all, and this last indignity should result in something except talk. He was present at the meeting in the Exchange and listened carefully to all that was said, feeling that he could add to that whirlwind of ideas, but forbearing on account of his youth. His mind, by now, was so mature that he reminded himself, with some difficulty, that he was but seventeen. He was as lively and as happy as ever, but that was temperamental and would endure through all things; mentally he had no youth in him, had had little since the day he began to ask questions.

The meeting in the Fields—at which it was hoped to effect a choice of delegates by the people at large—was called for the 6th of July, and a great multitude assembled. Alexander McDougall, the first patriot to have suffered imprisonment at the hands of the Tyrant, presided, and celebrated speakers harangued. It was here that Hamilton's impatience got rid of its curb. He heard much that was good, more that was bad, little that was new; and he found the radicals illogical and the conservatives timid. Nicolas Fish and Robert Troup pushed their way through the crowd to where Hamilton stood, his uplifted face expressing his thoughts so plainly to those who knew him that these friends determined to force him to the platform.

At first he protested; and in truth, the idea, shaping concretely, filled his very legs with terror; but the young men's insistence, added to his own surging ideas, conquered, and he found himself on the platform facing a boundless expanse of three-cornered hats. Beneath were the men who represented the flower as well as the weeds of the city, all dominated by the master passion of the civilized world. There was little shade in the Fields and the day was hot. It was a crowded, uncomfortable, humid mass whose attention he was about to demand, and their minds were already weary of many words, their calves of the ruthless mosquito. They stared at Hamilton in amazement, for his slender little figure and fair curling hair, tied loosely with a ribbon, made him look a mere boy, while his proud high-bred face, the fine green broadcloth of his fashionably cut garments, the delicate lawn of his shirt and the profusion of lace with which it was trimmed, particularly about his exquisite hands, gave him far more the appearance of a court favourite than a champion of liberty. Some smiled, others grunted, but all remained to listen, for the attempt was novel, and he was beautiful to look upon.

For a moment Hamilton felt as if the lower end of his heart had grown wings, and he began falteringly and in an almost inaudible voice. Pride hastened to his relief, however, and his daily debates in college had given him assurance and address. He recovered his poise, and as ideas swam from his brain on the tide of a natural eloquence, he forgot all but the great principle which possessed him in common with that jam of weary men, the determination to inspire them to renewed courage and greater activity. He rehearsed their wrongs, emphasized their inalienable rights under the British Constitution—from which the ministerial party and a foolish sovereign had practically divorced them. He insisted that the time had come in their history to revert to the *natural* rights of man—upon which all civil rights were founded—since they were no longer permitted to lead the lives of self-respecting citizens, pursuing the happiness which was the first instinct of the human intelligence; they had been reduced almost to the level of their own slaves, who soon would cease to respect them.

He paused so abruptly that the crowd held its breath. Then his ringing thrilling voice sounded the first note of the Revolution. "It is war!" he cried. "It is war! It is the battlefield or slavery!"

When the deep roar which greeted the startling words had

116

subsided, he spoke briefly of their immense natural advantages, in the event of war, the inability of England to gain any permanent advantage, and finally of the vast resources of the country, and its phenomenal future, when the "waves of rebellion, sparkling with fire, had washed back to the shores of England the wrecks of her power, her wealth, and her glory."

His manner was as fiery and impetuous as his discourse was clear, logical, and original. The great crowd was electrified. It was as if a blade of lightning had shot down from the hot blue sky to illuminate the doubting recesses of their understandings. They murmured repeatedly "It is a collegian," "a collegian," and they thundered their applause when he finished.

Troup and Fish bore him off in triumph to Fraunces' Tavern, where Stevens joined them immediately, hot, but exultant.

"I've just passed our president, looking like an infuriated bumblebee," he cried. "I know he heard your speech from some hidden point of vantage. It was a great speech, Alec. What a pity Hugh Knox, Mr. Lytton, and Benny Yard were not there to hear. I'll write them about it to-night, for St. Croix ought to burn a bonfire for a week. It was a hurricane with a brain in it that whirled you straight to these shores—as opportune for this country as for your own ambitions, for, unless I'm much mistaken, you're going to be a prime factor in getting rid of these pestiferous redcoats—we've a private room, so I can talk as I please. One tried to trip me up just now, thinking I was you."

Fish leaned across the table and looked penetratingly at Hamilton, who was flushed and nervous. The young New Yorker had a chubby face, almost feminized by a soft parted fringe, but his features were strong, and his eyes preternaturally serious.

"You've committed yourself, Hamilton," he said. "That was no college play. Whether you fight or not doesn't so much matter, but you must give us your pen and your speech. I'm no idle purveyor of compliments, but you are extraordinary, and there isn't a man living can do for the cause with his pen what you can do. Write pamphlets, and they'll be published without an hour's delay."

"Ah, I see!" cried Hamilton, gaily. "I was a bit bewildered. You think my new patriotism needs nursing. 'After all, he is a West Indian, born British, brought up under Danish rule, which is like being coddled by one's grandmother. He sympathizes with us, his mind is delighted with a new subject for analysis and discourse, but patriotism—that is impossible,' Is it not true?"

"You have read my thought," said Fish, with some confusion. "And you have a great deal to occupy your mind. I never have known anyone whose brain worked at so many things at once. I am selfish enough to want you to give a good bit of it to us."

"I never was one to make fierce demonstrations," said Alexander; "but fill up another bumper—the first has calmed my nerves, which were like to jump through my skin—and stand up, and I'll drink you a pledge."

The three other young men sprang to their feet, and stood with their glasses raised, their eyes anxiously fixed on young Hamilton. They had believed him to be preparing himself for a great career in letters, and knowing his tenacity and astonishing powers of concentration, had doubted the possibility of interesting him permanently in politics. They all had brains and experience enough—it was a hot quick time—to recognize his genius, and to conceive the inestimable benefit it could confer upon the colonial cause. Moreover, they loved him and wanted to see him famous as quickly as possible.

"Stand up on the table," cried Troup. "It is where you belong; and you're the biggest man in New York, to-day." As Hamilton, although self-confident, was modest, Troup put down his bumper, seized the hero in his big arms and swung him to the middle of the table. Then the three, raising their glasses again, stood in a semi-circle. Hamilton threw back his head and raised his own glass. His hand trembled, and his lips moved for a moment without speaking, after his habit when excited.

"The pledge! The pledge!" cried Fish. "We want it."

"It is this," said Hamilton. "I pledge myself, body and soul and brain, to the most sacred cause of the American colonies. I vow to it all my best energies for the rest of my life. I swear to fight for it with my sword; then when the enemy is driven out, and all the brain in the country needed to reconstruct these tattered colonies and unify them into one great state, or group of allied states, which shall take a respectable place among nations, to give her all that I have learned, all that my brain is capable of learning and conceiving. I believe that I have certain abilities, and I solemnly swear to devote them wholly to *my country*. And I further swear that never, not in a single instance, will I permit my personal ambitions to conflict with what must be the lifelong demands of this country."

He spoke slowly and with great solemnity. The hands of the three young men shook, as they gulped down a little of the wine. Hamilton rarely was serious in manner; even when discussing literature, politics, or any of the great questions before the world, his humour and wit were in constant play, a natural gift permitting this while detracting nothing from the weight of his opinions. But his words and his manner were so solemn to-day that they impressed his hearers profoundly, and they all had a vague presentiment of what the unborn Country would owe to that pledge.

"You'll keep that, Alexander," said Fish. "Perhaps it were better for you had you not made it so strong. I burn with patriotism, but I'd not have you sacrificed—"

"I've made my vows," cried Hamilton, gaily, "and I'll not have you mention the fact again that I'm not an American born. Here's not only to liberty, but to a united people under the firmest national constitution ever conceived by man."

"Amen," said Troup, "but that's looking well ahead. Hard as it will be to get England out, it will be harder still to make New York and New England love each other; and when it comes to hitching Massachusetts and Virginia about each other's necks, I vow my imagination won't budge."

"It will come," said Hamilton, "because in no other way can they continue to exist, much less become one of the nations of the earth. This war is but an interlude, no matter how long it may take. Then will come the true warfare of this country—the Great Battle of Ideas, and our real history will begin while it is raging, while we are experimenting; and there will be few greater chapters in any country. I shall take part in that battle; how, it is too soon to know, except that for union I shall never cease to strive until it is a fact. But it has grown cooler. Let us ride up to the village of Harlem and have supper under the trees."

XVI

It was not long after this that he wrote the pamphlets in reply to the tracts assailing the Congress and aimed particularly at setting the farmers against the merchants. These tracts were by two of the ablest men on the Tory side, and were clever, subtle, and insinuating. Hamilton's pamphlets were entitled, "A Full Vindication of the Measures of Congress from the Calumnies of Their Enemies," and "The Farmer Refuted; or a More Comprehensive and Impartial View of the Disputes between Great Britain and the Colonies, Intended as a Further Vindication of the Congress." It is not possible to quote these pamphlets, and they can be found in his "Works," but they were remarkable not only for their unanswerable logic, their comprehensive arraignment of Britain, their close discussion of the rights of the colonists under the British Constitution, their philosophical definition of "natural rights," and their reminder that war was inevitable, but for their anticipation of the future resources of the country, particularly in regard to cotton and manufactures, and for the prophecies regarding the treatment of the colonies by Europe. The style was clear, concise, and bold, and with a finish which alone would have suggested a pen pointed by long use.

These pamphlets, which created a profound sensation, were attributed to William Livingston and John Jay, two of the ablest men on the patriot side. That side was profoundly grateful, for they put heart into the timid, decided the wavering, and left the Tory writers without a leg to stand on. Nothing so brilliant had been contributed to the cause.

It was not long before the public had the author's name. Troup had been present at the writing of the pamphlets, and he called on Dr. Cooper, one day, and announced the authorship with considerable gusto.

"I'll not believe it," exclaimed the president, angrily; "Mr. Jay wrote those pamphlets, and none other. A mere boy like that—it's absurd. Why do you bring me such a story, sir? I don't like this Hamilton, he's too forward and independent—but I have no desire to hear more ill of him."

"He wrote them, sir. Mulligan, in whose house he lives, and I, can prove it. He's the finest brain in this country, and I mean you shall know it."

He left Dr. Cooper foaming, and went to spread the news elsewhere. The effect of his revelation was immediate distinction for Hamilton. He was discussed everywhere as a prodigy of intellect; messages reached him from every colony. "Sears," said Willets, one of the leaders of the Liberty party, "was a warm man, but with little reflection; McDougall was strong-minded; and Jay, appearing to fall in with the measures of Sears, tempered and controlled them; but Hamilton, after these great writings, became our oracle."

Congress met in May, 1775, and word having come that Chatham's conciliation bill had been rejected, and that Britain was about to send an army to suppress the American rebellion, this body assumed sovereign prerogatives. They began at once to organize an army; Washington was elected Commander-in-chief, and they ordered that five thousand men be raised to protect New York, as the point most exposed. The royal troops were expelled, and the city placed in command of General Charles Lee, an English soldier of fortune, who had fought in many lands and brought to the raw army an experience which might have been of inestimable service, had he been high-minded, or even well balanced. As it was, he very nearly sacrificed the cause to his jealousy of Washington and to his insane vanity.

Hamilton, meanwhile, published his two pamphlets on the Quebec Bill, and took part in a number of public debates. At one of these, as he rose to speak, a stranger remarked, "What brings that lad here? The poor boy will disgrace himself." But the merchants, who were present in force, listened intently to all he had to say on the non-importation agreement, and admitted the force of his arguments toward its removal, now that war practically had been declared. One of the most interesting of the phenomena in the career of Hamilton was the entire absence of struggle for an early hearing. People recognized his genius the moment they came in contact with it, and older men saw only the extraordinary and mature brain, their judgement quite unaffected by the boyish face and figure. Those who would not admit his great gifts were few, for except in the instances where he incurred jealous hate, he won everybody he met by his charming manner and an entire absence of conceit. He was conscious of his powers, but took them as a matter of course, and thought only of what he would do with them, having no leisure to dwell on their quality. In consequence, he already had a large following of unhesitating admirers, many of them men twice his age, and was accepted as the leading political philosopher of the country.

Dr. Cooper sent for him after his third pamphlet. He, too, was a patriot in his way, and although he bristled whenever Hamilton's name was mentioned, he had come in contact with too many minds not to recognize ability of any sort; he knew that Hamilton would be invaluable to the Royalist cause.

"Ask your own price, sir," he said, after suggesting the higher service to which he could devote his pen. "You will find us more liberal—" But Hamilton had bolted. It is impossible to knock down one's venerable president, and his temper was still an active member in the family of his faculties. To the numerous other offers he received from the Tory side he made no reply, beyond inserting an additional sting into his pen when writing for Holt's *Journal*. In the press he was referred to, now, as "The Vindicator of Congress," and it was generally conceded that he had done more to hasten matters to a climax, by preparing and whetting the public mind, than anyone else in America.

There is no doubt that the swiftness and suddenness of Hamilton's conversion, his abrupt descent from a background of study and alien indifference, gave him a clearer and more comprehensive view of the wrongs and needs of the colonists than they possessed themselves. They had been muttering ever since the passage of the first stamp tax, threatening, permitting themselves to be placated, hoping, despairing, hoping again. Hamilton, from the first moment he grasped the subject, saw that there was no hope in ministerial England, no hope in anything but war. Moreover, his courage, naturally of the finest temper, and an audacity which no one had ever discouraged, leapt out from that far background of the West Indies into an arena where the natives moved in an atmosphere whose damps of doubt and discouragement had corroded them for years. Even among men whose courage and independence were of the first quality, Hamilton's passionate energy, fearlessness of thought, and audacity of expression, made him remarkable at once; and they drew a long breath of relief when he uncompromisingly published what they had long agreed upon over the dining-table, or built up the doctrine of resistance with argument as powerful as it was new.

But the time rapidly approached for deeds, and Hamilton had been occupied in other ways than writing pamphlets. During the past six months he had studied tactics and gunnery, and had joined a volunteer corps in order to learn the practical details of military science. All his friends belonged to this corps, which called itself "Hearts of Oak," and looked very charming in green uniforms and leathern caps, inscribed

"Freedom or Death." They soon attracted the attention of General Greene, a superior man and an accomplished officer. He took an especial fancy to Hamilton, and great as was their disparity in years, they were close friends until the General's death. It was Greene who first attracted Washington's attention to the youngest of his captains, and Hamilton was able to render the older man, whose services and talents have even yet not been properly recognized by his country, exceptional service. The company exercised in the churchyard of St. George's chapel, early in the morning; for in spite of the swarms of recruits clad in every variety of uniform, deserted houses, and daily flights of the timid into Jersey, earthworks and fortifications, college went on as usual.

It was not long before the "Hearts of Oak" had an opportunity to distinguish themselves. The provincial committee ordered them to remove the cannon stationed at the Battery. In the harbour was the British war-ship, *Asia*, which immediately sent off a boat to enquire into this proceeding. A large number of armed citizens had escorted the little corps to the Battery, and several lost their heads and fired at the boat. There was an immediate broadside from the *Asia*. Three of the militia were wounded, and one fell dead by Hamilton's side. "It is child's play to a hurricane," he thought. "I doubt if a man could have a better training for the battlefield." They removed the guns.

The result of this attack was another explosion of New York's nerves. The Sons of Liberty made it unsafe for a Tory to venture abroad. They marched through the streets shouting vengeance, burning in effigy, and making alarming demonstrations before the handsome houses of certain loyalists. Suddenly, about ten o'clock at night, they were animated by a desire to offer up Dr. Cooper, and they cohered and swarmed down toward King's. Hamilton and Troup happened to be walking in the grounds when the sudden flare of torches and the approaching tide of sound, warned them of the invasion. They ran like deer to head them off, but reached the portico only a moment ahead of the mob, which knew that it must be sudden and swift to be victorious.

"I can talk faster than you," whispered Hamilton, "I'll harangue them, and it won't take Dr. Cooper long to understand and flee through the back door—and may the devil fly away with him."

"A moment!" he cried, "I've something to say, and I may not have another chance, war is so close upon us."

"Tis young Hamilton," cried someone in the crowd. "Well, make us a speech; we're always glad to hear you, but we'll not go home without old Cooper. Don't think it."

Hamilton never remembered what nonsense he talked that night. Fortunately words always came with a rush, and he could mix up politics, wrongs, the clergy, and patriotism, in so picturesque a jumble that an excited crowd would not miss his usual concise logic. "Do you suppose he's gone?" he whispered, pausing to take breath.

"Go on, go on," said Troup nervously, "I hear someone moving."

"Ah-h-h!"

There was a wild yell from the crowd, and a hoarse roar from above. Hamilton and Troup looked up. Dr. Cooper's infuriated visage, surrounded by a large frill, projected from his bedroom window. "Don't listen to him," he shrieked, thrusting his finger at Hamilton. "He's crazy! He's crazy!"

"The old fool," fumed Troup, "he thinks you're taking your just revenge. If I could get inside—"

Dr. Cooper was jerked back by a friendly hand and the window slammed. "Someone understands," whispered Troup, excitedly; "and they'll have him out in two minutes. Go on, for heaven's sake."

Hamilton, who had been tearful with laughter, began again:—

"I appeal to you, my friends, am I crazy?" Indignant shouts of "No! No!" "Then let me, I pray, make a few remarks on the possibility of holding New York against the advancing fleet, that you can testify to my sanity to-morrow, and save me from whatever unhappy fate this irascible gentleman has in store for me."

"Go ahead! Go ahead!" cried someone in the mob. "We won't let him touch you."

And again Hamilton harangued them, until Troup slipped round to the rear of the big building and returned with word that Dr. Cooper was safely over the back fence and on his way to the *Asia*. When Hamilton announced the flight, there was muttering, but more laughter, for the mob was in a better humour than when it came.

"Well, that silver tongue of yours did the old man a good turn to-night, but you shan't make fools of us again." And a few days later, when Alexander attempted to head off the same mob as it made for the press of Rivington, the Tory printer, they would not listen to him. But the effort raised him still higher in the estimation of the patriots, for they saw that his love of law and order was as great as his passion for war.

XVII

In January the convention of New York gave orders that a company of artillery be raised. Hamilton, through Colonel McDougall of the First New York regiment, at once applied for the captaincy, underwent an examination that convinced the Congress of his efficiency, and on the 14th of March was appointed Captain of the Provincial Company of Artillery. McDougall had already applied for "coarse blue cloth," with which to clothe in a semblance of uniform those who already had enlisted, and Hamilton took even better care of them. On May 26th he wrote a brief, pointed, and almost peremptory letter to the Congress, representing the injustice of paying his men less than the wages received by the Continental artillery, adding that there were many marks of discontent in his ranks, and that in the circumstances it was impossible for him to get any more recruits. "On this account I should wish to be immediately authorized to offer the same pay to all who may be inclined to recruit," he wrote. He then went on to demand ten shillings a head for every man he should be able to enlist, and that each man of his company be allowed a frock as a bounty.

Congress passed a resolution as soon as the letter was read, granting him all he asked for, but limiting his company to one hundred men. When it was recruited to his satisfaction, it numbered ninety-one, exclusive of himself and his four officers. Besides his Captain-Lieutenant, and first, second, and third Lieutenants, he had three sergeants, three corporals, six bombardiers, three gunners, two drummers, two fifers, a barber, and seventy-one matrosses, or assistant gunners.

He had his troubles, and Congress came to the rescue whenever it received one of his singularly unboyish letters, expressed, moreover, with little more diffidence than if he had been Commander-in-chief. But he knew what he wanted, and he never transcended courtesy; he was evidently a favourite with the Congress. On July 26th he wrote demanding a third more rations for his men, and on the 31st a resolution was passed which marked an end to the disposition to keep his little company on a level with the militia rather than with the regular army.

Thereafter he had no further complaints to carry to headquarters; but he was annoyed to discover that one of his officers was a hard drinker, and that the Lieutenant Johnson who had recruited the larger number of his men before he assumed command, had disobeyed orders and enlisted them for a year instead of for the term of war.

Meanwhile, although the very air quivered and every man went armed to the teeth, if a war-ship fired a gun the streets were immediately filled with white affrighted faces; and although redoubts were building day and night, still Congress came out with no declaration, and the country seemed all nerves and no muscle. The English fleet arrived and filled the bay,—a beautiful but alarming sight. Washington came and made New York his headquarters, called for more troops, and Brooklyn Heights were fortified, lest the English land on Long Island and make an easy descent on the city.

It is doubtful if the Americans have ever appreciated all they owe to Lord Howe. He sat out in the harbour day after day, while they completed their preparations, practically waiting until they announced themselves ready to fight. But no man ever went to the wars with less heart for his work, and he put off the ugly business of mowing down a people he admired, hoping from day to day for an inspired compromise. It was not until after the Declaration of Independence by the Congress, the wild enthusiasm it excited throughout the colonies, and the repeated declination of Washington to confer with Howe as a private citizen, that our Chief received word the British Commander was landing troops on Long Island, near Gravesend.

Several thousand troops were ordered across to reinforce the Brooklyn regiments, and Hamilton's artillery was among them. He stood up in his boat and stared eagerly at the distant ridge of hills, behind which some twenty thousand British were lying on their arms with their usual easy disregard of time, faint, perhaps, under the torrid sun of August. But they were magnificently disciplined and officered, and nothing in history had rivalled the rawness and stubborn ignorance of the American troops. Hamilton had not then met Washington, but he knew from common friends that the Chief was worried and disgusted by what he had seen when inspecting the Brooklyn troops the day before. Greene, second only to Washington in ability, who had been in charge of the Brooklyn contingent, knowing every inch of the ground, was suddenly ill. Putnam was in command, and the Chief was justified in his doubt of him, for nothing in the mistakes of the Revolution exceeded his carelessness and his errors of judgement during the battle of Long Island.

There were still two days of chafing inactivity, except in the matter of strengthening fortifications, then, beginning with dawn of the 28th, Hamilton had his baptism of fire in one of the bloodiest battlefields of the Revolution.

The Americans were outgeneralled and outnumbered. Their attention was distracted by land and water, while a British detachment, ten thousand strong, crept over the ridge of hills by night, and through the Bedford Pass, overpowering the guards before their approach was suspected. At dawn they poured down upon the American troops, surprising them, not in one direction, but in flank, in rear, and in front. The green woods swarmed with redcoats, and the Hessians acted with a brutality demoralizing to raw troops. Hamilton's little company behaved well, and he was in the thick of the fight all day. The dead were in heaps, the beautiful green slopes were red, there was not a hope of victory, but he exulted that the colonies were fighting at last, and that he was acting; he had grown very tired of talking.

He was driven from his position finally, and lost his baggage and a field-piece, but did not take refuge within the redoubts until nightfall. There, in addition to fatigue, hunger, a bed on the wet ground, and the atmosphere of hideous depression which pressed low upon the new revolutionists, he learned that Troup had been taken prisoner. Then he discovered the depths to which a mercurial nature could descend. He had been fiercely alive all day; the roar of the battle, the plunging horses, the quickening stench of the powder, that obsession by the devil of battles which makes the tenderest kill hot and fast, all had made him feel something more than himself, much as he had felt in the hurricane when he had fancied himself on high among the Berserkers of the storm. In his present collapse he felt as if he were in a hole underground.

Washington arrived on the scene next morning, and for forty-eight hours he barely left the saddle, encouraging the wretched men and exercising an unceasing vigilance. For two long days they were inactive in the rain. The Chief, having assured himself that the British aimed to obtain command of the river, determined upon the retreat which ranks as one of the greatest military achievements in history. On the night of the 29th, under cover of a heavy fog, the feat of embarking nine thousand men, with all the ammunition and field-pieces of the army, and ferrying them across the East River with muffled oars, was accomplished within earshot of the enemy. Washington rode from regiment to regiment, superintending and encouraging, finally taking his stand at the head of the ferry stairs. He stood there until the last man had embarked at four in the morning. The last man was Hamilton. His was one of the regiments, and the rear one, detailed to cover the retreat, to attract fire to itself if necessary. His position was on the Heights, just outside the intrenchments, at the point closest to the enemy. For nine hours he hardly moved, his ear straining for the first indication that the British heard the soft splashing of bare feet in the mud. The fog was so thick that he could see nothing, not even the battalions of retreating Americans; the forms of his own men were vague and gray of outline. He never had fancied an isolation so complete, but his nerves stood the strain; when they began to mutter he reminded himself of Mr. Cruger's store and St. Croix. There was a false summons, and after turning his back upon his post with a feeling of profound relief, he was obliged to return and endure it for two hours longer. Did the fog lift he would never see another. It was dawn when a messenger came with the news that his turn positively had come, and he marched his men down the slope to the ferry stairs. He passed close enough to Washington to see his dejected, haggard face.

On the 15th of the following month, after much correspondence with Congress, discussion, and voting, it was determined to abandon New York City, and intrench the army on the Heights of Harlem. Hamilton was bitterly disappointed; he wanted to defend the city, and so had three of the generals, but they were overruled, and the march began on a blazing Sunday morning. It was not only the army that marched, but all the inhabitants of the town who had not escaped to the Jersey shore. The retreat was under the command of General Putnam, and guided through all the intricacies of those thirteen winding miles by his aide-de-camp, Aaron Burr. The last man in the procession was Alexander Hamilton.

"So, you're covering again, Alexander," said Fish, as he passed him on his way to his own regiment,—the New York, of which he was brigade-major. "You can't complain that your adopted country doesn't make use of you. By the way, Troup is in the Jersey prison-ship, safe and sound."

"Can't we exchange him?" asked Hamilton, eagerly, "Do you think General Washington would listen to us?"

"If we have a victory. I shouldn't care to approach him at present. God! This is an awful beginning. The whole army is ready to dig its own grave. The only person of the lot who has any heart in him to-day is little Burr. He's like to burst with importance because he leads and we follow. He's a brave little chap, but such a bantam one must laugh. Well, I hate to leave you here, the very last man to be made a target of. You won't be rash?" he added anxiously.

"No, granny," said Hamilton, whose gaiety had revived as he heard of Troup's safety. "And I'd not exchange my position for any."

"Good-by."

Handshakes in those days were solemn. Fish feared that he never should see Hamilton again, and his fear was close to being realized.

It was a long, hot, dusty, miserable march; some lay down by the wayside and died. Hamilton had been bred in the heat of the Tropics, but he had ridden always, and to-day he was obliged to trudge the thirteen miles on foot. He had managed to procure horses for his guns and caissons, but none for himself and his officers.

It was on the Hoagland farm at the junction of the Kingsbridge and Bloomingdale roads that a serious skirmish occurred, and Hamilton and his men stood the brunt of it. The tired column was almost through the pass, when a detachment of British light infantry suddenly appeared on the right. Fortunately the cannon had not entered the pass, and were ready for action. Hamilton opened fire at once. There was a sharp engagement, but the British were finally driven off. Then the defenders of the column made good their own retreat, for they knew that by now the redcoats were swarming over the island.

Toward night a cold wind and rain swept in from the ocean. When the little army finally reached Harlem Heights they were obliged to sleep on the wet ground without so much as a tent to cover them, then arise at dawn and dig trenches. But by night they were men again, they had ceased to be dogged machines: the battle of Harlem Heights had been fought and won. The British had begun the battle in the wrong place and at the wrong time, and all the natural advantages of that land of precipices, forests, gorges, wooded hills, and many ravines, were with the Americans. Again Hamilton worked in the thick of the fight during the four hours it lasted, but like everybody else he went to sleep happy.

XVIII

He rose at dawn the next morning, and rousing his men, set them at work throwing up redoubts. He was standing some distance from them, watching the sun rise over the great valley they had been forced to abandon, with its woods and beautiful homes, now the quarters of British officers, when every nerve in his body became intensely aware that some one was standing behind him. He knew that it was a man of power before he whirled round and saw Washington.

"This is Captain Hamilton?" said the Chief, holding out his hand. "General Greene spoke to me, weeks ago, about you, but I have been in no mood until to-day for amenities. I know of your part in the retreat from Long Island, and I noticed you as you passed me on the ferry stairs. What a lad you are! I am very proud of you."

"I had asked for no reward, sir," cried Hamilton, with a smile so radiant that Washington's set face caught a momentary reflection from it, and he moved a step nearer, "but I feel as if you had pinned an order on my coat."

"I have heard a great deal more about you," said Washington, "and I want to know you. Will you come up and have breakfast with me?"

"*Oh, yes, I will*," said Hamilton, with such seriousness that they both laughed. Hamilton's personal pride was too great to permit him to feel deeply flattered by the attentions of any one, but the halo about Washington's head was already in process of formation; he stood aloft, whether successful or defeated, a strong, lonely, splendid figure, and he had fired Hamilton's imagination long since. At that time he was ready to worship the great Chief with all a boy's high enthusiasm, and although he came to know him too well to worship, he loved him, save at intervals, always. As for Washington, he loved Hamilton then and there, and it is doubtful if he ever loved any one else so well. When they were alone he called him "my boy," an endearment he never gave another.

On that September morning they breakfasted together, and talked for hours, beginning a friendship which was to be of the deepest

130

consequences to the country they both were striving to deliver.

During the following month Hamilton had much leisure, and he spent it in the library of the Morris house, which its owner, a royalist, had abandoned on the approach of the American troops, fleeing too hurriedly to take his books. The house was now General Washington's headquarters, and he invited Hamilton to make what use of the library he pleased. It was a cool room, and he found there many of the books he had noted down for future study. He also wrote out a synopsis of a political and commercial history of Great Britain. As the proclivities and furnishing of a mind like Hamilton's cannot fail to interest the students of mankind, a digression may be pardoned in favour of this list of books he made for future study, and of the notes scattered throughout his pay book:—

Smith's History of New York; Leonidas; View of the Universe; Millot's History of France; Memoirs of the House of Brandenburgh; Review of the Characters of the Principal Nations of Europe; Review of Europe; History of Prussia; History of France; Lassel's Voyage through Italy; Robertson's Charles V; Present State of Europe; Grecian History; Baretti's Travels; Bacon's Essays; Philosophical Transactions; Entick's History of the Late War; European Settlements in America; Winn's History of America.

The Dutch in Greenland have from 150 to 200 sail and ten thousand seamen.... It is ordered that in their public prayers they pray that it should please God to bless the Government, the Lords, the States, and their great and small fisheries.

Hamburg and Germany have a balance against England—they furnish her with large quantities of linen.

Trade with France greatly against England.... The trade with Flanders in favour of England.... A large balance in favour of Norway and Denmark.

Rates of Exchange with the several Nations in 52, viz.: To Venice, Genoa, Leghorn, Amsterdam, Hamburgh. To Paris—Loss, Gain.

Postlethwaite supposes the quantity of cash necessary to carry on the circulation in a state one third of the rents to the land proprietors, or one ninth of the whole product of the lands. See the articles, Cash and Circulation.

The par between land and labour is twice the quantity of land whose product will maintain the labourer. In France one acre and a half will maintain one. In England three, owing to the difference in the manner of living.

Aristotle's Politics, chap. 6, definition of money, &c.

The proportion of gold and silver, as settled by Sir Isaac Newton's proposition, was 1 to 14. It was generally through Europe 1 to 15. In China I believe it is 1 to 10.

It is estimated that the labour of twenty-five persons, on an average, will maintain a hundred in all the necessaries of life.

Postlethwaite, in his time, supposes six millions of people in England. The ratio of increase has been found by a variety of observations to be, that 100,000 people augment annually, one year with another to—. Mr. Kerseboom, agreeing with Dr. Halley, makes the number of people thirty-five times the number of births in a year.

Extracts from Demosthenes' Orations.

Philippic. "As a general marches at the head of his troops, so ought wise politicians, if I dare use the expression, to march at the head of affairs; insomuch that they ought not to wait *the event*, to know what measures to take; but the measures which they have taken ought to produce the *event*."

"Where attack him? it will be said. Ah, Athenians—war, war, itself will discover to you his weak sides, if you will seek them."

Sublimely simple. Vide Long. C. 16.

Are the limits of the several states and the acts on which they are founded ascertained, and are our ministers provided with them? What intelligence has been given to Congress by our ministers of the designs, strength by sea and land, actual interests and views of the different powers in Europe?

The government established (by Lycurgus) remained in vigour about five hundred years, till a thirst of empire tempted the Spartans to entertain foreign troops, and introduce Persian gold to maintain them; then the institutions of Lycurgus fell at once, and avarice and luxury succeeded.

He (Numa) was a wise prince, and went a great way in civilizing the Romans. The chief engine he employed for this purpose was religion, which could alone have sufficient empire over the minds of a barbarous and warlike people to engage them to cultivate the arts of peace.

Dr. Halley's Table of Observations exhibiting the probabilities of life; containing an account of the whole number of people of Breslau, capital of Silesia, and the number of those of every age, from one to a hundred. (Here follows the table with comments by A.H.)

When the native money is worth more than the par in foreign, exchange is high; when worth less, it is low.

Portugal trade — Spanish trade — Artificers — Money—Exchange — Par of exchange — Balance of trade — Manufactures — Foundry — Coin—Gold—Silver—Naval Power—Council of trade—Fishery.

Money coined in England from the reign of Queen Elizabeth.

Quere. Would it not be advisable to let all taxes, even those imposed by the States, be collected by persons of Congressional appointment; and would it not be advisable to pay the collectors so much per cent on the sums collected?

Hamilton was nineteen at this time, and while there are many instances of mental precocity in the history of mankind, it is doubtful if there is a parallel case of so great a *range* of intellectual curiosity, or such versatility combined with pursuit of knowledge as distinct from information. But the above notes are chiefly significant as showing that long before he could have dreamed of directing the finances of the United States, while he was wild with delight at the prospect of military excitement and glory, a part of his mind was imperiously attracted to the questions which were to become identified in American history with his name.

Washington often came in and sat for an hour with him; and although they talked military science and future campaigns invariably,— for Washington was a man of little reading and his thoughts moved in a constant procession to one tune,—this was perhaps the happiest period of their intercourse. The Chief demanded nothing, and his young friend was free to give or not, as he chose. In that interval nothing gave Hamilton such pleasure as to see Washington come into the cool library, his face softening.

"You have a streak of light in you that never goes out," said the man of many burdens once. "When I catch a spark of it, I am cheered for the rest of the day. When I am close to it for a time, I can feel the iron lid on my spirits lifting as if it were on a bubbling pot. I believe you are something more than human."

During the first of these conversations Hamilton suggested the advisability of keeping up the spirits of the raw troops by drawing the enemy in separate detachments into constant skirmishes, a plan in which the Americans were sure to have every advantage; and this policy was pursued until Washington fell back into Westchester County.

The American troops under Washington numbered about nineteen thousand men, in one-third of whom the Chief felt something like confidence. Many were grumbling at the prospect of a winter in the discomforts of camp life; others were rejoicing that their time of service drew to a close; all were raw. Nevertheless, he determined to give the British battle on the shore of the Bronx River, where they were camped with the intention of cutting him off from the rest of the country.

Both armies were near White Plains on the morning of the 28th of October. Most of the Americans were behind the breastworks they had thrown up, and the British were upon the hills below, on the opposite side of the Bronx. On the American side of the stream was an eminence called Chatterton's Hill, and on the evening of the 27th Colonel Haslet was stationed on this height, with sixteen hundred men, in order to prevent the enfilading of the right wing of the army. Early the next morning McDougall was ordered to reinforce Haslet with a small corps and two pieces of artillery under Hamilton, and to assume general command.

At ten o'clock the British army began its march toward the village, but before they reached it, Howe determined that Chatterton's Hill should be the first point of attack, and four thousand troops under Leslie moved off to dislodge the formidable looking force on the height.

Hamilton placed his two guns in battery on a rocky ledge about halfway down the hill, and bearing directly upon that part of the Bronx which the British were approaching. He was screened from the enemy by a small grove of trees. The Hessians, who were in the lead, refused to wade the swollen stream, and the onslaught was checked that a bridge might hastily be thrown together for their accommodation. Hamilton waited a half-hour, then poured out his fire. The bridge was struck, the workmen killed, the Hessians fell back in a panic. Leslie appealed to the loyalty of the British, forded the river at another point, and rushed up the hill with bayonets fixed, resolved to capture the guns. But the guns flashed with extraordinary rapidity. Both the British and the watching Americans were amazed. There were no tin canisters and grape-shot in the American army, even the round shot were exhausted. Loading cannon with musket balls was a slow process; but Hamilton was never without resource. He stood the cannon on end, filled his three-cornered hat with the balls, and loaded as rapidly as had he leaped a century. His guns mowed down the British in such numbers that Leslie fell back, and joining the Hessian grenadiers and infantry, who had now crossed the stream, charged up the southwestern declivity of the hill and endeavoured to turn McDougall's right flank. McDougall's advance opposed them hotly, while slowly retreating toward the crown of the eminence. The British cavalry attacked the American militia on the extreme right, and the raw troops fled ignominiously. McDougall, with only six hundred men and Hamilton's two guns, sustained an unequal conflict for an hour, twice repulsing the British light infantry and cavalry. But the attack on his flank compelled him to give way and retreat toward the intrenchments. Under cover of a heavy rainstorm and of troops despatched in haste, he retreated in good order with his wounded and artillery, leaving the victors in possession of a few inconsiderable breastworks.

Fort Washington was betrayed, and fell on the 16th of November. Then began that miserable retreat of the American army through the Jerseys, with the British sometimes in full pursuit, sometimes merely camping on the trail of the hapless revolutionists. For Washington's force was now reduced to thirty-five hundred, and they were ragged, half fed, and wretched in mind and body. Many had no shoes, and in one regiment there was not a pair of trousers. They left the moment their leave expired, and recruits were drummed up with great difficulty. Washington was obliged to write eight times to General Lee, who was at North Castle with a considerable force, before he was able to hope for relief in that quarter.

Hamilton had a horse at times, at others not. But his vitality was proof against even those endless days and nights of marching and countermarching, through forests and swamps, in the worst of late autumn and winter weather; and he kept up the spirits of his little regiment, now reduced from bullets, exposure, and the expiration of service to thirty men. Nevertheless, he held the British in check at the

Raritan River while the Americans destroyed the bridge, and when Washington, after having crossed the Delaware, determined to recross it on Christmas night and storm Trenton, he was one of the first to be chosen, with what remained of his men and guns.

As they crossed the Delaware that bitter night, the snow stinging and blinding, the river choked with blocks of ice, Hamilton for the first time thought on St. Croix with a pang of envy. But it was the night for their purpose, and all the world knows the result. The victory was followed on the 3d of January by the capture of Princeton; and here Hamilton's active military career came to an end for the present.

Well do I recollect the day [wrote a contemporary] when Hamilton's company marched into Princeton. It was a model of discipline. At their head was a boy, and I wondered at his youth; but what was my surprise, when, struck with his slight figure, he was pointed out to me as that Hamilton of whom we had heard so much.

I noticed [a veteran officer said many years after] a youth, a mere stripling, small, slender, almost delicate in frame, marching beside a piece of artillery, with a cocked hat pulled down over his eyes, apparently lost in thought; with his hand resting on a cannon, and every now and again patting it as if it were a favourite horse or a pet plaything.

BOOK III
THE LITTLE LION
—⟋⟍—

I

Hamilton's body succumbed to the climax of Trenton and Princeton upon months of hardship and exposure, and he was in hospital for a week with a rheumatic fever. But Troup, whose exchange had been effected, was with him most of the time, and his convalescence was made agreeable by many charming women. He was not the only brilliant young man in the army, for Troup, Fish, Burr, Marshall, were within a few months or, at most, a year or two of his age, and there were many others; men had matured early in that hot period before the Revolution, when small boys talked politics, and even the women thought of little else; but Hamilton, through no fault of his, had inspired his friends with the belief that he was something higher than human, and they never tired of sounding his praises. Moreover, Washington had not hesitated to say what he thought of him, and the mere fact that he had won the affection of that austere Chieftain was enough to give him celebrity. At all events, he was a dazzling figure, and pretty women soothed many a weary hour. As for Troup, who was unpleasantly anatomical, he had a fresh story for every day of the horrors of the prison cattle-ship *Mentor*, where half the prisoners had died of filth, starvation, and fever, from putrid water and brutal treatment.

But never was there a more impatient invalid than Hamilton. He was astonished and disgusted that his body should defy his mind, and at the first moment possible he was up and about his duties with the army at Morristown. Troup was ordered to join the army under Gates in the North.

Morristown was a natural fortress, a large fertile valley, protected by precipitous hills and forests, yet with defiles known to the Americans, through which they could retreat if necessary. It was within striking distance of New Brunswick and Amboy, in which towns Washington kept the British cooped up for months, not permitting them to cut a stick of forest wood without fighting for it. "Here was seen," to quote Hamilton, "the spectacle of a powerful army straitened within narrow limits by the phantom of a military force, and never permitted to transgress those limits with impunity; in which skill supplied the place of means, and disposition was the substitute for an army."

Congress had invested Washington with such extraordinary powers after the brilliant exploit at Trenton, that in Europe he was called "The Dictator of America." Therein lay the sole cause of the ultimate victory of the Revolutionists, and had the States been more generous, and less jealous of delegating powers to Congress, he would have driven out the British in short order.

Mrs. Washington had joined her General—she kept an eye on him—at Freeman's Tavern, which had been converted into comfortable headquarters, and he was happy in his military family: Colonel Harrison, indefatigable and fearless, affectionately known as "Old Secretary"; Tench Tilghman of Maryland, young, accomplished, cheerful, devoted to Washington and serving without pay, for his fortune was considerable; Richard Kidder Meade, sprightly, enthusiastic, always willing to slave; and John Fitzgerald,—all in an attitude of perpetual adoration. But he lacked a secretary of the requisite ability, and as soon as he heard of Hamilton's return to camp he sent for him.

Hamilton was feeling almost well, and he walked rapidly across the village green to headquarters, delighted at the prospect of seeing Washington again. He had acquired a military air and walked more erectly than ever, for he was somewhat sensitive of his juvenile appearance. He found Washington in a front room on the second floor. The General wore his usual blue and buff, and looked less harassed and worn than when he had last seen him. He rose and shook hands warmly with Hamilton, who thanked him again for the messages he had received while in hospital.

"I would have had you brought here if there had been any place to make you comfortable; and I am going to ask you to come and live with me now—as my aide and secretary."

Hamilton sprang to his feet impetuously. "Oh, sir!" he exclaimed, "I don't want to leave the regular line of promotion! I don't want to leave my men. I'm much attached to them. And I'll not deny my ambition, sir; I want opportunities to distinguish myself. I've already refused two generals. This war will last for years. There is no reason in the world why I should not be a general in three."

"No," said Washington, "there is none; there is every possibility of your becoming one of the most brilliant figures on the revolutionary battlefields. I admit that, and I understand your ambition. Nevertheless, I think I can prove to you that there is another way in which you can serve your country better. I know your uncompromising sense of duty and your high patriotism, and I am sure you will accept my invitation when I prove to you that while there are hundreds to fight valorously, even brilliantly, there is scarcely a man I can get to write my letters who can do more than punctuate properly or turn a sentence neatly. You must know the inexpressible value of a brilliant accomplished versatile secretary, with a brain capable of grasping every question that arises— and you can imagine how many of that sort have come my way. I have been driven nearly distracted, dictating, explaining, revising—when I have so much else to think of. Besides the constant correspondence with the Congress and the States, something else is always turning up—to-day it is the exchange of prisoners, a most important and delicate matter. Were you my secretary, you would also be my brain: a word would be sufficient. I could trust you so implicitly that if matters pressed I could confidently sign my name to whatever you wrote without reading it over. There is no one else living of whom I can say that. You are the most useful young man in America, and if you will give your great brain to this country from this time on, she will be far more grateful to you than if you merely continued to fight, splendidly as you have done that. And *I* need you—I have no words to tell you how much."

"Sir," said Hamilton, deeply touched, "no human being could withstand such an appeal, and your words of praise are glory enough. I will come as soon as you say, and do the best I can."

"Come at once. The British persist in treating us as rebels. It is for you, with your inspired pen, to force and coax them to regard us with the respect an educated thinking people—not a horde of ignorant rebels, as they imagine—deserve. If you do that, you will do a greater service to your country than if you rose to be first in military rank. Here are some notes. When you have finished, write to Congress and ask for the rank of

Lieutenant-Colonel; and move up here to-day, if possible. I cannot tell you how happy I shall be to have you a member of my family."

Washington had won his point. A shrewd judge of men, he had calculated upon Hamilton succumbing to an appeal to his sense of patriotic duty—the strongest passion in his passionate nature. Much as he loved Hamilton, he had no hesitation in using him, and our petted young hero was to learn what work meant for the first time in his life. He wrote most of the day, often half the night; but although he chafed angrily at the confinement, beat many a tattoo on the floor with his heels, and went for a hard ride more than once that he might keep his temper, the result was that mass of correspondence, signed "George Washington," which raised the commander of the American forces so high in the estimation of Europe, adding to his military renown the splendour of a profound and luminous intellect.

There was, also, some correspondence with the Congress regarding the disposition of his artillery men. He insisted upon definite provision for them, and they were permitted to enlist in the Continental Army. They loved him, and the final parting on March 18th, with cannon as well as men!—made him ill for half a day.

Otherwise his life at Headquarters was very pleasant Tilghman and Meade became two of the most congenial friends he ever made. The tavern was comfortable, and he had a room to himself for a time. The dining room reunions were agreeable in spite of their formality. Besides the amiable military family, and the most motherly of women, who knit him stockings and kept his wardrobe in order, there were frequent visitors. The Livingston girls were spending the winter with their aunt, Lady Sterling, and, with their beautiful cousin, the Lady Kitty Alexander, often drove over to a five o'clock dinner or the more informal supper. The Boudinots and Morgans, the generals in camp at Morristown and their wives, and the more distinguished officers, were frequently dined at Headquarters. Washington sat halfway in the table's length, with Mrs. Washington opposite. Hamilton was placed at the head of the table on the day of his arrival, a seat he retained while a member of the family. The Chief encouraged him to talk, and it must be confessed that he talked from the time he sat down till the meal finished. His ideas were always on the rush, and talking was merely thinking aloud. As he expressed himself with wit and elegance, and on subjects which interested them all profoundly, illuminating everything he touched, old men and young would lean forward and listen with respect to the wisdom of a young man who was yet an infant in the eyes of the law. How he escaped being insufferably spoiled can only be explained by the ceaseless activity of his brain, and the fact that the essence of which prigs are made was not in him. That he was utterly without commonplace conceit is indisputable, for he was the idol of the family. Harrison christened him "The Little Lion," a name his friends used for their aptest designation as long as he lived, and assumed a paternal relation which finished only with the older man's death. The Lady-in-chief made such a pet of him that he was referred to in the irreverent Tory press as "Mrs. Washington's Tom-cat."

"Alexander," said Kitty Livingston to him, one day, "have a care. You are too fortunate. The jealous gods will smite you."

But Hamilton, thinking of those terrible months in the previous year, of mental anxiety and physical hardship, when, in bitter weather, he had often gone hungry and insufficiently clothed, and of his present arduous duties, concluded there was a fine balance in his affairs which doubtless would placate the gods.

II

In May and July there were illustrious additions to Washington's family,—John Laurens and Lafayette. Both became the intimate friends of Hamilton, the former one of the few passionate attachments of his life. Although Hamilton was by no means indifferent to the affection he inspired in nine-tenths of the people he met, he did not himself love easily. He was too analytical, he saw people too precisely as they were, and his acquaintance with human nature had made him too cynical to permit the flood gates of his affections to open except under uncommon stress. He dreaded disappointment. For Troup, Fish, Stevens, Meade, and Tilghman he had a deep affection and served their interests ardently; for Washington a contradictory budget of emotions, which were sometimes to be headed "respectful affection," at others "irritated resentment," now and again a moment of adoration. While he could not pay sufficient tribute to Washington's magnanimity and generosity, he had by now seen him in too many tempers, had been ground too fine in

141

his greedy machine, to think on him always with unqualified enthusiasm. Lafayette, brilliant, volatile, accomplished, bubbling with enthusiasm for the cause of Liberty, and his own age within a few months, he liked sincerely and always. There was no end to the favours he did him, and Lafayette loved no one better in his long and various career. Women, Hamilton fancied sharply and forgot quickly.

But Laurens, the "young Bayard of the Revolution," fresh from the colleges and courts of Europe, a man so handsome that, we are told, people experienced a certain shock when he entered the room, courtly, accomplished to the highest degree, of flawless character, with a mind as noble and elevated as it was intellectual, and burning with the most elevated patriotism,—he took Hamilton by storm, capturing judgement as well as heart, and loving him as ardently in return.

Like Hamilton, Laurens was of Huguenot descent; he was born in South Carolina, of a distinguished family. Against the expressed wish of his father he had returned to America, made his way to Headquarters and offered his services to Washington, who immediately attached him to his military household. The unhappiest of men, praying for death on every battlefield, he lived long enough to distinguish himself by a bravery so reckless, by such startling heroic feats, that he was, beyond all question, the popular young hero of the Revolution. He worshipped Washington as one might worship a demi-god, and risked his life for him on two occasions. But Hamilton was the friend of his life; the bond between them was romantic and chivalrous. Each burned to prove the strength of his affection, to sacrifice himself for the other. Laurens slaved at Washington's less important correspondence, and Hamilton's turn came later. The age has passed for such friendships; but at that time, when young men were nurtured on great ideas, when they were sacrificing themselves in a sacred cause, and had seen next to nothing of the frivolities of life, they were understandable enough.

Hamilton was obliged to share his room with both the young men, and they slept on three little cots in a small space. When the nights were insufferably hot they would go out and lie on the grass and talk until they were in a condition to sleep anywhere. Hamilton would forecast the next movement of the enemy; Laurens and Lafayette would tell all they knew about military science in Europe; and then they would discuss the future of the liberated country and the great ideals which must govern her. And when men can be idealistic while fighting the Jersey mosquito, it must be admitted that they are of the stuff to serve their country well.

But all this delightful intercourse was interrupted in August. Washington gave battle to the British at Brandywine, was defeated, and in the following month surprised them at Germantown, and was defeated again. Nevertheless, he had astonished the enemy with his strength and courage so soon after a disastrous battle. To hold Philadelphia was impossible, however, and the British established themselves in the Capital of the colonies, making, as usual, no attempt to follow up their victories.

Washington went into temporary quarters near the village of Whitemarsh. His own were in a baronial hall at the head of a beautiful valley. Old trees shaded the house, and a spring of pure water bubbled in a fountain before the door. The men were encamped on the hills at the north.

There was a great hall through the centre of the mansion, and here Washington held his audiences and councils of war. The house throughout was of extreme elegance, and much to the taste of the younger members of the family, particularly of Hamilton, who spent the greater part of his leisure in the library. But his enjoyment of this uncommon luxury was brief.

Washington must have reinforcements or his next engagement might be his last. There was but one source from which he could obtain a considerable supply, and that was from the army of Gates in the North. But Gates was swollen with the victory of Saratoga and the capture of Burgoyne, and was suspected to be in the thick of an intrigue to dethrone Washington and have himself proclaimed Commander-in-chief. At the moment he was the idol of the army, and of the northern and eastern States, for his victories were tangible and brilliant, while Washington's surer processes were little appreciated. Therefore to get troops from him would be little less difficult than to get them from Lord Howe, short of a positive command, and this prerogative Washington did not think it politic to use. He called a council of war, and when it was over he went to his private office and sent for Alexander Hamilton.

He looked haggard, as if from sleepless nights, and for a moment after Hamilton entered the room, although he waved his hand at a chair, he stared at him without speaking. Hamilton divined what was coming—he attended all councils of war—and sat forward eagerly. The prospect of a holiday from clerical work would alone have filled him with youth, and he knew how great a service he might be able to render the cowering Republic.

"Hamilton," said Washington, finally, "you are as much in my secret thoughts as I am myself. If I attempted to deceive you, you would divine what I withheld. It is a relief to speak frankly to you. I dare not demand these troops from Gates, because there is more than a possibility he would defy me, and that the Congress and a large part of the army would sustain him. He has given sufficient evidence of his temper in sending me no official notice of the battle of Saratoga. But unless I am to meet with overwhelming disaster here, I must have reinforcements. It may be possible to extract these by diplomacy, and I have selected you for the mission, because I feel sure that you will not forget the issues at stake for a moment, because you never lose your head, and because you will neither be overawed by Gates's immediate splendour, nor will you have any young desire to assert the authority which I give you as a last resort. There is another point: If you find that Gates purposes to employ his troops on some expedition, by the prosecution of which the common cause will be more benefited than by their being sent down to reinforce this army, you must suspend your consideration for me. God knows I am tender of my reputation, and I have no wish to be disgraced, but we are or should be fighting for a common cause and principle, and should have little thought of individual glory. However, I do not believe in the disinterestedness of Gates, nor in his efficiency on a large scale. But I leave everything in your hands."

Hamilton stood up, his chest rising, and stared at his Chief.

"Sir," he said, after a moment, "do you appreciate that you are placing your good name and your future in my hands?" For a moment he realized that he was not yet of age.

"You are the only being to whom I can confide them, and who can save this terrible situation."

"And you have the magnanimity to say that if Gates has a chance of other victories to let him go unhindered?" He had one of his moments of adoration and self-abnegation for this man, whose particular virtues, so little called upon in ordinary affairs, gave him so lonely a place among men.

144

Washington jerked his head. There was nothing more to say. Hamilton's head dropped for a moment, as if he felt the weight of an iron helmet, and his lips moved rapidly.

"Are you saying your prayers when your lips work like that?" asked Washington, crossly.

Hamilton threw back his head with a gay laugh. His eyes were sparkling, his nostrils dilating; his whole bearing was imperious and triumphant. "Never mind that. I'll undertake this mission gladly, sir, and I think I'll not fail. My old friend Troup is his aide. He will advise me of many things. I'll bring you back those regiments, sir. One way or another a thing can always be managed."

The light in Hamilton's face was reflected on Washington's. "You are my good genius," he said shortly. "Take care of yourself. You will have to ride hard, for there is no time to lose, but be careful not to take cold. I shall give you orders in writing. Come back as soon as you can. I believe I am not lacking in courage, but I always have most when you are close by."

There is a print somewhere representing Hamilton setting forth on this mission. He is mounted on a handsome white horse, and wears a long green cloak, one end thrown over a shoulder. His three-cornered hat is pulled low over his eyes. In the rear is an orderly.

He started on the 30th of October, riding hard through the torn desolate country, toward Newburg on the Hudson. He was three days making the distance, although he snatched but a few hours' rest at night, and but a few moments for each meal. From Newburg he crossed to Fishkill and, acting on his general instructions, ordered Putnam to despatch southward three brigades; and on his own account despatched seven hundred Jersey militia on the same expedition.

He then started hot and hard for Albany, a dangerous as well as exhausting journey, for neither savage tribes nor redcoats could be far in the distance. His mental anxiety by now wore as severely as the physical strain. None knew better than he that his talents were not for diplomacy. He was too impatient, too imperious, too direct for its sinuous methods. On the other hand, he had a theory that a first-rate mind could, for a given time, be bent in any direction the will commanded, and he had acquired an admirable command of his temper. But the responsibility was terrific, and he was half ill when he reached Albany. He presented himself at General Gates's headquarters at once.

Gates, like Lee, was a soldier of fortune; and low-born, vain, weak, and insanely ambitious. He had been advised of Hamilton's coming, and had no intention of giving Washington an opportunity to rival his own achievements and reëstablish himself with the army and the Congress. He received Hamilton surrounded by several of his military family; and for the first time our fortunate hero encountered in high places active enmity and dislike. He had incurred widespread jealousy on account of his influence over Washington, and for the important part he was playing in national affairs. To the enemies of the Commander-in-chief he represented that exalted personage, and was particularly obnoxious. Never was a youth in a more difficult position.

"I cannot expose the finest arsenal in America," said Gates, pompously, "to the possibility of destruction. Sir Henry Clinton may return at any minute. Nor could I enterprise against Ticonderoga were my army depleted. Nor can I leave the New England States open to the ravages and the depredations of the enemy."

These statements made no impression on Hamilton, and he argued brilliantly and convincingly for his object, but Gates was inflexible. He would send one brigade and no more.

Hamilton retired, uneasy and dejected. Gates had an air of omnipotence, and his officers had not concealed their scorn. He hesitated to use his authority, for a bold defiance on the part of Gates might mean the downfall of Washington, perhaps of the American cause. That Washington was practically the American army, Hamilton firmly believed. If he fell, it was more than likely that the whole tottering structure would crumble.

Another reason inclined him not to press Gates too far. He had been able to order seventy-seven hundred troops from Fishkill, which was more than Washington had expected, although by no means so many as he needed. He therefore wrote to the Chief at length, sent for Troup, and threw himself on the bed; he was well-nigh worn out.

Troup was already in search of him, and met the messenger. Big and bronzed, bursting with spirits, he seemed to electrify the very air of the room he burst into without ceremony. Hamilton sat up and poured out his troubles.

"You have an affinity for posts of danger," said Troup. "I believe you to be walking over a powder-mine here. I am not in their confidence, for they know what I think of Washington, but I believe there is a cabal on foot, and that Gates may be in open rebellion any minute. But he's a coward and a bully. Treat him as such. Press your point and get your troops. He is but the tool of a faction, and I doubt if they could make him act when it came to the point. He wants to make another grand coup before striking. Look well into what regiment he gives you. Which are you to have?"

"General Patterson's."

"I thought as much. It is the weakest of the three now here, consists of but about six hundred rank and file fit for duty. There are two hundred militia with it, whose time of service is so near expiring that they will have dissolved ere you reach Headquarters."

Hamilton had sprung to his feet in a fury. He forgot his pains, and let his temper fly with satisfaction in the exercise. "If that is the case," he cried, when he had finished his anathema of Gates, "I'll have the men;" and he dashed at his writing materials. But he threw his pen aside in a moment. "I'll wait till to-morrow for this. I must be master of myself. Tell me of Saratoga. You distinguished yourself mightily, and no one was more glad than I."

Troup talked while Hamilton rested. That evening he took him to call at the Schuyler mansion, high on the hill.

Philip Schuyler was the great feudal lord of the North. He had served the colonial cause in many ways, and at the outbreak of the Revolution had been one of its hopes and props. But brilliant as his exploits had been, the intrigues of Gates, after the fall of Ticonderoga, had been successful, and he was deprived of the army of the North before the battle of Saratoga. The day of exoneration came, but at present he was living quietly at home, without bitterness. A man of the most exalted character, he drew added strength from adversity, to be placed at the service of the country the moment it was demanded. Mrs. Schuyler, herself a great-granddaughter of the first patroon, Killian Van Rensselaer, was a woman of strong character, an embodied type of all the virtues of the Dutch pioneer housewife. She had a lively and turbulent family of daughters, however, and did not pretend to manage them. The spirit of our age is feeble and bourgeois when compared with the independence and romantic temper of the stormy days of this Republic's birth. Liberty was in the air; there was no talk but of freedom and execration of tyrants; young officers had the run of every house, and Clarissa Harlowe was the model for romantic young "females." Angelica Schuyler, shortly before the battle of Saratoga, had run off with John Barker Church, a young Englishman of distinguished connections, at present masquerading under the name of Carter; a presumably fatal duel having driven him from England. Subsequently, both Peggy and Cornelia Schuyler climbed out of windows and eloped in a chaise and four, although there was not an obstacle worth mentioning to union with the youths of their choice. It will shock many good mothers of the present day to learn that all these marriages were not only happy, but set with the brilliance of wealth and fashion. When Hamilton was introduced to the famous white hall of the Schuyler mansion on the hill, Cornelia and Peggy were still free in all but fancy; Elizabeth, by far the best behaved, was the hope of Mrs. Schuyler's well-regulated soul and one of the belles of the Revolution. Hamilton was enchanted with her, although his mind was too weighted for love. Her spirits were as high as his own, and they talked and laughed until midnight as gaily as were Gates's army marching south. But Hamilton was a philosopher; nothing could be done before the morrow; he might as well be happy and forget. He had met many clever and accomplished American women by this, and Lady Kitty Alexander and Kitty and Susan Livingston were brilliant. He had also met Angelica Church, or Mrs. Carter, as she was called, one of the cleverest and most high-spirited women of her time. It had crossed his mind that had she been free, he might have made a bold dash for so fascinating a creature, but it seemed to him to-night that on the whole he preferred her sister. "Betsey" Schuyler had been given every advantage of education, accomplishment, and constant intercourse with the best society in the land. She had skill and tact in the management of guests, and without; being by any means a woman of brilliant parts, understood the questions of the day; her brain was informed with shrewd common sense. Hamilton concluded that she was quite clever enough, and was delighted with her beauty, her charm of manner, and style. Her little figure was graceful and distinguished, her complexion the honey and claret that artists extol, and she had a pair of big black eyes which were alternately roguish, modest, tender, sympathetic; there were times when they were very lively, and even suggested a temper. She was bright without attempting to be witty, but that she was deeply appreciative of wit Hamilton had soothing cause to know. And he had learned from the admiring Troup that she was as intrepid as she was wholly and daintily feminine. Altogether, Hamilton's fate was sealed when he bent over her hand that night, although he was far from suspecting it, so heavily did duty press the moment he was alone in his rooms.

On the following morning he asked for an interview with General Schuyler and several other military men whom he knew to be friendly to Washington, and they confirmed the advice of Troup. In the afternoon he wrote to Gates a letter that was peremptory, although dignified and circumspect, demanding the addition of a superior brigade. He expressed his indignation in no measured terms, and in more guarded phrases his opinion of the flimsiness of the victorious General's arguments. Gates sent the troops at once, and despatched a volume of explanation to Washington.

Hamilton set out immediately for New Windsor, Troup bearing him company the greater part of the way, for he was feeling very ill. But he forgot his ailments when he arrived. To his fury he discovered that not a regiment had gone south. Two of the brigades, which had received no pay for eight months, had mutinied, and he was obliged to ask Governor Clinton to borrow $5000, with which to pay them off. He had the satisfaction of despatching them, wrote a peremptory letter to Putnam, who had other plans brewing, another to Gates, asking for further reinforcements, then went to bed in Governor Clinton's house with fever and rheumatism. But he wrote to Washington, apprising him of a scheme among the officers of the northern department to recover the city of New York, and denouncing Putnam in the most emphatic terms. Two days later he recovered sufficiently to proceed to Fishkill, where he wrested troops from Putnam, and ascertained that heavy British reinforcements had gone from that neighbourhood to Howe. He wrote at once to Washington, advising him of his peril, and endeavoured to push on; but his delicate frame would stand no more, and on the 15th he went to bed in Mr. Kennedy's house in Peekskill, with so violent an attack of rheumatism that to his bitter disgust he was obliged to resign himself to weeks of inactivity. But he had the satisfaction to receive a letter from Washington approving all that he had done. And in truth he had saved the situation, and Washington never forgot it.

III

Hamilton rejoined the army at Valley Forge and soon recovered his health and spirits. It was well that the spirits revived, for no one else during that terrible winter could lay claim to any. The Headquarters were in a small valley, shut in by high hills white with snow and black with trees that looked like iron. The troops were starving and freezing and dying a mile away, muttering and cursing, but believing in Washington. On a hill beyond the pass Lafayette was comfortable in quarters of his own, but bored and fearing the worst. Laurens chafed at the inaction; he would have had a battle a day. As the winter wore on, the family succumbed to the depressing influence of unrelieved monotony and dread of the future, and only Hamilton knew to what depths of anxiety Washington could descend. But despair had no part in Hamilton's creed. He had perfect faith in the future, and announced it persistently. He assumed the mission of keeping the family in good cheer, and they gave him little time for his studies. As for Washington, even when Hamilton was not at his desk, he made every excuse to demand his presence in the private office; and Hamilton in his prayers humorously thanked his Almighty for the gift of a cheerful disposition. It may be imagined what a relief it was when he and Laurens, Meade, or Tilghman raced each other up the icy gorge to Lafayette's, where they were often jollier the night through than even a cheerful disposition would warrant. Hamilton, although he had not much of a voice, learned one camp-song, "The Drum," and this he sang with such rollicking abandon that it fetched an explosive sigh of relief from the gloomiest breast.

There were other duties from which Hamilton fled to the house on the hill for solace. Valley Forge harboured a heterogeneous collection of foreigners, whose enthusiasm had impelled them to offer swords and influence to the American cause: Steuben, Du Portail, De Noailles, Custine, Fleury, Du Plessis, the three brothers Armand, Ternant, Pulaski, and Kosciusko. They had a thousand wants, a thousand grievances, and as Washington would not be bothered by them, their daily recourse was Hamilton, whom they adored. To him they could lament in voluble French; he knew the exact consolation to administer to each, and when

150

it was advisable he laid their afflictions before Washington or the Congress. They bored him not a little, but he sympathized with them in their Cimmerian exile, and it was necessary to keep them in the country for the sake of the moral effect. But he congratulated himself on his capacity for work.

"I used to wish that a hurricane would come and blow Cruger's store to Hell," he said one day to Laurens, "but I cannot be sufficiently thankful for that experience now. It made me as methodical as a machine, gave my brain a system without which I never could cope with this mass of work. I have this past week dried the tears of seven Frenchmen, persuaded Steuben that he is not Europe, nor yet General Washington, and without too much offending him, written a voluminous letter to Gates calculated to make him feel what a contemptible and traitorous ass he is, yet giving him no chance to run, blubbering, with it to the Congress, and official letters *ad nauseum*. I wish to God I were out of it all, and about to ride into battle at the head of a company of my own."

"And how many widows have you consoled?" asked Laurens. He was huddled in his cot, trying to keep warm.

"None," said Hamilton, with some gloom. "I haven't spoken to a woman for three weeks."

It was a standing joke at Headquarters that Washington always sent Hamilton to console the widows. This he did with such sympathy and tact, such address and energy, that his friends had occasionally been forced to extricate him from complications. But it was an accomplishment in which he excelled as long as he lived.

"The Chief will never let you go," pursued Laurens. "And as there is no one to take your place, you really should not wish it. Washington may be the army, but you are Washington's brain, and of quite as much importance. You should never forget—"

"Come out and coast. That will warm your blood," interrupted Hamilton. His own sense of duty was not to be surpassed, but he had rebellious moods, when preaching suggested fisticuffs.

Outside they met a messenger from Lafayette, begging them to repair to his quarters at once. There they found him entertaining a party of charming women from a neighbouring estate; and a half-hour later the dignity and fashion of Washington's family might have been seen coasting down a steep hill with three Philadelphian exiles, who were as accomplished in many ways as they were satisfying to look upon.

It was one of those days when a swift freeze has come with a rain-storm. Hamilton had stood at the window of the office for an hour, early in the day, biting the end of his quill, and watching the water change to ice as it struck the naked trees, casing every branch until, when the sun came out, the valley was surrounded by a diamond forest, the most radiant and dazzling of winter sights. The sun was still out, its light flashed back from a million facets, the ground was hard and white, the keen cold air awoke the blood, and the three young men forgot their grumblings, and blessed the sex which has alleviated man's burdens so oft and well.

IV

In June the military ardours of this distinguished young trio were gratified to the point of temporary exhaustion. The British evacuated Philadelphia on the 18th, and proceeded up the Delaware in New Jersey. Captain Allan McLane had, as early as May 25th, reported to Washington the enemy's intention to change their quarters for New York, and Washington's desire was to crush them by a decisive blow. At a council of war, however, it was decided merely to hang upon the skirts of the retreating army and avoid an engagement. Lee was aggressive, almost insulting, in counselling inaction, Washington, much embarrassed, but hesitating to ignore the decisions of the council, followed the enemy by a circuitous route, until he reached the neighbourhood of Princeton. The British were in and about Allentown. Washington called another council of war, and urged the propriety of forcing an engagement before the enemy could reach the Heights of Monmouth. Again Lee overruled, being sustained by the less competent generals, who were in the majority. As soon as the council broke up, Hamilton sought out General Greene and led him aside, Greene was white and dejected, but Hamilton's face was hot, and his eyes were flashing.

"I believe that Lee is in the pay of the British or the Conway Cabal," he exclaimed. "I've always believed him ready at any minute to turn traitor. It's a pity he wasn't left to rot in prison. Washington must fight. His honour is at stake. If he lets the British walk off while we sit and whistle, his influence with the army will be gone, Europe will have no more of him, the Conway Cabal will have the excuse it's been watching at keyholes for, and Gates will be Commander-in-chief to-morrow. Will you come with me and persuade him to fight?"

"Yes," said Greene. "And I believe he will. You are like a sudden cold wind on an August day. Come on."

They walked rapidly toward Washington's tent. He was sitting on his camp-stool, but rose as they approached.

"Gentlemen," he said, "I anticipate the object of your visit. You wish me to fight."

"Yes!" exclaimed Hamilton. "As much as you wish it yourself. Why should you regard the councils of the traitorous and the timorous, who, for aught you know, may be in the pay of the Cabal? If the British retreat unmolested, the American army is disgraced. If Congress undertake to manage it, the whole cause will be lost, and the British will be stronger far than when we took up arms—"

"Enough," said Washington. "We fight"

He ordered a detachment of one thousand men, under General Wayne, to join the troops nearest the enemy. Lafayette was given the command of all the advance troops—Lee sulkily retiring in his favour—which amounted to about four thousand. Hamilton was ordered to accompany him and reconnoitre, carry messages between the divisions, and keep Washington informed of the movements of the enemy. There was but a chance that he would be able to fight, but the part assigned to him was not the least dangerous and important at Washington's disposal. The Chief moved forward with the main body of the army to Cranbury.

Clinton had no desire to fight, being encumbered with a train of baggage-wagons and bathorses, which with his troops made a line on the highroad twelve miles long. It being evident that the Americans intended to give battle, he encamped in a strong position near Monmouth Court-house, protected on nearly all sides by woods and marshes. His line extended on the right about a mile and a half beyond the Court-house, and on the left, along the road toward Allentown, for about three miles.

This disposition compelled Washington to increase the advance corps, and he ordered Lee to join Lafayette with two brigades. As senior officer, Lee assumed command of the whole division, under orders to

153

make the first attack. Both Lafayette and Hamilton were annoyed and apprehensive at this arrangement. "Washington is the shrewdest of men in his estimates until it is a matter of personal menace," said Hamilton, "and then he is as trusting as a country wench with a plausible villain. I thought we had delivered him from this scoundrel, and now he has deliberately placed his fortunes in his hands again. Mark you, Lee will serve us some trick before the battle is over."

Hamilton had been galloping back and forth night and day between Lafayette's division and Headquarters, wherever they happened to be, and reconnoitring constantly. The weather was intensely hot, the soil so sandy that his horse often floundered. He had not had a full night's sleep since Washington announced his decision to give battle, and he would have been worn out, had he not been too absorbed and anxious to retain any consciousness of his body. Early on the morning of the 28th, a forward movement being observed on the part of the enemy, Washington immediately put the army in motion and sent word to Lee to press forward and attack.

Lee looked uglier and dirtier than usual, and the very seat of his breeches scowled as he rode forward leisurely. In a few moments he halted, word having been brought him that the main body of the British was advancing.

"If we could but court-martial him on the spot," groaned Lafayette, whose delicate boyish face was crumpled with anxiety.

"He meditates treason!" exclaimed Hamilton. "It is writ all over him."

Having ascertained that the rumour was false, Lee consented to move on again, and the division entered the forest, their advance covered from the British on the plains beyond. For a time Lee manoeuvred so cleverly that Hamilton and Lafayette permitted themselves to hope. Under cover of the forest he formed a portion of his line for action, and with Wayne, Hamilton, and others, rode forward to reconnoitre. Concluding that the column of the British deploying on the right was only a covering party of two thousand, he manoeuvred to cut them off from the main army. Wayne was detached with seven hundred men to attack the covering party in the rear. Lee, with a stronger force, was to gain its front by a road to the left. Small detachments were concealed in the woods. At nine o'clock, the Queen's dragoons being observed upon an eminence near the wood, Lee ordered his light-horse to decoy them to the point where Wayne was posted. The dragoons appeared to fall into the trap, but upon being attacked from the wood, galloped off toward the main column. Wayne started in pursuit; his artillery was raking them, and he had ordered a charge at the point of the bayonet, when, to his amazement, he received an order from Lee to make but a feint of attack and pursuit. He had no choice but to obey, brilliant as might be the victory wrested from him. Lee, meanwhile, dawdled about, although his troops were on one foot with impatience.

Suddenly Sir Henry Clinton, learning that the Americans were marching in force on both his flanks, with the design of capturing his baggage, changed the front of his army by facing about in order to attack Wayne with such deadly fire that the enemy on his flanks would be obliged to fly to the succour of that small detachment. Lafayette immediately saw the opportunity for victory in the rear of the enemy, and rode up to Lee asking permission to make the attempt.

Lee swung his loose head about and scowled at the ardent young Frenchman. "Sir," he replied witheringly, "you do not know British soldiers. We cannot stand against them. We certainly shall be driven back at first. We must be cautious."

"It may be so, General," replied Lafayette, who would have given much to see that head rolling on the sands; "but British soldiers have been beaten, and they may be again. At any rate, I am disposed to make the trial."

Lee shrugged his shoulders, but as Lafayette sat immovable, his clear hazel eyes interrogating and astonished, he reluctantly gave the Marquis the order to wheel his column to the right and attack the enemy's left. He simultaneously weakened Wayne's detachment and went off to reconnoitre. He afterward claimed that he saw what looked to be the approach of the entire army, and he ordered his right to fall back. The brigades of Scott and Maxwell on the left were already moving forward and approaching the right of the Royal forces, when they received an order from Lee to reënter the wood. At the same time an order was sent to Lafayette to fall back to the Court-house. With a face as flaming as his unpowdered head, he obeyed. Upon reaching the Court-house he learned that a general retreat had begun on the right, under the immediate command of Lee. He had no choice but to follow.

Hamilton, hardly crediting that his worst fears were realized in this unwarranted retreat, galloped over to Lee and urged that possession be taken of a neighbouring hill that commanded the plain on which the enemy were advancing. But Lee protested violently that the Americans had not a chance against that solid phalanx, and Hamilton, now convinced that he meditated the disgrace of the American arms, galloped with all speed in search of Washington.

The retreat, by this, was a panic. The troops fled like an army of terrified rabbits, with that reversion to the simplicity of their dumb ancestors which induces the suspicion that all the manly virtues are artificial. In times of panic man seems to exchange his soul for a tail. These wretches trampled each other into the shifting sand, and crowded many more into the morass. The heat was terrific. They ran with their tongues hanging out, and many dropped dead.

Washington heard of the retreat before Hamilton found him. He was pushing on to Lee's relief when a country-man brought him word of the disgraceful rout. Washington refused to credit the report and spurred forward. Halfway between the meeting-house and the morass he met the head of the first retreating column. He commanded it to halt at once, before the panic be communicated to the main army; then made for Lee. Lee saw him coming and braced himself for the shock. But it was a greater man than Lee who could stand the shock of Washington's temper. He was fearfully roused. The noble gravity of his face had disappeared. It was convulsed with rage.

"Sir," he thundered, "I desire to know what is the reason of this? Whence arises this confusion and disorder?"

"Sir—" stammered Lee, "sir—" He braced himself, and added impudently: "I thought it best not to beard the enemy in such a situation. It was contrary to my opinion—"

"*Your* opinion!" And then the Chief undammed a torrent of profanity Washingtonian in its grandeur.

He wheeled and galloped to the rallying of the troops. At this moment Hamilton rode up. He had ridden through the engagement without a hat. It seemed to him that he could hear the bubbling of his brain, that the very air blazed, and that the end of all things had come. That day of Monmouth ever remained in his memory as the most awful and hopeless of his life. An ordinary defeat was nothing. But the

American arms branded with cowardice, Washington ignobly deposed, inefficient commanders floundering for a few months before the Americans were become the laughing-stock of Europe,—the whole vision was so hideous, and the day so hopeless in the light of those cowardly hordes, that he galloped through the rain of British bullets, praying for death; he had lost all sense of separate existence from the shattered American cause. He did not perceive that Washington had reached the column, and resolved to make one more appeal to Lee, he rode up to that withered culprit and exclaimed passionately:—

"I will stay with you, my dear General, and die with you! Let us all die here, rather than retreat!"

Lee made no reply. His brain felt as if a hot blast had swept it.

"At least send a detachment to the succour of the artillery," said Hamilton, with quick suspicion. And Lee ordered Colonel Livingston to advance.

At the same moment some one told Hamilton that Washington was in the rear, rallying the troops. He spurred his horse and found that the General had rallied the regiments of Ramsay and Stewart, after a rebuke under which they still trembled, and was ordering Oswald to hasten his cannon to the eminence which his aide had suggested to Lee. Hamilton himself was in time to intercept two retreating brigades. He succeeded in rallying them, formed them along a fence at hand, and ordered them to charge at the point of the bayonet. He placed himself at their head, and they made a brilliant dash upon the enemy. But his part was soon over. His horse was shot under him, and as he struck the ground he was overcome by the shock and the heat, and immediately carried from the field. But the retreat was suspended, order restored, and although the battle raged all day, the British gained no advantage. The troops were so demoralized by the torrid heat that at sunset both Commanders were obliged to cease hostilities; and Washington, who had been in the saddle since daybreak, threw himself under a tree to sleep, confident of a victory on the morrow.

"I had a feeling as if my very soul were exploding," said Hamilton to Laurens, as they bathed their heads in a stream in the woods, with the bodies of dead and living huddled on every side of them. "I had a hideous vision of Washington and the rest of us in a huge battle picture, in which a redcoat stood on every squirming variety of continental uniform, while a screeching eagle flew off with the Declaration of Independence. But after all, there is something magnificent in so absolutely identifying yourself with a cause that you go down to its depths of agony and fly to its heights of exaltation. I was mad to die when the day—and with it the whole Cause—seemed lost. Patriotism surely is the master passion. Nothing else can annihilate the ego."

Laurens, who had performed prodigies of valour, sighed heavily. "I felt as you did while the engagement lasted," he replied. "But I went into the battle with exultation, for death this time seemed inevitable. And the only result is a headache. What humiliation!"

"You are morbid, my dear," said Hamilton, tenderly. "You cannot persuade me that at the age of twenty-five naught remains but death—no matter what mistakes one may have made. There is always the public career—for which you are eminently fitted. I would begin life over again twenty times if necessary."

"Yes, because you happen to be a man of genius. I am merely a man of parts. There are many such. Not only is my life ruined, but every day I despair anew of ever attaining that high ideal of character I have set for myself. I want nothing short of perfection," he said passionately. "Could I attain that, I should be content to live, no matter how wretched. But I fall daily. My passions control me, my hatreds, my impulses of the moment. When a man's very soul aches for a purity which it is in man to attain if he will, and when he is daily reminded that he is but a whimperer at the feet of the statue, the world is no place for him."

"Laurens," said Hamilton, warmly, "you refine on the refinements of sensibility. You have brooded until you no longer are normal and capable of logic. Compare your life with that of most men, and hope. You are but twenty-five, and you have won a deathless glory, by a valour and brilliancy on these battlefields that no one else has approached. Your brain and accomplishments are such that the country looks to you as one of its future guides. Your character is that of a Bayard. It is your passions alone, my dear, which save you from being a prig. Passion is the furnace that makes greatness possible. If, when the mental energies are resting, it darts out tongues of flame that strike in the wrong place, I do not believe that the Almighty, who made us, counts them as sins. They are natural outlets, and we should burst without them. If one of those tongues of flame was the cause of your undoing, God knows you have paid in kind. As a rule no one is the worse, while most are better. A certain degree of perfection we can attain, but absolute perfection—go into a wilderness like Mohammed and fast. There is no other way, and even then you merely would have visions; you would not be yourself."

Laurens laughed. "It is not easy to be morbid when you are by. Acquit me for the rest of the night. And it is time we slept. There will be hot work to-morrow. How grandly the Chief rallied! There is a man!"

"He was in a blazing temper," remarked Hamilton. "Lee and Ramsay and Stewart were like to have died of fright. I wish to God he'd strung the first to a gibbet!"

They sought out Washington and lay down beside him. The American army slept as though its soul had withdrawn to another realm where repose is undisturbed. Not so the British army. Sir Henry Clinton did not share Washington's serene confidence in the morrow. He withdrew his weary army in the night, and was miles away when the dawn broke.

Once Washington awoke, raised himself on his elbow, and listened intently. But he could hear nothing but the deep breathing of his weary army. The stars were brilliant. He glanced about his immediate vicinity with a flicker of amusement and pleasure in his eyes. The young men of his household were crowded close about him; he had nearly planted his elbow on Hamilton's profile. Laurens, Tilghman, Meade, even Lafayette, were there, and they barely had left him room to turn over. He knew that these worshipping young enthusiasts were all ready and eager to die for him, and that in spite of his rigid formality they were quite aware of his weak spot, and did not hesitate to manifest their affection. For a moment the loneliest man on earth felt as warmly companioned as if he were raising a family of rollicking boys; then he gently lifted Hamilton out of the way, and slept again. He was bitterly disappointed next morning; but to pursue the enemy in that frightful heat, over a sandy country without water, and with his men but half refreshed, was out of the question.

The rest of the year was uneventful, except for the court-martialling of Lee and his duel with Laurens, who challenged him for his defamation of Washington. Then came the eventful winter of 1779-80, when the army went into quarters at Morristown, Washington and his military family taking possession of a large house belonging to the Widow Ford.

V

"Alexander!" cried a musical but imperious voice.

Hamilton was walking in the depths of the wood, thinking out his financial policy for the immediate relief of the country. He started and faced about. Kitty Livingston sat on her horse, a charming picture in the icy brilliance of the wood. He ran toward her, ripped off her glove, kissed her hand, replaced the glove, then drew back and saluted.

"You are a saucy boy," said Miss Livingston, "and I've a mind to box your ears. I've brought you up very badly; but upon my word, if you were a few years older, I believe I'd marry you and keep you in order, something no other woman will ever be able to do. But I've a piece of news for you—my dear little brother. Betsey Schuyler is here."

Alexander, much to his annoyance, blushed vividly. "And how can you know that I have ever even seen Miss Schuyler?" he asked, rather sulkily.

"*She* told me all about it, my dear. And I inferred from the young lady's manner that she lived but to renew the experience. She is down at Surgeon-General Cochraine's. Mrs. Cochraine is her aunt. Seriously, I want you to be a good little beau, and keep her here as long as possible. She is a great addition to our society; for she is not only one of the belles of the country, accomplished and experienced, but she has an amazing fine character, and I am anxious to know her better. You are still too young to marry, *mon enfant*, but you are so precocious and Miss Schuyler is so charming—if you will marry at your absurd age, you could not do better; for you'll get fine parents as well as a wife, and I've never known a youth more in need of an entire family."

Hamilton laughed. "If I accumulate any more parents," he said, "I shall share the fate of the cat. This morning Colonel Harrison—one of my fathers—almost undressed me to see if my flannels were thick enough, Mrs. Washington gave me a fearful scolding because I went out without a muffler, and even the General is always darting edged glances at the soles of my boots. Yesterday, Laurens, who is two-thirds English, tried to force an umbrella into my hand, but at that I rebelled. If I marry, it will be for the pleasure of taking care of someone else."

He escorted Miss Livingston out to the highroad, and returned to Headquarters, his imagination dancing. He had by no means forgotten Miss Schuyler. That merry roguish high-bred face had shone above many dark horizons, illuminated many bitter winter nights at Valley Forge. He was excited at the prospect of seeing her again, and hastened to arrange a dinner, to which she must be bidden. The young men did as they chose about entertaining, sure of Washington's approval.

"Ah, I know Miss Schuyler well," exclaimed Tilghman, when Hamilton remarked that they should immediately show some attention to the daughter of so illustrious a man as General Schuyler. "I've fetched and carried for her—in fact I once had the honour to be despatched by her mamma to buy her a pair of stays. I fell at her little feet immediately. She has the most lively dark good-natured eyes I ever saw—Good God, Hamilton, are you going to run me through?"

Hamilton for the moment was so convulsed with jealous rage that his very fingers curved, and he controlled them from his friend's throat with an effort. Tilghman's words brought him to his senses, and he laughed heartily. "I was as jealous as Othello, if you'll have the truth, and just why, I vow I don't know, for I met this young lady only once, and that a year ago. I was much attracted, but it's not possible I'm in love with her."

"It's love, my dear boy," said Tilghman, gravely. "Go and ask Steuben if I am not right. Laurens and I will arrange the dinner. You attend to your case immediately."

Hamilton, much concerned, repaired to the house of Baron Steuben. This old courtier and rake was physician in ordinary to all the young men in their numerous cardiacal complications. Hamilton found him in his little study, smoking a huge meerschaum. His weather-beaten face grinned with delight at the appearance of his favourite, but he shook his head solemnly at the revelation.

"I fear this time you are shot, my dear little Hamilton," he said, with much concern. "Have you told me all?"

"All that I can think of." Hamilton was sitting forward on the edge of the chair in considerable dejection. He had not expected this intrication, had hoped the Baron would puff it away.

"Has she a neat waist?"

Hamilton admitted, with some surprise, that her waist was exceptional.

"And her eyes?—I have heard of them—benevolent, yet sparkling;—and a daughter of the Schuylers. Hamilton, believe me, there are worse things than love."

"But I have affairs of the utmost moment on hand at present. I'm revolving a whole financial system, and the correspondence grows heavier every day. I've no time for love."

"My boy," said the former aide to the great Frederick, with emphasis, "when you can work in the sun, why cling to the cold corner of a public hearth? Your brain will spin the faster for the fire underneath. You will write great words and be happy besides. Think of that. What a combination! Mein Gott! You will be terribly in love, my son, but your balance is so extraordinary that your brain will work on just the same. Otherwise I would not dare give such counsel, for without you General Washington would give up, and your poor old Steuben would not have money for tobacco. Give me just one half-sovereign," he added coaxingly.

Hamilton examined the big tobacco pouch and found it two-thirds full. "Not a penny," he said gaily. "The day after to-morrow I will buy you some myself, but I know where that last sovereign went to."

Hamilton took care of the old spendthrift's money, and not only then but as long as he lived. "The Secretary of the Treasury is my banker," said Steuben, years after. "My Hamilton takes care of my money when he cannot take care of his own."

Hamilton retired in some perturbation, and the result of much thinking was that he spent an unconscionable time over his toilet on the evening of the dinner. In his nervousness he tore one of his lace ruffles. Laurens attempted to mend it, and the rent waxed. Hamilton was forced to knock at Mrs. Washington's door and ask her to repair the injury. She was already dressed, in a black lutestring, her hair flat and natural. She looked approvingly at Hamilton, who, not excepting Laurens, was always the most faultlessly dressed member of the family. To-night he wore dark green velvet, fitting closely and exquisitely cut, white silk stockings, and a profusion of delicate lace. His hair was worn in a queue and powdered. It was not till some years later that he conformed to the prevailing fashion and wore a wig.

Mrs. Washington mended the lace, retied the bow of his queue, kissed him and told him to forget the cares of war and correspondence, and enjoy himself. Hamilton retired, much comforted.

It was an imposing family which, a half-hour later, awaited the guests in the drawing-room. Washington was in black velvet and silk stockings, his best white wig spreading in two symmetrical wings. It was a cold grave figure always, and threw an air of solemnity over every scene it loomed upon, which only Hamilton's lively wit could dispel. Laurens wore plum-coloured velvet and much lace, a magnificent court costume. His own figure was no less majestic than Washington's, but his brown eyes and full mouth were almost invariably smiling, despite the canker. He wore a very close wig. Tilghman was in blue, the other men in more sober dress. Lafayette some time since had departed for France, Hamilton having suggested that the introduction of a French military force of six or seven thousand troops would have a powerful effect upon the American army and people.

Lady Sterling arrived with Lady Kitty—the bride of Colonel William Duer since July—her undistinguished homeliness enhancing the smart appearance of her daughter, who was one of the beauties of the time. Lady Kitty had a long oval face, correct haughty little features, and a general air of extreme high breeding. Her powdered hair was in a tower, and she had the tiniest waist and stood upon the highest heels of all the belles. She wore white satin over an immense hoop, a flounce of Spanish lace and a rope of pearls. Kitty Livingston wore yellow which outshone the light of the candles. Susan Boudinot and the other girls were dressed more simply. Mr. Boudinot's eyes were as keen and as kind as ever, his nose seemed longer, and the flesh was accumulating beneath his chin.

The Cochraines and Miss Elizabeth Schuyler were the last to arrive. The northern belle's wardrobe had been an object of much concern to the young ladies now cut off from New York shops, and lamenting the demoralized condition of those in Philadelphia. In Albany all things were still possible. Miss Schuyler wore a pink brocade of the richest and most delicate quality, and a bertha of Brussels lace. The pointed bodice and large paniers made her waist look almost as small as Kitty Duer's, and her feet were the tiniest in the world. She turned them in and walked with a slight shuffle. Hamilton had never seen a motion so adorable. Her hair was rolled out from her face on both sides as well as above, and so thickly powdered that her eyes looked as black as General Washington's coat, while her cheeks and lips were like red wine on pale amber. She blushed as Hamilton bowed before her and offered his arm, and then she felt his heart thump. As for Hamilton, he gave himself up for lost the moment she entered the room, and with the admission, his feelings concentrated with their usual fiery impetuosity. As it was too soon for an outlet, they rushed to his eyes and camped there, to Miss Schuyler's combined discomfort and delight.

For once Hamilton was content to listen, and Miss Schuyler was not loath to entertain this handsome young aide, of whom all the world was talking, and who had haunted her dreams for a year. She had read Milton, Shenstone, and Dodsworth, "The Search after Happiness," by Hannah More, the works of Madame de Genlis, the "Essay on Man," and Shakespeare's lighter plays. Her learning was not oppressive, merely sufficient to give distinction to her mind, and Hamilton was enchanted once more; but he found her most interesting when relating personal anecdotes of encounters with savage warriors in that dark northern land where she had been born and bred, of hideous massacres of which her neighbours had been the victims, of adventurous journeys she had taken with her father, of painted chieftains they had been forced to entertain. She talked with great spirit and no waste of words, and it was evident that she was both sensible and heroic. Hamilton ate little and forgot that he was in a company of twenty people. He was recalled by an abraded shin.

He turned with a jump and encountered Meade's agonized face thrust across Susan Livingston, who sat between them.

"For God's sake, Hamilton, come forth and talk," said Meade, in a hoarse whisper. "There hasn't been a word said above a mutter for three-quarters of an hour. Tilghman gave out long ago. Unless you come to the rescue we'll all be moaning in each other's arms in three minutes."

Hamilton glanced about the table. Washington, looking like himself on a monument, was making not a pretence to entertain poor Lady Sterling, who was almost sniffling. Lord Sterling, having gratified, an hour since, Mrs. Washington's polite interest in his health, was stifling yawn after yawn, and his chubby little visage was oblong and crimson. Tilghman, looking guilty and uncomfortable,—it was his duty to relieve Hamilton at the table,—was flirting with Miss Boudinot. Lady Kitty and Baron Steuben always managed to entertain each other. Laurens and Kitty Livingston were sitting back and staring at each other as they had stared many times before. The others were gazing at their plates or at Hamilton. It was, indeed, a Headquarters dinner at the worst.

It has been remarked that Hamilton had a strong sense of duty. He felt himself unable, even with the most charming girl on the continent beside him, to resist the appeal of all those miserable eyes, and launched forth at once upon the possibilities of Lafayette returning with an army. Everybody responded, and he had many subjects of common interest to discourse brilliantly upon until the long meal finished. Even Washington gave him a grateful glance, and the others reattacked their excellent food with a lost relish, now that the awful silence and sense of personal failure were dispelled by their "bright particular star," as the letters of the day from Morristown and the vicinity cleped our hero. But with Miss Schuyler he had no further word that night, and he retired with the conviction that there were times when there was no satisfaction whatever in doing one's duty.

VI

But a few nights later there was a subscription ball in the commissary storehouse, and Hamilton danced with Miss Schuyler no less than ten times, to the merciless amusement of the family. The ball, the first of any size since the war began, was a fine affair, and had been organized by Tilghman, Meade, and several of the Frenchmen; they were determined upon one gay season, at least. The walls were covered with flags and holly; the women wore their most gorgeous brocades; feathers and jewels were on becoming white wigs or on the towers of powdered hair. All the foreigners were in full regimentals, Steuben, in particular, being half covered with gold lace and orders; the music and supper were admirable. Even Washington looked less careworn than usual, and as he stood apart with Lord Sterling, General Knox, and General Greene, he shed no perceptible chill. Miss Schuyler wore white, with a twist of black velvet in her powdered hair and another about her throat, and would have been the belle of the party had Hamilton permitted other attentions. But she gave him all the dances he demanded, and although her bright manner did not lapse toward sentiment for a moment, he went home so elated that he sat scribbling poetry until Laurens pelted him with pillows and extinguished the candle.

The next day there was a sleighing party to Lord Sterling's, and he drove Miss Schuyler, her aunt, and the wife of General Knox through the white and crystal and blue of a magnificent winter day. Mrs. Cochraine made no secret of her pride in her niece's capture of Washington's celebrated favourite, and assured him of a hearty welcome at her house if he felt disposed to call. He promptly established the habit of calling every evening.

But although he was seriously and passionately in love, and quite sure that Miss Schuyler loved him in return, he hesitated for the first time in his life before precipitating a desired consummation. That he had no money did not worry him in the least, for he knew himself capable of earning any amount, and that the Republic, when free, would bristle with opportunities for young men of parts. But he was in honour bound to tell her of the irregularity of his birth. And in what manner would she regard a possible husband with whose children she never could discuss their father's parents? She was twenty-two, a small woman-of-the-world, not a romantic young miss incapable of reason. And the Schuylers? The proudest family in America! Would they take him on what he had made of himself, on the promise of his future, or would their family pride prove stronger than their common sense? He had moments of frantic doubt and depression, but fortunately there was no time for protracted periods of lover's misery. Washington demanded him constantly for consultation upon the best possible method of putting animation into the Congress and extracting money for the wretched troops. He frequently accompanied the General, as at Valley Forge, in his visits to the encampment on the mountain, where the emaciated tattered wretches were hutting with all possible speed against the severity of another winter. The snow was already on the ground, and every prospect of a repetition of the horrors of Valley Forge. The mere sight of Washington put heart into them, and Hamilton's lively sallies rarely failed to elicit a smile in return.

It so happened that for a fortnight the correspondence with Congress, the States, the Generals, and the British, in regard to the exchange of prisoners, was so heavy, the consultations with Washington so frequent, that Hamilton saw nothing of Miss Schuyler, and had little time for the indulgence of pangs. When he emerged, however, his mind was the freer to seek a solution of the problem which had tormented him, and he quickly found it. He determined to write the truth to Miss

166

Schuyler, and so save the embarrassment he had dreaded for both. To think was to act. He related the facts of his birth and of his ancestry in the briefest possible manner, adding a description of his mother which would leave no question of the place she held in his esteem. He then stated, with the emphasis of which he was master, that he distractedly awaited his dismissal, or Miss Schuyler's permission to declare what he had so awkwardly concealed.

He sent the letter by an orderly, and attacked his correspondence with a desire to put gunpowder on his quill. But Miss Schuyler was a tender-hearted creature and had no intention that he should suffer. She scrawled him a hasty summons to come to her at once, and bade the orderly ride as for his life. Hamilton, hearing a horse coming up the turnpike at runaway pace, glanced out of the window to see what neck was in danger, then flung his quill to the floor and bolted. He was out of the house before the orderly had dismounted, and secured possession of the note. When he had returned to his office, which was in a log extension at the back of the building, he locked the door and read what he could of Miss Schuyler's illegible chirography. That it was a command to wait upon her at once he managed to decipher, but no more at the moment; and feeling as if the heavens had opened, he despatched a hasty note, telling her that he could not leave his work before night, when he would hasten with the pent-up assurances of a love which had been his torment and delight for many weeks. And then he answered a summons to Washington's office, and discussed a letter to the Congress as if there were no such person in the world as Elizabeth Schuyler, as indeed for the hour there was not, nor for the rest of the afternoon.

But at eight o'clock he presented himself at the Cochraine quarters, and Miss Schuyler was alone in the drawing-room. It was some time before they arrived at the question which had weighed so heavily on Hamilton's mind. When, however, they came down to conversation, Miss Schuyler remarked:—

"I am sure that it will make no difference with my dear father, who is the most just and sensible of men. I had never thought of your parentage at all. I should have said you had leapt down from the abode of the gods, for you are much too remarkable to have been merely born. But if he should object—why, we'll run away."

Her eyes danced at the prospect, and Hamilton, who had vowed that nothing should induce him to enter a family where he was not welcome, was by now so hopelessly in love that he was ready to order the chaise and four at once. He remained until Mrs. Cochraine sent him home, then walked up the hill toward Headquarters, keeping to the road by instinct, for he was deep in a reverie on the happiness of the past hours. His dreams were cruelly shattered by the pressure of a bayonet against his breast.

"What?" he demanded. "Oh, the countersign." He racked his memory. It had fled, terrified, from his brain under the rush of that evening's emotions.

"I can't remember it," he said haughtily; "but you know who I am. Let me pass." The sentry stood like a fate.

"This is ridiculous!" cried Hamilton, angrily, then the absurdity of the situation overcame him, and he laughed. Once more he searched his brain for the countersign, which he remembered having given to little Ford just after dinner. Mrs. Ford and her son retained two rooms in the house, and Hamilton frequently gave the youngster the word, that he might play in the village after dark. Suddenly he saw him approaching. He darted down the road, secured the password, and returned in triumph to the sentry.

"Sir," exclaimed the soldier, in dismay, "is this quite regular? Will you give me your word, sir, that it is all right?"

"I vow that no harm shall come to you," said Hamilton. "Shoulder your musket." And there the incident ended, so far as the soldier was concerned, but young Ford carried the story to Headquarters, and it was long before Hamilton heard the last of it.

There was no sleep in him that night. He went to his office and laboured for hours over a verse which should adequately express the love consuming him, and then he awoke Laurens and talked into that sympathetic ear until it was time to break the ice and freshen himself for work.

His work that day was of a vastly different character from the impassioned trifle of the night before. He obtained exemption from other duty, and ordered luncheon and dinner brought to his office. One of the most remarkable examples of Hamilton's mature genius at this age of twenty-three is his long and elaborate letter to Robert Morris on the financial condition of the country, written during the earliest period of his love for Elizabeth Schuyler. As passionate and impatient as he was tender, alive in every part of his nature to the joy of a real affection and to the prospect of a lasting happiness, he yet was able for twelve hours at a time to shut his impending bride in the remotest cupboard of his mind, nor heed her sighs. But there was an older love than Elizabeth Schuyler: a ragged poverty-stricken creature by this, cowering before dangers within and without, raving mad at times, imbecile at others, filling her shattered body with patent nostrums, yet throughout her long course of futilities and absurdities making a desperate attempt to shade the battered lamp of liberty from the fatal draught. Her name was the United States of America, and never was there a more satiric misnomer. If the States chose to obey the requisitions of the Congress, they obeyed them; but as a rule they did not. There was no power in the land to enforce obedience; and they hated each other. As the Congress had demonstrated its inefficiency to the most inactive in public affairs, the contempt of the States is hardly to be wondered at. It is not too much to say that troops were recruited by Washington's influence alone, and kept from mutiny by his immortal magnetism. The finances of the Revolution were in such a desperate condition that Sir Henry Clinton built his hopes of success—now he had discovered that no victory gave him a permanent advantage—upon the dissolution of the American army, possibly an internal war. With depreciated bills in circulation amounting to one hundred and sixty millions of dollars, a public debt of nearly forty millions in foreign and domestic loans, the Congress had, in March, ordered a new emission of bills; the result had been a season of crazy speculation and the expiring gasp of public credit. In addition to an unpaid army, assurances had been given to the French minister that not less than twenty-five thousand men should be ready for the next campaign; and how to force the States to recruit them, and how to pay them when in the field, was the present question between Headquarters and Congress.

From the time that Hamilton's mind had turned to finance, in his nineteenth year, he had devoted the greater part of his leisure to the study and thought of it. Books on the subject were few in those days; the science of political economy was unborn, so far as Hamilton was concerned, for Adam Smith's "Wealth of Nations," published in 1776, had not made its way to America. He assimilated all the data there was to be found, then poured it into the crucible of his creative faculty, and gradually evolved the great scheme of finance which is the locomotive of the United States to-day. During many long winter evenings he had talked his ideas over with Washington, and it was with the Chief's full approval that he finally went to work on the letter embodying his scheme for the immediate relief of the country. It was addressed to Robert Morris, the Financier of the Revolution.

The first part of the letter was an essay on inflated and depreciated currency, applied personally, the argument based on the three following points: There having been no money in the country, Congress had been unable to avoid the issuance of paper money. The only way to obtain and retire this immense amount of depreciated paper money was to obtain real money. Real money could be obtained in one way only,—by a foreign loan. He then elaborately disposed of the proposed insane methods of applying this projected loan which were agitating the Congress. But he was an architect and builder as well as an iconoclast, and having shown the futility of every financial idea ever conceived by Congress, he proceeded to the remedy. His scheme, then as ever, was a National Bank, to be called The Bank of the United States; the capital to be a foreign loan of two millions sterling.

This letter, even in its details, in the knowledge of human nature it betrays, and in its scheme to combine public and private capital that the wealthy men of the country should, in their own interests, be compelled to support the government, reads like an easy example in arithmetic to-day; but a hundred and twenty years ago it was so bold and advanced that Morris dared to adopt several of its suggestions in part only, and founded the bank of Pennsylvania on the greater plan, by way of experiment. No one but Hamilton could carry out his own theories.

Hamilton, who often had odd little attacks of modesty, signed the letter, James Montague; address, Morristown. He read it to Washington before posting.

The Chief, whose men were aching, sighed heavily.

"They will pick a few crumbs out of it," he said. "But they will not make a law of it in toto; the millennium is not yet come. But if it gives them one idea we should be thankful, it being a long and weary time since they have experienced that phenomenon. If it does not, I doubt if these men fight another battle. I wonder if posterity will ever realize the indifference of their three million ancestors to the war which gave them their independence—if we accomplish that end. I ask for soldiers and am treated much as if I had asked for my neighbour's wife. I ask for money to keep them from starving and freezing and am made to feel like an importunate beggar."

"I had a letter from Hugh Knox not so long since," said Hamilton, in his lightest tone; for Washington was on the verge of one of his attacks of infuriated depression, which were picturesque but wearing. "He undertakes to play the prophet, and he is an uncommon clever man, sir: he says that you were created for the express purpose of delivering America, to do it single-handed, if necessary, and that my proud destiny is to be your biographer. The first I indorse, so does every thinking man in the country. But for the second—alas! I am not equal to a post of such exalted honour."

Washington smiled. "No one knows better than your old Chief that your destiny is no such ha'penny affair as that. But at least you wouldn't make an ass of me. God knows what is in store for me at the hands of scribblers."

"You lend yourself fatally well to marble and stone, sir," said Hamilton, mischievously. "I fear your biographers will conceive themselves writing at the feet of a New World Sphinx, and that its frozen granite loneliness will petrify their image of you."

"I like the prospect! I am unhappily conscious of my power to chill an assemblage, but the cold formality of my manner is a safeguard, as you know. My nature is one of extremes; if I did not encase myself, I should be ramming every man's absurd opinions down his throat, and letting my cursed temper fly at each of the provocations which constantly beset me. I have not the happy gift of compromise; but I am not unhuman, and I like not the prospect of going down to posterity a wooden figurehead upon some emblematic battle-ship. Perhaps, my boy, you, who best know me, will be moved by charity to be my biographer, after all."

"I'll make it the business of my old age, sir; I pledge you my word, and no one loves you better nor can do you such justice as I. When my work in the National Family is done, then shall I retire with my literary love, an old and pleasant love; and what higher subject for my pen?"

He spoke in a tone of badinage, for he was bent on screwing up

171

Washington's spirits, but he made his promise in good faith, nevertheless, and Washington looked at him with deep affection.

"My mind is certainly easier," he said, in a tone that was almost light.

"Go now and post your letter, and give your evening to Miss Schuyler. Present my compliments to her."

"I became engaged to her last night, sir."

"Ah! had you forgotten to tell me?"

"No, sir; I have but just remembered it."

Washington laughed heartily. "Mind you never tell her that," he said. "Women love the lie that saves their pride, but never an unflattering truth. You have learned your lesson young,—to put a tempting face aside when duty demands every faculty; it is a lesson which takes most men longest to learn. I could tell you some amusing stories of rough and tumbles in my mind between the divine image of the hour and some affair of highest moment. But to a brain like yours all things are possible."

He rose, and took Hamilton's hand and shook it warmly.

"God bless you," he said. "Your future unrolls to my vision, brilliant and happy. I deeply wish that it may be so."

VII

The letter from General Schuyler, giving his consent to the engagement, has not been preserved; but some time after he had occasion to write Hamilton a business letter, in which the following passage occurs:—

You cannot, my dear sir, be more happy at the connexion you have made with my family than I am. Until the child of a parent has made a judicious choice, his heart is in continual anxiety; but this anxiety was removed on the moment I discovered it was on you she had placed her affections. I am pleased with every instance of delicacy in those who are so dear to me; and I think I read your soul on the occasion you mention. I shall therefore only entreat you to consider me as one who wishes in every way to promote your happiness.

General Schuyler was ordered by Congress to Morristown to confer with Washington. He took a house, sent for his family, and remained until late in the summer. The closest friendship was formed between

Schuyler and Hamilton, which, with common political interests and deepening sympathy, increased from year to year. The good fairies of Nevis who had attended Hamilton's birth never did better for him than when they gave him Elizabeth Schuyler for wife and Philip Schuyler for father and friend. And they had blasted the very roots of the chief impediment to success, for he triumphed steadily and without effort over what has poisoned the lives of many men; and triumphed in spite of the fact that the truth was vaguely known always, and kept in the quiver of his enemies.

As Hamilton was absent from Headquarters but seldom during General Schuyler's sojourn, the lovers met almost every evening, and occasionally Washington, who possessed certain sympathies based on long experience, would give Hamilton a morning free, and suggest a ride through the woods. Never were two people happier nor more inherently suited. Hamilton's instinct had guided him safely past more brilliant women to one who willingly would fold herself round his energetic individuality of many parts, fitting into every division and crevice. She was receptive, sympathetic, adaptive, with sufficient intelligence to appreciate the superlative brain of the man whom she never ceased to worship and to regard as a being of unmortal clay. A brilliant ambitious wife in the same house with Hamilton might have written a picturesque diary, but the domestic instrument would have twanged with discords. Hamilton was unselfish, and could not do enough for those he loved; but he was used to the first place, to the unquestioned yielding of it to his young high-mightiness by his clever aspiring friends, by the army of his common acquaintance, and in many ways by Washington himself. Had he married Angelica Schuyler, that independent, high-spirited, lively, adorable woman, probably they would have boxed each other's ears at the end of a week.

Hamilton made the dash on Staten Island with Lord Sterling, and in March went with General St. Clair and Colonel Carrington to negotiate with the British commissioners for the exchange of prisoners; before the battle of Springfield he was sent out to reconnoitre. Otherwise his days were taken up bombarding the Congress with letters representing the necessity of drafting troops to meet the coming emergencies.

He and Miss Betsey Schuyler had a very pretty plan, which was nothing less than that they should go to Europe on their wedding tour, Congress to find his presence necessary at the Court of France. The suggestion originated with Laurens, who had been asked to go as secretary to Franklin. He had no wish to go, and knowing Hamilton's ardent desire to visit Europe and growing impatience with his work, had recommended his name to the Congress. General Schuyler would have procured a leave of absence for his impending son-in-law, and sent the young couple to Europe with his blessing and a heavy wallet, but Hamilton would as soon have forged a man's name as travelled at his expense. He hoped that the Congress would send him. He was keenly alive to the value of studying Europe at first hand before he was called upon to help in the modelling of the new Republic, and the vision of wandering in historic lands with his bride kept him awake at night. Moreover, he was desperately tired of his life at Headquarters. When the expedition to Staten Island was in question, he asked Washington, through Lafayette, to give him the command of a battalion which happened to be without a field-officer. Washington refused, partly from those motives of policy to which he ever showed an almost niggling adherence, but more because he could not spare his most useful aide. Hamilton, who was bursting for action of any sort, retired to his detested little office in angry disappointment. But he was a philosopher. He adjusted himself to the Inevitable, and dismissed the matter from his mind, after registering a vow that he would take advantage of the first excuse which might offer to resign his position.

The Schuylers returned to Albany. The French fleet arrived, and hovered well beyond the range of British guns, having no desire to risk an engagement until reinforced. Its Admiral, Count Rochambeau, having a grievance, Hamilton advised a personal conference.

"We might suggest that he meet us halfway—say at Wethersfield, near Hartford," he added. "That would save us something in travelling expenses."

Washington sighed heavily. "We are worse off than you think," he said.

"I might scrape together money enough for half the journey, but no more. Lafayette and his aide must go with us—to say nothing of the escort. Think of the innkeepers' bills, for ourselves and horses. What to do I confess I do not know, for I should confer with this Frenchman at once."

"Go we must, sir," said Hamilton, decidedly, "if we have to take up a collection—why not? If an object cannot be accomplished one way, try another." He stood up and emptied the contents of his pockets on the table. "Only five hundred beggarly continentals," he said ruefully. "However, who knows what treasures may line more careful pockets than mine? I know they will come forth as spontaneously. Have I your permission to try, sir?"

Washington nodded, and Hamilton ran downstairs, pressed Meade into service, and together they made the round of the officers' quarters. He returned at the end of an hour and threw a huge bundle of paper on the table. "Only eight thousand dollars, sir," he said. "It's the best that any man could do. But I think it may carry us through."

"It will have to," said Washington. "Remind me, my dear boy, if you see me eating too much. I have such an appetite!"

They set out on their journey a week later, having communicated with Rochambeau, who agreed to meet them at Wethersfield. All went well, for the wretched inns were not exorbitant, until they reached Hartford. They arrived late in the afternoon, weary and ravenous. After a bath and a glimpse of luxurious beds, they marched to the dining room and sat down to a sumptuous repast, whose like had greeted neither nostril nor palate for many a day. The wines were mellow, the tobacco green, the conversation gay until midnight. Hamilton sang "The Drum," and many another song rang among the rafters. Washington retired first, bidding the youngsters enjoy themselves. The young men arose at their accustomed hour next morning, with appetites renewed, but waited in vain for their Chief. Hamilton finally knocked at his door. There was no response, and a servant told him that the General had gone out nearly an hour before. He went in search, bidding Lafayette and M'Henry remain behind. As he had anticipated, he found Washington in a secluded nook, engaged in prayer. He waited a few moments, then coughed respectfully. Washington immediately rose, his harassed face showing little relief.

"Is anything wrong, sir?" asked Hamilton, anxiously.

"Alas!" said the General, "I wonder that you, too, are not driven to prayer, to intercede for help in this distressing predicament. Think of that extravagant repast we consumed last night. God help me, but I was so famished I never gave a thought to consequences. Unquestionably, the breakfast will be on a like scale. *And we have but eight thousand dollars with which to pay the bill!*"

"It is true! I never gave the matter a thought—I am cursedly extravagant. And we must get home! I suppose we shall have to fast all the way. Well, we've fasted before, and the memory of last night's dinner may sustain us—"

"But this man's bill! How are we to meet it?"

"Shall I speak to him, sir? Tell him unreservedly our predicament—that these wretched eight thousand dollars are all we have in the world? Perhaps he is a good patriot, and will call the account square."

"Do," said Washington, "and come here and tell me what he says. I am too mortified to show my face. I shall not enter the house again."

Hamilton walked slowly to the house, little caring for his errand. He returned on a dead run.

"We are saved, sir!" he cried, almost in Washington's arms. "Governor Trumbull has sent word to all the hostelries that we are to be his guests while we are in the state of Connecticut!"

Washington said his prayers again, and ate two chickens for breakfast.

On the return from this conference, when approaching the house of General Benedict Arnold, opposite West Point, where they were invited for breakfast, Washington suddenly decided to accompany Lafayette, who wished to inspect some earthworks.

"You need not come," he said to Hamilton and M'Henry. "I know that you are both in love with Mrs. Arnold. Go on. We will join you presently."

The young men were greeted with effusion by the pretty hostess, with absent reserve by her husband. Mrs. Arnold left the room to order that the breakfast be delayed. While she was absent, a note was brought to Arnold. He opened it, turned green, and rising hastily, announced that his presence was demanded at West Point and left the room. The sound of a smothered scream and fall came from above. A moment later the aides heard the sound of galloping hoofs.

Their suspicions aroused, they ran outside. A messenger, with a despatch from Colonel Jameson, awaited Washington's arrival. Hamilton tore open the paper. It contained the news that a British spy had been captured within the lines. In an instant Hamilton and

M'Henry were on their horses and off in pursuit of the fugitive. That Arnold was a traitor and had fled to the British war-ship, *Vulture*, hovering in Haverstraw Bay, a slower wit than Hamilton's would have assumed. The terrified scoundrel was too quick for them. He had ridden over a precipice to the shore below, and under protection of a flag of truce was far down the river when his pursuers sighted him. They returned with all speed.

I shall not repeat the oft-told tale of André's capture, trial, and death. Nowhere has it been so well told as by Hamilton himself, in a letter to Laurens, printed at the time and universally read. It is only necessary here to allude to his share in that unhappiest episode of the war. When Washington reached the house his aide was engaged in consoling Mrs. Arnold, who was shrieking and raving, weeping and fainting; imposing on Hamilton a task varied and puzzling, even to one of his schooling. But she was very young, very charming, and in a tragic plight. Washington himself wiped away a tear, and for a moment forgot the barely averted consequences of her husband's treason, while he assisted Hamilton in assuaging a grief so bitter and so appealing. As soon as was possible he sent her through the British lines.

But Hamilton quickly forgot Mrs. Arnold in his sympathy and admiration for the unfortunate André. He conceived a quick and poignant friendship for the brilliant accomplished young Englishman, with the dreamy soft face of a girl, and a mettle which had brought him to destruction. Hamilton did all he could to save him, short of suggesting to André to ask Sir Henry Clinton to offer Arnold in exchange. He enlisted the sympathy of the officers at West Point in the prisoner's behalf, gave up his leisure to diverting André's mind, and persuaded Washington to delay the execution and send an indirect suggestion to Clinton to offer the exchange himself. When all hope was over, he personally begged Washington to heed André's request for a soldier's death, and not condemn such a man to the gibbet. Washington gladly would have saved his interesting prisoner's life, and felt deeply for him, but again those motives of policy prevailed, and André was executed like a common malefactor.

VIII

Washington was in temporary quarters—a cramped and wretched

tavern—at Liberty Pole, New Jersey. The inaction being oppressive, Hamilton concentrated his thoughts on the condition and needs of the country.

I am sorry that the same spirit of indifference to public affairs prevails, [he wrote to Sears]. It is necessary we should rouse and begin to do our business in earnest, or we shall play a losing game. We must have a government with more power. We must have a tax in kind. We must have a foreign loan. We must have a bank on the true principles of a bank. We must have an administration distinct from Congress, and in the hands of single men under their orders. We must, above all things, have an army for the war.... We are told here there is to be a Congress of the neutral powers at the Hague for meditating of peace. God send it may be true. We want it; but if the idea goes abroad, ten to one if we do not fancy the thing done, and fall into a profound sleep till the cannon of the enemy waken us next campaign. This is our national character.

Hamilton, the High Priest of Energy, had long since declared war against the genius of the American people, who believed in God and the art of leisure. Hamilton believed in God and a cabinet of zealous ministers. He was already a thorn in the side of estimable but hesitant patriots, and in times to come his unremitting and remorseless energy was to be a subject of reproach by associates and enemies alike. Even Jefferson, that idol of the present as of the past democracy, had timidly declared against separation in 1774, while Hamilton, a boy of seventeen, had been the first to suggest the resort to arms, and incessant in his endeavours until the great result was accomplished. He had countless other schemes, and he knew that eventually he would succeed in driving the American people before the point of his quill. That his task would be long and arduous did not daunt him for a moment. By this time he knew every want of the country, and was determined upon the reorganization of the government. The energy which is one of the distinguishing characteristics of the American nation to-day was generated by Hamilton, might, indeed, be said to be the persistence and diffusion of his ego. For the matter of that, all that is greatest in this American evolution of a century was typified in Hamilton. Not only his formidable energy, but his unqualified honour and integrity, his unquenchable optimism, his extraordinary nimbleness of mind and readiness of resource, his gay good-nature, high spirits, and buoyancy, his light philosophy effervescing above unsounded depths, his inability to see when he was beaten, his remorseless industry, his hard common sense, combined with a versatile cleverness which makes for shallowness in another race, his careless generosity, his aptitude for detail and impatience of it, his reckless bravery in war and intrepidity in peace, even his highly strung nerves, excitability, and obliging readiness at all times for a fight, raise him high above history as the genius of the American race. The reverse side of the national character we owe to the greatest of his rivals; as will be seen hereafter.

During the sojourn at Liberty Pole, Washington and he sat through many nights discussing the imperative need of the reorganization of the government, and the best methods by which it could be accomplished. The result was Hamilton's letter to James Duane, an important member of the Congress.

This letter, no doubt the most remarkable of its kind ever written, and as interesting to-day as when Hamilton conceived it, is far too long to be quoted. It began with an exhaustive analysis of the reasons for the failure of Congress to cope with a situation which was becoming more threatening every hour, and urged the example of the Grecian republics and the Swiss cantons against the attempted confederation of the States without a strong centralized government. Lacking a common tie of sufficient strength, the States would inevitably drift toward independent sovereignty, and they had given signal proof in the matter of raising troops, contributing money, and in their everlasting disputes about boundary lines, as to the absolute lack of any common public spirit. His remedy, in brief, was a convention of the States for the purpose of creating a Federal Constitution, the distributing of the powers of government into separate departments, with Presidents of War, Marine, and Trade, a secretary of Foreign Affairs, and a Financier, defining their prerogatives; the States to have no privileges beyond an internal police for the protection of the property and the rights of individuals, and to raise money by internal taxes; the army to be recruited on a permanent establishment. In addition, there was an elaborate system of taxation, by which the country could be supported in all its emergencies. His favourite plan of a National Bank was elaborated in minute detail, the immediate necessity for a foreign loan dwelt upon with sharp reproof, and examples given of the recruiting of armies in European states.

Out of a multitude of suggestions a few were adopted within a short time, but the great central suggestion, the calling of a convention for the purpose of creating a Federal Constitution, was to be hammered at for many weary years before jealous States and unconfident patriots could be persuaded to a measure so monarchical and so bold. But the letter is on record, and nothing more logical, far-sighted, and comprehensive ever was written. It contained the foundation-stones upon which this government of the United States stands to-day. Congress put on its spectacles and read it with many grunts, magnanimously expressing admiration for a youth who had fearlessly grappled with questions which addled older brains; but its audacious suggestions of a government greater than Congress, and of a bank which would add to their troubles, were not taken seriously for a moment.

Hamilton also found time to write a good many love letters. Here is one of them:—

I would not have you imagine, Miss, that I write you so often to gratify your wishes or please your vanity; but merely to indulge myself, and to comply with that restless propensity of my mind which will not be happy unless I am doing something in which you are concerned. This may seem a very idle disposition in a philosopher and a soldier, but I can plead illustrious examples in my justification. Achilles liked to have sacrificed Greece and his glory to a female captive, and Anthony lost a world for a woman. I am very sorry times are so changed as to oblige me to go to antiquity for my apology, but I confess, to the disgrace of the present time, that I have not been able to find as many who are as far gone as myself in the laudable Zeal of the fair sex. I suspect, however, if others knew the charm of my sweetheart as I do, I could have a great number of competitors. I wish I could give you an idea of her. You can have no conception of how sweet a girl she is. It is only in my heart that her image is truly drawn. She has a lovely form and still more lovely mind. She is all goodness, the gentlest, the dearest, the tenderest of her sex. Ah, Betsey, how I love her!

His reiterated demand for a foreign loan, and the sending of a special envoy to obtain it, at last wrung a reluctant consent from Congress. Lafayette was his politic suggestion, and Congress would have indorsed it, but that adventurous young hero had not come to America to return and beg money on his own doorstep. There was a prospect of fighting in the immediate future, and he was determined to add to his renown. The choice then lay between Hamilton and Laurens, who had received the thanks of Congress for his distinguished services in the field, and whose father had been a president of that body. Lafayette and all the Frenchmen were anxious that the mission be given to Hamilton. The former went to Philadelphia and talked to half the Congress. He offered Hamilton private letters which would introduce him to the best society of Europe; adding, "I intend giving you the *key* of the cabinet, as well as of the societies which influence them."

Laurens, by this time, was eager to go. His father, who had started for Holland as Minister Plenipotentiary, had been captured by the British and confined in the Tower of London; the foreign mission would give him an opportunity to attempt his liberation. Moreover, life was very dull at present, and he knew himself to be possessed of diplomatic talents. But he was also aware of Hamilton's ardent desire to visit Europe, all that it would mean to that insatiate mind, his weariness of his present position. Washington would give his consent to the temporary absence of Hamilton, for the French money was the vital necessity of the Republic's life, and he knew that his indomitable aide would not return without it Therefore Laurens wrote to Hamilton, who was in Albany awaiting his wedding-day, that he should resign in his favour, and congratulated him on so brilliant and distinguished a honeymoon.

The struggle in Hamilton's mind was brief. The prospect of sailing with his bride on a long and delightful journey that could not fail to bring him highest honour had made his blood dance. Moreover, in the previous month Washington had again refused his request for an independent command. It took him but a short time to relinquish this cherished dream when he thought of the unhappy plight of Mr. Laurens, and remembered the deep anxiety of the son, often expressed. He wrote to Laurens, withdrawing in the most decisive terms. Laurens was not to be outdone. He loved his father, but he loved Hamilton more. He pressed the appointment upon his friend, protesting that the affairs of the elder Laurens would be quite as safe in his hands. Hamilton prevailed, and Congress, having waited amiably while the two martial youths had it out, unanimously appointed Laurens. He could not sail until February, and as soon as the matter was decided obtained leave of absence and repaired in all haste to Albany, to be present at Hamilton's wedding.

IX

The wedding of Alexander Hamilton and Elizabeth Schuyler was the most notable private event of the Revolution. The immense social and political consequence of the Schuylers, and the romantic fame of the young aide, of whom the greatest things possible were expected, brought the aristocracy of New York and the Jersies to Albany despite the inclement winter weather. The large house of the Schuylers gave a prolonged hospitality to the women, and the men lodged in the patriarchal little town. But although Hamilton was glad to see the Livingstons, Sterlings, and Boudinots again, the greater number of the guests interested him far less than a small group of weather-beaten soldiers, of which this occasion was the happy cause of reunion. Troup was there, full of youth and honours. He had received the thanks of Congress for his services at Saratoga, and been appointed secretary of the Board of War. Recently he had resigned from the army, and was completing his law studies. Nicolas Fish came with Lafayette, whose light artillery he commanded. He was known as a brave and gallant soldier, and so excellent a disciplinarian that he had won the approval and confidence of Washington. He still parted his little fringe in the middle, and his face was as chubby as ever, his eyes as solemn. Lafayette, who had brought a box full of clothes that had dazzled Paris, embraced Hamilton with tears, but they were soon deep in conjectures of the next campaign. Laurens, looking like a king in exile, wrung many hearts. Hamilton's brother aides, unfortunately, were the more closely bound by his absence, but they had despatched him with their blessing and much chaffing.

The hall of the Schuyler mansion was about twenty feet square and panelled in white. It was decorated with holly, and for three nights before the wedding illuminated by hundreds of wax candles, while the young people danced till three in the morning. The Schuyler house, long accustomed to entertaining, had never been gayer, and no one was more content than the chatelaine. Although she had been reasonably sure of Elizabeth, there was no telling at what moment the maiden might yield to the romantic mania of the time, and climb out of her window at night while Hamilton stood shivering below. Now all danger was past, and Mrs. Schuyler moved, large, placid, and still handsome, among her guests, beaming so affectionately whenever she met Mrs. Carter's flashing eyes that Peggy and Cornelia renewed their vows to elope when the hour and the men arrived. General Schuyler, once more on the crest of public approval, was always grave and stern, but he, too, breathed satisfaction and relief. He was a tall man of military appearance, powerful, muscular, slender; but as his nose was large and fleshy, and he wore a ragged-looking wig with wings like Washington's, he could not be called handsome. It was a noble countenance, however, and his black eyes flashed and pierced.

As for Hamilton and Miss Schuyler, who had a trunk full of charming new gowns, they were as happy as two children, and danced the night through. They were married on the 20th, in the drawing-room, in front of the splendid mantel, which the housewives had spent much time in admiring. The bride wore the white which became her best, made with a long pointed bodice and paniers, and lace that had been worn by the wife of the first patroon. She had risen to the dignity of a wig, and her mass of black hair was twisted mercilessly tight under the spreading white monstrosity to which her veil was attached. Hamilton wore a black velvet coat, as befitting his impending state. Its lining and the short trousers were of white satin. His shapely legs were in white silk, his feet in pumps with diamond buckles, the present of Lafayette. He, too, wore a wig,—a close one, with a queue,—but he got rid of it immediately after the ceremony, for it heated his head.

Hamilton had then reached his full height, about five feet six. His bride was perhaps three inches shorter. The world vowed that never had there been so pretty a couple, nor one so well matched in every way. Both were the perfection of make, and the one as fair and fresh as a Scot, the other a golden gipsy, the one all fire and energy, the other docile and tender, but with sufficient spirit and intelligence. It is seldom that the world so generously gives its blessing, but it might have withheld it, for all that Hamilton and his bride would have cared.

Hamilton's honeymoon was brief. There was a mass of correspondence awaiting him, and no place for a bride in the humble Dutch house at New Windsor where Washington had gone into winter quarters. But the distance was not great, and he could hope for flying leaves of absence. Washington was not unsympathetic to lovers; he had been known to unbend and advise his aides when complications threatened or a siege seemed hopeless; and he had given Hamilton the longest leave possible. Nevertheless, the bridegroom set forth, one harsh January morning, on his long journey, over roads a foot deep in snow, and through solitary winter forests, with any thing but an impassioned desire to see General Washington again. Had he been returning to the command of a corps, with a prospect of stirring events as soon as the snow melted, he would have spurred his horse with high satisfaction, even though he left a bride behind him; but to return to a drudgery which he hated the more for having escaped it for three enchanted weeks, made his spirit turn its back to the horse's head. He resolved anew to resign if an opportunity offered. Four years of that particular sort of devotion to the patriot cause were enough. He wished to demonstrate his patriotism in other ways. He had accomplished the primary object for which Washington had pressed him into service, and he believed that the war was nearing its finish; there was nothing he could now do at Headquarters which the other aides could not do as well, and he wanted military excitement and renown while their possibilities existed.

X

The first task awaiting him upon his arrival at Headquarters was to draw up a letter of instruction for Laurens, a task which required minute care; for on its suggestions, as much as on Laurens's brilliant talents, depended the strength of a mission whose failure might mean that of the American arms. Laurens had requested the letter, and told Hamilton that he should be guided by it. He did not anticipate a royal condition of mind which would prompt him practically to carry off the French money-bags under the king's astonished nose, and he knew Hamilton's command of every argument connected with the painful subject of financial needs. Hamilton drew up a lucid and comprehensive letter, in nine parts, which Laurens could study at his leisure on the frigate, *Alliance*; then attacked his accumulated duties. They left him little leisure to remember he was a bridegroom, although he occasionally directed his gaze toward the North with some longing. His freedom approached, however, and it was swift and unexpected.

It came on the 16th of February. His office was in his bedroom. He had just completed a letter containing instructions of an important nature for the commissary, and started in search of Tilghman, whose duty it was to see it safely delivered. On the stairs he passed Washington, whose brow was heavy. The General, with that brevity which was an indication of his passionate temper fighting against a self-control which he must have knocked flat with great satisfaction at times, ejaculated that he wished to speak with him at once. Hamilton replied that he would wait upon him immediately, and hastened to Tilghman's office, wondering what had occurred to stir the depths of his Chief. He was but a moment with Tilghman, but on the stairs he met Lafayette, who was in search of him upon a matter of business. It is possible that Hamilton should not have permitted himself to be detained, but at all events he did, for perhaps two minutes. Suddenly he became conscious that Washington was standing at the head of the stairs, and wondering if he had awaited him there, he abruptly broke off his conversation with Lafayette, and ran upward. Washington looked as if about to thunder anathema upon the human race. He had been annoyed since dawn, and his passions fairly flew at this last indignity.

"Colonel Hamilton!" he exclaimed. "You have kept me waiting at the head of the stairs these ten minutes. I must tell you, sir, you treat me with disrespect."

Hamilton's eyes blazed and his head went back, but his quick brain leapt to the long-desired opportunity. He replied as calmly as if his heart were not thumping, "I am not conscious of it, sir, but since you have thought it necessary to tell me so, we part."

"Very well, sir!" replied Washington, "if it be your choice!" He turned his back and strode to his office.

Hamilton went to his room with a light heart, feeling as if the pigeon-holes were marching out of his brain. The breach was Washington's; he himself had answered with dignity, and could leave with a clear conscience. He had not kept Washington waiting above four minutes, and he did not feel that an apology was necessary.

"Oh," he thought aloud, "I feel as if I had grown wings." He would return to his bride for a few weeks, then apply once more for a command.

There was a knock, and Tilghman entered. The young men looked at each other in silence for a moment; Tilghman with an almost comical anxiety, Hamilton with alert defiance.

"Well?" demanded Hamilton.

"I come from the Chief—ambassador extraordinary. Look out of the window, or I shall not have courage to go on. He's put the devil to bed and is monstrous sorry this misunderstanding has occurred—"

"Misunderstanding?" snorted Hamilton.

"You know my love of euphony, Hamilton. Pray let me finish. I'd rather be Laurens on my way to beg. What is a king to a lion? But seriously, my dear, the Chief is desperately sorry this has occurred. He has deputed me to assure you of his great confidence in your abilities, integrity, and usefulness, and of his desire, in a candid conversation, to heal a difference which could not have happened but in a moment of passion. Do go and see him at once, and then we shall all sleep in peace to-night."

But Hamilton shook his head decidedly. "You know how tired I am of all this," he said, "and that I can be as useful and far more agreeably active in the field. If I consent to this interview, I am lost. I have never doubted the Chief's affection for me, but he is also the most astute of men, and knows my weakness. If, arguments having failed, he puts his arm about my shoulders and says, 'My boy, *do* not desert me,' I shall melt, and vow that neither bride nor glory could beckon me from him. So listen attentively, mon ami, and deliver my answer as follows: 1st. I have taken my resolve in a manner not to be revoked, 2d. As a conversation could serve no other purpose than to produce explanations, mutually disagreeable, though I certainly will not refuse an interview if he desires it, yet I should be happy if he would permit me to decline it. 3d. That, though determined to leave the family, the same principles which have kept me so long in it will continue to direct my conduct toward him when out of it. 4th. That I do not wish to distress him or the public business by quitting him before he can derive other assistance by the return of some of the gentlemen who are absent. 5th. And that in the meantime it depends on him to let our behaviour to each other be the same as if nothing had happened."

Tilghman heaved a deep sigh. "Then you really mean to go?" he said. "Heartless wretch! Have you no mercy on us? Headquarters will be a tomb, with Washington reposing on top. Think of the long and solemn breakfasts, the funereal dinners, the brief but awful suppers. Washington will never open his mouth again, and I never had the courage to speak first. If ever you deign to visit us, you will find that we have lost the power of speech. I repeat that you have no heart in your body."

Hamilton laughed. "If you did not know that I love you, you would not sit there and revile me. No family has ever been happier than ours. In four years there has not been a quarrel until to-day. I can assure you that my heart will ache when the time comes to leave you, but I really had got to the end of my tether. I have long felt as if I could not go on another day."

"'Tis grinding, monotonous work," admitted Tilghman, "and we've all wondered how you have stood it as long as this—every bit of you was made for action. Well, I'll take your message to the Chief."

Washington consented to waive the explanation and sent Hamilton another message, thanking him for consenting to remain until Harrison and Meade returned.

XI

Little Mrs. Hamilton was delighted with the course affairs had taken, and pleaded for resignation from the army. But to this Hamilton would not hearken. Anxious as he was for the war to finish, that he might begin upon the foundations of home and fortune, he had no intention of deserting a cause to which he had pledged himself, and in which there still was a chance for him to achieve distinction. So far, his ambitions were wholly military. If the profound thought he had given to the present and future needs of the Republic was not wholly impersonal; if he took for granted that he had a part to play when the Revolution finished, it was little more than a dream at present. His very temperament was martial, the energy and impetuosity of his nature were in their element on the battlefield, and he would rather have been a great general than the elder Pitt. But although there is no reason to doubt that he would have become a great general, had circumstance favoured his pet ambition, yet Washington was a better judge of the usefulness of his several abilities than he was himself. Not only had that reader of men made up his mind that a brain like his favourite's should not be wasted on the battlefield,—left there, perhaps, while dolts

187

escaped, for Hamilton had no appreciation of fear or danger,—but he saw in him the future statesman, fertile, creative, executive, commanding; and he could have no better training than at a desk in his office. Phenomenally precocious, even mature, as Hamilton's brain had been when they met that morning on the Heights of Harlem, these four years had given it a structural growth which it would not have acquired in camp life, and to which few men of forty were entitled. Of this fact Hamilton was appreciative, and he was too philosophical to harbour regrets; but that period was over now, and he wanted to fight.

On April 27th he wrote to Washington, asking for employment during the approaching campaign, suggesting the command of a light corps, and modestly but decidedly stating his claims.

Washington was greatly embarrassed. Every arbitrary appointment caused a ferment in the army, where jealousies were hotter than martial ardours. Washington was politic above all things, but to refuse Hamilton a request after their quarrel and parting was the last thing he wished to do. He felt that he had no choice, however, and wrote at once, elaborating his reasons for refusal, ending as follows:—

My principal concern rises from an apprehension that you will impute my refusal of your request to other motives than those I have expressed, but I beg you to be assured I am only influenced by the reasons I have mentioned.

Hamilton knew him too well to misunderstand him, but he was deeply disappointed. He retired into the library behind the drawing-room of the Schuyler mansion, and wrote another and a more elaborate letter to Robert Morris. He began with a reiteration of the impotence of Congress, its loss of the confidence of this country and of Europe, the necessity for an executive ministry, and stated that the time was past to indulge in hopes of foreign aid. The States must depend upon themselves, and their only hope lay in a National Bank. There had been some diffidence in his previous letter. There was none in this, and he had a greater mastery of the subject. In something like thirty pages of close writing, he lays down every law, extensive and minute, for the building of a National Bank, and not the most remarkable thing about this letter is the psychological knowledge it betrays of the American people. Having despatched it, he wrote again to Washington, demonstrating that his case was dissimilar from those the Chief had quoted. He disposed of each case in turn, and his presentation of his own claims was equally unanswerable. Washington, who was too wise to enter into a controversy with Hamilton's pen, did not reply to the letter, but made up his mind to do what he could for him, although still determined there should be no disaffection in the army of his making.

Meanwhile Hamilton received letters from Lafayette, begging him to hasten South and share his exile; from Washington, asking advice; and from members of the family, reminding him of their affection and regret. Tilghman's is characteristic:—

Headquarters, 27th April.

MY DEAR HAMILTON: Between me and thee there is a gulf, or I should not have been thus long without seeing you. My faith is strong, but not strong enough to attempt walking on the waters. You must not suppose from my dealing so much in Scripture phrase that I am either drunk with religion or with wine, though had I been inclined to the latter I might have found a jolly companion in my lord, who came here yesterday. We have not a word of news.... I must go over and see you soon, for I am not yet weaned from you, nor do I desire to be. I will not present so cold words as compliments to Mrs. Hamilton. She has an equal share of the best wishes of

Your most affectionate

TILGHMAN.

The following was from Laurens:—

I am indebted to you, my dear Hamilton, for two letters: the first from Albany, as masterly a piece of cynicism as ever was penned; the other from Philadelphia, dated the second March; in both you mention a design of retiring, which makes me extremely unhappy. I would not wish to have you for a moment withdraw from the public service; at the same time my friendship for you, and knowledge of your value to the United States, makes me most ardently desire that you should fill only the first offices of the Republic. I was flattered with an account of your being elected a delegate from New York, and am much mortified not to hear it confirmed by yourself. I must confess to you that at the present stage of the war, I should prefer your going into Congress, and from thence becoming a minister plenipotentiary for peace, to your remaining in the army, where the dull system of seniority, and the *tableau*, would prevent you from having the important commands to which you are entitled; but, at any rate, I will not have you renounce your rank unless you entered the career above mentioned. Your private affairs cannot require such immediate and close attention. You speak like a *paterfamilias* surrounded with a numerous progeny.

On the 26th of May he had an appreciative letter from Robert Morris, thanking him for his suggestions, and assuring him of their acceptability. He promises a bank on Hamilton's plan, although with far less capital; still it may afterward be increased to any extent.

The northern land was full of amenities, the river gay with pleasure barges. The French gardens about the Schuyler mansion were romantic for saunterings with the loveliest of brides; the seats beneath the great trees commanded the wild heights opposite. Forty of the finest horses in the country were in General Schuyler's stables, and many carriages. There was a constant stream of distinguished guests. But Hamilton, who could dally pleasurably for a short time, had no real affinity for anything but work. There being no immediate prospect of fighting, he retired again to the library and began that series of papers called *The Continentalist*, which were read as attentively as if peace had come. They examined the defects of the existing league of states, their jealousies, which operated against the formation of a Federal government, then proceeded to enumerate the powers with which such a government should be clothed.

Hamilton did not wait with any particular grace, but even the desired command came to him after a reasonable period of attempted patience. At Washington's request he accompanied him to Newport to confer with Rochambeau. Although the Chief did not allude to Hamilton's last letter, their intercourse on this journey was as natural and intimate as ever; and Washington did not conceal his pleasure in the society of this the most captivating and endearing of his many young friends. After the conference was over, Hamilton returned to Albany for a brief visit, then determined to force Washington to show his hand. He joined the army at Dobbs Ferry, and sent the Chief his commission. Tilghman returned with it, express haste, and the assurance that the General would endeavour to give him a command, nearly such as he could desire in the present circumstance of the army, Hamilton had accomplished his object. He retained his commission and quartered with General Lincoln.

When Washington arrived at Dobbs Ferry and went into temporary quarters, he gave a large dinner to the French officers, and invited Hamilton to preside.

His graceful manners and witty speeches provoked universal admiration [runs the pen of a contemporary]. He was the youngest and smallest man present. His hair was turned back from the forehead, powdered, and queued at the back. His face was boyishly fair, and lighted up with intelligence and genius. Washington, grave, elegant and hospitable, sat at the side of the table, with the accomplished Count de Rochambeau on his right. The Duke de Luzerne occupied a seat opposite. General Knox was present, and so was Baron Steuben.

Shortly afterward, Hamilton attended a council of war, at Washington's invitation. The squadron of De Grasse was approaching the coast of Virginia. For the second time, Washington was obliged to give up his cherished scheme of marching on New York, for it was now imperative to meet Cornwallis in the South. The Chief completely hoodwinked Clinton as to his immediate plans, Robert Morris raised the funds for moving the army, and Hamilton obtained his command. To his high satisfaction, Fish was one of his officers. Immediately before his departure for the South he wrote to his wife. He had attained his desire, but he was too unhappy to be playful. A portion of the letter is as follows:—

A part of the army, my dear girl, is going to Virginia, and I must, of necessity, be separated at a much greater distance from my beloved wife. I cannot announce the fatal necessity without feeling everything that a fond husband can feel. I am unhappy;—I am unhappy beyond expression. I am unhappy because I am to be so remote from you; because I am to hear from you less frequently than I am accustomed to do. I am miserable because I know you will be so; I am wretched at the idea of flying so far from you, without a single hour's interview, to tell you all my pains and all my love. But I cannot ask permission to visit you. It might be thought improper to leave my corps at such a time and upon such an occasion. I must go without seeing you—I must go without embracing you:—alas! I must go.

The allied armies moved on the 22d of August and arrived within two miles of the enemy's works at York Town, on the 28th of September. Hamilton's light infantry was attached to the division of Lafayette, who joined the main army with what was left of his own. Laurens was also in command of a company of light infantry in the young French general's division. He had acquitted himself brilliantly in France, returning, in spite of all obstacles and the discouragement of Franklin, with two and a half million livres in cash, part of a subsidy of six millions of livres granted by the French king; but he felt that to be in the field again with Washington, Hamilton, Lafayette, and Fish was higher fortune than successful diplomacy.

The allied army was twelve thousand strong; Cornwallis had about seventy-eight hundred men. The British commander was intrenched in the village of York Town, the main body of his troops encamped on the open grounds in the rear. York Town is situated on a peninsula formed by the rivers York and James, and into this narrow compass Cornwallis had been driven by the masterly tactics of Lafayette. The arrival of De Grasse's fleet cut off all hope of retreat by water. He made but a show of opposition during the eight days employed by the Americans in bringing up their ordnance and making other preparations. On the 9th the trenches were completed, and the Americans began the bombardment of the town and of the British frigates in the river. It continued for nearly twenty-four hours, and so persistent and terrific was the cannonading, that the British, being unfortunate in their embrasures, withdrew most of their cannon and made infrequent reply. On the night of the 11th new trenches were begun within two and three hundred yards of the British works. While they were completing, the enemy opened new embrasures, from which their fire was far more effective than at first. Two redoubts flanked this second parallel and desperately annoyed the men in the trenches. It was determined to carry them by assault, and the American light infantry and De Viomenil's grenadiers and chasseurs were ordered to hold themselves in readiness for the attack. Laurens, with eighty men, was to turn the redoubt in order to intercept the retreat of the garrison, but Hamilton, for the moment, saw his long-coveted opportunity glide by him. Washington had determined to give it to our hero's old Elizabethtown tutor, Colonel Barber, conceiving that the light infantry which had made the Virginia campaign was entitled to precedence. Hamilton was standing with Major Fish when the news of this arrangement was brought to him. He reached the General's tent in three bounds, and poured forth the most impetuous appeal he had ever permitted himself to launch at Washington. But he was terribly in earnest, and the prospect of losing this magnificent opportunity tore down the barriers of his self-possession. "It is my right to attack, sir!" he concluded passionately, "I am the officer on duty!" Washington had watched his flushed nervous face and flashing eyes, which had far more command in their glances than appeal, and he never made great mistakes: he knew that if he refused this request, Hamilton never would forgive him.

"Very well," he said. "Take it."

Hamilton ran back to Fish, crying: "We have it. We have it;" and immediately began to form his troops. The order was issued to advance in two columns, and after dark the march began, Hamilton leading the advance corps. The French were to attack the redoubt on the right.

The signal was a shell from the American batteries, followed by one from the French. The instant the French shell ascended, Hamilton gave the order to advance at the point of the bayonet; then his impatience, too long gnawing at its curb, dominated him, and he ran ahead of his men and leaped to the abatis. For a half moment he stood alone on the parapet, then Fish reached him, and together they encouraged the rest to come on. Hamilton turned and sprang into the ditch, Fish following. The infantry was close behind, and surmounting the abatis, ditch, and palisades, leaped into the work. Hamilton had disappeared, and they feared he had fallen, but he was investigating; he suddenly reappeared, and formed the troops in the redoubt. It surrendered almost immediately. The attack took but nine minutes, so irresistible was the impetuosity of the onslaught. Hamilton gave orders at once to spare every man who had ceased to fight. When Colonel Campbell advanced to surrender, one of the American captains seized a bayonet and drew back to plunge it into the Englishman's breast. Hamilton thrust it aside, and Campbell was made prisoner by Laurens. Washington was delighted. "Few cases," he said, "have exhibited greater proofs of intrepidity, coolness, and firmness than were shown on this occasion." On the 17th, when Washington received the proposition for surrender from Cornwallis, he sent for Hamilton and asked his opinion of the terms. To Laurens was given the honour of representing the American army at the conference before the surrender. Tilghman rode, express haste, to Philadelphia with the first news of the surrender of Cornwallis and his army.

Hamilton's description of his part in the conquest that virtually put an end to the war is characteristic.

Two nights ago, my Eliza [he wrote], my duty and my honour obliged me to take a step in which your happiness was too much risked. I commanded an attack upon one of the enemy's redoubts; we carried it in an instant and with little loss. You will see the particulars in the Philadelphia papers. There will be, certainly, nothing more of this kind; all the rest will be by approach; and if there should be another occasion, it would not fall to my turn to execute it.

"It is to be hoped so," she said plaintively to her mother. "Else shall I no longer need to wear a wig."

XII

The next few years may be passed over quickly; they are not the most interesting, though not the least happy of Hamilton's life. He returned home on furlough after the battle of York Town and remained in his father-in-law's hospitable home until the birth of his boy, on the 22d of January. Then, having made up his mind that there was no further work for him in the army, and that Britain was as tired of the war as the States, he announced his intention to study for the bar. His friends endeavoured to dissuade him from a career whose preparation was so long and arduous, and reminded him of the public offices he could have for the asking. But Hamilton was acquainted with his capacity for annihilating work, and at this time he was not conscious of any immediate ambition but of keeping his wife in a proper style and of founding a fortune for the education of his children. His military ambition had been so possessing that the sudden and brilliant finish at York Town of his power to gratify it had dwarfed for a while any other he may have cherished.

He took a little house in the long street on the river front, and invited Troup to live with him. They studied together. He had been the gayest of companions, the most courted of favourites, since his return from the wars. For four months even his wife and Troup had, save on Sundays, few words with him on unlegal matters. His brain excluded every memory, every interest. For the first time he omitted to write regularly to Mrs. Mitchell, Hugh Knox, and Peter Lytton. All day and half the night he walked up and down his library, or his father-in-law's, reading, memorizing, muttering aloud. His friends vowed that he marched the length and width of the Confederacy. He never gave a more striking exhibition of his control over the powers of his intellect than this. The result was that at the end of four months he obtained a license to practise as an attorney, and published a "Manual on the Practice of Law," which, Troup tells us, "served as an instructive grammar to future students, and became the groundwork of subsequent enlarged practical treatises." If it be protested that these feats were impossible, I can only reply that they are historic facts.

It was during these months of study that Aaron Burr came to Albany.

This young man, also, was not unknown to fame; and the period of the Revolution is the one on which Burr's biographers should dilate, for it was the only one through which he passed in a manner entirely to his credit. He was now in Albany, striving for admittance to the bar, but handicapped by the fact that he had studied only two years, instead of the full three demanded by law.

While Burr did not belong to the aristocracy of the country, his family not ranking by any means with the Schuylers, Van Rensselaers, Livingstons, Jays, Morrises, Roosevelts, and others of that small and haughty band, still he came of excellent and respectable stock. His father had been the Rev. Aaron Burr, President of Princeton College, and his mother the daughter of the famous Jonathan Edwards. He was quick-witted and brilliant; and there is no adjective which qualifies his ambition. He was a year older than Hamilton, about an inch taller, and very dark. His features were well cut, his eyes black, glittering, and cold; his bearing dignified but unimposing, for he bent his shoulders and walked heavily. His face was not frank, even in youth, and grew noticeably craftier. He and Hamilton were the greatest fops in dress of their time; but while the elegance and beauty of attire sat with a peculiar fitness on Hamilton, seeming but the natural continuation of his high-bred face and easy erect and graceful bearing, Burr always looked studiously well-dressed. In regard to their height, a similar impression prevailed. One never forgot Burr's small stature, and often commented upon it. Comment upon Hamilton's size was rare, his proportions and motions were so harmonious; when he was on the platform, that ruthless test of inches, he dominated and controlled every brain in the audience, and his enemies vowed he was in league with the devil.

Burr brought letters to General Schuyler, and was politely given the run of the library. He and Hamilton had met casually in the army, but had had no opportunity for acquaintance. At this time the law was a subject of common interest, and they exchanged many opinions. There was no shock of antagonism at first, and for that matter they asked each other to dinner as long as Hamilton lived. But Hamilton estimated him justly at once, although, as Burr was as yet unconscious of the depths of his own worst qualities, the most astute reader of character hardly would suspect them. But Hamilton read that he was artificial and unscrupulous, and too selfish to serve the country in any of her coming needs. Still, he was brilliant and fascinating, and Hamilton asked him to his home. Burr, at first, was agreeably attracted to Hamilton, whose radiant disposition warmed his colder nature; but when he was forced to accept the astounding fact that Hamilton had prepared himself for the bar in four months, digesting and remembering a mountain of knowledge that cost other men the labour of years, and had prepared a Manual besides, he experienced the first convulsion of that jealousy which was to become his controlling passion in later years. Indeed, he established the habit with that first prolonged paroxysm, and he asked himself sullenly why a nameless stranger, from an unheard-of Island, should have the unprecedented success which this youth had had. Social victory, military glory, the preference of Washington, the respect and admiration of the most eminent men in the country, a horde of friends who talked of him as if he were a demi-god, an alliance by marriage with the greatest family in America, a father-in-law to advance any man's ambitions, a fascination which had kept the women talking until he married, and finally a memory and a legal faculty which had so astounded the bar—largely composed of exceptional men—that it could talk of nothing else: it was enough for a lifetime, and the man was only twenty-five. What in heaven's name was to be expected of him before he finished? The more Burr brooded, the more enraged he became. He had been brought up to think himself extraordinary, although his guardian had occasionally birched him when his own confidence had disturbed the peace; he was intensely proud of his military career, and aware of his fitness for the bar. But in the blaze of Hamilton's genius he seemed to shrivel; and as for having attempted to prepare himself for practice in four months, he might as well have grafted wings to his back and expected them to grow. It was some consolation to reflect that, as aide and confidential secretary for four years to Washington, Hamilton had been a student of the law of nations, and that thus his mind was peculiarly fitted to grasp what confronts most men as a solid wall to be taken down stone by stone; also that himself acknowledged no rival where the affections of women were concerned. But while he lifted the drooping head of his pride, and tied it firmly to a stake with many strong words, he chose to regard Hamilton as a rival, and the idea grew until it possessed him.

In July Robert Morris, after some correspondence, persuaded Hamilton to accept the office of Continental Receiver for a short time.

Your former situation in the army [he wrote], the present situation of that very army, your connexions in the state, your perfect knowledge of men and measures, and the abilities with which heaven has blessed you, will give you a fine opportunity to forward the public service.

Hamilton, who had no desire to interrupt his studies, was placed in a position which gave him no choice; his sense of public duty grew steadily.

For my part [he wrote to Morris], considering the late serious misfortune to our ally, the spirit of reformation, of wisdom, and of unanimity, which seems to have succeeded to that of blunder and dissension in the British government, and the universal reluctance of these states to do what is right, I cannot help viewing our situation as critical, and I feel it the duty of every citizen to exert his faculties to the utmost.

But in spite of the onerous and disagreeable duties of his position, he continued to pursue the course of study necessary for admission to the bar as a counsellor. He also found time to write a letter to Meade. The following extract will show that the severity of his great task was over, and that he was once more alive to that domestic happiness to which so large a part of his nature responded.

You reproach me with not having said enough about our little stranger. When I wrote last I was not sufficiently acquainted with him to give you his character. I may now assure you that your daughter, when she sees him, will not consult you about her choice, or will only do it in respect to the rules of decorum. He is truly a very fine young gentleman, the most agreeable in conversation and manners of any I ever knew, nor less remarkable for his intelligence and sweetness of temper. You are not to imagine by my beginning with his mental qualifications that he is defective in personal. It is agreed on all hands that he is handsome; his features are good, his eye is not only sprightly and expressive, but it is full of benignity. His attitude in sitting is, by connoisseurs, esteemed graceful, and he has a method of waving his hand that announces the future orator. He stands, however, rather awkwardly, and as his legs have not all the delicate slimness of his father's, it is feared he may never excel as much in dancing, which is probably the only accomplishment in which he will not be a model. If he has any fault in manners, he laughs too much. He has now passed his seventh month.

Happy by temperament, Hamilton was at this time happier in his conditions—barring the Receivership—than any vague, wistful, crowded dream had ever presaged. His wife was adorable and pretty, sprightly and sympathetic, yet accomplished in every art of the Dutch housewife; and although he was far too modest to boast, he was privately convinced that his baby was the finest in the Confederacy. He had a charming little home, and Troup, the genial, hearty, and solid, was a member of it. In General and Mrs. Schuyler he had found genuine parents, who strove to make him forget that he had ever been without a home. He had been forced to refuse offers of assistance from his father-in-law again and again. He would do nothing to violate his strong sense of personal independence; he had half of the arrears of his pay, Troup his share of the expenses of the little house. He knew that in a short time he should be making an income. The cleverest of men, however, can be hoodwinked by the subtle sex. The great Saratoga estate of the Schuylers furnished the larder of the Hamiltons with many things which the young householder was far too busy to compare with his slender purse.

He heard constantly from his friends in the army, and finally was persuaded to sit for a portrait, to be the common property of six or eight of them. Money was desperately tight, they could not afford a copy apiece, but each was to possess it for two months at a time so long as he lived; he who survived the others to dispose of it as he chose. For

Hamilton to sit still and look in one direction for half an hour was nothing short of misery, even with Betsey, Troup, and the Baby to amuse him; and only the head, face, stock, and front of the coat were finished. But the artist managed to do himself justice with the massive spirited head, the deep-set mischievous eyes, whose lightnings never were far from the surface; the humour in the remarkable curves of the mouth, the determination and suppressed energy of the whole face. It was a living portrayal, and Betsey parted from it with tears. When she saw it again her eyes were dim with many tears. The last of its owners to survive fell far into poverty, and sold it to one of her sons. It is to-day as fresh, as alive with impatient youth and genius, as when Hamilton estimated portrait painters thieves of time.

Meanwhile a compliment was paid to him which upset his plans, and placed him for a short time in the awkward position of hesitating between private desires and public duty: he was elected by the New York legislature, and almost unanimously, a delegate to Congress. Troup brought him the news as he was walking on the broad street along the river front, muttering his Blackstone, oblivious of his fellow-citizens.

"Go to Congress!" he exclaimed. "Who goes to that ramshackle body that is able to keep out of it? Could not they find someone else to send to distinguish himself by failure? I've my living to make. If a man in these days manages to support his wife and child, there is nothing else he can do which so entitles him to the esteem of his fellow-citizens."

"True," said Troup, soothingly; "there certainly is nothing in that body of old women and lunatics, perpetually bickering with thirteen sovereign, disobedient, and jealous States, to tempt the ambition of any man; nor, ordinarily, to appeal to his sense of usefulness. But just at present there are several questions before it with which it is thought you can cope more successfully than any man living. So I think you ought to go, and so does General Schuyler. I know all that you will sacrifice, domestic as well as pecuniarily—but remember, you solemnly dedicated yourself to the service of this country."

"I'm not likely to forget it, and I am willing to sacrifice anything if I am convinced of my usefulness in a given direction, but I see no chance of accomplishing aught in Congress, of doing this country any service until it is a nation, not a sack of scratching cats."

Not only was great pressure brought to bear upon him, but he was not long convincing himself that it was his duty to take his knowledge of certain subjects vexing the Confederation, to the decrepit body which was feebly striving to save the country from anarchy. He had given little attention to the general affairs of the country during the past six months, but an examination of them fired his zeal. He accepted the appointment, and returned to his law books and his dispiriting struggle with the taxes.

In the autumn Hamilton received the second of those heavy blows by which he was reminded that in spite of his magnetism for success he was to suffer like other mortals. Laurens was dead—killed in a petty skirmish which he was so loath to miss that he had bolted to it from a sick-bed. Hamilton mourned him passionately, and never ceased to regret him. He was mercurial only among his lighter feelings. The few people he really loved were a part of his daily thoughts, and could set his heartstrings vibrating at any moment. Betsey consoled, diverted, and bewitched him, but there were times when he would have exchanged her for Laurens. The perfect friendship of two men is the deepest and highest sentiment of which the finite mind is capable; women miss the best in life.

In October Hamilton resigned the Receivership, having brought an honourable amount of order out of chaos and laid down the law for the guidance of future officials. November came, and he set off for Philadelphia philosophically, though by no means with a light heart. The baby was too young to travel; he was obliged to send his little family to General Schuyler's, with no hope of seeing them again for months, and a receding prospect of offering them a home in New York. His father-in-law, not unmindful that consolation was needed, drove him two-thirds of the distance, thus saving him a long ride, or its alternative, the heavy coach. In Philadelphia he found sufficient work awaiting him to drive all personal matters out of his head.

It was during this year of hard work and little result that he renewed an acquaintance with James Madison, Jr., afterward fourth President of the United States, and Gouverneur Morris, one of the most brilliant and disinterested young men in the country, now associated with Robert Morris in the Department of Finance. With the last the acquaintance ripened into a lifelong and intimate friendship; with Madison the friendship was equally ardent and intimate while it lasted.

Madison had the brain of a statesman, energy and persistence in crises, immense industry, facility of speech, a broad contempt for the pretensions and mean bickerings of the States, and a fairly national outlook. As Hamilton would have said, he "thought continentally." But he lacked individuality. He was too patriotic, too sincere to act against his principles, but his principles could be changed by a more powerful and magnetic brain than his own, and the inherent weakness in him demanded a stronger nature to cling to. It happened that he and Hamilton, when they met again in Congress, thought alike on many subjects, and they worked together in harmony from the first; nevertheless, he was soon in the position of a double to that towering and energetic personality, and worshipped it. In their letters the two young men sign themselves, "yours affectionately," "yours with deep attachment," which between men—I suppose—means something. So noticeable was Madison's devotion to the most distinguished young man of the day, and a few years later so absorbed was he into the huge personality of his early friend's bitterest enemy, that John Randolph once exclaimed in wrath, "Madison always was some great man's mistress—first Hamilton's, then Jefferson's:" a remark which was safe in the days of our ancestors, when life was all work and no satiety.

Gouverneur Morris had sacrificed home, inheritance, and ties in the cause of the Revolution, most of his family remaining true to the crown. His education was thorough, however, and subsequently he had nine years of Europe, of which he left to posterity an entertaining record. Tall, handsome, a wit, a beau, notable for energy in Congress, erratic, caustic, cynical, but the warmest of friends, he was a pet of society, a darling of women, and trusted by all men. He and Hamilton had much in common, and to some degree he took Laurens's place; not entirely, for Laurens's idealism gave him a pedestal in Hamilton's memory which no other man but Washington ever approached; and Morris was brutal in his cynicism, placing mankind but a degree higher than the beasts of the forest. But heart and brain endeared him to Hamilton, and no man had a loftier or more burning patriotism. As for himself, he loved and admired Hamilton above all men. He was as strong in his nationalism, believing Union under a powerful central government to be the only hope of the States. Both he and Madison were leaders; but both, even then, were willing to be led by Hamilton, who was several years their junior.

The three young enthusiasts made a striking trio of contrasts as they sat one evening over their port and walnuts in a private room of a coffee-house, where they had met to discuss the problems convulsing the unfortunate country. Madison had the look of a student, a taciturn intellectual visage. He spoke slowly, weightily, and with great precision. Morris had, even then, an expression of cynicism and contempt on his handsome bold face, and he swore magnificently whenever his new wooden leg interfered with his comfort or dignity. Hamilton, with his fair mobile face, powerful, penetrating, delicate, illuminated by eyes full of fire and vivacity, but owing its chief attraction to a mouth as sweet as it was firm and humorous, made the other men look almost heavy. Madison was carelessly attired, the other two with all the picturesque elegance of their time.

"A debt of $42,000,000," groaned Morris, "interest $2,400,000; Robert Morris threatening to resign; delirious prospect of panic in consequence; national spirit with which we began the war, a stinking wick under the tin extinguisher of States' selfishness, stinginess, and indifference—caused by the natural reversion of human nature to first principles after the collapse of that enthusiasm which inflates mankind into a bombastic pride of itself; Virginia pusillanimous, Rhode Island an old beldam standing on the village pump and shrieking disapproval of everything; Jay, Adams, and Franklin, after years of humiliating mendicancy, their very hearts wrinkled in the service of the stupidest country known to God or man, shoved by a Congress not fit to black their boots under the thumb of the wiliest and most disingenuous diplomatist in Europe—much France cares for our interests, provided we cut loose from Britain; Newburg address and exciting prospect, in these monotonous times, of civil war, while peace commission is sitting in London; just demands of men who have fought, starving and naked, for a bare subsistence after the army disbands, modest request for arrears of pay,—on which to relieve the necessities of their families turned out to grass for seven years,—pleasantly indorsed by the Congress, which feels safe in indorsing anything, and rejected by the States, called upon to foot the bill, as a painful instance of the greed and depravity of human nature—there you are: no money, no credit, no government, no friends,—for Europe is sick of us,—no patriotism; immediate prospects, bankruptcy, civil war, thirteen separate meals for

Europe. What do you propose, Hamilton? I look to you as your Islanders flee to a stone house in a hurricane. You are an alien, with no damned state roots to pull up, your courage is unhuman, or un-American, and you are the one man of genius in the country. Madison is heroic to a fault, a roaring Berserker, but we must temper him, we must temper him; and meanwhile we will both defer to the peculiar quality of your mettle."

Madison, who had not a grain of humour, replied gravely, his rich southern brogue seeming to roll his words down from a height: "I have a modest hope in the address I prepared for the citizens of Rhode Island, more in Hamilton's really magnificent letter to the Governor. Nothing can be more forcible—nay, beguiling—than his argument in that letter in favour of a general government independent of state machinery, and his elaborate appeal to that irritating little commonwealth to consent to the levying of the impost by Congress, necessary to the raising of the moneys. I fear I am not a hero, for I confess I tremble. I fear the worst. But at all events I am determined to place on record that I left no stone unturned to save this miserable country."

"You will go down to posterity as a great man, Madison, if you are never given the chance to be one," replied the father of American humour and coinage; "for it is not in words but in acts that we display the faith that is not in us. Well, Hamilton?"

"I must confess," said Hamilton, "that Congress appears to me, as a newcomer, rooted contentedly to its chairs, and determined to do nothing, happy in the belief that Providence has the matter in hand and but bides the right moment to make the whole world over. But I see no cause to despair, else I should not have come to waste my time. I fear that Rhode Island is too fossilized to listen to us, but I shall urge that we change the principle of the Confederation and vote to make the States contribute to the general treasury in an equal proportion to their means, by a system of general taxation imposed under continental authority. If the poorer States, irrespective of land and numbers, could be relieved, and the wealthier taxed specifically on land and houses, the whole regulated by continental legislation, I think that even Rhode Island might be placated. It may be that this is not agreeable to the spirit of the times, but I shall make the attempt—"

"Considering there is no spirit *in* the times, we might as well expect to inform its skull with genius by means of a lighted candle. You think too well of human nature, my boy; expect nothing, that ye be not disappointed, especially in the matter of revenue."

"I have no exalted opinion of human nature, but if I did not think more hopefully of it than you do, I should yield up that enthusiasm without which I can accomplish nothing. You have every gift, but you will end as a dilettante because your ideal is always in the mud; and it is only now and again that you think it worth while to pick it up and give it a bath."

"Right, right," murmured Morris, good-naturedly. "Would that I had your unquenchable belief in the worth while. Allied to your abilities it will make the new world over and upset the wicked plans of the old. Analyst and disbeliever in man's right to his exaggerated opinion of himself, how do you keep enthusiasm abreast with knowledge of human kind? Tell me, Hamilton, how do you do it?"

"I fear 'tis the essence of which I am made. My energies will have outlet or tear me to pieces. When there is work to do, my nostrils quiver like a war-horse's at the first roar and smoke—"

"Your modesty does you infinite honour; the truth is, you have the holy fire of patriotism in an abnormal degree. I have it, but I still am normal. I have made sacrifices and shall make more, but my ego curls its lip. Yours never does. That is the difference between you and most of us. Hundreds of us are doggedly determined to go through to the bitter end, sacrifice money, youth and health; but you alone are happy. That is why we love you and are glad to follow your lead. But, I repeat, how can you labour with such undying enthusiasm for the good of human kind when you know what they amount to?"

"Some are worth working for, that is one point; I don't share your opinion of general abasement, for the facts warrant no such opinion. And the battle of ideas, the fight for certain stirring and race-making principles,—that is the greatest game that mortals can play. And to play it, we must have mortals for puppets. To create a new government, a new race, to found what may become the greatest nation on the earth,—what more stupendous destiny? Even if one were forgotten, it would be worth doing, so tremendous would be the exercise of the faculties, so colossal the difficulties. I would have a few men do it all; I have no faith in the uneducated. The little brain, half opened by a village schoolmaster, is pestilential; but in the few with sufficient power over the many,—from whom will be evolved more and more to rank with the first few,—in those I have faith, and am proud to work with them."

"Good. I'd not have a monarchy, but I'd have the next thing to it, with a muzzle on the rabble. Perhaps I, too, have faith in a few,—in yourself and George Washington; and in Madison, our own Gibraltar. But the pig-headed, selfish, swinish—well, go on with your present plans. 'Tis to hear those we met to-night, not to analyze each other. Tell us all, that we may not only hope, but work with you."

"The army first. If retirement on half pay is impossible, then full pay for, say six years,—and the arrears,—paid upon the disbanding of the army. Washington, by the exercise of the greatest moral force, but one, that has appeared in this world, has averted a civil war—I am persuaded that horror is averted, and I assume that the country does not care eternally to disgrace itself by letting its deliverers, who have suffered all that an army can suffer, return to their ruined homes without the few dollars necessary for another start in life. I have resigned my claim to arrears of pay, that my argument may not be weakened. Then a peace establishment. Fancy leaving our frontiers to the mercy of state militia! I shall urge that the general government have exclusive power over the sword, to establish certain corps of infantry, artillery, cavalry, dragoons, and engineers, a general system of land fortifications, establishment of arsenals and magazines, erection of founderies and manufactories for arms, of ports and maritime fortifications—with many details with which I will not bore you. I shall urge the necessity of strengthening the Federal government through the influence of officers deriving their appointment directly from Congress—always, always, the necessity of strengthening the central government, of centralizing power, and of putting the States where they belong. It is federation or anarchy. Then—moderate funds permanently pledged for the security of lenders. I have preached that since I have dared to preach at all, and that is the only solution of our present distress, for we'll never get another foreign loan—"

"We've accepted your wisdom, but we can't apply it," interposed Morris.

"Our only hope lies in your national government—but go on."

"A moment," said Madison. "This, in regard to the peace

establishment: Do we apply a war congress to a state of peace, I fear we shall too clearly define its limits. The States may refuse obedience, and then the poor invalided body will fall into greater disrepute than ever."

"I have thought of that," replied Hamilton, "and if the worst comes to the worst, I have a radical plan to propose,—that Congress publish frankly its imperfections to the country—imperfections which make it impossible to conduct the public affairs with honour to itself or advantage to the United States; that it ask the States to appoint a convention, with full powers to revise the Confederation, and to adopt and propose all necessary alterations—all to be approved or rejected, in the last instance, by the legislatures of the several States. That would be the first step toward a national government. With that, all things would be possible,—the payment of our foreign loan, of our army, duties on foreign goods, which is a source of revenue to which they are incredibly blind; the establishment of a firm government, under which all will prosper that are willing to work, of a National Bank, of a peace army—"

"Of Utopia!" exclaimed Morris. "Hamilton, you are the least visionary man in this country, but you are God knows how many years ahead of your times. If we are ever on two legs again, you will put us there; but your golden locks will thin in the process, and that rosy boyish face we love will be lined with the seams of the true statesman. Only you could contemplate imbuing these fossilized and commonplace intellects, composing our Congress of the Confederation—mark the ring of it!—with a belief in its own impotency and worthlessness. You are not mortal. I always said it. When Duane gave me your letter to read, I remarked: 'He withdrew to heaven, and wrote that letter on the knee of the Almighty; never on earth could he have found the courage and the optimism.' No, Hamilton, I would embrace you, did my wooden leg permit me to escape your wrath, but I can give you no encouragement. You will fail here—gloriously, but you will fail. Mark my words, the army will go home cursing, and scratch the ground to feed its women. The States will have no peace establishment to threaten their sovereign rights, we will pay nobody, and become more and more poverty-stricken and contemptible in our own eyes, and in the eyes of Europe; we will do nothing that is wise and everything that is foolish—"

"And then, when the country is sick unto death," interrupted Hamilton, "it will awake to the wisdom of the drastic remedy and cohere into a nation."

"Query," said Madison, "would it not be patriotic to push things from bad to worse as quickly as possible? It might be a case of justifiable Jesuitism."

"And it might lead to anarchy and the jaws of Europe," said Hamilton. "It is never safe to go beyond a certain point in the management of human affairs. What turn the passions of the people may take can never be foretold, nor that element of the unknown, which is always under the invisible cap and close on one's heels. God knows I have not much patience in my nature, and I do not believe that most of my schemes are so far in advance of even this country's development; but certain lessons must be instilled by slow persistence. I have no faith in rushing people at the point of the bayonet in times of peace."

"I think you are right there," said Morris. "But mark my words, you'll propagate ideas here, and the result in time will be the birth of a nation—no doubt of that; but you must rest content to live on hope for the present. I was a fettered limb in this body too long. I know its inertia."

He knew whereof he spoke. Hamilton won little but additional reputation, much admiration, half resentful, and many enemies. The army went home unpaid; the peace establishment consisted of eighty men; little or nothing was done to relieve the national debt or to carry on the business of government. Even his proposition to admit the public to the galleries of Congress, in the hope of interesting it in governmental affairs, only drew upon him the sneer that he could go out on the balcony and make his speeches if he feared his eloquence was wasted. He was accused of writing the Newburg address inciting the officers to civil war, because it was particularly well written, and of hurrying Congress to Trenton, when threatened by a mutinous regiment. But he worked on undaunted, leaving his indelible mark; for he taught the States that their future prosperity and happiness lay in giving up to the Union some part of the imposts that might be levied on foreign commodities, and incidentally the idea of a double government; he proposed a definite system of funding the debts on continental securities, which gradually rooted in the common sense of the American people, and he inveighed with a bitter incisiveness, which was tempered by neither humour nor gaiety, against the traitorous faction in the pay of

207

France. He dissuaded Robert Morris from resigning, and introduced a resolution in eulogy of Washington's management of his officers in the most critical hour of the Union's history. But his immediate accomplishment was small and discouraging, although his foresight may have anticipated what George Ticknor Curtis wrote many years later:—

The ideas of a statesman like Hamilton, earnestly bent on the discovery and inculcation of truth, do not pass away. Wiser than those by whom he was surrounded, with a deeper knowledge of the science of government than most of them, and constantly enunciating principles which extended far beyond the temporizing policy of the hour, the smiles of his opponents only prove to posterity how far he was in advance of them.

The following extract from a letter of James M'Henry, Lafayette's former aide, and a member of the Congress, is interesting as a commentary on the difficulties of our hero's position while a member of that body.

DEAR HAMILTON: The homilies you delivered in Congress are still remembered with pleasure. The impressions they made are in favour of your integrity; and no one but believes you a man of honour and of republican principles. Were you ten years older and twenty thousand pounds richer, there is no doubt but that you might obtain the suffrages of Congress for the highest office in their gift. You are supposed to possess various knowledge, useful, substantial, and ornamental. Your very grave and your cautious, your men who measure others by the standard of their own creeping politics, think you sometimes intemperate, but seldom visionary: and that were you to pursue your object with as much cold perseverance as you do with ardour and argument, you would become irresistible. In a word, if you could submit to spend a whole life in dissecting a fly you would be, in their opinion, one of the greatest men in the world. Bold designs; measures calculated for their rapid execution; a wisdom that would convince from its own weight; a project that would surprise the people into greater happiness, without giving them an opportunity to view it and reject it, are not adapted to a council composed of discordant elements, or a people who have thirteen heads, each of which pay superstitious adorations to inferior divinities.

Adieu, my dear friend, and in the days of your happiness drop a line to your

M'HENRY.

At the end of 1783 Hamilton was convinced that he was of no further immediate use to the country, and refused a reelection to the Congress, despite entreaty and expostulation, returning to the happiness of his domestic life and to his neglected law-books. The British having evacuated New York, he moved his family there and entered immediately upon the practice of his profession.

BOOK IV

"ALEXANDER THE GREAT"
INCLUDING THE STRANGE ADVENTURES OF THE
CONSTITUTION OF THE UNITED STATES

—ᙡ—

I

It was the autumn of 1786. New York had risen from her charred and battered ruins. There were cows on her meadows, a lake with wooded shores as merely traditional, groves, gardens, orchards, fields, and swamps; but her business houses and public buildings were ambitious once more, her spires more lofty and enduring, her new dwelling-houses, whether somewhat crowded in Wall Street and Broadway, or on the terraces of less busy streets, or along the river fronts and facing a wild and lovely prospect, were square, substantial, and usually very large. And every street was an avenue of ancient trees. Mrs. John Jay, with her experience of foreign courts, her great beauty, and the prestige of her distinguished husband, was the leader of society, holding weekly receptions, and the first to receive the many distinguished strangers. Although society was not quite as gay as it became three years later, under a more settled government and hopeful outlook, still there was quiet entertaining by the Hamiltons, who lived at 58 Wall Street, the Duers, Watts, Livingstons, Clintons, Duanes, Jays, Roosevelts, Van Cortlandts, and other representatives of old New York families, now returned to their own. Congress was come to New York and established in the City Hall in Wall Street. It had given the final impetus to the city, struggling under the burden of ruins and debt left by the British; and society sauntered forth every afternoon in all the glory of velvet and ruffles, three-cornered hats recklessly laced, brocades, hoopskirts, and Rohan hats, to promenade past the building where the moribund body was holding its last sessions. The drive was down the Broadway into the shades of the Battery, with the magnificent prospect of bay and wooded shores beyond. Politics, always epidemic among men and women alike, had recently been animated by Hamilton's coup at Annapolis, and the prospect of a general convention of the States to consider the reorganization of a government which had reduced the Confederation to a condition fearfully close to anarchy, the country to ruin, and brought upon the thirteen sovereign independent impotent and warring States the contempt of Europe and the threat of its greed.

A group of men, standing on a corner of Wall Street and the Broadway, were laughing heartily: a watch was dragging off to jail two citizens who had fallen upon each other with the venom of political antithesis; the one, a Nationalist, having called Heaven to witness that Hamilton was a demi-god, begotten to save the wretched country, the other vociferating that Hamilton was the devil who would trick the country into a monarchy, create a vast standing army, which would proclaim him king and stand upon the heads of a people that had fought and died for freedom, while the tyrant exercised his abominable functions.

The men in the group were Governor Clinton, Hamilton's bitterest opponent, but sufficiently amused at the incident; William Livingston, Governor of New Jersey, now with but a few hairs on the top of his head and a few at the base, his nose more penetrating, his eye more disapproving, than ever; James Duane, Mayor of New York; John Jay, the most faultless character in the Confederation, honoured and unloved, his cold eyes ever burning with an exalted fire; and John Marshall of Virginia, munching an apple, his attire in shabby contrast to the fashionable New Yorkers, the black mane on his splendid head unpowdered and tossing in the ocean breeze.

"I like your Hamilton," he announced, "and I've come to the conclusion that I think with him on all matters. He's done more to educate the people up to a rational form of government during the last seven years than all the rest of us put together. He's shone upon them like a fixed star. Other comets have come and gone, whirling them forward to destruction, but they have always been forced to turn and look at him again and again, and he has always shone in the same place."

"Sir," exclaimed Clinton, who was flushed with rage, "are you aware that I am present, and that I entirely disapprove of Mr. Hamilton's attempt to reduce the States to a condition of ignominious subserviency to an ambitious and tyrannical central power?"

"I had heard of you, sir," replied Marshall, meekly, "and I am glad to have the opportunity to ask you what *your* remedy is for the existing state of things? You will admit that there must be a remedy, and quickly. If not a common government with a Constitution empowering it to regulate trade, imposts, reduce the debt, enter into treaties with foreign powers which will not be sneered at, administer upon a thousand details which I will not enumerate, and raise the country from its slough of contempt, then what? As the personage who has taken the most decided stand against the enlightened and patriotic efforts of Mr. Hamilton, I appeal to you for a counter suggestion as magnificent as his. I am prepared, sir, to listen with all humility."

Clinton, whose selfish fear of his own downfall with that of State supremacy was so well known that a smile wrinkled across the polite group of gentlemen surrounding him, deepened his colour to purple under this assault, and stammered: "Sir, have I not myself proposed an enlargement of the powers of Congress, in order to counteract the damnable policy of Britain? Did not your Hamilton harangue that crowd I sanctioned till he got nearly all he asked for?"

"But he knew better than to ask for too much, in the conditions," replied Marshall, suavely. "May I suggest that you have not answered my humble and earnest questions?"

"I answer no questions that I hold to be impertinent and unimportant!" said Clinton, pompously, and with a dignified attempt to recover his poise. He swept his hat from his head; the New Yorkers were as punctilious; Marshall lifted his battered lid from the wild mass beneath, and the popular Governor sauntered down the street, saluted deferentially by Nationalists and followers alike. When he had occasion to sweep his gorgeous hat to his knees, the ladies courtesied to the ground, their draperies taking up the entire pavement, and His Excellency was obliged to encounter the carriages in the street.

"If Clinton were sure of figuring as powerfully in a national government as he does in the state of New York, he would withdraw his opposition," said Livingston, contemptuously. "He has been Governor for nine years. New York is his throne. He is a king among the common people, who will elect him indefinitely. Were it not for Hamilton, he would be New York, and the awful possibilities lying hidden in the kernel of change haunt his dreams at night. You embarrassed him in a manner that rejoiced my heart, Mr. Marshall. I beg you will do me the honour to dine with me to-night. I beg to assure you that your fame is as known to me as were I a Virginian."

"I'll accept the invitation with pleasure," replied Marshall, whose manners were all that his attire was not. "I shall be glad to talk with you on many subjects. To-morrow I shall pay my respects to Mr. Hamilton. His has been a trying but not a thankless task. He has addressed himself to the right class of men all over the country, winning them to his sound and enlightened views, giving them courage, consolidating them against the self-interested advocates of State sovereignty. That he has so often neglected a legal practice which must bring him a large income, as well as sufficient personal glory, out of a sincere pity for and patriotic interest in this afflicted country, gives New York deep cause for congratulation that she was in such close communication with that Island of his youth. I wish that fate had steered him to Virginia."

"Surely you have enough as it is," said Duane, laughing: "Washington, yourself, Patrick Henry, Jefferson, Madison, Randolph. Spare us Hamilton. We shall need him badly enough. The Clinton faction is very strong. That the Hamilton embraces the best spirits of the community means that it is in the minority, and needs the unremitting exercise of his genius to counteract the disadvantage in numbers."

"I think that what I admire most in Hamilton," remarked a newcomer, a small dark man of vivid personality, "are his methods of manipulation. He picks out his own men, Duer, Troup, Malcolm, has them sent to the legislature, where they blindly and indefatigably obey his behest and gain the consent of that body to the convention at Annapolis, then see that he is elected as principal delegate. He goes to Annapolis ostensibly to attend a commercial convention: while its insufficient numbers are drowsing, he springs upon them an eloquent proposal for a national convention for reforming the Union, and forces it through before they know what they are about. Certainly Mr. Hamilton is a man of genius."

"Do I understand. Mr. Burr," said Jay, from his glacial height, "that you are impugning the purity of Mr. Hamilton's motives?"

"No, sir," replied Burr, whom an archangel could not have rebuked. "In the present condition of things all methods are justifiable. Hamilton is great but adaptable. I respect him for that quality above all others, for he is quite the most imperious character in America, and his natural instinct is to come out and say, 'You idiots, fall into line behind me and stop twaddling. I will do your thinking; be kind enough not to delay me further.' On the other hand, he is forced to be diplomatic, to persuade where he would command, to move slowly instead of charging at the point of the bayonet. So, although I have no sympathy with his pronounced monarchical inclinations, I respect his acquired methods of getting what he wants."

"What do you mean by pronounced monarchical inclinations?" snorted Governor Livingston, who could not endure Burr.

Burr gave his peculiar sardonic laugh. "Will you deny it, sir?"

"Deny it? I certainly am in Mr. Hamilton's confidence to no such extent, and I challenge you to indicate one sentence in his published writings which points to such a conclusion."

"Ah, he is too clever for that; but his very walk, his whole personality expresses it, to say nothing of the fact that he never thinks of denying his admiration of the British Constitution. And did he not defend the Tories after the evacuation, when no other lawyer would touch them? I admired his courage, but it was sufficient evidence of the catholicity of his sentiments."

"Mr. Hamilton defended the abstract principle of right against wrong in defending the wretched Tories against the persecutions of an unmagnanimous public sentiment," said Jay, witheringly. "I should advise you, young gentleman, to become a disciple of Mr. Hamilton. I can recommend no course which would prove so beneficial." And he turned on his heel.

He had hit Burr. The jealousy born in Albany had thriven with much sustenance since. Hamilton was by far the most prominent figure at the New York bar, and was hastening to its leadership. Burr was conspicuous for legal ability, but never would be first while Hamilton was in the race. Moreover, although Hamilton had not then reached that dizzy height from which a few years later he looked down upon a gaping world, he was the leader of a growing and important party, intelligently followed and worshipped by the most eminent men in the Confederation, many of them old enough to be his father; and he was the theme of every drawing-room, of every coffee-house group and conclave. His constant pamphlets on the subject nearest to all men's hearts, his eloquent speeches on the same theme upon every possible occasion, and the extraordinary brilliance of his legal victories, gave people no time to think of other men. When he entered a drawing-room general conversation ceased, and the company revolved about him so long as he remained. When he spoke, all the world went to hear. For an ambitious young man to be told to attach himself to the train of this conquering hero was more than poor Burr could stand, and he replied angrily:—

"I have the privilege of being true to my own convictions, I suppose. They are not Mr. Hamilton's and never will be. I do not impugn the purity of his motives, but I have no desire to see George Washington king, nor Hamilton, neither. I wish you good day, sirs," and he strode up Broadway to the Fields with dignity in every inch of him.

"This constant talk of Hamilton's monarchical principles makes my gorge rise," said Livingston. "Did he not fight as hard as he was permitted, to drive monarchy out of the country? Was he not the first to sound the call to arms?"

"Hamilton's exact attitude on that question is not clearly understood," replied Duane, soothingly, for the heat of Livingston's republicanism had never abated. "I fancy it is something like this: So far no constitution has worked so well as the British. Montesquieu knew whereof he praised. The number of men in this country equal to the great problem of self-government are in a pitiful minority. The anarchic conditions of the States, the disgrace which they have brought upon us, their inefficiency to cope with any problem, the contemptible depths of human nature which they have revealed to the thinking members of the community—all these causes inspire Hamilton, incomparably the greatest brain in the country, with a dread of leaving any power whatever in their hands. He believes firmly in the few of tried brain and patriotism. I very much doubt if he has considered the subject of actual monarchy for a moment, for he is no dreamer, and he knows that even his followers have been Republicans too long. But that he will fight for the strongest sort of national government, with the least possible power vested in the States—oh, no doubt of that."

"Our people are hopeless, I fear," said Livingston, with a sigh. "This period of independency seems to have demoralized them when it should have brought out their best elements. Well, Mr. Marshall, what say you? You have been modestly silent, and we have been rudely voluble when so distinguished a guest should have had all the floor."

"I have been deeply entertained," replied Marshall, with a grin. "My visit to New York is by no means wasted. I envy Mr. Hamilton; but let him look out for Mr. Burr. There are just five feet seven inches of jealous hate in that well-balanced exterior, and its methods would be sinuous, I fancy, but no less deadly. But Hamilton has had many escapes. What was that atrocious story I heard of a duelling cabal? When the rolling stone of gossip reaches Virginia from New York, it has gathered more moss than you would think."

"It would be difficult to exaggerate that story," snorted Livingston." Hamilton defended his course in regard to the Tories in two pamphlets, signed 'Phocion.' They were answered by a Mr. Ledyard, who signed himself 'Mentor,' and was a conspicuous advocate of the damnable spirit of revenge possessing this country. It is a bold man indeed who enters into a conflict of the pen with Hamilton, and 'Mentor' was left without a leg to stand on. Forthwith, a club of Ledyard's friends and sympathizers, enraged by defeat, and fearing the growing ascendency of Hamilton over men's minds, deliberately agreed to challenge him in turn until he was silenced forever. This atrocious project would undoubtedly have been carried out, had not Ledyard himself repudiated it with horror. Can you show me a greater instance of the depravity of human nature, sir?"

"We are in a ferment of bitter passions," said Marshall, sadly, "and I fear they will be worse before they are better. I only hope that Hamilton will not be swept into their current, for upon his keeping his balance depends the future greatness of this country. I am at your service, sir, for I will confess my two legs are tired."

II

As the three men turned into Broadway they saluted a man who was entering Wall Street. It was Hamilton, hastening home to his family after the day's work. He had lost his boyish slenderness; his figure had broadened and filled out sufficiently to add to his presence while destroying nothing of its symmetry or agile grace, and it was dressed with the same care. His face was as gay and animated as ever, responded with the old mobility to every passing thought, but its lines and contours showed the hard work and severe thought of the last four years.

216

When he was taking a brief holiday with his friends, or tumbling about the floor with his little brood, he felt as much a boy as ever, but no one appreciated more fully than he the terrible responsibility of his position in the Confederation. His abilities, combined with his patriotism, had forced him to the head of the Nationalist Party, for whose existence he was in greatest measure responsible; and he hardly dared to think of his personal ambitions, nor could he hesitate to neglect his lucrative practice whenever the crying needs of the country demanded it. He had also given much time to the creating and organization of the Bank of New York. But Burr was not far wrong when he accused him of impatience. His bearing was more imperious, his eye flashed more intolerantly, than ever. To impute to him monarchical ambitions was but the fling of a smarting jealousy, but it is quite true that he felt he knew what was best for the country, and would have liked to regulate its affairs without further hindrance.

His house, beyond the dip of Wall Street and within sight of the bay, was of red brick, and as unbeautiful architecturally as other New York houses which had risen at random from the ruins. But within, it was very charming. The long drawing-room was furnished with mahogany, and rose-coloured brocade, with spindle-legged tables and many bibelots sent by Angelica Church, now living in London. The library was filling with valuable books, and the panelled whiteness of the dining room glittered with silver and glass, which in quantity or value was not exceeded in the home of any young couple in America; the world had outdone itself at the most interesting wedding of the Revolution. Betsey's sitting room was behind the drawing-room, and there Hamilton found her counting the moments until his return. She had lost nothing of her slimness, and except on dress occasions wore her mass of soft black hair twisted in a loose knot and unpowdered. She looked younger and prettier than with powder or wig, and Hamilton begged her to defy the fashion; but yielding in all else, on this point she was inflexible. "I am wiser than you in just a few things," she would say, playfully, for she firmly believed him infallible; "my position would suffer, were I thought eccentric. You cannot stand in rank without a uniform. I shall not yield to Sarah Jay nor even Kitty Duer. I am a little Republican, sir, and know my rights. And I know how to keep them."

Today, after her usual prolonged and unmitigated greeting, she remarked: "Speaking of eccentric people, I met to-day, at Lady Sterling's, that curious person, Mrs. Croix, or Miss Capet, as some will call her. Her hair was built up quite a foot and unpowdered. On top of it was an immense black hat with plumes, and her velvet gown was at least three yards on the floor. She certainly is the handsomest creature in town, but, considering all the gossip, I think it odd Lady Sterling should take her up, and I believe that Kitty is quite annoyed. But Lady Sterling is so good-natured, and I am told that Dr. Franklin went personally and asked her to give this lady countenance. He calls her his Fairy Queen, and to-day saluted her on the lips before all of us. Poor dear Dr. Franklin is by now quite in the class with Caesar's wife, but still I think his conduct rather remarkable."

"Who is this woman?" asked Hamilton, indifferently.

"Well!" exclaimed his wife, with a certain satisfaction, "you *are busy*. She has been the talk of the town for quite three months, although she never went *anywhere* before to-day."

"I hear all my gossip from you," said Hamilton, smiling from the hearth rug, "and considering the labours of the past three months—but tell me about her. I believe I love you best when gossiping. Your effort to be caustic is the sweetest thing in the world."

She threw a ball of wool at him, which he caught and pulled apart, then showered on her head. It was yellow wool, and vastly becoming on her black hair. "You must have a yellow hat at once, with plumes," he said, "but go on."

"You shall wind that this evening, sir. Well, she came here about three months ago with Captain Croix of the British army, and rumour hath it that he left a wife in England, and that this lady's right to the royal name of Capet is still unchallenged. The story goes that she was born about eighteen years ago, on a French frigate bound for the West Indies, that her mother died, and that, there being no one else of that royal name on board, the Captain adopted her; but that a baby and a ship being more than he could manage, he presented the baby to a humble friend at Newport, by the name of Thompson, who brought her up virtuously, but without eradicating the spirit of the age, and one fine day she disappeared with Colonel Croix, and after a honeymoon which may have been spent in the neighbourhood of any church between here and Rhode Island, or of none, they arrived in New York, and took the finest lodgings in town. I suppose Dr. Franklin was a friend of her humble guardian, he is so philanthropic, and that he is willing to take my lady's word that all is well—and perhaps it is. I feel myself quite vicious in repeating the vaguest sort of gossip—active, though. Who knows, if she had worn a wig, or an inch of powder, and employed the accepted architect for her tower, she would have passed without question? Another pillar for my argument, sir."

"As it is, you are even willing to believe that she is a daughter of the house of France," said Hamilton, with a hearty laugh. "Would that the world were as easily persuaded of what is good for it as of what tickles its pettiness. Shall you ask this daughter of the Capets to the house?"

"I have not made up my mind," said Mrs. Hamilton, demurely.

The two older children, Philip and Angelica, came tumbling into the room, and Hamilton romped with them for a half-hour, then flung them upon their mother, and watched them from the hearth rug. Betsey was lovely with her children, who were beautiful little creatures, and Hamilton was always arranging them in groups. The boy and girl pulled down her hair with the yellow wool, until all her diminutive figure and all her face, but its roguish black eyes, were extinguished; and Hamilton forgot the country.

Elizabeth Schuyler was a cleverer woman than her meed of credit has led the world to believe. She understood Hamilton very well even then, although, as his faults but added to his fascination in the eyes of those that loved him, the knowledge did not detract from her happiness. In many ways she made herself necessary to him; at that time she even kept his papers in order. He talked to her freely on every subject that interested him, from human nature to finance, taxes, and the law, and she never permitted a yawn to threaten. He read aloud to her every line he wrote, and while she would not have presumed to suggest, her sympathy was one of his imperative needs. When his erratic fancy flashed him into seductive meshes, she pulled a string and back he came. Perhaps this is the reason why no specific account of his numerous alleged amours have come down to us. He is vaguely accused of being the Lothario of his time, irresistible and indefatigable; but of all famous men whose names are enlivened with anecdotes of gallantry in the vast bulk of the world's unwritten history, he alone is the hero of much mysterious affirmation but of no particular romance. The

Reynolds affair is open history and not a case in point. It is probable that, owing to inherent fickleness and Betsey's gentle manipulation, his affairs rarely lasted long enough to attract attention. It is one of the accidents of life that the world barely knew of his acquaintance with Eliza Croix, she who has come down to us as Madame Jumel; and such a thing could not happen twice. But whether or not he possessed in all their perfection the proclivities of so great and impetuous and passionate a genius, it is certain that he loved his wife devotedly, and above all other women, so long as his being held together. His home was always his Mecca, and he left it only when public duty compelled his presence in exile.

III

In February he went to the Assembly to fight Clinton's opposition to the harassing need of conferring a permanent revenue upon Congress. He had already written a memorial, distributed over the State, setting forth the dangerous position of the country. But Clinton was lord of the masses, and their representatives in the Legislature had been trained to think as he thought. They honoured him because he had made New York the greatest State in the Union, not yet realizing that he had brought her into disrepute at home and abroad, and that his selfish policy was now hastening her to her ruin. To increase the power of Congress was to encourage the spirit of Nationalism, and that meant the sure decline of the States and of himself. The fight was hot and bitter. Clinton won; but the thinking men present took Hamilton's words home and pondered upon them, and in time they bore fruit.

After many delays the Convention was summoned to meet at Philadelphia on the 14th of May. History calls it the Constitutional Convention, but its promoters were careful to give the States-right people no such guide to contravention. The violent oppositionists of all change slumbered peacefully, while the representatives of the more enlightened were appointed to the Convention under moderately worded and somewhat vague resolutions; and some of them went as vaguely. Congress, after a characteristic and selfish hesitation, and a thorough fright induced by the Massachusetts rebellion, was finally persuaded to give her official sanction to the proposed Convention. Hamilton secured his appointment as a delegate,—after a hard fight to have New York represented at all,—and found himself saddled with two Clintonians, Robert Yates and John Lansing, Jr. But the first great step for which he had struggled, since his Morristown letter to the Financier of the Revolution seven years before, was assured at last.

Shortly before the Convention opened, Gouverneur Morris and James Madison, Jr. met by appointment at Hamilton's house to discuss the plan of campaign and make sure of their leader's wishes. General Schuyler and Robert Troup were also present.

Morris was a delegate from Pennsylvania, but was about to return to New York, having bought the family estate at Morrisania from his brother, Staats Long Morris, and was involved in business enterprises which resulted in a large fortune. He awaited the settlement of the country's affairs before sailing for Europe in his private interests. Troup, now a successful lawyer at the New York bar, was an able politician and devoted to Hamilton's interests. Philip Schuyler was entirely in his son-in-law's confidence, working for and with him always, occupying the double position of adviser and follower. Madison, who had forced the Convention at Annapolis, had had his breath taken away by Hamilton's coup, but now was delighted that he had been the instrument which made it possible. He had composed his somewhat halting mind to the determination to concentrate his energies upon wringing from the Convention a national scheme of government after Hamilton's model, provided that model were not too extreme: he was no monarchist, and knew the people very thoroughly. But he was deeply anxious to have Hamilton's views and plans for his guidance, even if modification were necessary. He knew Hamilton's complete mastery of the science of government, and that his broad structure was bound to be right, no matter what its frills.

The company assembled in the library, whose open windows overhung a garden full of lilacs, dogwood, and maples. There was a long table in the room, about which the guests mechanically seated themselves, so accustomed were they to the council table. Hamilton had greeted them in the hall, and sent them on to the library, while he went to fetch some papers his wife had promised to copy for him.

"So this is the room in which the government of the United States is to be born," said Troup, glancing about at the familiar books and at the desk stuffed with papers. "I shall always smell lilacs in the new Constitution."

"If we get one," observed Morris. "'Conceive' would be a better word than 'born,' Twelve states,—for my part I am glad the refusal of Rhode Island to send delegates makes one less,—each wanting its own way, and the North inevitably pitted against the South: I confess that 'still-born' strikes me as a better word than any."

"We'll have a Constitution," said Madison, doggedly, "I've made up my mind to that. There are a sufficient number of able and public-spirited men on their way to Philadelphia to agree upon a wise scheme of government and force it through—besides Hamilton and ourselves there are Washington, Governor Randolph, William Livingston, Rufus King, Roger Sherman, Dr. Franklin, James Wilson, George Wythe, the Pinckneys, Hugh Williamson—to mention but a few."

"They are not a bad lot," admitted Morris, "if they had all seen more of the world and less of their native or adopted State—all this State patriotism makes me sick. Half were not born in the State they vociferate about, are not certain of ending their days in it, nor of which their children may adopt as intemperately."

"Travel is not the only cure for provincialism," said General Schuyler. "Dr. Franklin, I happen to know, is bent upon a form of government little firmer than the one now existing; and Hamilton, whose travels are limited to campaigning in the different States, has a comprehensive grasp of European political machinery, and the breadth of vision such knowledge involves, which could gain nothing by personal contact."

"Dr. Franklin was too long a mendicant at foreign courts not to be besottedly in love with their antithesis, and Hamilton has a brain power and an intellectual grasp which quite remove him from the odiums of comparison," said Morris. "I think myself he is fortunate in never having visited Europe, deeply as he may regret it; for with his faculty of divination he goes straight for what is best only—or most essential. Had he lived there, the details and disappointments might have blocked his vision and upset the fine balance of his mind. There she is!"

He was at the window as quickly as he could have flung a book to the lilacs, despite his wooden leg; and he was followed by Troup and General Schuyler, demanding "Who?"

"Mrs. Croix—there. Did anything so lovely ever dawn upon a distracted American's vision? 'Tis said she is an unregistered daughter of the house of Capet, and I vow she looks every inch a princess. I stared at her so long last night in Vauxhall that she was embarrassed; and I never saw such poise, such royal command of homage. How has she developed it at the age of eighteen? I half believe this tale of royal birth; although there are those who assert that she is nothing less than the daughter of our highest in honour."

"'Tis said that she had an opportunity to acquire her aplomb in the village of Rutland, Massachusetts, where for some years she enlivened the exile and soothed the domestic yearnings of many British officers," said Troup. "One told me that he would vow she was none other than the famous vagrant 'Betsey.'"

"But I am told that she comes of a respectable Rhode Island family named Bowen," observed General Schuyler, who was not romantic. "That she was wayward and ran off with Colonel Croix, of whose other wife there is no proof, but that none of these fancy stories are true."

"Then wherein lies her claim to the name of Capet?" demanded Morris. "'Twould be nothing remarkable were she a daughter of Louis V., and I'm told she signs her name Eliza Capet Croix."

"I don't know," said Schuyler, meekly. "'Tis easy enough to assume a name, if you have it not. I am told that Lady Sterling is assured of her respectability. She certainly shines upon us like a star at this moment. I did not know that women had such hair."

"Is this what we came here to discuss?" asked a voice, dropped to the register of profound contempt. They turned about with a laugh and faced Madison's ascetic countenance, pale with disgust. "We have the most important work to do for which men ever met together, and we stand at the window and talk scandal about a silly woman and her hair."

"You did not, my dear James," said Morris, lightly; "and thereby you have missed the truly divine stimulus for the day's work. Don't you realize, my friend, that no matter how hard a man may labour, some woman is always in the background of his mind? She is the one reward of virtue."

"I know nothing of the sort," replied Madison, contemptuously. "I can flatter myself that I at least am independent of what appears to men like you to be the only motive for living."

"Right, my boy, but great as you are, you don't know what you might have been."

The door opened, and Hamilton entered the room, his hands full of papers, his face as gay and eager as if he were about to read to his audience a poem or a lively tale. Perhaps one secret of his ascendency over those who knew him best was that he never appeared to take himself seriously, even when his whole being radiated power and imperious determination. When he descended to the depths of seriousness and his individuality was most overwhelming, his unsleeping sense of humour saved him from a hint of the demagogue.

"While my wife was finishing, I heard you gossiping from the window above," he said, "but I had by far the best view. The lilac bushes—"

"Do you know her?" asked Morris, eagerly.

"Alas, I do not. It is incalculable months since I have had time to look so long at a woman. What is the matter, Madison?"

"I am nauseated. I had thought that *you*—"

Here even General Schuyler laughed, and Hamilton hurriedly arranged his papers.

He sat down when he began to talk, but was quickly on his feet and shaking his papers over the table. To him, also, the council table was the most familiar article of furniture in his world, but he was usually addressing those it stood for, and he was too ardent a speaker, even when without the incentive of debate, to keep to his chair.

"I know what you are wondering," he said. "No, it is not the British Constitution. What I have done so distempered as to impress people with the belief that I am blind to the spirit of this country, I am at a loss to conjecture. The British Constitution is the best form which the world has yet produced; in the words of Necker, it is the only government 'which unites public strength with individual security,' Nevertheless, no one is more fully convinced than I that none but a republican government can be attempted in this country, or would be adapted to our situation. Therefore, I propose to look to the British Constitution for nothing but those elements of stability and permanency which a republican system requires, and which may be incorporated into it without changing its characteristic principles. There never has been, and there never will be, anything in my acts or principles inconsistent with the spirit of republican liberty. Whatever my private predilections, it would be impossible for me, understanding the people of this country as I do, to fail to recognize the authority of that people as the source of all political power. Therefore you will find many departures from the British Constitution in the rough draft I am about to read. I have neither the patience nor the temper to dogmatize upon abstract theories of liberty, and our success will lie in adapting to our particular needs such principles of government as have been tried and not found wanting, our failure in visionary experiments. The best and wisest effort we can make will be a sufficient experiment, for whose result we must all tremble.

"It is going to be difficult to persuade this Convention to unite upon any constitution very much stronger than the one Dr. Franklin will propose, or to accomplish its ratification afterward. Nevertheless, I have prepared a draft of the strongest constitution short of monarchy which it is possible to conceive, and which I shall propose to the Convention for reasons I will explain after I have read it to you. Do you care to listen?"

"Hurry up!" exclaimed Morris. The audience leaned forward. Madison shook his head all through the reading; Morris jerked his with emphatic approval.

The radical points in which Hamilton's constitution differed from that under which we live, was in the demand for a President, to be elected by property holders, and who should hold office during good behaviour; senators possessing certain property qualifications and elected on the same principle; and governors of States appointed and removable by the President. Practically the author of the dual government, he believed emphatically in subserving the lesser to the greater, although endowing the States with sufficient power for self-protection. The Executive was to be held personally responsible for official misconduct, both he and the senators subject to impeachment and to removal from office. The whole scheme was wrought out with the mathematical complexity and precision characteristic of Hamilton's mind.

"Would that it were possible," exclaimed Morris, when Hamilton had finished. "But as well expect the Almighty to drive the quill. You will weaken your influence, Hamilton, and to no effect."

"Ah, but I have calculated upon two distinct points, and I believe I shall achieve them. I have not the most distant hope that this paper will be acceptable to five men in the Convention,—three, perhaps, would round the number,—Washington, yourself, myself. Nevertheless, I shall introduce it and speak in its favour with all the passion of which I am master, for these reasons: I believe in it; its energy is bound to give a tone that might be lacking otherwise; and—this is the principal point—*there must be something to work back from.* If I alarm with the mere chance of so perilous a menace to their democratic ideals, they will go to work in earnest at *something* in order to defeat me, and they will not go back so far in the line of vigour as if I had suggested a more moderate plan; for, mark my words, they would infallibly incline to weaker measures than *any* firm government which should first be proposed. In the management of men one of the most important things to bear in mind is their proneness to work forward from the weak, and backward from the strong. On the quality of the strength depends its magnetism over the weak. All reformers are ridiculed or outlawed, and their measures are never wholly successful; but they awaken men's minds to something of approximate worth, and to a desire for a divorce from the old order of things. So, while I expect to be called a monarchist, I hope to instil subtly the idea of the absolute necessity of a strong government, and implant in their minds a distrust of one too weak."

"Good," said Morris. "And it is always a delight to see your revelation of yourself in a new light. I perceive that to your other accomplishments you add the cunning of the fox."

"You are right to call it an accomplishment," retorted Hamilton. "We cannot go through life successfully with the bare gifts of the Almighty, generous though He may have been. If I find that I have need of cunning, or brutality,—than which nothing is farther from my nature,—or even nagging, I do not hesitate to borrow and use them."

"Let us call this sagacity," said Troup. "'Tis a prettier word. Or the canniness of the Scot. But there is one thing I fear," he added anxiously. "You may injure your chances of future preferment. Your ambition will be thought too vaulting, particularly for so young a man, and, besides, you may be thought a menace to the commonwealth."

"That is a point to be considered, Hamilton," said General Schuyler.

"I have an end to gain, sir, and I mean to gain it. Moreover, this is no time to be considering private interests. If this be not the day for patriotism to stifle every personal ambition, then there is little hope for human nature. I believe the result of this paper will be a constitution of respectable strength, and I shall use all the influence I wield to make the people accept it. So, if you worry, consider if the later effort will not outweigh the first."

"Hamilton," said Madison, solemnly, "you are a greater man even than I thought you. You have given me a most welcome hint, and I shall take upon myself to engineer the recession from your constitution. I shall study its effect with the closest attention and be guided accordingly, I am heart and soul in this matter, and would give my life to it if necessary. I never should have thought of anything so astute," he added, with some envy, "but perhaps if I had, no one else would be so peculiarly fitted as myself to work upon its manifold suggestions. I hope I do not strike you as conceited," he said, looking around anxiously, "but I *feel* that it is in me to render efficient service in the present crisis."

Before Morris could launch his ready fling, Hamilton hastened to assure Madison of his belief that no man living could render services so great. He underrated neither Madison's great abilities nor the danger of rankling arrows in that sensitive and not too courageous spirit. They then discussed a general plan of campaign and the best methods of managing certain members of the Convention. Morris was the first to rise.

"Adieu," he said. "I go to ruminate upon our Captain's diplomacy, and to pursue the ankle of Mrs. Croix. Be sure that the one will not interfere with the other, but will mutually stimulate."

The other gentlemen adjourned to the dining room.

IV

The story of the Convention has been told so often that only the merest outline is necessary here; those who have not before this read at least one of the numberless reports, would be the last to wish its multigenerous details. To the students of history there is nothing new to tell, as may be the case with less exploited incidents of Hamilton's career. Someone has said that it was an assemblage of hostile camps, and it certainly was the scene of intense and bitter struggles, of a heterogeneous mass blindly striving to cohere, whilst a thousand sectional interests tugged at the more familiar of the dual ideal; of compromise after compromise; of a fear pervading at least one-half that the liberties of republicanism were menaced by every energetic suggestion; of the soundest judgement and patriotism compelled to

227

truckle to meaner sentiments lest they get nothing; of the picked men of the Confederacy, honourable, loyal, able, and enlightened, animated in the first and last instance by a pure and common desire for the highest welfare of the country, driven to war upon one another by the strength of their conflicting opinions; ending—among the thirty-nine out of the sixty-one delegates who signed the Constitution—in a feeling as closely resembling general satisfaction as individual disappointments would permit.

At first so turbulent were the conditions, that Franklin, who troubled the Almighty but little himself, arose and suggested that the meetings be opened with prayer. After this sarcasm, and the submission of his mild compromise with the Confederation, he sat and watched the painted sun behind Washington's chair, pensively wondering if the artist had intended to convey the idea of a rise or a setting. Hamilton presented his draft at the right moment, and the startled impression it made quite satisfied him, particularly as his long speech to the Committee of the Whole was received with the closest attention. Nothing could alter his personal fascination, and even his bitterest enemies rarely left their chairs while he spoke. The small figure, so full of dignity and magnetizing power that it excluded every other object from their vision, the massive head with a piercing force in every line of its features, the dark eyes blazing and flashing with a fire that never had been seen in the eyes of a mere mortal before, the graceful rapid gestures, and the passionate eloquence which never in its most apparently abandoned moments failed to be sincere and logical, made him for the hour the glory of friend and enemy alike, although the reaction was correspondingly bitter. Upon this occasion he spoke for six hours without the interruption of a scraping heel; and what the Convention did not know about the science of government before he finished with them, they never would learn elsewhere. Although he made but this one speech, he talked constantly to the groups surrounding him wherever he moved. To his original scheme he had too much tact to make further allusion; but his general opinions, ardently propounded, his emphatic reiteration of the demoralized country's need for a national government, and of the tyrannies inherent in unbridled democracies, wedged in many a chink. Nevertheless, he was disgusted and disheartened when he left for New York, at the end of May. The

Convention was chaos, but he could accomplish nothing more than what he hoped he might have done; the matter was now best in the hands of Madison and Gouverneur Morris, and his practice could no longer be neglected.

But although he returned to a mass of work,—for he handled most of the great cases of the time,—he managed to mingle daily with the crowd at Fraunces' and the coffee-houses, in order to gauge the public sentiment regarding the proposed change of government, and to see the leading men constantly. On the whole, he wrote to Washington, he found that both in the Jerseys and in New York there was "an astonishing revolution for the better in the minds of the people."

Washington replied from the depths of his disgust:—

... In a word I almost despair of seeing a favourable issue to the proceedings of the Convention, and do, therefore, repent having any agency in the business. The men who oppose a strong and energetic government are, in my opinion, narrow-minded politicians, or are under the influence of local views. The apprehension expressed by them that the *people* will not accede to the form proposed, is the *ostensible*, not the real cause of the opposition; but admitting that *present* sentiment is as they prognosticate, the question ought nevertheless to be, is it, or is it not, the best form? If the former, recommend it, and it will assuredly obtain, maugre opposition. I am sorry you went away; I wish you were back.

To Washington, who presided over that difficult assemblage with a superhuman dignity, to Hamilton who breathed his strong soul into it, to Madison who manipulated it, to Gouverneur Morris, whose sarcastic eloquent tongue brought it to reason again and again, and whose accomplished pen gave the Constitution its literary form, belong the highest honours of the Convention; although the services rendered by Roger Sherman, Rufus King, James Wilson, R.R. Livingston, and Charles Cotesworth Pinckney entitle them to far more than polite mention.

When Hamilton signed the Constitution, on the 17th of September, it was by no means strong enough to suit him, but as it was incomparably better than the Articles of Confederation, which had carried the country to the edge of anarchy and ruin, and was regarded by a formidable number of people and their leaders as so strong as to be a menace to the liberties of the American citizen, he could with consistency and ardour exert himself to secure its ratification. After all, it was built of his stones, chipped and pared though they might be; had he not gone to the Convention, the result might have been a constitution for which his pen would have refused to plead.

Manhattan Island, Kings and Westchester counties had long since accepted his doctrines, and they stood behind him in unbroken ranks; but the northern counties and cities of New York, including Albany, were still under the autocratic sway of Clinton. Hamilton's colleagues, Yates and Lansing, had resigned their seats in the Great Convention. Among the signatures to the Constitution his name stood alone for New York, and the fact was ominous of his lonely and precarious position. But difficulties were ever his stimulant, and this was not the hour to find him lacking in resource.

"The Constitution terrifies by its length, complexity, frigidity, and above all by its novelty," he said to Jay and Madison, who met by appointment in his library. "Clinton, in this State, has persuaded his followers that it is so many iron hoops, in which they would groan and struggle for the rest of their lives. To defeat him and this pernicious idea, we must discuss the Constitution publicly, in the most lucid and entertaining manner possible, lay every fear, and so familiarize the people with its merits, and with the inseparable relation of its adoption to their personal interests, that by the time the elections for the State Convention take place, they will be sufficiently educated to give us the majority. And as there is so much doubt, even among members of the Convention, as to the mode of enacting the Constitution, we must solve that problem as quickly as possible. My purpose is to publish a series of essays in the newspapers, signed, if you agree with me, Publius, and reaching eighty or ninety in number, which shall expound and popularize the Constitution of the United States; and if you will give me your inestimable help, I am sure we shall accomplish our purpose."

"If you need my help, I will give it to you to the best of my ability, sir," said Jay, "but I do not pretend to compete with your absolute mastery of the complex science of government, and I fear that my weaker pen may somewhat counteract the vigour of yours; but, I repeat, I will do my best with the time at my disposal."

Hamilton laughed, "You know how anxious I am to injure our chances of success," he said. "I hope all things from your pen."

Jay bowed formally, and Hamilton turned to Madison. "I know you must feel that you have done your share for the present," he said, "and there is hard work awaiting you in your State Convention, but the subject is at your finger tips; it hardly can be too much trouble."

"I am not very well," said Madison, peevishly, "but I realize the necessity,—and that the papers should be read as extensively in Virginia as here. I will write a few, and more if I can."

But, as it came to pass, Madison wrote but fourteen separate papers of the eighty-five, although he collaborated with Hamilton on three others, and Jay wrote five only. The remaining sixty-three, therefore, of the essays, collected during and after their publication under the title of "The Federalist," which not only did so much to enlighten and educate the public mind and weaken the influence of such men as Clinton, but which still stand as the ablest exposition of the science of government, and as the parent of American constitutional law, were the work of Hamilton.

"It is the fortunate situation of our country," said Hamilton, a few months later, at Poughkeepsie, "that the minds of the people are exceedingly enlightened and refined." Certainly these papers are a great tribute to the general intelligence of the American race of a century and more ago. Selfish, petty, and lacking in political knowledge they may have been, but it is evident that their mental *tone* was high, that their minds had not been vulgarized by trash and sensationalism. Hamilton's sole bait was a lucid and engaging style, which would not puzzle the commonest intelligence, which he hoped might instruct without weighing heavily on the capacity of his humbler readers. That he was addressing the general voter, as well as the men of a higher grade as yet unconvinced, there can be no doubt, for as New York State was still seven-tenths Clintonian, conversion of a large portion of this scowling element was essential to the ratification of the Constitution. And yet he chose two men of austere and unimaginative style to collaborate with him; while his own style for purity, distinction, and profundity combined with simplicity, has never been excelled.

Betsey was ailing, and her doors closed to society; the children romped on the third floor or on the Battery. Hamilton wrote chiefly at night, his practice occupying the best of the hours of day, but he was sensible of the calm of his home and of its incentive to literary composition; it never occurred to him to open his office in the evening. Betsey, the while she knitted socks, listened patiently to her brilliant husband's luminous discussions on the new Constitution—which she could have recited backward—and his profound interpretation of its principles and provisions. If she worried over these continuous labours she made no sign, for Hamilton was racing Clinton, and there was not a moment to lose. Clinton won in the first heat. After a desperate struggle in the State Legislature the Hamiltonians succeeded in passing resolutions ordering a State Convention to be elected for the purpose of considering the Constitution; but the result in April proved the unabated power and industry of Clinton,—the first, and not the meanest of New York's political "bosses,"—for two-thirds of the men selected were his followers. The Convention was called for the 17th of June and it was rumoured that the Clintonians intended immediately to move an adjournment until the following year. According to an act of Congress the ratification of only nine States was necessary to the adoption of the Constitution. The others could come into the Union later if they chose, and there was a disposition in several States to watch the experiment before committing themselves. Hamilton, who knew that such a policy, if pursued by the more important States, would result in civil war, was determined that New York should not behave in a manner which would ruin her in the present and disgrace her in history, and wrote on with increasing vigour, hoping to influence the minds of the oppositionists elected to the Convention as well as the people at large. Even he had never written anything which had attracted so wide admiring and acrimonious attention. The papers were read in all the cities of the Confederation, and in such hamlets as boasted a mail-bag. When they reached England and France they were almost as keenly discussed. That they steadily made converts, Hamilton had cause to know, for his correspondence was overwhelming. Troup and General Schuyler attended to the greater part of it; but only himself could answer the frequent letters from leaders in the different states demanding advice. He thought himself fortunate in segregating five hours of the twenty-four for sleep. The excitement throughout the country was intense, and it is safe to say that nowhere and for months did conversation wander from the subject of politics and the new Constitution, for more than ten minutes at a time. In New York

Hamilton was the subject of constant and vicious attack, the Clintonians sparing no effort to discredit him with the masses. New York City was nicknamed Hamiltonopolis and jingled in scurrilous rhymes. In the midst of it all were two diversions: the fourth of his children, and a letter which he discovered before General Schuyler or Troup had sorted his mail. As the entire Schuyler family were now in his house, and his new son was piercingly discontented with his lot, he took refuge in his chambers in Garden Street, until Betsey was able to restore peace and happiness to his home. The postman had orders to bring his mail-bag thither, and it was on the second morning of his exile that the perfume of violets caused him to make a hasty journey through the letters.

He found the spring sweetness coincidentally with a large square, flowingly superscribed. He glanced at the clock. His devoted assistants would not arrive for half an hour. He broke the seal. It was signed Eliza Capet Croix, and ran as follows:—

MY DEAR SIR: Do you care anything for the opinion of my humble sex, I wonder? The humblest of your wondering admirers is driven beyond the bounds of feminine modesty, sir, to tell you that what you do not write she no longer cares to read. I was the first to detect—I claim that honour—such letters by Publius as were not by your hand, and while I would not disparage efforts so conscientious, they seem to me like dawn to sunrise. Is this idle flattery? Ah, sir! I too am greatly flattered. I do not want for admirers. Nor can I hope to know—to know—so great and busy a man. But my restless vanity, sir, compels me to force myself upon your notice. I should die if I passed another day unknown to the man who gives me the greatest pleasures of my life—I have every line you have had printed that can be found, and half the booksellers in the country searching for the lost copies of the *Continentalist*—I should die, I say, if you were longer ignorant that I have the intelligence, the ambition, and the erudition to admire you above all men, living or dead. For that is my pride, sir. Perchance I was born for politics; at all events you have made them my passion, and I spend my days converting Clintonians to your cause. Do not scorn my efforts. It is not every day that a woman turns a man's thoughts from love to patriotism; I have heard that 'tis oftenest the other way. But I take your time, and hasten to subscribe myself, my dear sir,

Your humble and obd't servant

ELIZA CAPET CROIX.

The absence of superfluous capitals and of underscoring in this letter, alone would have arrested his attention, for even men of a less severe education than himself were liberal in these resources, and women were prodigal. The directness and precision were also remarkable, and he recalled that she was but nineteen. The flattery touched him, no doubt, for he was very human; and despite the brevity of his leisure, he read the note twice, and devoted a moment to conjecture.

"She is cleverer, even, than Lady Kitty, or Susan and Kitty Livingston, by this," he mused. "She would be worth knowing, did a driven mortal but have the time to idle in the wake of so much intelligence—and beauty. Not to answer this were unpardonable—I cannot allow the lady to die." He wrote her a brief note of graceful acknowledgement, which caused Mrs. Croix to shed tears of exultation and vexation. He acknowledged her but breathed no fervid desire for another letter. It is not to be expected that maturest nineteen can realize that, although a busy man will find time to see a woman if it be worth his while, the temptations to a romantic correspondence are not overwhelming.

Hamilton tore up the letter and threw it into the waste basket. Its perfume, delicate but imperious, intruded upon his brief. He dived into the basket as he heard Troup's familiar whistle, and thrust the pieces into a breast pocket. In a moment he remembered that Betsey's head would be pillowed upon that pocket at five in the afternoon, and he hastily extracted the mutilated letter, and applied a match to it, consigning women to perdition. Troup sniffed as he entered the room.

"Violets and burnt paper," remarked he. "'Tis a combination I have noticed before. I wonder will some astute perfumer ever seize the idea? It would have its guilty appeal for our sex—perchance for t'other; though I'm no cynic like you and Morris."

"Shut up," said Hamilton, "and get to work if you love me, for I've no time to write to St. Croix, much less waste five seconds on any woman."

That afternoon he wasted half an hour in search of a bunch of redolent violets to carry home to his wife. He pinned three on his coat.

V

When the 17th of June approached, Hamilton, John Jay, Chancellor Livingston, and James Duane, started on horse for Poughkeepsie, not daring, with Clinton on the spot, and the menace of an immediate adjournment, to trust to the winds of the Hudson. General Schuyler had promised to leave even a day sooner from the North, and the majority of Federal delegates had gone by packet-boat, or horse, in good season.

The old post road between New York and Albany was, for the greater part of the way, but a rough belt through a virgin forest. Occasionally a farmer had cleared a few acres, the lawns of a manor house were open to the sun, the road was varied by the majesty of Hudson and palisade for a brief while, or by the precipitous walls of mountains, so thickly wooded that even the wind barely fluttered their sombre depths. Man was a moving arsenal in those long and lonely journeys, for the bear and the panther were breeding undisturbed. But the month was hot, and those forest depths were very cool; the scenery was often as magnificent as primeval, and a generous hospitality at many a board dispelled, for an interval, the political anxiety of Hamilton and his companions.

Hamilton, despite a mind trained to the subordination of private interests to public duty, knew that it was the crisis of his own destiny toward which he was hastening. He had bound up his personal ambitions with the principles of the Federalist party—so called since the publication in book form of the Publius essays; for not only was he largely responsible for those principles, but his mind was too well regulated to consider the alternative of a compromise with a possibly victorious party which he detested. Perhaps his ambition was too vaulting to adapt itself to a restricted field when his imagination had played for years with the big ninepins of history; at all events, it was inseparably bound up with nationalism in the boldest sense achievable, and with methods which days and nights of severe thought had convinced him were for the greatest good of the American people. Union meant Washington in the supreme command, himself with the reins of government in both hands. The financial, the foreign, the domestic policy of a harmonious federation were as familiar to his mind as they are to us to-day. Only he could achieve them, and only New York could give him those reins of power.

It is true that he had but to move his furniture over to Philadelphia to be welcomed to citizenship with acclamation by that ambitious town; but not only was his pride bound up in the conquest of New York from Clintonism to Federalism, but New York left out of the Union, dividing as she did New England from the South and North, of the highest commercial importance by virtue of her central position and her harbour, meant civil war at no remote period, disunion, and the undoing of the most careful and strenuous labours of the nation's statesmen. That New York should be forced into the Union at once Hamilton was determined upon, if he had to resort to a coup which might or might not meet with the approval of the rest of the country. Nevertheless, he looked forward to the next few weeks with the deepest anxiety. An accident, an illness, and the cause was lost, for he made no mistake in estimating himself as the sole force which could bear Clinton and his magnificent organization to the ground. Hamilton was no party manipulator. He relied upon his individual exertions, abetted by those of his lieutenants,—the most high-minded and the ablest men in the country,—to force his ideas upon the masses by their own momentum and weight. Indeed, so individual did he make the management of the Federalist party, that years later, when the "Republican" leaders determined upon its overthrow, they aimed all their artillery at him alone: if he fell the party must collapse, on top of him; did he retain the confidence of the people, he would magnetize their obedience, no matter what rifts there might be in his ranks.

He had established a horse-express between Virginia and Poughkeepsie, and between New Hampshire and the little capital. Eight States having ratified, the signature of New Hampshire, the next in order, would mean union and a trial of the Constitution, a prospect which could not fail to influence the thinking men of the anti-Federal party; but it was from the ratification of Virginia that he hoped the greatest good. This State occupied much the same position in the South that New York did in the North, geographically, commercially, historically, and in the importance of her public men. And she was as bitterly opposed to union, to what a narrow provincialism held to be the humiliation of the States. Patrick Henry, her most powerful and eloquent leader, not through the selfish policy of a Clinton, but in the limitations of a too narrow genius, was haranguing with all his recuperated might against the sinister menace to the liberties of a people who had freed themselves of one despotism so dearly; and even Randolph, with characteristic hesitancy when approaching a point, was deficient in enthusiasm, although he intimated that he should vote for the unconditional adoption of the Constitution he had refused to sign. He and Marshall were Madison's only assistants of importance against the formidable opponent of union, and it was well understood among leaders that Jefferson, who was then American minister in France, gave the Constitution but a grudging and inconsistent approval, and would prefer that it failed, were not amendments tacked on which practically would nullify its energies. But although Hamilton had such lieutenants as John Jay, Philip Schuyler, Duane, and Robert Livingston, Madison had the inestimable, though silent, backing of Washington. The great Chief had, months since, forcibly expressed his sentiments in a public letter; and that colossal figure, the more potent that it was invisible and mute, guided as many wills as Madison's strenuous exertions and unanswerable dispassionate logic.

But Washington, although sufficiently revered by New Yorkers, was not their very own, as was he the Virginians'; was by no means so impinging and insistent as his excellency, Governor Clinton, he whose powerful will and personality, aided by an enterprise and wisdom that were not always misguided, for eleven years had compelled their grateful submission. It was difficult to convince New Yorkers that such a man was wholly wrong in his patriotism, particularly when their own interests seemed bound so firmly to his. It was this dominant, dauntless, resourceful, political nabob that Hamilton knew he must conquer single-handed, if he conquered him at all; for his lieutenants, able as they were, could only second and abet him; they had none of his fertility of resource. As he rode through the forest he rehearsed every scheme of counterplay and every method that made for conquest which his fertile brain had conceived. He would exercise every argument likely to appeal to the decent instincts of those ambitious of ranking as first-class citizens, as well as to the congenital selfishness of man, which could illuminate the darker recesses of their Clintonized understandings, and effect their legitimate conversion; then, if these higher methods failed, coercion.

"What imperious method are you devising, Hamilton?" asked

Livingston. "Your lips are set; your eyes are almost black. I've seen you like that in court, but never in good company before. You look as if considering a challenge to mortal combat."

Hamilton's brow cleared, and he laughed with that mercurial lightness which did more to preserve the balance of what otherwise would have been an overweighted mind than any other quality it possessed.

"Well, am I not to fight a duel?" he asked. "Would that I could call Clinton out and settle the question as easily as that. I disapprove of duelling, but so critical a moment as this would justify anything short of trickery. We'll leave that to Clinton; but although there is no vast difference between my political and my private conscience, there are recourses which are as fair in political as in martial warfare, and I should be found ingenuous and incapable did I fail to make use of them."

"Well, you love a fight," said Jay, without experiencing the humour of his remark. "I believe you would rather fight than sit down in good company at any time, and you are notoriously convivial. But easy conquest would demoralize you. If I do not mistake, you have the greatest battle of your career, past or present, immediately ahead of you—and it means so much to all of us—I fear—I fear—"

"I will listen to no fears," cried Hamilton, who at all events had no mind to be tormented by any but his own. "Are we not alive? Are we not in health? Are not our intellectual powers at their ripest point of development? Can Clinton, Melancthon Smith, Yates, Lansing, Jones, make a better showing?"

"We are nineteen against forty-six," said Jay, with conceivable gloom.

"True. But there is no reason why we should not shortly be forty-six against nineteen."

"We certainly are Right against the most unstatesman-like Selfishness the world has ever seen," observed Duane.

"Would that experience justified us in thinking well enough of the human race to gather courage from that fact," replied Hamilton. "It is to the self-interest of the majority we shall have to appeal. Convince them that there is neither career nor prosperity for them in an isolated State, and we may drag them up to a height which is safer than their mire, simply because it is better, or better because it is safer. This is a time to practice patriotism, but not to waste time talking about it."

"Your remarks savour of cynicism," replied Jay, "but I fear there is much truth in them. It is only in the millennium, I suppose, that we shall have the unthinkable happiness of seeing on all sides of us an absolute conformity to our ideals."

In spite of the close, if somewhat formal, friendship between Jay and Hamilton, the latter was often momentarily depressed by the resemblance of this flawless character to, and its rigid contrasts from, his dead friend Laurens. Jay was all that Laurens had passionately wished to be, and apparently without effort; for nature had not balanced him with a redeeming vice, consequently with no power to inspire hate or love. Had he been a degree greater, a trifle more ambitious, or had circumstances isolated him in politics, he would have been an even lonelier and loftier figure than Washington, for our Chief had one or two redeeming humanities; as it was, he stood to a few as a character so perfect that they marvelled, while they deplored his lack of personal influence. But his intellect is in the rank which stands just beneath that of the men of genius revealed by history, and he hangs like a silver star of the tropics upon the sometimes dubious fields of our ancestral heavens. Nevertheless, he frequently inspired Hamilton with so poignant a longing for Laurens that our impetuous hero was tempted to wish for an exchange of fates.

"In the millennium we will all tell the truth and hate each other," answered Hamilton. "And we either shall all be fools, or those irritants will be extinct; in any case we shall be happy, particularly if we have someone to hate."

"Ah, now you jest," said Duane, smiling. "For you are logical or nothing. *You* may be happy when on the warpath, but the rest of us are not. And you are the last man to be happy in a millennium by yourself."

They all laughed at this sally, for Hamilton was seldom silent. He answered lightly:—

"Someone to fight. Someone to love. Three warm friends. Three hot enemies. A sufficiency of delicate food and wine. A West Indian swimming-bath. Someone to talk to. Someone to make love to. War. Politics. Books. Song. Children. Woman. A religion. There you have the essence of the millennium, embroider it as you may."

"And scenery," added Jay, devoutly.

The road for the last quarter of an hour had led up a steep hill, above which other hills piled without an opening; and below lay the Hudson. As they paused upon the bare cone of the elevation, the river looked like a chain of Adirondack lakes, with dense and upright forests rising tier beyond tier until lost in the blue haze of the Catskills. The mountains looked as if they had pushed out from the mainland down to the water's edge to cross and meet each other. So close were the opposite crags that the travellers could see a deer leap through the brush, the red of his coat flashing through the gloomy depths. Below sped two packet-boats in a stiff breeze.

"Friends or enemies?" queried Livingston. "I wish I were with them, for I must confess the pleasures of horse travel for seventy-five miles must be the climax of a daily habit to be fully appreciated. It is all very well for Hamilton, who is on a horse twice every day; but as I am ten years older and proportionately stiffer, I shall leave patriotism to the rest of you for a day or two after our arrival."

Hamilton did not answer. He had become conscious of the delicate yet piercing scent of violets. Wild violets had no perfume, and it was long past their season. He glanced eagerly around, but without realizing what prompted a quick stirring of his pulses. There was but one tree on the crag, and he stood against it. Almost mechanically his glance sought its recesses, and his hand reached forward to something white. It was a small handkerchief of cambric and lace. The other men were staring at the scenery. He hastily glanced at the initials in the corner of the scented trifle, and wondered that he should so easily decipher a tangled E.C.C. But he marvelled, nevertheless, and thrust the handkerchief into his pocket.

They reached Poughkeepsie late in the afternoon. Main Street, which was the interruption of the post road, and East Street, which terminated the Dutchess turnpike, were gaily decorated with flags and greens, the windows and pavements crowded with people whose faces reflected the nervous excitement with which the whole country throbbed. The capital for ten years, the original village had spread over the hills into a rambling town of many avenues, straight and twisted, and there were pretentious houses and a certain amount of business. Hamilton and his party were stared at with deep curiosity, but not cheered, for the town was almost wholly Clintonian. The Governor had

240

his official residence on the Dutchess turnpike, a short distance from town; and this was his court. Nevertheless, it was proudly conscious of the dignity incumbent upon it as the legislative centre of the State, and no matter what the suspense or the issue, had no mind to make the violent demonstrations of other towns. Nearly every town of the North, including Albany, had burned Hamilton in effigy, albeit with battered noses, for he had his followers everywhere; but here he was met with a refreshing coolness, for which the others of his party, at least, were thankful.

They went first to Van Kleek's tavern, on the Upper Landing Road, not far from the Court-house, to secure the rooms they had engaged; but finding an invitation awaiting them from Henry Livingston to make use of his house during the Convention, repaired with unmixed satisfaction to the large estate on the other side of the town. The host was absent, but his cousin had been requested to do the honours to as many as he would ask to share a peaceful retreat from the daily scene of strife.

"And it has the advantage of an assured privacy," said Hamilton. "For here we can hold conference nightly with no fear of eavesdropping. Moreover, to get a bath at Van Kleek's is as easy as making love to Clinton."

General Schuyler joined them an hour later. He had been in town all day, and had held several conferences with the depressed Federalists, who, between a minority which made them almost ridiculous, and uncomfortable lodgings, were deep in gloomy forebodings. As soon as they heard of their Captain's arrival they swarmed down to the Livingston mansion. Hamilton harangued them cheerfully in the drawing-room, drank with them, in his host's excellent wine, to the success of their righteous cause; and they retired, buoyant, confirmed in their almost idolatrous belief in the man who was responsible for all the ideas they possessed.

VI

Although Hamilton and Clinton had no liking for each other, they were far from being the furious principals in one of those political hatreds which the times were about to engender,—an intellectual cataclysm which Hamilton was to experience in all its blackness, of which he was to be the most conspicuous victim. He had by no means plumbed his depths as yet. So far he had met with few disappointments, few stumbling blocks, never a dead wall. Life had smiled upon him as if magnetized. At home he found perfect peace, abroad augmenting ranks of followers, sufficient work to use up his nervous energies, and the stimulant of enmity and opposition that he loved. It was long since he had given way to rage, although he flew into a temper occasionally. He told himself he was become a philosopher, and was far from suspecting the terrible passions which the future was to undam. His mother, with dying insight, had divined the depth and fury of a nature which was all light on the surface, and in its upper half a bewildering but harmonious intermingling of strength, energy, tenderness, indomitability, generosity, and intense emotionalism: a stratum so large and so generously endowed that no one else, least of all himself, had suspected that primeval inheritance which might blaze to ashes one of the most nicely balanced judgements ever bestowed on a mortal, should his enemies combine and beat his own great strength to the dust.

But when Hamilton and Clinton approached the Court-house from opposite directions, on the morning of the 17th, they did not cross the street to avoid meeting, although they bowed with extreme formality and measured each other with a keen and speculative regard. Clinton was now forty-nine years old, his autocratic will, love of power, and knowledge of men, in their contemptuous maturity. He was a large man, with the military bearing of the born and finished martinet, a long hard nose, and an irritated eye. The irritation kindled as it met Hamilton's, which was sparkling with the eager determination of a youth which, although desirable in itself, was become a presumption when pitted against those eighteen additional distinguished years of the Governor of New York. That there was a twinkle of amusement in the Federalist's eye was also to his discredit.

"The young fop," fumed Clinton, as he brushed a fleck of mud from his own magnificent costume of black ducape, "he is the *enfant gâté* of politics, and I shall settle him here once for all. It will be a public benefaction."

The Court-house, which stood halfway up the hill, on the corner of Main and East streets, and was surrounded by the shade of many maples, was a two-story building of rough stones welded together by a ruder cement. The roof sloped, and above was a belfry. The Convention was held in the upper story, which was unbroken by partition; and with the windows open upon what looked to be a virgin forest, so many were the ancient trees remaining in the little town, the singing of birds, the shrilling of crickets, the murmur of the leaves in an almost constant breeze, the old Court-house of Poughkeepsie was by no means a disagreeable gathering-place. Moreover, it was as picturesque within as it was arcadian without; for the fine alert-looking men, with their powdered hair in queues, their elaborately cut clothes of many colours, made for the most part of the corded silk named ducape, their lawn and ruffles, made up the details of a charming picture, which was far from appealing to them, but which gives us a distinct pleasure in the retrospect.

Governor Clinton was elected the President of the Convention. On the right of the central table sat his forty-five henchmen, with Melancthon Smith, one of the most astute and brilliant debaters of the time, well to the front. Opposite sat Hamilton, surrounded by General Schuyler, Jay, Duane, and Robert Livingston, the rest of his small following close to the windows, but very alert, their gaze never ranging far from their leader. Beyond the bar crowded the invited guests, many of them women in all the finery of the time.

If the anti-Federalists had entertained the idea of an immediate and indefinite adjournment, they appear to have abandoned it without waste of time; perhaps because long and tedious journeys in midsummer were not to be played with; perhaps because they were sure of their strength; possibly because Clinton was so strongly in favour of arranging Hamilton's destinies once for all.

Certainly at the outset the prospects of the Federalists were almost ludicrous. The anti-Federalists were two-thirds against one-third, fortified against argument, uncompromisingly opposed to union at the expense of State sovereignty, clever and thinking men, most of them, devoted to Clinton, and admirably led by an orator who acknowledged no rival but Hamilton. The latter set his lips more than once, and his heart sank, but only to leap a moment later with delight in the mere test of strength.

Clinton's first move was to attempt a vote at once upon the Constitution as a whole, but he was beaten by Hamilton and many in his own ranks, who were in favour of the fair play of free debate. The Governor was forced to permit the Convention to go into a Committee of the Whole, which would argue the Constitution section by section. Hamilton had gained a great point, and he soon revealed the use he purposed to make of it.

It is doubtful if his own followers had anticipated that he would speak almost daily for three weeks, receiving and repelling the brunt of every argument; and certainly Clinton had looked for no such feat.

The contest opened on the Clintonian side, with the argument that an amended Confederation was all that was necessary for the purposes of a more general welfare. The plan advanced was that Congress should be given the power to compel by force the payment of the requisitions which the States so often ignored. Hamilton demolished this proposition with one of his most scornful outbursts.

Coerce the States! [he cried]. Never was a madder project devised! Do you imagine that the result of the failure of one State to comply would be confined to that State alone? Are you so willing to hazard a civil war? Consider the refusal of Massachusetts, the attempt at compulsion by Congress. What a series of pictures does this conjure up? A powerful State procuring immediate assistance from other States, particularly from some delinquent! A complying State at war with a non-complying State! Congress marching the troops of one State into the bosom of another! This State collecting auxiliaries and forming perhaps a majority against its Federal head! And can any reasonable man be well disposed toward a government which makes war and carnage the only means of supporting itself?—a government that can exist only by the sword? And what sort of a State would it be which would suffer itself to be used as the instrument of coercing another? ... A Federal standing army, then, must enforce the requisitions or the Federal treasury will be left without supplies, and the government without support.... There is but one cure for such an evil—to enable the national laws to operate on individuals like the laws of the States. To take the old Confederation as the basis of a new system, and to trust the sword and the purse to a single assembly organized upon principles so defective, giving it the full powers of taxation and the national forces, would result in what— Despotism! To avoid the very issue which appears to be held in such abject terror, a totally different government from anything into which the old Confederation can be twisted, or fitted out with wings and gables, must be established with proper powers and proper checks and balances.

His words created a palpable uneasiness. The outburst was the more effective for following and preceding close passionless and pointed reasoning, a trenchant review of other republics ancient and modern, and an elaborate argument in favour of the representation prescribed by the new Constitution.

Hamilton was not only the most brilliant, resourceful, and unanswerable orator of his time, but he was gifted with an almost diabolical power over the emotions of men, which he did not hesitate to use. At this momentous assembly he kept them in exercise; when he chose, he made his audience weep; and the Clintonians weakened daily. Had not many years of trouble and anxiety made their emotions peculiarly susceptible, Hamilton would have attempted their agitation more sparingly; and had he been theatrical and rhetorical in his methods, he would have lost his control of them long before the end of the session. But he rarely indulged in a trope or a flight, never in bathos nor in bursts of ill-balanced appeal. Nothing ever was drier than the subjects he elucidated day after day for three weeks: for he took the Constitution to pieces bit by bit, and compelled them to listen to an analysis which, if propounded by another, would have bored them to distraction, vitally interested as they were. But he not only so illuminated the cold pages of the Constitution that while they listened they were willing to swear it was more beautiful than the Bible, but the torrent of his eloquence, never confusing, so sharp was every feature of the Constitution to his own mind, the magic of his personality, and his intense humanity in treating the driest sections of the document, so bewitched his audience that, even when he talked for six hours without pausing on the subject of taxation, perhaps the baldest topic which the human understanding is obliged to consider, there was not a sign of impatience in the ranks of the enemy.

He by no means harrowed them daily; he was far too astute for that. There were days together when he merely charmed them, and they sat with a warm unconscious smile while he demolished bit by bit one of Melancthon Smith's clever arguments, in a manner so courteous that even his victim could only shrug his shoulders, although he cursed him roundly afterward. Then, when his audience least expected an assault, he would treat them to a burst of scorn that made them hitch their chairs and glance uneasily at each other, or to a picture of future misery which reduced them to pulp.

Clinton was infuriated. Even he often leaned forward, forgetting his own selfish ambitions when Hamilton's thrilling voice poured forth a rapid appeal to the passions of his hearers; but he quickly resumed the perpendicular, and set his lips to imprison a scarlet comment. He saw that his men were weakening, and as much to the luminous expounding of the Constitution, to the logic of the orator, as to a truly satanic eloquence and charm. He held long private sessions at his mansion on the turnpike, where he was assisted by much material argument. But even Melancthon Smith, who distinguished himself in almost daily debate, acknowledged more than once that Hamilton had convinced him; and others asserted, with depression, that their minds, which they had supposed to be their own,—or Clinton's,—seemed to be in a process of remaking.

After all, for the most part, they were sincere and earnest; and although it is difficult for us of the present day to comprehend that enlightened men ever could have been so mad as to believe that the country would prosper without union, that a mere State should have been thought to be of greater importance than a Nation, or that a democratic constitution, which permits us to coddle anarchists in our midst, and the lower orders to menace the liberties of the upper, was ever an object of terror to men of bitter republican ideals, yet the historic facts confront us, and we wonder, when reading the astonishing arguments of that long and hard-fought contest, if Hamilton's constitution, had it passed the Great Convention, would not have ratified with a no more determined opposition.

Melancthon Smith was one of the brightest and most conspicuous men of his time, but his name is forgotten to-day. He was sincere; he was, in his way, patriotic; he was a clever and eloquent orator. Moreover, he was generous and manly enough to admit himself beaten, as the sequel will show. To insure greatness, must the gift of long foreknowledge be added to brilliant parts and an honest character? If this be the essential, no wonder Melancthon Smith is forgotten. We have him asserting that in a country where a portion of the people live more

246

than twelve hundred miles from the centre, one body cannot legislate for the whole. He apprehends the abolition of the State constitutions by a species of under-mining, predicts their immediate dwindling into insignificance before the comprehensive and dangerous power vested in Congress. He believes that all rich men are vicious and intemperate, and sees nothing but despotism and disaster in the Federal Constitution.

But, like most of the speakers of that day, he was trenchant and unadorned, so that his speeches are as easy reading as they must have been agreeable to hear. It is a curious fact that the best speakers of to-day resemble our forefathers in this respect of trenchant simplicity. Mediocrity for half a century has ranted on the stump, and given foreigners a false impression of American oratory. Those who indulge in what may be called the open-air metaphor, so intoxicating is our climate, may find consolation in this flight of Mr. Gilbert Livingston, who had not their excuse; for the Court-house of Poughkeepsie was hot and crowded. He is declaiming against the senatorial aristocrats lurking in the proposed Constitution. "What," he cries, "what will be their situation in a Federal town? Hallowed ground! Nothing so unclean as State laws to enter there, surrounded as they will be by an impenetrable wall of adamant and gold, the wealth of the whole country flowing into it!" "*What*? What WALL?" cried a Federal. "A wall of gold, of adamant, which will flow in from all parts of the continent." The joyous roar of our ancestors comes down to us.

Hamilton's speech, in which he as effectually disposed of every argument against the Senate as Roger Sherman had done in the Great Convention, is too long to be quoted; but it is as well to give the precise words in which he defines the vital difference between republics and democracies.

It has been observed by an honourable gentleman [he said] that a pure democracy, if it were practicable, would be the most perfect government. Experience has proved that no position in politics is more false than this. The ancient democracies, in which the people themselves deliberated, never possessed one feature of good government. Their very character was tyranny; their figure deformity. When they assembled, the field of debate presented an ungovernable mob, not only incapable of deliberation, but prepared for every enormity. In these assemblies the enemies of the people brought forward their plans of ambition systematically. They were opposed by their enemies of another party; and it became a matter of contingency, whether the people subjected themselves to be led blindly by one tyrant or another.

Again he says, in reply to Melancthon Smith:—

It is a harsh doctrine that men grow wicked as they improve and enlighten their minds. Experience has by no means justified us in the supposition that there is more virtue in one class of men than in another. Look through the rich and the poor of this community, the learned and the ignorant—Where does virtue predominate? The difference indeed consists not in the quantity, but kind of vices which are incident to various classes; and here the advantage of character belongs to the wealthy. Their vices are probably more favourable to the prosperity of the State than those of the indigent; and partake less of moral depravity.

More than once Hamilton left his seat and went up to the belfry to strain his eyes down the Albany post road or over the Dutchess turnpike, and every afternoon he rode for miles to the east or the south, hoping to meet an express messenger with a letter from Madison, or with the good tidings that New Hampshire had ratified. Madison wrote every few days, sometimes hopefully, sometimes in gloom, especially if he were not feeling well. Each letter was from ten to twelve days old, and it seemed to Hamilton sometimes that he should burst with impatience and anxiety. On the 24th of June, as he was standing in the belfry while Chancellor Livingston rained his sarcasms, he thought he saw an object moving rapidly down the white ribbon which cut the forest from the East. In five minutes he was on his horse and the Dutchess turnpike. The object proved to be the messenger from Rufus King, and the letter which Hamilton opened then and there contained the news of the adoption of the Constitution by New Hampshire.

There was now a Nation, and nine States would be governed by the new laws, whether New York, Virginia, North Carolina, and Rhode Island sulked unprotected in the out-skirts, or gracefully entered the league before dragged in or driven. It was a glittering and two-edged weapon for Hamilton, and he flashed it in the faces of the anti-Federalists until they were well-nigh blinded. Nevertheless, he did not for a moment underrate Clinton's great strength, and he longed desperately for good news from Virginia, believing that the entrance of that important State into the Union would have more influence upon the opposition than all the arts of which he was master.

VII

And through it all Hamilton was sensible that someone was working for him, and was not long attributing the influence to its proper source. Mysterious hints were dropped of political reunions in a house on a thickly wooded hill, a quarter of a mile behind the Governor's, the fortunate guests to which enchanted abode being sworn to secrecy. That it was the nightly resort of Clintonians was an open secret, but that Federalism was being intelligently interpreted, albeit with deepest subtlety, was guessed by few of the visitors themselves, and Hamilton divined rather than heard it. If converts were not actually made, they were at least undergoing a process of education which would make them the more susceptible to Hamilton's final effort. Even before he caught a glimpse of radiant hair among the maples, when riding one day along the lane at the foot of the hill, he suspected that Mrs. Croix had preceded the Convention with the deliberate intention of giving him the precious assistance of a woman with a talent for politics and a genius for men. He was touched, interested, intrigued, but he resisted the temptation to precipitate himself into the eddies of her magnetism. Croix was in England, but even before his departure, which among men was regarded as final, she had achieved a reputation as a lady of erratic impulse and imperious habit. That she was also the most brilliant and fascinating woman in America, as well as the most beautiful, were facts as publicly established. Hamilton had resisted the temptation to meet her, the temptation receiving no help from indifference on the part of the lady; he had answered more than one note of admirable deftness. But he had no intention of being drawn into an intrigue which would be public gossip in a day and ruin the happiness of his wife. To expect a man of Hamilton's order of genius to keep faith with one woman for a lifetime would be as reasonable as to look for such genius without the transcendent passions which are its furnace; but he was far from being a man who sought adventure. Under certain conditions his horizon abruptly contracted, and life was dual and isolated; but when the opportunity had passed he dismissed its memory with contrite philosophy, and was so charming to Betsey that he persuaded himself, as her, that he wished never to behold the face of another woman. Nor did he—overwhelming temptation being absent: he was the most driven man in the United States, with no time to run about after women, had such been his proclivity; and his romantic temperament, having found high satisfaction in his courtship and marriage with one of the most bewitching and notable girls in America, was smothered under a mountain of work and domestic bliss. So, although well aware that his will must perish at times in the blaze of his passions, he was iron against the temptation that held itself sufficiently aloof. To an extreme point he was master of himself. He knew that it would be no whirlwind and forgetting with this mysterious woman, who had set the town talking, and yet whose social talents were so remarkable that she managed women as deftly as she did men, and was a welcome guest in many of the most exclusive houses in New York; the men were careful to do none of their gossiping at home, and the women, although they criticised, and vowed themselves scandalized, succumbed to her royal command of homage and her air of proud invincibility. That she loved him, he had reason to know, and although he regarded it as a young woman's romantic passion for a public man focussing the attention of the country, and whom, from pressure of affairs, it was almost impossible to meet, still the passion existed, and, considering her beauty and talents, was too likely to communicate itself to the object, were he rash enough to create the opportunity. Hamilton's morals were the morals of his day,—a day when aristocrats were libertines, receiving as little censure from society as from their own consciences. His Scotch foundations had religious shoots in their grassy crevices, but religion in a great mind like Hamilton's is an emotional incident, one of several passions which act independently of each other. He avoided temptation, not because he desired to shun a torment of conscience or an accounting with his Almighty,—to Whom he was devoted,—but because he was satisfied with the woman he had married and would have sacrificed his ambitions rather than deliberately cause her unhappiness. Had she been jealous and eloquent, it is more than probable that his haughty intolerance of restraint would have driven him to assert the pleasure of his will, but she was only amused at his occasional divagations, and had no thought of looking for meanings which might terrify her. He was quite conscious of his good fortune and too well balanced to risk its loss. So Mrs. Croix might be driven to rest her hopes on a trick of chance or a *coup de théâtre*. But she was a very clever woman; and she was not unlike Hamilton in a quite phenomenal precocity, and in the torrential nature of her passions.

Having a considerable knowledge of women and some of Mrs. Croix, he inferred that sooner or later she would cease to conceal the light of her endeavour. Nevertheless, he was taken aback to receive one day a parcel, which, in the seclusion of his room, he found to contain a dainty scented handkerchief, the counterpart of the one hidden in the tree by the post road.

"Can she have put it there on purpose?" he thought. "Did she take for granted that I would pause to admire the scenery, and that I would recognize the perfume of her violets? Gad! she's deeper than I thought if that be true. The wider the berth, the better!"

He gave no sign, and, as he had expected, a note arrived in due course.
It ran:—

THE MAPLES, 8th July—4 in the morning.

DEAR SIR: I fear I am a woman of little purpose, for I intended to flit here like a swallow and as noiselessly flit again, accomplishing a political trifle for you meanwhile, of which you never should be the wiser. But alas! I am tormented by the idea that you never *will* know, that in this great crisis of your career, you think me indifferent when I understand so well your terrible anxieties, your need for stupendous exertion, and all that this convention means to this great country and to yourself; and heart and soul and brain, at the risk of my popularity,— that I love, sir,—and of a social position grudgingly acquired me, but which I demand by right of an inheritance of which the world knows less than of my elevation by Colonel Croix,—at the risk of all, I am here and working for you. Perhaps I love power. Perhaps this country with its strange unimaginable future. Perhaps I merely love politics, which you have glorified—perhaps—well, when we do meet, sir, you will avoid me no longer. Do you find me lacking in pride? Reflect how another woman would have pursued you with love-letters, persecuted you. I have exercised a restraint that has left its mark, not only out of pride for myself, but out of a deep understanding of your multitude of anxieties and interests; nor should I dare to think of you at all were I not so sure of my power to help you—now and always. Think, sir, of what such a partnership—of which the world should never be cognizant—would mean. I purpose to have a *salon*, and it shall be largely composed of your enemies. Not a secret but that shall yield to me, not a conspiracy but that you shall be able to forestall in time. I believe that I was born devoted to your interests. Heart and soul I shall be devoted to them as long as I live, and whether I am permitted to know you or not. I could ruin you if I chose. I feel that I have the power within me even for that. But God forbid! I should have gone mad first. But ask yourself, sir, if I could not be of vital assistance to your career, did we work in common. And ask yourself other things—and truthfully. E.C.C

P.S. In a meeting held here last night the two generals poured vials of their own molten iron into the veins of the rank and file, belted them together in a solid bunch, vowed that you were a dealer in the black arts and reducing them to knaves and fools. Their words sank, no doubt of that. But I uprooted them, and blew them away. For I professed to be seized with an uncontrollable fit of laughter at the nonsense of forty-seven men—*the flower of the State*—terrified of a bare third, and of a man but just in his thirties. I rapidly recounted your failures in your first Congress, dwelling on them, harping on them; and then I stood up like a Chorus, and proclaimed the victories of C's career. C, who had scowled when I went off into hysterics, almost knelt over my hand at parting; and the rest departed secure in your fancied destiny, their waxen brains ready for your clever fingers. At least you will acknowledge the receipt of this, sir? Conceive my anxiety till I know it has not fallen into the wrong hands!

A messenger brought the note directly after breakfast, and Hamilton hastily retreated with it to the privacy of his room. His horse awaited him, but he read the epistle no less than four times. Once he moved uneasily, and once he put his hand to his neck as if he felt a silken halter. He smiled, but his face flushed deeply. Her bait, her veiled threat, affected him little. But all that was unsaid pulled him like a powerful magnet. He struggled for fully twenty minutes with the temptation to ride to that paradise on the hill as fast as his horse would carry him. But although he usually got into mischief when absent from Betsey, contradictorily he was fonder of his wife when she was remote; moreover, her helplessness appealed to him, and he rejected the idea of deliberate disloyalty, even while his pulses hammered and the spirit of romance within him moved turbulently in its long sleep. He glanced out of the window. Beyond the tree-tops gleamed the river; above were the hills, with their woods and grassy intervals. It was an exquisite country, green and primeval; a moderate summer, the air warm but electric. The nights were magnificent. Hamilton dreamed for a time, then burned the letter in a fit of angry impatience.

"I have nothing better to do!" he thought. "Good God!"

An answer was imperative. He took a long ride first, however, then scrawled a few hasty lines, as if he had found just a moment in which to read her letter, but thanking her warmly for her interest and information; ending with a somewhat conscience-stricken hope for the instructive delight of her personal acquaintance when he should find the leisure to be alive once more. So rested the matter for a time.

VIII

That afternoon the very memory of Eliza Croix fled before a mounted messenger, who came tearing into town with word of Virginia's ratification, of the great excitement in the cities of Richmond, Philadelphia, Baltimore, and New York, the processions in honour of this important conquest. There were tales also of fray and bloodshed, in which the Federals had retained the field; but, on the whole, the country seemed wild with delight.

But although this news did not produce the visible effect upon the opposition for which Hamilton had hoped, the anti-Federalist leaders were as fearful of hurrying the matter to the final vote as the Constitutionalists. Clinton stood like a rock, but he feared defections at the last moment, was conscious that his dominance over the minds of the men who had come to the Convention believing implicitly in his doctrine that union was unnecessary, concurring in his abhorrence of the new Constitution, was snapping daily, as Hamilton's arguments and acute logic fermented in their clarifying brains. Many began to avoid their chief. They talked in knots by themselves. They walked the forest roads alone for hours, deep in thought. It was evident that Hamilton had liberated their understandings from one autocrat, whether he had brought them under his own despotic will or not.

There was no speaking, and little or no business for several days. A few more amendments would be suggested, then an adjournment. It was like the lull of the hurricane, when nervous people sit in the very centre of the storm, awaiting the terrors of its final assault.

Hamilton had much leisure for several days, but he was too deeply anxious to give more than a passing thought to Mrs. Croix, although he was grateful for the help he knew she was rendering him. "If we were Turks," he thought once, "she would be an invaluable member of a harem. She never could fill my domestic needs, which are capacious; most certainly I should never, at any time, have chosen her for the mother of my children; but as an intellectual and political partner, as a confidante and counsellor, she would appeal to me very keenly. I talk to Betsey, dear child, because I must talk, because I have an egotistical craving for response, but I must bore her very often, and I am not conscious of ever having received a suggestion from her—however, God knows I am grateful for her sympathy. As the children grow older I shall have less and less of her; already I appreciate the difference. She will always have the core of my soul and the fealty of my heart, but it is rather a pity that man should be given so many sides with their corresponding demands, if no one woman is to be found able to respond to all. As for this remarkable creature, I could imagine myself in a state of mad infatuation, and seeking her constantly for the delight of mental companionship besides; but the highest and best, if I have them—oh, no! Perhaps the Turks are wiser than we, after all, for their wives suffer only from jealousy, while—most men being Turks on one plan or another—the women of the more advanced races suffer from humiliation, and are wounded in their deepest sentiments. All of which goes to prove, that the longer I delay a meeting with this high-priestess the better."

In a day or two he was hard at work again fighting the last desperate battle. The oppositionists had brought forward a new form of conditional ratification, with a bill of rights prefixed, and amendments subjoined. This, it would seem, was their proudest achievement, and, in a long and adroit speech, Melancthon Smith announced it as their final decision. That was at midday. Hamilton rose at once, and in one of the most brilliant and comprehensive speeches he had yet made, demonstrated the absurdity of conditional ratification, or the power of Congress to indorse it. It was a close, legal, and constitutional argument, and with the retorts of the anti-Federalists occupied two days, during which Hamilton stood most of the time, alert, resourceful, master of every point of the vast subject, to which he gave an almost embarrassing simplicity. On the third day occurred his first signal triumph and the confounding of Clinton: Melancthon Smith stood up and admitted that Hamilton had convinced him of the impossibility of conditional ratification. Lansing immediately offered as a substitute for the motion withdrawn, another, by which the State ratify but reserve to itself the right to secede after a certain number of years, unless the amendments proposed should previously be submitted to a general convention.

Adjournment followed, and Hamilton and his leaders held a long consultation at the Livingston mansion, as a result of which he wrote that night to Madison, now in New York, asking his advice as to the sort of ratification proposed by the enemy. It was a course he by no means approved, but it seemed the less of two evils; for if, by hook or crook, the Constitution could be forced through, the good government which would ensue was bound to break up the party of the opposition. He had a trump, but he hesitated to resort to a coercion so high-handed and arbitrary. His supposed monarchical aspirations were hurled at him daily, and he must proceed with the utmost caution, lest his future usefulness be impaired at the outset.

Madison replied at once that such a proposition could not be considered, for only unconditional ratification was constitutional; but before his letter arrived Hamilton and Smith had had another hot debate, at the end of which the anti-Federalist leader declared himself wholly beaten, and announced his intention to vote for the unconditional acceptance of the Constitution.

But although there was consternation in the ranks of the anti-Federalists at this momentous defection, Clinton stood like an old lion at bay, with his other leaders behind him, his wavering ranks still coherent under his practised manipulation. For several days more the battle raged, and on the night before what promised to be the day of the final vote, Hamilton received a note from Mrs. Croix.

July 24.

DEAR SIR: The case is more desperate than you think. The weakening caused by the defection of the great Lieutenant has been counteracted in large measure by the General. His personal influence is enormous, his future like yours is at stake; he is desperate. It all rests with you. Make your great and final effort to-morrow. It is a wonderful responsibility, sir—the whole future of this country dependent upon what flows from your brain a few hours hence, but as you have won other great victories by efforts almost unprecedented, so you will win this. I am not so presumptuous as to write this to inspire you, merely to assure you of a gravity, which, after so long and energetic a contest, you might be disposed to underrate.

Hamilton was very grateful for this note, and answered it more warmly than had been his habit. His friends were deep in gloomy prognostications, for it was impossible to delay twenty-four hours longer. He had made converts, but not enough to secure a majority; and his followers did not conceive that even he could put forth an effort more convincing or more splendid than many of his previous achievements. In consequence, his susceptible nature had experienced a chill, for he was Gallic enough to compass greater things under the stimulus of encouragement and prospective success; but this unquestioning belief in him by a woman for whose mind he was beginning to experience a profound admiration, sent his quicksilver up to a point where he felt capable of all things. She had scored one point for herself. He felt that it would be unpardonable longer to accept such favours as she showered upon him unsought, and make no acknowledgment beyond a civil note: he expressed his desire to call upon her when they were both in New York once more. "But not here in Arcadia!" he thought. "I'll call formally at her lodgings and take Troup or Morris with me. Morris will doubtless abduct her, and that will be the end of it."

IX

On the following day every shop was closed in Poughkeepsie. The men, even many of the women, stood for hours in the streets, talking little, their eyes seldom wandering from the Court-house, many of them crowding close to the walls, that they might catch a ringing phrase now and again. By this time they all knew Hamilton's voice, and they confessed to a preference for his lucid precision. In front of the Court-house, under a tree, an express messenger sat beside his horse, saddled for a wild dash to New York with the tidings. The excitement seemed the more intense for the heat of the day, which half suppressed it, and all longed for the snap of the tension.

Within the upper room of the Court-house the very air vibrated. Clinton, who always grunted at intervals, and blew his nose stentoriously when fervescent, was unusually aggressive. Beyond the bar men and women stood; there was no room for chairs, nor for half that desired admittance. In the very front stood the only woman whose superb physique carried her through that trying day without smelling-salts or a friendly shoulder. She was a woman with the eyes of an angel, disdainful of men, the mouth of insatiety, the hair and skin of a Lorelei, and a patrician profile. Her figure was long, slender, and voluptuous. Every man within the bar offered her his chair, but she refused to sit while other women stood; and few were the regrets at the more ample display of her loveliness.

Hamilton and Lansing debated with a lively exchange of acrimonious wit. Smith spoke in behalf of the Constitution. Then Hamilton rose for what all felt was to be a grand final effort, and even his friends experienced an almost intolerable excitement. On the other side men trembled visibly with apprehension, not so much in fear of the result as of the assault upon their nervous systems. They hardly could have felt worse if on their way to execution, but not a man left his seat; the fascination was too strong to induce even a desire to avoid it.

Hamilton began dispassionately enough. He went over the whole Constitution rapidly, yet in so emphatic a manner as to accomplish the intelligent subservience of his audience. Then, with the unexaggerated eloquence of which he was so consummate a master, he pictured the beauty, the happiness, the wealth of the United States under the new Constitution; of the peace and prosperity of half a million homes; of the uninterrupted industry of her great cities, their ramifications to countless hamlets; of the good-will and honour of Europe; of a vast international trade; of a restored credit at home and abroad, which should lift the heavy clouds from the future of every ambitious man in the Republic; of a peace between the States which would tend to the elevation of the American character, as the bitter, petty, warring, and perpetual jealousies had incontestably lowered it; of, for the beginning of their experiment, at least eight years of harmony under George Washington.

He spoke for two hours in the glowing terms of a prophecy and an optimism so alluring, that load after load seemed to roll from the burdened minds opposite, although Clinton snorted as if about to thrust down his head and paw the earth. When Hamilton had made his hearers thoroughly drunk with dreams of an ecstatic future, he advanced upon them suddenly, and, without a word of warning transition, poured upon them so terrible a picture of the consequences of their refusal to enter the Union, that for the first few moments they were ready to leap upon him and wrench him apart. The assault was terrific, and he plunged on remorselessly. He sketched the miseries of the past eleven years, the poverty, the dangers, the dishonour, and then by the most precise and logical deduction presented a future which, by the commonest natural and social laws, must, without the protection of a high and central power, be the hideous finish. The twilight came; the evening breeze was rustling through the trees and across the sultry room. As Hamilton had calculated, the moment came when he had his grip on the very roots of the enemy's nerves. Chests were rising, handkerchiefs appearing. Women fainted. Clinton blew his nose with such terrific force that the messenger below scrambled to his feet. Hamilton waited during a breathless moment, then charged down upon them.

"Now listen, gentlemen," he said. "No one so much as I wishes that this Constitution be ratified to the honour of the State of New York; but upon this I have determined: that the enlightened and patriotic minority shall not suffer for the selfishness and obstinacy of the majority. I therefore announce to you plainly, gentlemen, that if you do not ratify this Constitution, with no further talk of impossible amendments and conditions, that Manhattan Island, Westchester, and Kings counties shall secede from the State of New York and form a State by themselves, leaving the rest of your State without a seaport, too contemptible to make treaties, with only a small and possibly rebellious militia to protect her northern boundaries from the certain rapacity of Great Britain, with the scorn and dislike of the Union, and with no hope of assistance from the Federal Government, which is assured, remember, no matter what her straits. That is all."

It was enough. He had won the day. The Constitution was ratified without further parley.

X

Hamilton reëntered New York to the blaze of bonfires, the salute of cannon, and the deafening shouts of a multitude that escorted him to his doorway. Betsey was so proud of him she hardly could speak for a day, and his library was flooded with letters of congratulation from all parts of the Union. For several days he shut himself up with his family and a few friends, for he needed the rest; and the relaxation was paradisal. He played marbles and spun tops with his oldest boys, and dressed and undressed Angelica's doll as often as his imperious daughter commanded. Troup and Fish, now the dignified Adjutant-General of State, with his bang grown long and his hair brushed back, spent hours with him in the heavy shades of the garden, or tormenting a monkey on the other side of the fence. Madison came at once to wrangle with him over the temporary seat of government, and demanded the spare bedroom, protesting he had too much to say to waste time travelling back and forth. He was a welcome guest; and he, too, sat on the floor and dressed Angelica's doll.

The city was *en fête*, and little business was transacted except at the public houses. Bands of citizens awoke Hamilton from his sleep, shouting for "Alexander the Great." Anti-Federalists got so drunk that they embraced the Federalists, and sang on Hamilton's doorstep. The hero retreated to the back room on the top floor. The climax came on the 5th of August, in the great procession, with which, after the fashion of other triumphant cities, New York was to demonstrate in honour of the victory of the Constitution.

But, unlike its predecessors, this procession was as much in honour of one man as of the triumph of a great principle. To have persuaded New York, at that time, that Hamilton had not written the Constitution, and secured its ratification in the eleven States of the Union by his unaided efforts, would have been a dissipation of energy in August which even Clinton would not have attempted. To them Hamilton was the Constitution, Federalism, the genius of the new United States. And he was their very own. "Virginia has her Madison," they reiterated,

"Massachusetts her Adamses—and may she keep them and be damned; other States may think they have produced a giant, and those that do not can fall back on Washington; but Hamilton is ours, we adore him, we are so proud of him we are like to burst, and we can never express our gratitude, try as we may; so we'll show him an honour that no other State has thought of showing to any particular man."

And of the sixth of New York's thirty thousand inhabitants that turned out on that blazing August day and marched for hours, that all the eager city might see, at least two-thirds bore a banner emblazoned with Hamilton's portrait or name, held on high. The procession was accompanied by a military escort; and every profession, every trade, was represented. A large proportion of the men who marched were gentlemen. Nicolas Fish was on the staff of the grand marshal, with six of his friends. Robert Troup and two other prominent lawyers bore, on a cushion, the new Constitution, magnificently engrossed. Nicolas Cruger, Hamilton's old employer, again a resident of New York, led the farmers, driving a plough drawn by three yoke of oxen. Baron Polnitz displayed the wonders of the newly perfected threshing-machine. John Watts, a man who had grown gray in the highest offices of New York, before and since the Revolution, guided a harrow, drawn by horses and oxen. The president, regents, professors, and students of Columbia College, all in academic dress, were followed by the Chamber of Commerce and the members of the bar. The many societies, led by the Cincinnati, followed, each bearing an appropriate banner.

And in the very centre of that pageant, gorgeous in colour and costume, from the green of the foresters to the white of the florists, was the great Federal ship, with HAMILTON, HAMILTON, HAMILTON, HAMILTON, emblazoned on every side of it. In the memory of the youngest present there was to be but one other procession in New York so imposing, and that, too, was in honour of Hamilton.

He stood on a balcony in the Broadway, with his family, Madison, Baron Steuben, and the Schuylers, bowing constantly to the salutes and cheers. Nicolas Cruger looked up and grinned. Fish winked decorously, and Troup attempted a salaam, and nearly dropped the Constitution. But Hamilton's mind served him a trick for a moment; the vivid procession, with his face and name fluttering above five thousand heads, the compact mass of spectators, proud and humble, that crowded the pavements and waved their handkerchiefs toward him, the patriotically decorated windows filled with eager, often beautiful, faces, disappeared, and he stood in front of Cruger's store on Bay Street, with his hands in his linen pockets, gazing out over a blinding glare of water, passionately wishing for the war-ship which never came, to deliver him from his Island prison and carry him to the gates of the real world beyond. He had been an ambitious boy, but nothing in his imaginings had projected him to the dizzy eminence on which he stood to-day. He was recalled by the salute of the Federal ship's thirteen guns to the president of the Congress and its members, who stood on the fort in the Battery.

After all, perhaps it was the proudest and the happiest day of his career, for the depths in his nature still slumbered, the triumph was without alloy; and he knew that there were other heights to scale, and that he should scale them. It was the magnificent and spontaneous tribute of an intelligent people to an enlightened patriotism, to years of severe and unselfish thought; and hardly an enemy grudged him his deserts. The wild feeling of exultant triumph which surged behind his smiling face receded before the rising swell of the profoundest gratitude he had ever known.

The day finished with a great banquet at Mr. Bayard's country-seat, near Grand Street, where tables were spread for six thousand persons, in a pavilion surmounted by an image of Fame, and decorated with the colours of the nations that had formed treaties with the United States. Later, there was a grand display of fireworks.

XI

On the following day Hamilton went to Albany to march at the head of a Federal procession with General Schuyler, then returned to "Hamiltonopolis" and such legal work as he was permitted to accomplish; for not only were leaders consulting him on every possible question from the coming elections to the proper seat for the new government, and his duties as a member of Congress pressing, but Edward Stevens, now established as a doctor in Philadelphia, paid him a visit of a week, and they talked the night through of St. Croix and old times. One of the pleasantest results of these years of supremacy was the unqualified delight of his Island friends. Hugh Knox was so proud of

261

him, and of himself and the debt which Hamilton acknowledged, that he wrote explosive reams describing the breathless interest of St. Croix in his career, and of the distinguished gatherings at the Governor's when he arrived with one of their lost citizen's infrequent epistles. Mrs. Mitchell, poor soul, wrote pathetically that she would no longer regret his loss could she love him less. Hamilton wrote to her as often as he could find the time, and Betsey selected a present for her several times a year. Gratitude is the privilege of a great soul, and Hamilton had a full measure of it. Even his father and brother wrote occasionally, respectfully, if with no great warmth; and if their congratulations were usually accompanied by the experimental sigh of poverty, Hamilton was glad to respond, for at this period he was making a good deal of money.

His promised bow to Mrs. Croix he deferred from day to day, pleading to himself the pressure of work, which was submerging; but while he reproached himself for ingratitude, he knew that he dreaded the meeting: the old spirit of adventure within him, long quiescent, tapped alluringly on the doors of his prudence. That she did not write again, even to congratulate him as other friends had done, but added to his discomfort, for he knew that her pride was now in arms, and that she must be deeply wounded. He heard of her constantly, and at the procession in his honour he had seen her, leaning on the arm of General Knox, a dazzling, but angelic vision in blue and white, at which even the bakers, wig-makers, foresters, tanners, and printers had turned to stare. One of the latter had leaped down from the moving platform on which he was printing a poem of occasion by William Duer, and begged her on his knee to deign to receive a copy. She held weekly receptions, which were attended by two-thirds of the leading men in town, and Hamilton's intimate friends discoursed of her constantly. Croix was supposed to have been seized with a passion for travelling in savage jungles, and it was the general belief that his death would be announced as soon as the lady should find it convenient to go into mourning. It was plain to the charitable that he had left her with plenty of money, for she dressed like the princess she looked, and her entertainments lacked no material attraction. The gossip was more furious than ever, but the most assiduous scandal-monger could connect no one man with her name, nor trace her income to other than its reputed source. More than once Hamilton had passed her coach, and she had bowed gravely, with neither challenge nor reproach in her sweet haughty eyes. After these quick passings Hamilton usually gave her a few moments of intense thought. He marvelled at her curious intimate knowledge of him, not only of the less known episodes of his career, but of more than one of his mental processes. It is true, she might have led Troup or Fish into gossip and analysis, but her sympathy counted heavily. She drew him by many strings, and sometimes the response thrilled him unbearably. He felt like a man who stood outside the gates of Paradise, bolting them fast. Still, he could quite forget her in his work; and it is probable that but for chance he never would have met her, that one of the greatest disasters in history would have been averted.

Betsey, who had not been well for some time, went to the northern forests of her old home to strive for "spring" and colour. She took the children with her, and Hamilton, who hated to live alone, filled his deserted rooms with Troup, Fish, and Baron Steuben, whose claims he had been pressing upon Congress for years, practically supporting him meanwhile. The old soldier felt keenly the ingratitude of the country he had served, but in time it made him ample compensation; meanwhile the devotion of a few friends, and the lionizing of society, helped him to bear his lot with considerable fortitude. He spent hours in the nursery of the little Hamiltons, and was frequently seen in the Broadway with one in his arms and the other three attached to his person.

All the talk was of Washington and the first administration, Hamilton having carried his point in Congress that New York should be the temporary seat of government; there was jealousy and wrangling over this, as over most other matters involving state pride, but Hamilton believed that should the prize fall to Philadelphia, she would not relinquish it as lightly as New York, which geographically was the more unfit for a permanent gathering, and that the inconvenience to which most of the members, in those days of difficult travel over a vast area, would be subjected, would force them the sooner to agree upon a central and commonly agreeable locality,—one, moreover, which would not meet with the violent opposition of New York. Madison, who had been in favour of Philadelphia, finally acknowledged Hamilton's sagacity and gave him his influence and vote.

That point settled, all eyes were turned to Mount Vernon. The masses took for granted that Washington would respond to every call of duty the public chose to make, and it was inconceivable that anyone else should fill the first term of that great executive experiment. The universal confidence in Washington and belief that he was to guide the Constitution over the more critical of its shoals, had operated more than any other factor in the ratification of that adventurous instrument. It was a point upon which Hamilton had harped continually. That a whole country should turn, as a matter of course, to a man whom they revered for his virtues rather than for any brilliant parts he may have effectually hidden within his cold and silent exterior, their harmonious choice unbroken by an argument against the safety and dignity of the country in the hands of such a man, certainly is a manifest of the same elevation of tone that we infer from the great popularity of the writings of Hamilton and the deference to such men as Jay and Philip Schuyler. But although they had all the faults of human nature, our forefathers, and were often selfish and jealous to a degree that imperilled the country, at least they had the excuse, not only of being mere mortals, but of living in an era of such changes, uncertainty, and doubt, that public and private interests seemed hopelessly tangled. They were not debased by political corruption until Jefferson took them in hand, and sowed the bountiful crop which has fattened so vast and so curious a variation upon the original American.

The Federal leaders by no means shared the confidence of the people in Washington's response to their call, and they were deeply uneasy. They knew that he had been bombarded with letters for a year, urging upon him the acceptance of the great office which would surely be offered him, and that he had replied cautiously to each that he could not share their opinion of his indispensability, that he had earned the repose he loved after a lifetime spent in the service of his country, and had no desire to return to public life. Hamilton, at least, knew the motive that lay behind his evasion; without ambition, he was very jealous of his fame. That fame now was not only one of the most resplendent in history, but as unassailable as it was isolated. He feared the untried field in which he might fail.

One evening, late in September, as Hamilton and his temporary household were entering the dining room, Gouverneur Morris drove down Wall Street in his usual reckless fashion, scattering dogs and children, and pulling his nervous sweating horses almost to their haunches, as he reached Hamilton's door. As he entered the house, however, and received the enthusiastic welcome to which he was accustomed, his bearing was as unruffled as if he had walked down from Morrisania reading a breviary.

"I grow desperately lonely and bored out on my ancestral domain, and long for the glare and glitter, the intrigues and women, of Europe— our educated ones are so virtuous, and the others write such shockingly ungrammatical notes," he announced, as he took his seat at the board. "Educated virtue is beneficial for the country, but we will all admit that politics are our only excitement, and my blood dances when I think of Europe. However, I did not come tearing through the woods on a hot night to lament the virtue of the American woman. I've written to Washington, and he won't listen to me. We all know how many others have written, including Lafayette, I hear. And we all know what the consequences will be if—say John or Sam Adams, Hancock, or Clinton should be our first president. I long for Paris, but I cannot leave the country while she is threatened with as grave a peril as any that has beset her. Would that he had a grain of ambition—of anything that a performer upon the various chords of human nature could impress. I suppose if he were not so desperately perfect, we should not be in the quandary we are, but he would be far easier to manage. As I awoke from my siesta just two hours ago, my brain was illuminated by the idea that one man alone could persuade him; and that was Alexander Hamilton. He likes us, but he loves you. If he has a weak spot, it has yearned over you since you were our infant prodigy in uniform, with your curls in your eyes. You must take him in hand."

"I have mentioned it to him, when writing of other things."

"He is only too glad of the excuse to evade a mere mention. You must write to him as peremptorily as only you dare to write to that majestic presence. Don't mince it. Don't be too respectful—I was, because he is the one being I am afraid of. So are all the others. Besides, you have the most powerful and pointed pen in this country. We have spoiled you until you are afraid of no one—if you ever were. And you know him as no one else does; you will approach him from precisely the right sides. Your duty is clear, and the danger is appalling. Besides, I want to go to Europe. Promise me that you will write to-night."

"Very well," said Hamilton, laughing. "I promise." And, in truth, his mind had opened at once to the certainty that the time was come for him to make the final effort to insure Washington's acceptance. He had felt, during the last weeks, as if burrowing in the very heart of a mountain of work; but his skin chilled as he contemplated the opening of the new government without Washington in the presidential Chair.

Two hours after dinner Morris escorted him to the library and shut him in, then went, with his other friends, to Fraunces' tavern, and the house was quiet. Hamilton's thoughts arranged themselves rapidly, and before midnight he had finished his letter. Fortunately it has been preserved, for it is of as vital an interest as anything he ever wrote, not only because it was the determining factor in Washington's acceptance of an office toward which he looked with reluctance and dread, but because of its consummate sagacity and of its peremptory tone, which no man but Hamilton would have dared to assume to Washington.

It ran:—

NEW YORK, September, 1788.

... I should be deeply pained, my dear sir, if your scruples in regard to a certain station should be matured into a resolution to decline it; though I am neither surprised at their existence, nor can I but agree in opinion, that the caution you observe in deferring an ultimate determination, is prudent. I have, however, reflected maturely on the subject, and have come to a conclusion (in which I feel no hesitation), that every public and personal consideration will demand from you an acquiescence in what will *certainly* be the unanimous wish of your country. The absolute retreat which you meditated at the close of the late war was natural, and proper. Had the Government produced by the Revolution gone on in a *tolerable* train, it would have been most advisable to have persisted in that retreat. But I am clearly of opinion that the crisis which brought you again into public view, left you no alternative but to comply; and I am equally clear in the opinion, that you are by that act *pledged* to take a part in the execution of the Government. I am not less convinced, that the impression of this necessity of your filling the station in question is so universal, that you run no risk of any uncandid imputation by submitting to it. But even if this were not the case, a regard to your own reputation, as well as to the public good, calls upon you in the strongest manner, to run that risk.

266

It cannot be considered as a compliment to say, that on your acceptance of the office of President, the success of the new Government, in its commencement, may materially depend. Your agency and influence will be not less important in preserving it from the future attacks of its enemies, than they have been in recommending it, in the first instance, to the adoption of the people. Independent of all considerations drawn from this source, the point of light in which you stand at home and abroad will make an infinite difference in the respectability with which the Government will begin its operations, in the alternative of your being or not being at the head of it. I forbear to urge considerations which might have a more personal application. What I have said will suffice for the inferences I mean to draw.

First. In a matter so essential to the well being of society, as the prosperity of a newly instituted government, a citizen, of so much consequence as yourself to its success, has no option but to lend his services if called for. Permit me to say it would be inglorious, in such a situation, not to hazard the glory, however great, which he might have previously acquired.

Secondly. Your signature to the proposed system pledges your judgement for its being such an one as, upon the whole, was worthy of the public approbation. If it should miscarry (as men commonly decide from success, or the want of it), the blame will, in all probability, be laid on the system itself; and the framers of it will have to encounter the disrepute of having brought about a revolution in government, without substituting anything that was worthy of the effort. They pulled down one Utopia, it will be said, to build up another. This view of the subject, if I mistake not, my dear sir, will suggest to your mind greater hazard to that fame, which must be and ought to be dear to you, in refusing your future aid to the system, than in affording it. I will only add, that in my estimate of the matter, that aid is indispensable.

I have taken the liberty to express these sentiments, and to lay before you my view of the subject. I doubt not the considerations mentioned have fully occurred to you, and I trust they will finally produce in your mind the same result which exists in mine. I flatter myself the frankness with which I have delivered myself will not be displeasing to you. It has been prompted by motives which you could not disapprove. I remain, my dear sir,

With the sincerest respect and regard,
Your obedient and humble servant,

A. HAMILTON.

XII

Hamilton folded and sealed the letter, then determined to take it to the post-office himself. The night was hot and his head was throbbing: he had worked, dined, wined, talked, and written, since eight in the morning, with no interval for fresh air or exercise. He was not tired, but very nervous, and after he had disposed of his letter, he set off for a stroll along the river front, and walked for two miles up the quiet road on the east side, listening to the lap of the water, and pausing to watch the superb effect of the moonlight on the bright ripples and on the wooded heights of Long Island. The little village of Brooklyn twinkled here and there for a time, then lay like a sombre shadow in the silences of her forest. As he returned, there was not a light anywhere, except now and again at a masthead, for it was very late. The clock in Trinity steeple struck one as he reëntered the town. He moved through the narrow dark and crooked streets with a lagging step, although he had walked briskly for the past hour. There seemed to be no sleep in him, and the idea of his quiet room was an irritation.

"That woman is on my nerves," he thought. "I've written a letter to-night that may bridge this country over another crisis, and I should be sleeping the sleep of the self-sufficient statesman, or at least excogitating upon weighty matters; and for the last hour I've given no thought to anything but an unknown woman, who has electrified my imagination and my passions. Is there, perhaps, more safety in meeting her and laying the ghost? Imagination plays us such damnable tricks. She may have a raucous voice, or too sharp a wit; or she may love another by this. I'll ask Nick to take me there to-morrow."

The drawing-room windows of the dwellings were but a few feet above the ground, and many of them abutted on the pavement. The narrow street was almost dark, in spite of the moonlight, but Hamilton saw that some one sat at a lower window but a few feet ahead of him. It was a woman, for her arm hung over the sill There was nothing to arrest his attention in the circumstance, beyond the vague beauty of the arm and hand, for on these dog nights many sat at their windows until the chill of early morning; but he suddenly remembered that he was in Pearl Street. For a moment he meditated retreat; with no enthusiasm, however. He shrugged his shoulders and walked on, but his breath was short. As he approached he could see that she was watching him, although her face was almost invisible. He paused beneath the window, half in defiance, his eyes striving to pierce the heavy shade of the room. The hand closed abruptly about the lower part of his face. It trembled, but there was as much determination as warmth in the finger tips; and he seemed to have been transported suddenly to a field of violets.

XIII

"Nick," said Hamilton, a few evenings later as they were peeling walnuts, "This is the night on which Mrs. Croix receives, is it not? Do you attend? I will go with you. The lady has kindly been at pains to let me know that I shall not be unwelcome."

Troup pushed back his plate abruptly, and Baron Steuben burst into a panegyric. Fish replied that he had not intended to go, but should change his mind for the sake of the sensation he must create with such a lion in tow. He left the table shortly after, to dress, followed by Steuben, who announced his intention to make one of the party. The host and Troup were left alone.

"What is the matter?" asked Hamilton, smiling. "I see you disapprove of something. Surely you have not lost your heart—"

"Nonsense," exclaimed Troup, roughly, "but I have always hoped you would never meet her."

"*Have* you?"

"If you want to know the truth she has pumped me dry about you. She did it so adroitly that it was some time before I discovered what she was up to. At first I wondered if she were a spy, and I changed my first mind to avoid her, determined to get to the bottom of her motives. I soon made up my mind that she was in love with you, and then I began to tremble, for she is not only a very witch of fascination, but she has about forty times more power of loving, or whatever she chooses to call it, than most women, and every mental attraction and fastidious refinement, besides. There is not a good woman in the country that could hold her own against her. I have no wish to slander her, and have never discussed her before; but my instincts are strong enough to teach me that a woman whose whole exterior being is a promise, will be driven by the springs of that promise to redeem her pledges. And the talk of you banishes all that regal calm from her face and lets the rest loose. I suppose I am a fool to tell you this, but I've been haunted by the idea from the first that if you know this woman, disaster will come of it. I do not mean any old woman's presentiment, but from what I know of her nature and yours. You do astonishingly few erratic things for a genius, but in certain conditions you are unbridled, and my only hope has been that the lightning in you would strike at random without doing much harm—to you, at all events. But this volcano has a brain in it, and great force of character. She will either consume you, ruining your career, or if you attempt to leave her she will find some way to ruin you still. God knows I'm no moralist, but I am jealous for your genius and your future. This has been a long speech. I hope you'll forgive it."

Hamilton had turned pale, and he hacked at the mahogany with the point of his knife. He made no attempt to laugh off Troup's attack, Troup watched him until he turned pale himself. "You have met her," he said abruptly.

Hamilton rose and pushed back his chair. "I promise you one thing," he said: "that if I happen to lose my nethermost to Mrs. Croix, the world shall never be the wiser. That I explicitly promise you. I dislike extremely the position in which I put the lady by these words, but you will admit that they mean nothing, that I am but striving to allay your fears—which I know to be genuine. She will probably flout me. I shall probably detest her conversation. But should the contrary happen, should she be what you suspect, and should a part of my nature which has never been completely accommodated, annihilate a resistance of many months, at least you have my assurance that worse shall not happen."

Troup groaned. "You have so many sides to satisfy! Would that you could have your truly phenomenal versatility of mind with a sweet simplicity of character. But we are not in the millennium. And as you have not the customary failings of genius,—ingratitude, morbidity, a disposition to prevaricate, a lack of common-sense, selfishness, and irresponsibility,—it is easy for us to forgive you the one inevitable weakness. Come to me if you get into trouble. She'd have no mercy at my hands. I'd wring her neck."

Many people were at their country-seats, but politics kept a number of men in town, and for this political and wholly masculine *salon* of Mrs. Croix, Gouverneur Morris drove down from Morrisania, Robert Livingston from Clermont; Governor Clinton had made it convenient to remain a day longer in New York. Dr. Franklin had been a guest of my lady for the past two days. They were all, with the exception of Clinton, in the drawing-room, when Hamilton, Steuben and Fish arrived; and several of the Crugers, Colonel Duer, General Knox, Mayor Duane, Melancthon Smith, Mr. Watts, Yates, Lansing, and a half-dozen lesser lights. Mrs. Croix sat in the middle of the room, and her chair being somewhat higher and more elaborate than its companions, suggested a throne: Madame de Staël set the fashion in many affectations which were not long travelling to America. In the house, Mrs. Croix discarded the hoopskirt, and the classic folds of her soft muslin gown revealed a figure as superb in contour as it was majestic in carriage. Her glittering hair was in a tower, and the long oval of her face gave to this monstrous head-dress an air of proportion. Her brows and lashes were black, her eyes the deepest violet that ever man had sung, childlike when widely opened, but infinitely various with a drooping lash. The nose was small and aquiline, fine and firm, the nostril thin and haughty. The curves of her mouth included a short upper lip, a full under one, and a bend at the corners. There was a deep cleft in the chin. Technically her hair was auburn; when the sun flooded it her admirers vowed they counted twenty shades of red, yellow, sorrel, russet, and gold. Even under the soft rays of the candles it was crisp with light and colour. The dazzling skin and soft contours hid a jaw that denoted both strength and appetite, and her sweet gracious manner gave little indication of her imperious will, independent mind, and arrogant intellect. She looked to be twenty-eight, but was reputed to have been born in 1769. For women so endowed years have little meaning. They are born with what millions of their sex never acquire, a few with the aid of time and experience only. Nature had fondly and diabolically equipped her to conquer the world, to be one of its successes; and so she was to the last of her ninety-six years. Her subsequent career was as brilliant in Europe as it had been, and was to be again, in America. In Paris, Lafayette was her sponsor, and she counted princes, cardinals, and nobles among her conquests, and died in the abundance of wealth and honours. If her sins found her out, they surprised her in secret only. To the world she gave no sign, and carried an unbroken spirit and an unbowed head into a vault which looks as if not even the trump of Judgement Day could force its marble doors to open and its secrets to come forth. But those doors closed behind her seventy-seven years later, when the greatest of her victims had been dust half a century, and many others were long since forgotten. To-night, in her glorious triumphant womanhood she had no thought of vaults in the cold hillside of Trinity, and when Hamilton entered the room, she rose and courtesied deeply. Then, as he bent over her hand: "At last! Is it you?" she exclaimed softly. "Has this honour indeed come to my house? I have waited a lifetime, sir, and I took pains to assure you long since of a welcome."

"Do not remind me of those wretched wasted months," replied Hamilton, gallantly, and Dr. Franklin nodded with approval. "Be sure, madam, that I shall risk no reproaches in the future."

She passed him on in the fashion of royalty, and was equally gracious to Steuben and Fish, although she did not courtesy. The company, which had been scattered in groups, the deepest about the throne of the hostess, immediately converged and made Hamilton their common centre. Would Washington accept? Surely he must know. Would he choose to be addressed as "His Serene Highness," "His High Mightiness," or merely as "Excellency"? Would so haughty an aristocrat lend himself agreeably to the common forms of Republicanism, even if he had refused a crown, and had been the most jealous guardian of the liberties of the American people? An aristocrat is an aristocrat, and doubtless he would observe all the rigid formalities of court life. Most of those present heartily hoped that he would. They, too, were jealous of their liberties, but had no yearning toward a republican simplicity, which, to their minds, savoured of plebianism. Socially they still were royalists, whatever their politics, and many a coat of arms was yet in its frame.

"Of course Washington will be our first President," replied Hamilton, who was prepared to go to Mount Vernon, if necessary. "I have had no communication from him on the subject, but he would obey the command of public duty if he were on his death-bed. His reluctance is natural, for his life has been a hard one in the field, and his tastes are those of a country gentleman,—tastes which he has recently been permitted to indulge to the full for the first time. Moreover, he is so modest that it is difficult to make him understand that no other man is to be thought of for these first difficult years. When he does, there is no more question of his acceptance than there was of his assuming the command of the army. As for titles they come about as a matter of course, and it is quite positive that Washington, although a Republican, will never become a Democrat. He is a grandee and will continue to live like one, and the man who presumes to take a liberty with him is lost."

Mrs. Croix, quite forgotten, leaned back in her chair, a smile succeeding the puzzled annoyance of her eyes. In this house her words were the jewels for which this courtly company scrambled, but Hamilton had not been met abroad for weeks, and from him there was always something to learn; whereas from even the most brilliant of women—she shrugged her shoulders; and her eyes, as they dwelt on Hamilton, gradually filled with an expression of idolatrous pride. The new delight of self-effacement was one of the keenest she had known.

The bombardment continued. The Vice-President? Whom should Hamilton support? Adams? Hancock? Was it true that there was a schism in the Federal party that might give the anti-Federalists, with Clinton at their head, a chance for the Vice-Presidency at least? Who would be Washington's advisers besides himself? Would the President have a cabinet? Would Congress sanction it? Whom should he want as confreres, and whom in the Senate to further his plans? Whom did he favour as Senators and Representatives from New York? Could this rage for amendments be stopped? What was to be the fate of the circular letter? Was all danger of a new Constitutional Convention well over? What about the future site of the Capital—would the North get it, or the South?

All these, the raging questions of the day, it took Hamilton the greater part of the evening to answer or parry, but he deftly altered his orbit until he stood beside Mrs. Croix, the company before her shrine. He had encountered her eyes, but although he knew the supreme surrender of women in the first stages of passion, he also understood the vanities and weaknesses of human nature too well not to apprehend a chill of the affections under too prolonged a mortification.

Clinton entered at midnight; and after almost bending his gouty knee to the hostess, whom he had never seen in such softened yet

273

dazzling beauty, he measured Hamilton for a moment, then laughed and held out his hand.

"You are a wonderful fighter," he said, "and you beat me squarely. We'll meet in open combat again and again, no doubt of it, and I hope we will, for you rouse all my mettle; but I like you, sir, I like you. I can't help it."

Hamilton, at that time of his life the most placable of men, had shaken his hand heartily. "And I so esteem and admire you, sir," he answered warmly, "that I would I could convert you, for your doctrines are bound to plunge this country into civil war sooner or later. The Constitution has given the States just four times more power than is safe in their hands; but if we could establish a tradition at this early stage of the country's history that it was the duty of the States always to consider the Union first and themselves as grateful assistants to a hard-working and paternal central power, we might do much to counteract an evil which, if coddled, is bound to result in a trial of strength."

"That is the first time I ever heard you croak, except in a public speech where you had a point to gain," said Livingston. "Do you mean that?"

"What of it?" asked Clinton. "Under Mr. Hamilton's constitution— for if it be not quite so monarchical as the one he wanted, it has been saddled upon the United States through his agency more than through any other influence or group of influences—I say, that under Mr. Hamilton's constitution all individualism is lost. We are to be but the component parts of a great machine which will grind us as it lists. Had we remained thirteen independent and sovereign States, with a tribunal for what little common legislation might be necessary, then we might have built up a great and a unique nation; but under what is little better than an absolute monarchy all but a small group of men are bound to live and die nonentities."

"But think of the excited competition for a place in that group," said Hamilton, laughing. The disappointed Governor's propositions were not worthy of serious argument.

"I do not think it is as bad as that, your Excellency," said Dr. Franklin, mildly. "I should have favoured a somewhat loose Confederation, as you know, but the changes and the development of this country will be so great that there will be plenty of room for individualism; indeed, it could not be suppressed. And after a careful study of this instrument that you are to live under—my own time is so short that my only rôle now is that of the prophet—I fail to see anything of essential danger to the liberties of the American people. I may say that the essays of "The Federalist" would have reassured me on this point, had I still doubted. I read them again the other week. The proof is there, I think, that the Constitution, if rigidly interpreted and lived up to, must prove a beneficent if stern parent to those who dwell under it."

Clinton shrugged his shoulders. "I would I could share your optimism," he said. "What a picture have we! The most venerable statesman in the country finding some hope for individual liberty in this Constitution; the youngest, an optimist by nature and habit, sanguine by youth and temperament, trembling for the powers it may confer upon a people too democratically inclined. This is true, sir—is it not?"

"Yes," said Hamilton. "Democracy is a poison, just as Republicanism is the ideal of all self-respecting men. I would do all I could to vitalize the one and nullify the other. The spirit of democracy exists already, no doubt of it. If we could suppress it in time, we should also suppress the aspirations of encouraged plebianism,—a dangerous factor in any republic. It means the mixing of ignoble blood with good, a gradual lowering of ideals until a general level of sordidness, individualism in its most selfish and self-seeking form, and political corruption, are the inevitable results. You, your Excellency, are an autocrat. It is odd that your principles should coincide so closely with the despotism of democracy."

"Oh, I can't argue with you!" exclaimed Clinton, impatiently. "No one can. That is the reason you beat us when we clearly were in the right. What says Madam? She is our oracle." "If she would but bring him under her foot!" he said to Yates. "She is heart and soul with us. I augur well that he is here at last."

"It is long since our fairy queen has spoken," Franklin was saying; gallant to all women, he was prostrate before this one. "Her genius directs her to the most hidden kernels."

"What do you wish?" she asked lightly. "A prophecy? I am no Cassandra. Unlike Dr. Franklin, I am too selfish to care what may happen when I am dead. At this date we are assured of two elements in government: unselfish patriotism and common-sense. There never has been a nobler nor a more keenly intelligent group of men in public life than General Washington will be able to command as assistants in forming a government. And should our Governor lead his own party to victory," she added, turning to Clinton with so brilliant a smile that it dissipated a gathering scowl, "it would be quite the same. The determined struggle of the weaker party for the rights which only supremacy can insure them is often misconstrued as selfishness; and power leads their higher qualities as well as their caution and conservatism to victory. I am a philosopher. I disapproved the Constitution, and loved the idea of thirteen little sovereignties; but I bow to the Inevitable and am prepared to love the Constitution. The country has too much to accomplish, too much to recover from, to waste time arguing what might have been; it is sure to settle down into as complacent a philosophy as my own, and adjust itself to its new and roomy crinoline."

"Crinoline is the word," growled Clinton, who accepted her choice of words as a subtle thrust at Hamilton. "It is rigid. Wherever you move it will move with you and bound your horizon."

"Oh, well, you know," said Hamilton, who was tired of the conversation, "like a crinoline it can always be broken."

XIV

Washington was President of the United States. He had come over grandly from the Jersey shore in a magnificent barge manned by twelve oarsmen in white uniform, escorted by other barges but a shade less imposing. A week later he had taken the oath of office on the new Broad Street gallery of Federal Hall, amidst the breathless silence of thousands, surrounded by the dignitaries of state and three personal friends, Hamilton, Steuben, and Knox. The anti-Federalists were crushed, no longer of dignity as a party, although with ample resources for obstruction and annoyance. The country, after an interval of rejoicing, had settled down to another period of hope and anxiety.

And Hamilton had incurred the dislike of Adams and the hostility of the Livingstons. He had thought it best to scatter the votes for the Vice-President, lest there be the slightest risk of Washington's defeat; and Adams who thought quite as much of himself as he did of George Washington, and had expected to be elected with little less than unanimity, instead of by a bare thirty-four votes, never forgave Hamilton the humiliation. "I have seen the utmost delicacy used toward others," he wrote to a friend, "but my feelings have never been regarded." He knew that Hamilton believed him to have been in sympathy with the Conway Cabal,—a suspicion of which he never cleared himself,—and attributed to the Federal leader the motive of wishing to belittle his political significance, lest he should endeavour to use his power as President of the Senate to hamper and annoy the Administration. Perhaps he was right. Far be it from anyone to attempt a journey through the utmost recesses of Hamilton's mind. He was frank by nature and habit, but he had resolved that the United States government should succeed, and had no mind to put weapons into the hands of Washington's rivals. He believed in Adams's general integrity, patriotism, and federalism, however, and brought him to power in his own fashion. He achieved his objects with little or no thought of personal consequences; and although this has been characterized as one of the great political mistakes of his career, it must be remembered that it was a time for nervousness and exaggerated fears. Washington had enemies; no other man was believed, by the men who did the thinking for the country, to be able to hold the United States together until they were past their shoals, and the method of election was precarious: each elector casting two votes without specification, the higher office falling to the candidate who received the larger number of votes.

The Livingstons had desired a seat in the Senate of the new Congress for one of their powerful family, and Hamilton had given the prize to Rufus King. No gift could have been more justly bestowed; but the Livingstons felt themselves flouted, their great services to the country unrewarded. Their open hostility roused all the haughty arrogance of Hamilton's nature, and he made no effort to placate them. When the great office of Chief Justice of the United States was given to John Jay, instead of to Robert Livingston, they attributed the discrimination to Hamilton's influence over Washington; and the time came when this strong and hostile faction lent themselves to the scheming of one of the subtlest politicians that has ever lived.

The contest for the prizes of the two Houses had been hot and bitter, and Hamilton had never been more active. As a result, the Federalists controlled the Senate, and they had elected four of the six

Representatives. Philip Schuyler had drawn the short term in the Senate, and the antagonism of the Livingstons to Hamilton enabled Burr to displace him two years later. The signal mistakes of Hamilton's political career were in his party management. One of the greatest leaders in history, cool and wise, and of a consummate judgement in all matters of pure statesmanship, he was too hot-headed and impetuous, too obstinate when his righting blood was up, for the skilful manipulation of politics. But so long as the Federal party endured, no other leader was contemplated: his integrity was spotless, his motives unquestioned, his patriotism and stupendous abilities the glory of his party; by sheer force of genius he carried everything before him, whether his methods were approved by the more conservative Federalists or not.

Madison, who mildly desired an office, possibly in the Cabinet, he despatched South to get himself elected to Congress, for he must have powerful friends in that body to support the great measures he had in contemplation; and that not unambitious statesman, after a hot fight with Patrick Henry, was obliged to content himself with a seat in the House. Before he went to Virginia he and Hamilton had talked for long and pleasant hours over the Federal leader's future schemes. In all things he was in accord with his Captain, and had warmly promised his support.

It was some weeks before Hamilton had a private interview with Washington, although he had dined at his house, entertained him, and been present at several informal consultations on such minor questions as the etiquette of the Administration. But delicacy held him from embarrassing Washington in a familiar interview until he had been invited formally to a position in the contemplated cabinet. He knew that Washington wished him to be Secretary of the Treasury, but he also knew that that most cautious and conscientious of men would not trust to his own judgement in so grave a matter, nor take any step without weeks of anxious thought. The more deeply were Washington's affections or desires engaged, the more cautious would he be. He was not a man of genius, therefore fell into none of the pitfalls of that terrible gift; he was great by virtue of his superhuman moral strength— and it is safe to say that in public life he never experienced a temptation—by a wisdom that no mental heat ever unbalanced, by an unrivalled instinct for the best and most useful in human beings, and by a public conscience to which he would have unhesitatingly sacrificed himself and all he loved, were it a question of the nation's good. But Hamilton knew whom he would consult, and devoted himself to his legal work without a qualm for the future. As he had anticipated, Washington wrote to Robert Morris for advice, and the reply of that eminent financier, that "Hamilton was the one man in the United States competent to cope with the extreme difficulties of that office," pleasantly ended the indecision of the President, and he communicated with Hamilton at once.

Hamilton answered by letter, for Washington was wedded to the formalities, but he followed it with a request for a private interview; and after the lapse of eight years Washington and Hamilton met once more for a purely personal colloquy.

Washington was occupying temporarily the house of Walter Franklin, on the corner of Cherry Street and Franklin Square, a country residence at which society grumbled, for all the world lived between the present site of the City Hall and Battery Park. Hamilton rode up on horseback, and was shown into the library, which overlooked a pleasant garden. The President, in the brown suit of home manufacture which he had worn at the inauguration, as graceful and erect as ever, although with a more elderly visage than in the days of war, entered immediately, closed the door carefully, then took both Hamilton's hands in his enormous grasp. The austere dignity of his face relaxed perceptibly.

"Oh!" he said. "I am glad to see you!"

"It is not a return to old times, alas!" said Hamilton, gaily; "for what we all had to do then was a bagatelle to this, and you have made the supreme sacrifice of your life."

Washington seated himself in an arm-chair, motioning Hamilton to one opposite. "I wrote Knox," he said, "that I felt as if setting out to my own execution; and I swear to you, Hamilton, that if it had not been for you I doubt if my courage would not have failed me at the last moment. I had a moment of nervous dread this morning before I opened your letter, but I believed that you would not fail me. It is a colossal enterprise we are embarked upon, this constructing of a great nation for all time. God knows I am not equal to it, and although I shall always reserve to myself the final judgement, I expect a few of you to think for me—you, in particular. Then with the Almighty's help we may succeed, but I can assure you that it has cost me many wakeful nights—and cold sweats."

He spoke with his usual slow impressiveness, but he smiled as he watched Hamilton's flashing eyes and dilating nostrils. "You look but little older," he added. "Not that you still look a stripling, controlling your temper with both hands while I worked you half to death; but you have the everlasting youth of genius, I suppose, and you look to me able to cope with anything."

Hamilton laughed. "I am far older in many things, sir. I fear I often seemed ungrateful. I have blessed you many times, since, for the discipline and the invaluable knowledge I gained in those years."

"Ah!" exclaimed Washington. "Ah! I am very glad to hear you say that. It is like your generosity, and I have had many anxious moments, wondering if there might not still be a grudge. But not only were your peculiar gifts indispensable to this country, but, I will confess, now that it is over, I mortally dreaded that you would lose your life. You and Laurens were the most reckless devils I ever saw in the field. Poor Laurens! I felt a deep affection for him, and his death was one of the bitterest blows of the war. If he were here now, and Lafayette, how many pleasant hours I should look forward to; but I have you, and God knows I am grateful. Lafayette, I am afraid, has undertaken too great a business for his capacity, which is admirable; but he is not strong enough to be a leader of men."

"I wish he were here, and well out of it."

"I have not sufficiently thanked you for the letter you wrote me last September. It was what I had earnestly hoped for. My position was most distressing. It was impossible for me not only to ask the advice of anyone, but the temper of the public mind regarding myself. To assume that I must be desired—but I need not explain to you, who know me better than anybody living, the extreme delicacy of my position, and the torments of my mind. Your letter explained everything, told me all I wished to know, made my duty clear—painfully clear. You divined what I needed and expressed yourself in your usual frank and manly way, without the least hesitation or fear. I take this occasion to assure you again of my deep appreciation."

"Oh, sir," said Hamilton, who was always affected unbearably by Washington's rare moments of deep feeling, "I was merely the selected instrument to give you what you most needed at the moment; nothing more. This was your destiny; you would be here in any case. It is my pride, my reward of many years of thought and work, that I am able to be of service to your administration, and conspicuous enough to permit you to call me to your side. Be sure that all that I have or am is yours, and that I shall never fail you."

"If I did not believe that, I should indeed be deep in gloomy forebodings. Jay will officiate as Secretary of State for the present; Knox, as Secretary at War. I contemplate inviting Randolph to act as Attorney-General, and Jefferson as permanent Secretary of State, if he will accept; thus dividing the appointments between the North and the South. What do you think of the wisdom of appointing Mr. Jefferson? He is a man of great abilities, and his long residence abroad should make him a valuable Secretary of State, his conspicuous services acceptable to both sections of the country. It is the selection over which I have hesitated longest, for it is a deep and subtle nature, a kind I have no love of dealing with, but so far as I know it is not a devious one, and his talents command my respect."

"I am unable to advise you, sir, for he is not personally known to me," said Hamilton, who was not long wishing that he had had a previous and extensive knowledge of Thomas Jefferson. "Madison thinks well of him—is a close personal friend. He has rendered great services to the State of Virginia, his experience is wide, and he possesses a brilliant and facile pen—I can think of no one better fitted for the position. His record for personal bravery is not untarnished, but perhaps that will insure peace in the Cabinet."

Washington laughed. "Jefferson would slide under the table if you assaulted him," he said. "It is you only that I fear, as it is you only upon whom I thoroughly rely, and not for advice in your own department alone, but in all. I think it would perhaps be better not to hold collective meetings of the Cabinet, but to receive each of you alone. It is as well the others do not know that your knowledge and judgement are my chief reliance."

XV

Hamilton, on his way home, stopped in at the chambers of Troup.

"Bob," he said, "you are to wind up my law business. I am to be Secretary of the Treasury."

Troup half rose with an exclamation of impatience. "Good heavens!" he exclaimed. "Have you not an introductory line in your nature? It has been bad enough to have been anticipating this, without having it go straight through one like a cannon-ball. Of course it is no use to reason with you—I gave that up just after I had assumed that you were a small boy whom it was the duty of a big collegian to protect, and you nearly demolished my not too handsome visage with your astonishing fists for contradicting you. But I am sorry. Remain at the bar and you have an immediate prospect of wealth, not too many enemies, and the highest honours. Five years from now, and you would lead not only the bar of New York but of the whole country. Jay may be the first Chief Justice, but you would be the second—."

"Nothing would induce me to be Chief Justice. I should be bored to death. Can you fancy me sitting eternally and solemnly in the middle of a bench, listening to long-winded lawyers? While I live I shall have action—."

"Well, you will have action enough in this position; it will burn you out twenty years before your time. And it will be the end of what peace and happiness a born fighter could ever hope to possess; for you will raise up enemies and critics on every side, you will be hounded, you will be the victim of cabals, your good name will be assailed—."

"Answer this: do you know of anyone who could fill this office as advantageously to the country as I?"

"No," said Troup, unwillingly. "I do not."

Hamilton was standing by the table. He laid his hand on a volume of Coke, expanding and contracting it slowly. It was perhaps the most beautiful hand in America, and almost as famous as its owner. But as Troup gazed at it he saw only its superhuman suggestion of strength.

"The future of this country lies there," said Hamilton. "I know, and you know, that my greatest gift is statesmanship; my widest, truest knowledge is in the department of finance; moreover, that nothing has so keen and enduring a fascination for me. I could no more refuse this invitation of Washington's than I could clog the wheels of my mind to inaction. It is like a magnet to steel. If I were sure of personal consequences the most disastrous, I should accept, and without hesitation. For what else was the peculiar quality of my brain given me? To what other end have I studied this great question since I was a boy of

282

nineteen—wild as I was to fight and win the honours of the field? Was ever a man's destiny clearer, or his duty?"

"I have no more to say," said Troup, "but I regret it all the same. Have you heard from Morris—Gouverneur?"

"Oh, yes, I had a long screed, in almost your words, spiced with his own particular impertinence. Will you wind up my law business?"

"Oh, of course," said Troup.

The new Congress, made up, though it was, of many of the ablest men in the country, had inherited the dilatory methods of the old, and did not pass an act establishing the Treasury Department until the 2d of September. Hamilton's appointment to this most important portfolio at the disposal of the President was looked upon as a matter of course. It created little discussion, but so deep a feeling of security, that even before the reading of his famous Report business had revived to some extent. This Report upon the public credit was demanded of him at once, but it was not until the recess of Congress that he could work uninterruptedly upon it; for that body, floundering in its chaos of inherited difficulties, turned to the new Secretary for advice on almost every problem that beset it. I cannot do better here than to quote from the monograph on Hamilton by Henry Cabot Lodge, who puts with admirable succinctness a series of facts important to the knowledge of every American:—

In the course of a year he was asked to report, and did report with full details, upon the raising, management, and collection of the revenue, including a scheme for revenue cutters; as to the estimates of income and expenditure; as to the temporary regulation of the chaotic currency; as to navigation laws, and the regulation of the coasting trade, after a thorough consideration of a heap of undigested statistics; as to the post-office, for which he drafted a bill; as to the purchase of West Point; on the great question of public lands and a uniform system of managing them; and upon all claims against the government. Rapidly and effectively the secretary dealt with all these matters, besides drawing up as a voluntary suggestion a scheme for a judicial system. But in addition to all this multiplicity of business there were other matters like the temporary regulation of the currency, requiring peremptory settlement. Money had to be found for the immediate and pressing wants of the new government before any system had been or could be adopted, and the only resources were the empty treasury and broken credit of the old confederacy. By one ingenious expedient or another, sometimes by pledging his own credit, Hamilton got together what was absolutely needful, and without a murmur conquered those petty troubles when he was elaborating and devising a far-reaching policy. Then the whole financial machine of the Treasury Department, and a system of accounting, demanded instant attention. These intricate problems were solved at once, the machine constructed, and the system of accounts devised and put into operation; and so well were these difficult tasks performed that they still subsist, developing and growing with the nation, but at bottom the original arrangements of Hamilton. These complicated questions, answered so rapidly and yet so accurately in the first weeks of confusion incident to the establishment of a new government, show a familiarity and preparation, as well as a readiness of mind of a most unusual kind. Yet while Hamilton was engaged in all this bewildering work, he was evolving the great financial policy, at once broad, comprehensive, and minute, and after the recess in January he laid his ground plan before Congress in his first report on public credit; a state paper which marks an era in American history, and by which the massive corner-stone, from which the great structure of the Federal government has risen, was securely laid.

New York, meanwhile, had blossomed to her full. Houses had been renovated, and with all the elegance to be commanded. Many had been let, by the less ambitious, to the Members of Congress from other States, and all were entertaining. General Schuyler occupied a house close to Hamilton, and his daughters Cornelia and Peggy—Mrs. Stephen Van Rensselaer—were lively members of society. The Vice-President had taken the great house at Richmond Hill, and General Knox as imposing a mansion as he could find. Washington, after a few months, moved to the McComb house in lower Broadway, one of the largest in town, with a reception room of superb proportions. Here Mrs. Washington, standing on a dais, usually assisted by Mrs. Adams and Mrs. Hamilton, received, with the rigid formality of foreign courts, all who dared to attend her levees. She had discarded the simplicity of campaigning days, and attired herself with a magnificence which was emulated by her "Court." It was yet too soon to break from tradition, and the Washingtons conducted themselves in accordance with their strong aristocratic proclivities. Nor did it occur to anyone, even the most ardent Republican, that dignity and splendour were inconsistent with a free and enlightened Republic, until Jefferson began his steady and successful system of plebeianizing the country.

Washington's levees were frigid; but I have not observed any special warmth at the White House upon public occasions in my own time. The President, after the company had assembled, entered in full official costume: black velvet and satin, diamond knee-buckles, his hair in a bag and tied with ribbons. He carried a military hat under his arm, and wore a dress sword in a green shagreen scabbard. He made a tour of the room, addressing each guest in turn, all being ranged according to their rank. At his wife's levees he attended as a private individual and mingled more freely with the guests; but his presence always lowered every voice in the room, and women trembled with anxiety lest he should not engage them in conversation, while dreading that he might. The unparalleled dignity, the icy reserve of his personality, had always affected the temperature of the gatherings he honoured; but at this time, when to the height of a colossal and unique reputation was added the first incumbency of an office, bestowed by a unanimous sentiment, which was to raise the United States to the plane of the great nations of Europe, he was instinctively regarded as superhuman, rather as a human embodiment of the Power beyond space. He was deeply sensitive to the depressing effect he produced, and not a little bored by the open-mouthed curiosity he excited. A youngster, having run after him for quite a block, one day, panting from his exertions, Washington wheeled about suddenly, and made a bow so profound and satirical that his pursuer fled with a yell of terror.

The President was very fond of the theatre, and invited a party once a week to accompany him to John Street. He entertained at table constantly, and dined out formally and intimately. Congress, he attended in great state. He had brought to New York six white horses of the finest Virginian breed, and a magnificent cream-coloured coach, ornamented with cupids and festoons. For state occasions the horses were covered over night with a white paste, and polished next morning until they shone like silver. The hoofs were painted black. When Washington drove through the city on his way to Congress, attended by postilions and outriders, it is little wonder that he had a royal progress through proud and satisfied throngs.

The Adamses, who had counselled all the usages of foreign courts, but had been outvoted by Hamilton and Jay, entertained but little less than the President; and so did the Schuylers, Livingstons, Jays, and half the town. The Hamiltons, of necessity, entertained far more simply; but Betsey received every Wednesday evening, when her rooms were a crush of fashion and politics, eager for a glimpse of Hamilton and to do court to her popular self. They gave at least one dinner a week, but Betsey as a rule went out with her parents, for her husband was too busy for society.

The world saw little of Hamilton at this time, and Betsey but little more. He worked in his library or office for fourteen hours of the day, while the country teemed with conjectures of his coming Report. A disposition to speculate upon it was already manifest, and more than one friend endeavoured to gain a hint of its contents. Not even Madison, to whom he had talked more freely than to anyone, knew aught of the details of that momentous Report, what recommendations he actually should make to Congress; for none knew better than he that a hint derived from him which should lead to profitable speculation would tarnish his good name irretrievably. Careless in much else, on the subject of his private and public integrity he was rigid; he would not have yielded a point to retain the affection of the best and most valued of his friends. Fastidious by nature on the question of his honour, he knew, also, that other accusations, even when verified, mattered little in the long run; a man's actual position in life and in history was determined by the weight of his brain and the spotlessness of his public character. He worked in secret, with no help from anyone; nor could blandishments extract a hint of his purpose. Against the rock of his integrity passion availed nothing. As for Betsey, between her growing children, the delicacy which had followed the birth of her last child, and her heavy social duties, she would have had little time to assist him had he confided even in her. Moreover, to keep up a dignified position upon $3500 a year cost her clever little Dutch head much anxious thought. It is true that some money had been put aside from the income of her husband's large practice, but he was the most careless and generous of men, always refusing the fees of people poorer than himself, and with no talent for personal, great as was his mastery of political, economy. If General Schuyler often came to the rescue his son-in-law never knew it.

Hamilton had a vague idea that Betsey could manage somehow, and was far too absorbed to give the matter a thought. Betsey, it would seem, had her own little reputation, for it was about this time that M'Henry finished a letter to Hamilton, as follows:—

Pray present me to Mrs. Hamilton. I have learned from a friend of yours that she has, as far as the comparison will hold, as much merit as your treasurer as you have as treasurer of the wealth of the United States.

XVI

Congress reassembled, and on the 2d of January Hamilton sent in his Report on Public Credit. By this time excitement and anxiety, to say nothing of cupidity, were risen to fever pitch. All realized that they were well in the midst of a national crisis, for the country was bankrupt, and her foreign and domestic debts footed up to quite eighty millions of dollars—a stupendous sum in the infancy of a nation, when there was little specie in the country, and an incalculable amount of worthless paper, with long arrears of interest besides. If Hamilton could cope with this great question, and if Congress, with its determined anti-government party, would support him, the Union and its long-suffering patriots would enter upon a season of prosperity and happiness. If the one were inadequate to meet the situation, or the other failed in its national duty, the consequences must be deeper wretchedness and disaster than anything they yet had endured. The confidence in Hamilton was very widespread, for not only were his great abilities fully recognized, but his general opinions on the subject had long been known, and approved by all but the politicians on the wrong side. The confidence had been manifested in a manner little to his liking: speculators had scoured the country, buying up government securities at the rate of a few shillings on the pound, taking advantage of needy holders, who dwelt, many of them, in districts too remote from the centre of action to know what the Government was about. And even before this "signal instance of moral turpitude," the fact that so many old soldiers who had gone home with no other pay than government securities, to be exchanged for specie at the pleasure of a government which nobody had trusted, had sold out for a small sum, was one of the agitating themes of the country; and opinion was divided upon the right of the assignees to collect the full amount which the new government might be prepared to pay, while the moral rights of the worthy and original holder were ignored. It was understood, however, that Hamilton had given no more searching thought to any subject than to this.

The public was not admitted to the galleries of Congress in those days, but a great crowd packed Wall and Broad streets while the Report was reading and until some hint of its contents filtered through the guarded doors. Hamilton himself was at home with his family, enjoying a day of rest. It is one of the most curious incidents in his career, as well as one of the highest tributes to his power over men, that Congress, after mature deliberation, decided that it would be safer to receive his Report in writing than in the form of a personal address from a man who played so dangerously upon the nerve-board of the human nature. There hardly could be any hidden witchery in a long paper dealing with so unemotional a subject as finance; but no man could foresee what might be the effect of the Secretary's voice and enthusiasm,—which was perilously communicable,—his inevitable bursts of spontaneous eloquence. But Hamilton had a pen which served him well, when he was forced to substitute it for the charm of his personality. It was so pointed, simple, and powerful, it classified with such clarity, it expressed his convictions so unmistakably, and conveyed his subtle appeals to human passions so obediently, that it rarely failed to quiver like an arrow in the brain to which it was directed. And this particular report was vitalized by the author's overwhelming sense of the great crisis with which he was dealing. Reading it to-day, a hundred and eleven years after it was written, and close to the top of a twelve-story building, which is a symbol of the industry and progress for which he more than any man who has ever dedicated his talents to the United States is responsible, it is so fresh and convincing, so earnest, so insistent, so courteously peremptory, that the great century which lies between us and that empire-making paper lapses from the memory, and one is in that anxious time, in the very study of the yet more anxious statesman; who, on a tropical island that most of his countrymen never will see, came into being with the seed of an unimagined nation in his brain.

To condense Hamilton is much like attempting to increase the density of a stone, or to reduce the alphabet to a tabloid. I therefore shall make no effort to add another failure to the several abstracts of this Report. The heads of his propositions are sufficient. The Report is accessible to all who find the subject interesting. The main points were these: The exploding of the discrimination fallacy; the assumption of the State debts by the Government; the funding of the entire amount of the public debt, foreign, domestic, and State; three new loans, one to the entire amount of the debt, another of $10,000,000, a third of $12,000,000; the prompt payment of the arrears and current interest of the foreign loan on the original terms of the contract; the segregating of the post-office revenue, amounting to about a million dollars, for a sinking fund, that the creation of a debt should always be accompanied by the means of extinguishment; increased duties on foreign commodities, that the government might be able to pay the interest on her new debts and meet her current expenses; and more than one admonition for prompt action, as the credit of the nation was reaching a lower level daily, besides sinking more hopelessly into debt through arrears of interest. The indebtedness he divided as follows: The foreign debt, $10,070,307, with arrears of interest amounting to $1,640,071. The liquidated domestic debt, $27,383,917, with arrears of interest amounting to $13,030,168. The unliquidated part he estimated at $2,000,000, and the aggregate debt of the State at $25,000,000; making a total of nearly $80,000.000.

He also hinted at his long-cherished scheme of a National Bank, and a possible excise law, and gave considerable space to the miserable condition of landed property and the methods by which it might be restored to its due value.

XVII

The talk in the drawing-room of Mrs. Croix that night was of little else but the Secretary's Report. Mrs. Croix, so said gossip, had concluded that this was the proper time for the demise of her recalcitrant officer, and had retired to weeds and a semi-seclusion while Mrs. Washington pondered upon the propriety of receiving her. Her court cared little for the facts, and vowed that she never had looked so fair or so proud; Hamilton, that she shone with the splendour of a crystal star on the black velvet skies of the Tropics. She wore, this evening, a few yards of black gauze which left bare a crescent of her shining neck and the lower arms. Her bright hair was arranged in a mass of ringlets, after a fashion obtaining in Europe, and surmounted by a small turban of gauze fastened with a diamond sun. Many of the men who visited her habitually called her Lady Betty, for she was one of those women who invite a certain playful familiarity while repelling intimacy. Hamilton called her, as the fancy moved him, Egeria, Boadicea, or Lady Godiva.

Clinton came in fuming. "It is not possible," he cried, "that the Congress can be so mad as to be hoodwinked by this deep political scheme for concentrating the liberties of the United States under the executive heel. 'To cement more closely the union of the States and to add to their security against foreign attack!' Forsooth! This assumption plan is nothing more nor less than another of his dastardly schemes to squeeze out of the poor States what little liberty he left them under the Constitution. He could not obtain at Philadelphia all he wished for, but now that Washington has given him both reins, he laughs in our faces. I regret that I ever offered him my hand."

"Then our party in Congress will fight him on political grounds?" asked Mrs. Croix.

"You may put it that way if you choose. It certainly will not be blinded by his speciousness and aid him in his subtle monarchism. 'Contribute in an eminent degree to an orderly, stable, and satisfactory arrangement of the Nation's finances!' 'Several reasons which render it probable that the situation of the State creditors will be worse than that of the creditors of the Union, if there be not a national assumption of the State debts!' And then his plan of debit and credit, with 'little doubt that balances would appear in favour of all the States against the United States!' My blood has boiled since I read that paper. I have feared apoplexy. He is clever, that West Indian,—do they grow many such?— but he did not select a country composed entirely of fools to machinate in."

"My dearest Governor," whispered Mrs. Croix, "calm yourself, pray. Only you can cope with Mr. Hamilton. You must be the colossal spirit without the walls of Congress to whom all will look for guidance. If you become ill, the cause is lost."

Clinton composed himself promptly, and asked Elbridge Gerry, of Massachusetts, which, section of the Report he expected to attack first. There were no Federalists present.

Gerry shrugged his shoulders and shot a narrow glance of contempt at the Governor. "Give me time, your Excellency, pray. Mr. Hamilton's paper has the thought of a decade in it. It merits at least a week of thought on our part. I never could agree with him in all things, but in some I am at one with him; and I acknowledge myself deeply in his debt, insomuch as he has taught me, among thousands of others, to 'think continentally,' I certainly agree with him that to pay to present holders the full value of their certificates, without discrimination, is a matter of constitutional law, a violation of which would be a menace to the new government. I shall support him on that point at the risk of being accused of speculation."

Stone, of Maryland, was striding up and down, but a degree less agitated than the Governor of New York.

"The man is cleverer than all the rest of us put together!" he exclaimed. "Let us not forget that for an instant. A greater thought than this of assumption has never been devised by man. If it be carried into execution,—which God forbid,—it will prove a wall of adamant to the Federal government, impregnable to any attempt on its fabric or operations."

"Oh, is it so bad as that?" asked Gerry. "Every fort falls if the siege be sufficiently prolonged. I apprehend no such disaster, and I confess I see much promise in at least two of Mr. Hamilton's schemes. After all, the redemption of the country is what we must look to first."

"You are a trimmer. Cannot you see that if the whole revenue of the States be taken into the power of Congress, it will prove a band to draw us so close together as not to leave the smallest interstice for separation?"

"But do you meditate separation?" asked Mrs. Croix. "Surely that would be as great a crime as Mr. Hamilton's monarchical manoeuvres— if it be true he practises such."

"He is bold enough about them," snorted Clinton. "I do the man justice to recognize his insolent frankness."

"Those I cannot say I have observed," said Gerry. "Nor do I think that we meditate separation. We are struggling out of one pit. It would be folly to dig a deeper. And Massachusetts has a great debt, with decreasing revenue for interest and redemption. I am not sure that assumption would not be to her advantage. She stood the brunt of the war. It is but fair that she should have relief now, even at the expense of other States whose debt is insignificant; and she is able to take care of herself against the Federal government—"

"The brunt of the war!" exclaimed the Attorney-General of the Cabinet, who, with the Speaker of the House, had just entered, and who had controlled himself with difficulty for several seconds. "I beg to assure you, sir, that Virginia may claim that honour. Her glorious patriotism, her contributions in men and money—they exceeded those of any State in the Union, sir."

Gerry laughed. "I have no means of comparison by which patriotism may be measured, Mr. Randolph," he said. "But we can produce figures, if necessary, to prove our title to supremacy in the other matters you mention. As you have reduced your debt, however, by an almost total repudiation of your paper money—"

"How about Mr. Madison?" asked Mrs. Croix, hurriedly. "He is your fellow-statesman, Mr. Randolph, but he is Mr. Hamilton's devoted friend and follower. Virginia may be sadly divided."

"My fears have decreased on that point," said Randolph, drily. "Mr. Madison's loyalty toward his State increases daily."

"So does his ambition," observed Muhlenberg. "If I am not mistaken, he has begun to chafe at Hamilton's arrangement of his destinies—and a nature like that is not without deep and sullen jealousies. To be a leader of leaders requires a sleepless art; to lead the masses is play by comparison. Hamilton is a magician, but he is arrogant and impatient. With all his art and control of men's minds, he will lose a follower now and again, and not the least important would be—will be—Madison."

"Have you proof?" asked Clinton, eagerly. "He would be of incomparable value in our ranks. By the way, Aaron Burr is working to the front. He is a born politician, if I am not mistaken, and is in a rapid process of education. I feel sure that I have attached him to our cause by appointing him Attorney-General of the Staite. He should make an invaluable party man."

"He will be attached to no cause," said Gerry. "He is, as you say, a politician. There is not a germ of the statesman in him; nor of the honest man, either, unless I am deeply mistaken. He is the only man of note in the country who has not one patriotic act to his credit. He fought, but so did every adventurous youth in the country; and had there been anything more to his interest to do at the time, the

Revolution could have taken care of itself. But during all our trying desperate years since—did he go once to Congress? Did he interest himself in the Constitution, either at Philadelphia or Poughkeepsie? What record did he make in the State Legislature during his one term of infrequent attendance? While other men, notably Hamilton, of whom he betrays an absurd jealousy, have been neglecting their private interests in the public cause, he has been distinguishing himself as a femalist, and thinking of nothing else but making money at the bar. I admit his brilliancy, his intrepidity, and the exquisite quality of his address, but I don't believe that an honest man who comes into contact with him instinctively trusts him."

"Oh, let us not indulge in such bitter personalities," cried Mrs. Croix, who took no interest at that time in the temporary husband of her old age. "Surely this coming legislation should compel every faculty. What of the other debts?—of funding? Or, if it is still too soon to talk of these matters with equilibrium," she added hastily, as Clinton turned purple again, "pray tell me that the great question of deciding upon a site for the Capital is nearing a solution. It has been such a source of bitter agitation. I wish it were settled."

"The House may or may not pass this bill for ten years in Philadelphia, and the banks of the Potomac thereafter," growled the Senator from North Carolina. "The Federalists have the majority, and they are determined to keep the seat of government in the North, as they are determined to have their monarchical will in everything. Madison hopes for some fortuitous coincidence, but I confess I hardly know what he means."

Gerry laughed. "When Madison takes to verbiage," he said, "I should resort to a plummet and line."

"Sir!" cried Randolph, limping toward the door in angry haste. "Mr. Madison is one of the loftiest statesmen in the country!"

"Has been. Centrifugal forces are in motion."

"How everybody in politics does hate everybody else!" said Mrs. Croix, with a patient sigh.

XVIII

The next morning Mrs. Croix sent a peremptory summons to Hamilton.

Although at work upon his "Additional Estimates," he responded at once.

The lady was combing her emotional mane in the sunshine before the mirror of her boudoir when he arrived, and the maid had been dismissed.

"Well, Egeria," he said, smiling down upon this dazzling vision, "what is it? What warning of tremendous import have you to deliver, that you rout a busy Secretary from his work at eleven in the morning? I dared not loiter, lest your capricious majesty refuse me your door upon my next evening of leisure—"

"It is not I who am capricious!" cried Mrs. Croix. She pouted charmingly. "Indeed, sir, I never am quite sure of you. You are all ardour to-day, and indifference to-morrow. For work I am always put aside, and against your family demands I do not exist."

"My dear Boadicea," said Hamilton, drily, "I am a mere creature of routine. I met you after my habits of work and domesticity were well established. You are the fairest thing on earth, and there are times when you consume it, but circumstances isolate you. Believe me, I am a victim of those circumstances, not of caprice."

"My dear Hamilton," replied Mrs. Croix, quite as drily, "you have all the caprice of a woman combined with all the lordly superiority of the male. I well know that although I bewitch you, I can do so at your pleasure only. You are abominably your own master, both in your strength and your weakness. But there is no one like you on earth, so I submit. And I work and burrow for you, and you will not even accept my precious offerings."

"I will not have you playing the rôle of spy, if that is what you mean. I do not like this idea of confessing my enemies when they think themselves safe in your house, I prefer to fight in the open, and they reveal themselves to me sooner or later. What should I think of myself and you if I permitted you to act as a treacherous go-between."

"You will not permit me to help you! And I could do much! I could tell you so much now that would put you on your guard. I could help you immeasurably. I could be your fate. But you care for nothing but my beauty!" And she dropped dismally into her pocket-handkerchief.

Hamilton was not one of those men who dread a woman's tears. He had dried too many. His immediate and practical consolation but

294

appeared to deepen her grief, however, and he was obliged to resort to eloquence.

"Where do I find such hours of mental companionship as here?" he demanded. "I say nothing of art and literature; do I not discuss with you the weightiest affairs of State—everything, in fact, upon which my honour does not compel silence? Never have I thought of asking the advice, the opinion, of a woman before. You are my Egeria, and I am deeply grateful for you. If at times I remember nothing but your beauty, would you have it otherwise? I flatter myself that you would not. Have you really anything to reproach me for, because I will not hear of your committing an act which I would not commit myself? I suppose it is hopeless to talk of honour to the cleverest of women, but you must accept this dictum whether you understand it or not: I will listen to none of the confidences of your trusting anti-Federalists. Why cannot you come out honestly and declare your true politics? You could do far more good, and I leave you no excuse to perpetrate this lie."

"I will not," sobbed his Egeria, obstinately. "I may be able to be of service to you, even if you will not let me warn you of Madison's treachery."

She had scored her point, and Hamilton sprang to his feet, his face as white as her petticoats. "Madison's treachery!" he exclaimed. "It is true he comes near me but seldom this Congress. I had attributed his coldness to temperament. Can it be? So many forces would operate. There is much jealousy and ambition in him. He can never lead my party. Is he capable of deserting that he might lead another? One expects that sort of thing of a Burr; but Madison—I have thought him of an almost dazzling whiteness at times—then I have had lightning glimpses of meaner depths. He is easily influenced. Virginia opposes me so bitterly! Will he dare to continue to defy her? Can he continue to rise if she combines against him? Oh, God! If he only had more iron in his soul!"

It was characteristic of him that he had forgotten his audience. He was thinking aloud, his thought leaping from point to point as they sprang into the brilliant atmosphere of his mind; or using its rapid divining rod. He threw back his head. "I'll not believe it till I have proof!" he exclaimed defiantly. "Why, I should feel as if one of the foundations of the earth had given way. Madison—we have been like brothers. I have confided deeply in him. There is little in that Report of yesterday that I have not discussed with him a hundred times—nothing but the ways and means, which I dared confide to no one. He has always been in favour of assumption, of paying the whole debt. It is understood that he is to support me in Congress. I'll hear no more. Dry your tears. You have accomplished your object with a woman's wit. I believe you did but shed those tears to enhance your loveliness, my Lady Godiva."

XIX

The immediate consequences of Hamilton's Report were a rise of fifty per cent in the securities of the bankrupt Confederation, and a bitter warfare in Congress. All were agreed upon the propriety of paying the foreign loan, but the battle raged about every other point in turn. One of the legacies of the old Congress was the principle of repudiating what it was not convenient to redeem, and the politicians of the country had insensibly fallen into the habit of assuming that they should start clear with the new government, and relegate the domestic debt to the limbo which held so many other resources best forgotten. They were far from admitting the full measure of their inheritance, however, and opened the battle with a loud denouncement of the greedy speculator who had defrauded the impoverished soldier, to whose needs they had been indifferent hitherto. Most of this feeling concentrated in the opposition, but many Federalists were so divided upon the question of discrimination that for a time the other great questions contained in the Report fell back. Feeling became so bitter that those who supported the assignees were accused of speculation, and personalities were hot and blistering. Many of the strongest men, however, ranged with Hamilton, and were in sight of victory, when Madison, who had hoped to see the question settle itself in favour of the original holders without his open support, came out with a double bomb; the first symptom of his opposition to the Federal party, and an unconstitutional proposition that the holders by assignment should receive the highest market-price yet reached by the certificates, by which they would reap no inconsiderable profit, and that the balance of the sum due, possibly more than one-half, should be distributed among the original holders. For a time the reputation for statemanship which Madison had won was clouded, for his admission of the claims of the assignees nullified any argument he could advance in favour of the original holders. But he had his limitations. There was nothing of the business man in his composition. One of the most notable and useful attributes of Hamilton's versatile brain was excluded from his, beyond its comprehension. His proposition was rejected by thirty-six votes to thirteen.

Then the hostile camps faced each other on the questions of the domestic debt and assumption. In regard to the former, common decency finally prevailed, but the other threatened to disrupt the Union, for the Eastern States threw out more than one hint of secession did the measure fail. Madison, without further subterfuge, came forth at the head of his State as the leader of the anti-assumptionists. He offered no explanation to his former chief and none was demanded. For a time Hamilton was bitterly disgusted and wounded. He shrugged his shoulders, finally, and accepted his new enemy with philosophy, though by no means with amiability and forgiveness; but he had seen too much of the selfishness and meanness of human nature to remain pained or astonished at any defection.

When June came, however, he was deeply uneasy. On March 29th the resolutions providing for the foreign debt and for paying in full the principal of the domestic debt to the present holders passed without a division. So did the resolution in favour of paying the arrears of interest in like manner with the principal of the domestic debt. But the resolution in favour of assumption was recommitted. The next day the friends of assumption had the other resolutions also recommitted, and the furious battle raged again. Finally, on June 2d, a bill was passed by the House, which left the question of assumption to be settled by a future test of strength.

The anti-assumptionists were triumphant, for they believed the idea would gain in unpopularity. But they reckoned without Hamilton.

XX

Jefferson had arrived on March 21st, and entered at once upon his duties as Secretary of State. He disapproved of the assumption measure, but was so absorbed in the perplexing details of his new office, in correspondence, and in frequent conferences with the President on the subject of foreign affairs, that he gave the matter little consecutive thought. Moreover, he was dined every day for weeks, all the distinguished New Yorkers, from Hamilton down, vying with each other in attentions to a man whose state record was so enlightened, and whose foreign so brilliant, despite one or two humiliating failures. He rented a small cottage in Maiden Lane, and looked with deep disapproval upon the aristocratic dissipations of New York, the frigid stateliness of Washington's "Court." The French Revolution and the snub of the British king had developed his natural democratism into a controlling passion, and he would have preferred to find in even the large cities of the new country the homely bourgeois life of his highest ideals.

No one accused him of inconsistency in externals. With his shaggy sandy hair, his great red face, covered with freckles, his long loose figure, clad in red French breeches a size too small, a threadbare brown coat, soiled linen and hose, and enormous hands and feet, he must have astounded the courtly city of New York, and it is certain that he set Washington's teeth on edge. It is no wonder that when this vision rises upon the democratic horizon of to-day, he is hailed as a greater man than Washington or Hamilton.

Shortly after the final recommitment of the resolution in favour of assumption, the Federalist leader met this engaging figure almost in front of Washington's door, and a plan which had dawned in his mind a day or two before matured on the instant. He had no dislike for Jefferson at the time, and respected his intellect and diplomatic talents, without reference to differences of opinion. Jefferson grinned as Hamilton approached, and offered his great paw amiably. He did not like his brother secretary's clothes, and his hitherto averted understanding was gradually moving toward the displeasing fact that Hamilton was the Administration; but he had had little time for reflection, and he succumbed temporarily to a fascination which few resisted.

Hamilton approached him frankly. "Will you walk up and down with me a few moments?" he asked. "I have intended to call upon you. You have returned at a most opportune time. Do you realize, sir, that the whole business of this nation is at a deadlock? There is nothing in this talk of the North seceding, but so great is the apprehension that the energies of the country are paralyzed, and no man thinks of anything but the possible failure of the Government. I am convinced that assumption is not only necessary to permanent union, to the solution of the financial problem, but to the prosperity of the States themselves." He then proceeded to convince Jefferson, who listened attentively, wondering, with a sigh, how any man could pour out his thoughts so rapidly and so well. "Will you turn this over in your mind, and let me see you again in a day or two?" asked Hamilton, as he finished his argument. "Let me reiterate that there is no time to lose. The Government is at a standstill in all matters concerning the establishment of the country on a sound financial basis, until this subordinate matter is settled."

"You alarm and deeply interest me," said Jefferson. "I certainly will give the matter my attention. Will you dine with me to-morrow? We can then discuss this matter at leisure. I will ask one or two others."

The next day, at Mr. Jefferson's epicureous board, Hamilton played his trump. Having again wrought havoc with his host's imagination, but by no means trusting to the permanence of any emotion, he proposed a bargain: if Jefferson would use his influence with the Virginians and other Southern anti-assumptionists in Congress, he and Robert Morris would engage to persuade obstinate Northerners to concede the Capital city to the South. Hamilton made no sacrifice of conviction in offering this proposition. There was no reason why the Government should not sit as conveniently on the banks of the Potomac as elsewhere, and if he did not carry the Union through this new crisis, no one else would. All his great schemes depended upon his bringing the hostile States to reason, and with his usual high-handed impatience he carried his object in his own way.

Jefferson saw much virtue in this arrangement. The plan was an almost immediate success. White and Lee of Virginia were induced to change their votes, and assumption with some modifications passed into a law. The Government, after a ten years' sojourn in Philadelphia, would abide permanently upon the Potomac.

XXI

Mrs. Hamilton, albeit she had not a care in the world, sighed heavily. She was standing before her mirror, arrayed in a triumph of art recently selected by Mrs. Church, in London. On her head was an immense puff of yellow gauze, whose satin foundation had a double wing in large plaits. The dress was of yellow satin, flowing over a white satin petticoat, and embellished about the neck with a large Italian gauze handkerchief, striped with white. Her hair was in ringlets and unpowdered. She was a very plate of fashion, but her brow was puckered.

"What is it?" asked her husband, entering from his room. "You are a vision of loveliness, my dear Eliza. Is there a rose too few, or a hoop awry?"

"No, sir, I am well enough pleased with myself. I am worrying lest General Washington ask me to dance. It will be bad enough to go out with Mr. Adams, who snaps at me every time I venture a remark, but he at least is not a giant, and I do not feel like a dwarf. When the President leads me out—that is to say, when he did lead me out at the Inauguration ball, I was like to expire of mortification. I felt like a little polar cub trotting out to sea with a monster iceberg. And he never opened his lips to distract my mind, just solemnly marched me up and down, as if I had done something naughty and were being exhibited. I saw Kitty Livingston giggle behind her fan, and Kitty Duer drew herself up to her full height, which is quite five feet six, and looked down upon me with a cruel amusement. Women are so nasty to each other. Thank heaven I have a new gown for to-night—anyhow!"

Hamilton laughed heartily; she always amused him, she was half his wife, half the oldest of his children. "And you are fresher far than any of them; let that console you," he said, arranging her necklace. "I am sure both the President and the Vice-President will take you out; they hardly would have the bad taste not to. And you look very sweet, hanging on to Washington's hand. Don't imagine for a moment that you look ridiculous. Fancy, if you had to walk through life with either of them."

Betsey shuddered and smoothed her brow. "It *would* be a walk with the dear General," she said. "I dare not dwell upon what it would be with Mr. Adams—or anyone else! You are amazing smart, yourself, to-night."

"This new costume depressed me for a moment, for it is very like one Laurens used to wear upon state occasions, but I had not the courage to wear the light blue with the large gilt buttons, and the pudding cravat Morris inconsiderately sent me; not with Jefferson's agonized eye to encounter. The poor man suffers cruelly at our extravagance and elegance."

"He is an old fright," quoth Betsey, "and I'd not dance with him, not if he went on his knees."

She looked her husband over with great pride. He wore a coat of plum-coloured velvet, a double-breasted Marseilles vest, white satin breeches, white silk stockings, and pumps. There were full ruffles of lace on his breast and wrists. A man of to-day has to be singularly gifted by nature to shine triumphant above his ugly and uniform garb, whereas many a woman wins a reputation for beauty by a combination of taste with the infinite range modern fashion accords her. In the days of which we write, a man hardly could help looking his best, and while far more decorative than his descendant, was equally useful. And as all dressed in varying degrees of the same fashion, none seemed effeminate. As for Hamilton, his head never looked more massive, his glance more commanding, than when he was in full regalia; nor he more ready for a fight. All women know the psychological effect of being superlatively well dressed. In the days of our male ancestors' external vanities it is quite possible that they, too, felt unconquerable when panoplied in their best.

The ball that night was at Richmond Hill, the beautiful home of the Vice-President and his wife, Abigail Adams, one of the wisest, wittiest, and most agreeable women of her time. This historic mansion, afterward the home of Aaron Burr during his successful years, was a country estate where Varick Street now crosses Charlton in the heart of the city. It stood on an eminence overlooking the Hudson, surrounded by a park and commanding a view of the wild Jersey shore opposite. The Adamses were ambitious people and entertained constantly, with little less formality than the President. The early hours of their receptions, indeed, were chilling, and many went late, after dancing was, begun or the company had scattered to the card-tables. The Vice-President and his wife stood at the head of the long drawing-room and said good evening, and no more, as the women courtesied to the ground, or the men bowed as deeply as their varying years would permit. The guests then stood about for quite an hour and talked in undertones; later, perhaps, the host and hostess mingled with them and conversed. But although Mrs. Adams was vastly popular, her distinguished husband was less so; he was not always to be counted upon in the matter of temper. This grim old Puritan, of an integrity which makes him one of the giants of our early history, despite the last hours of his administration when he was beating about in the vortex of his passions, and always honest in his convictions, right or wrong, had not been gifted by nature with a pleasing address, although he could attach people to him when he chose. He was irascible and violent, the victim of a passionate jealous nature, without the saving graces of humour and liveliness of temperament. But his sturdy upright figure was very imposing; his brow, which appeared to end with the tip of his nose, so bold was the curve, would have been benevolent but for the youthful snapping eyes. His indomitability and his capacity for hatred were expressed in the curves of his mouth. He was always well dressed, for although a farmer by birth, he was as pronounced an aristocrat in his tastes as Washington or Hamilton. At this time, although he liked neither of them, he was the staunch supporter of the Government. He believed in Federalism and the Constitution, insignificant as he found his rewards under both, and he was an ally of inestimable value.

When the Hamiltons entered his drawing-room to-night they found many people of note already there, although the minuet had not begun. The President, his graceful six feet in all the magnificence of black velvet and white satin, his queue in a black silk bag, stood beside his lady, who was as brave as himself in a gown of violet brocade over an immense hoop. Poor dame, she would far rather have been at Mount Vernon in homespun, for all this pomp and circumstance bored and isolated her. She hedged herself about with the etiquette which her exalted position demanded, and froze the social aspirant of insufficient pretensions, but her traditions and her propensities were ever at war; she was a woman above all things, and an extremely simple one.

John Jay, now Chief Justice of the United States, was there, as ever the most simply attired personage in the Union. His beautiful wife, however, beaming and gracious, but no less rigid than "Lady Washington," in her social statutes, looked like a bird of paradise beside a graven image, so gorgeous was her raiment. Baron Steuben was in the regalia of war and a breastplate of orders. Kitty Livingston, now Mrs. Matthew Ridley, had also received a fine new gown of Mrs. Church's selection, for the two women still were friends, despite the rupture of their families. Lady Kitty Duer, so soon to know poverty and humiliation, was in a gown of celestial blue over a white satin petticoat, her lofty head surmounted by an immense gauze turban. General and Mrs. Knox, fat, amiable, and always popular, although sadly inflated by their new social importance, were mountains of finery. Mrs. Ralph Izard,

Mrs. Jay's rival in beauty, and Mrs. Adams's in wit, painted by Gainsborough and Copley, wore a white gown of enviable simplicity, and a string of large pearls in her hair, another about her graceful throat. Mrs. Schuyler, stout and careworn, from the trials of excitable and eloping daughters, clung to the kind arm of her austere and silent husband. Fisher Ames, with his narrow consumptive figure and his flashing ardent eyes, his eloquent tongue chilled by this funereal assemblage, had retreated to an alcove with Rufus King, where they whispered politics. Burr, the target of many fine eyes, was always loyal to his wife in public; she was a charming and highly respected woman, ten years his senior. Burr fascinated women, and adorned his belt with their scalps; but had it not been for this vanity, which led him to scatter hints of infinite devilment and conquest, it is not likely that he would have been branded, in that era of gallantry, a devirginator and a rake. All that history is concerned with is his utter lack of patriotism and honesty, and the unscrupulous selfishness, from which, after all, he suffered more than any man. His dishonesties and his treasonable attempts were failures, but he left a bitter legacy in his mastery of the arts of political corruption, and in a glittering personality which, with his misfortunes, has begodded him with the shallow and ignorant, who know the traditions of history and none of its facts. He was a poor creature, with all his gifts, for his life was a failure, his old age one of the loneliest and bitterest in history; and from no cause that facts or tradition give us but the blind selfishness which blunted a good understanding to stupidity. Selfishness in public life is a crime against one's highest ambitions.

Mrs. Hamilton kept a firm hold on her husband's arm, and her glance shot apprehensively from Washington to the Vice-President. The latter could not dance at present; the former looked as if petrified, rooted in the floor. Betsey had a clever little head, and she devised a scheme at once. She was the third lady in the land, and although many years younger than Mrs. Adams, had entertained from her cradle. No one else immediately following the entrance of her husband and herself, she did not move on after her courtesy, but drew Mrs. Adams into conversation, and the good lady by this time was glad of a friendly word.

"You will be detained here for an hour yet," said Betsey, sweetly. "Can I help you? Shall I start the minuet? Dear Mr. Adams will be too tired to dance to-night. Shall I choose a partner and begin?"

"For the love of heaven, do," whispered Mrs. Adams. "Take out Colonel Burr. He matches you in height, and dances like a courtier."

Other people entered at the moment, and Betsey whispered hurriedly to Hamilton: "Go—quickly—and fetch Colonel Burr. I breathe freely for the first time since the clock struck six, but who knows what may happen?"

Hamilton obediently started in quest of Burr. But alas, Ames and King darted at him from their hiding-place behind a curtain, and he disappeared from his wife's despairing vision. Ten minutes later he became aware of the familiar strains of the minuet, and guiltily glanced forth. Betsey, her face composed to stony resignation lest she disgrace herself with tears, was solemnly treading the measure with the solemnest man on earth, clutching at his hand, which was on a level with her turban. A turn of her head and she encountered her husband's contrite eye. Before hers he retreated to the alcove, nor did he show himself in the ball-room again until it was time to take his wife to their coach.

He escaped from the room by a window, and after half the evening in the library with a group of anxious Federalists,—for it was but a night or two after his dinner with Jefferson,—he retired to a small room at the right of the main hall for a short conference with the Chief Justice. He was alone after a few moments, and was standing before the half-drawn tapestry, watching the guests promenading in the hall, when Kitty Livingston passed on the arm of Burr. Their eyes met, and she cut him. His spirits dropped at once, and he was indulging in reminiscences tinged with melancholy, for he had loved her as one of the faithful chums of his youth, niching her with Troup, Fish, and other enthusiastic friends of that time, when to his surprise she entered abruptly, and drew the tapestry behind her.

"You wicked varlet!" she exclaimed. "What did you sow all this dissension for, and deprive me of my best friends?" Then she kissed him impulsively. "I shall always love you, though. You were the dearest little chap that ever was—and that is why I am going to tell you something to-night, although I may never speak to you again, Aaron Burr is burrowing between my family and the Clinton faction. He hopes to make a strong combination, defeat General Schuyler at the next election, and have himself elected senator in his place. Why, why did you alienate us? We are nine in public life—did you forget that?—and what was Rufus King to you or to the country compared with our combined strength? Why should John be preferred to Robert? You are as high-handed and arrogant as Lucifer himself; and generally you win, but not always. Burr has seen his first chance for political preferment, and seized it with a cunning which I almost admire. He has persuaded both the Livingstons and the Clintons that here is their chance to pull you down, and he is only too willing to be the instrument—the wretched little mole! I shall hate myself to-morrow for telling you this, for God knows I am loyal to my people, but I have watched you go up—up—up. I should feel like your mother would if I saw you in the dust. I am afraid it is too late to do anything now. These two hostile parties will not let slip this chance. But get Burr under your foot when you can, and keep him there. He is morbid with jealousy and will live to pull you down."

"My dear girl," exclaimed Hamilton, who was holding her hand between both his own, "do not let your imagination run away with you. I am very well with Burr, and he is jealous by fits and starts only. Why in the name of heaven should he be jealous? He has never given a thought to the welfare of the country, and I have devoted myself to the subject since boyhood. If I reap the reward—and God knows the future is precarious enough—why should he grudge me a power for which he has never striven? I know him to be ambitious, and I believe him to be unscrupulous, and for that reason I have been glad that he has hitherto kept out of politics; for he would be of no service to the country, would not hesitate to sacrifice it to his own ends—unless I am a poor student of character. But as to personal enmity against me, or jealousy because I occupy a position he has never sought,—and he is a year older than I, remember,—I find that hard to believe, as well as this other; he is not powerful enough to unite two such factions."

"He has a tongue as persuasive from its cunning as yours is in its impetuosity, and he has convinced greater men than himself of his usefulness. Believe me, Alexander, I speak of what I know, not of what I suspect. Accept the fact, if you will not be warned. You always underrate your enemies. Your confidence in your own genius—a confidence which so much has occurred to warrant—blinds you to the power of others. Remember the old adage: Pride goeth before a fall—although I despise the humble myself; the world owes nothing to them. But I have often trembled for the time when your high-handed methods and your scorn of inferior beings would knock the very foundations from under your feet. Now, I will say no more, and we part for ever. Perhaps if you had not worn that colour to-night, I should not have betrayed my family—heaven knows! We women are compounded of so many contradictory motives. Thank your heaven that you men are not half so complex."

"My dear friend," said Hamilton, drily, "you women are not half so complex as men. You may lay claim to a fair share because your intelligence is above the average, but that is the point—complexity is a matter of intelligence, and as men are, as a rule, far more intelligent than women, with far more densely furnished brains—"

But here she boxed his ears and left the room. She returned in a moment.

"You have not thanked me!" she exclaimed. "I deserve to be thanked."

Hamilton put his arm about her and kissed her affectionately.

"From the bottom of my heart," he said. "I deeply appreciate the impulse—and the sacrifice."

"But you won't heed," she said, with a sigh. "Good-by, Alexander! I think Betsey is looking for you."

XXII

Hamilton for many months was far too busy with the reports he sent to Congress in rapid succession, above all with the one concerning the establishment of a National Bank, to be presented at the opening of the next Session, and with the routine of business connected with his department, to interfere in politics. He warned General Schuyler, however, and hoped that the scandal connected with the State lands, in which Burr was deeply implicated, would argue for the statesman in his contest with a mere politician. But Burr, in common with the other commissioners, was acquitted, although no satisfactory explanation of their astounding transactions was given, and General Schuyler lost the election as much through personal unpopularity as through the industry of Burr and the determined efforts of the Livingstons. Schuyler, the tenderest of men in his friendships, was as austere in his public manner as in his virtues, and inflexible in demanding the respect due to his rank and position. Of a broad intelligence, and a statesman of respectable stature, he knew little of the business of politics and cared less. He took his defeat with philosophy, regretting it more for the animosity toward his son-in-law it betokened than because it removed him temporarily from public life, and returned with his family to Albany, Hamilton was annoyed and disgusted, and resolved to keep his eye on Burr in the future. While he himself was in power the United States should have no set-backs that he could prevent, and if Burr realized his reading of his character he should manage to balk his ambitions if they threatened the progress of the country. Kitty Livingston he did not see again for many months, for her father died on July 25th. Hamilton heard of William Livingston's death with deep regret, for Liberty Hall was among the brightest of his memories; but events and emotions were crowding in his life as they never had crowded before, and he had little time for reminiscence.

Congress adjourned on the 12th of August to meet in Philadelphia in December. New York followed Washington to the ferry stairs upon the day of his departure, weeping not only for that great man's loss, but for the glory that went with him. "That vile Philadelphia," as Angelica Church, in a letter to Betsey of consolatory lament, characterized the city where Independence was born, was to be the capital of the Nation once more, New York to console herself with her commerce and the superior cleanliness of her streets. Those who could, followed the "Court," and those who could not, travelled the weary distance over the corduroy roads through the forests, and over swamps and rivers, as often as circumstances would permit. Of the former was Mrs. Croix, whose particular court protested it must have the solace of her presence in a city to which few went willingly. Clinton heaped her with reproaches, but she argued sweetly that he was outvoted, and that she should ever go where duty called. "She felt politics to be her mission," and in truth she enjoyed its intrigues, the double game she played, with all her feminine soul. Hamilton would not help himself in her valuable storehouse, but it pleased her to know that she held dangerous secrets in her hands, could confound many an unwary politician. And she had her methods, as we have seen, of springing upon Hamilton many a useful bit of knowledge, and of assisting him in ways unsuspected of any. She established herself in lodgings in Chestnut Street, not unlike those in which she had spent so many happy hours for two years past, inasmuch as they were situated on the first floor and communicated with a little garden. Her removal was looked upon as quite natural, and so admirably did she deport herself that even Mrs. Washington received her in time.

Philadelphia was a larger city than New York, with wide ill-kept streets, good pavements, and many fine houses and public buildings. Chestnut Street was the great thoroughfare, shopping district, and promenade. It was a city renowned for social activity and "crucifying expenses." Naturally its press was as jubilant over the revival of its ancient splendour as that of disappointed New York was scurrilous and vindictive. When the latter was not caricaturing Robert Morris, staggering off with the Administration on its back, or "Miss Assumption and her bastard brats," its anti-Federal part was abusing Hamilton as the arch-fiend who had sold the country, and applying to him every adjective of vituperation that fury and coarseness could suggest. There were poems, taunts, jibes, and squibs, printed as rapidly as the press and ingenuity could turn them out. If our ancestors were capable of appreciating the literary excellence of their pamphleteers, as many of those who have replaced them to-day could not, it must be admitted that we do not rage and hate so violently. The most hysteric effusions of our yellow press, or the caustic utterances of our reputable newspapers, are tame indeed before the daily cyclones of a time when everybody who did not love his political neighbor hated him with a deadly virulence of which we know little to-day. We may be improved, merely commercialized, or more diffuse in our interests. In those days every man was a politician first and himself after.

The violence of party feeling engendered once more by the debates over Hamilton's Report spread over the country like a prairie fire, and raged until, in the North at least, it was met by the back fire of increasing prosperity. As the summer waned farmers and merchants beheld the prices of public securities going up, heard that in Holland the foreign loan had gone above par, and that two hundred and seventy-eight thousand dollars of the domestic debt had been purchased and cancelled at a cost of one hundred and fifty thousand, saw trade reviving, felt their own burdens lighten with the banishment of the State debt. To sing the praises of the Assumption Bill was but a natural sequence, and from thence to a constant panegyric of Hamilton. The anti-Federalist press was drowned in the North by the jubilance of the

Federal and its increasing recruits, but in the South everything connected with the Government in general and Hamilton in particular was unholy, and the language in which the sentiment was expressed was unholier.

Meanwhile, Hamilton was established in a little house in Philadelphia, at work upon his second Report on the Public Credit, and elaborating his argument in favour of a National Bank. Betsey had been more fortunate than many in getting her house in order within a reasonable time, for others were camping in two rooms while the carpenters hammered over the rest of the neglected mansions. Washington arrived in November and took possession of the stately home of Robert Morris, although he grumbled that the stables would hold but twelve horses. It was a splendid mansion, however, and filled not only with the fine collections of the rich merchant, but with many beautiful works of art that the President brought from Mount Vernon. Congress opened on the 6th of December.

If Hamilton had given only an occasional half-amused, half-irritated attention to the journalistic and pamphlet warfare in which he had been the target, he now found a domestic engagement confronting him which commanded his attentions and roused all the fighting Scotch blood in his composition. Jefferson had done much and distressful thinking during the summer recess. In the leisure of his extensive, not to say magnificent, Virginia estates, and while entertaining the neighbouring aristocracy, he had moved slowly to the conclusion that he approved of nothing in the Administration, and that Hamilton was a danger to the Nation and a colossus in his path. Assumption he held to be a measure of the very devil, and fumed whenever he reflected upon his part in its accomplishment. "I was made to hold a candle!" he would explain apologetically. "He hoodwinked me, made a fool of me."

For a statesman of forty-seven, and one of the most distinguished and successful men in the country, the literary author of The Declaration of Independence, the father of many beneficent and popular laws in his own State, a minister to foreign courts and one of the deepest and subtlest students of human nature of his century, to find himself fooled and played with by a young man of thirty-three, relegated by him to a second place in the Cabinet and country, means—meant in those days, at least—hate of the most remorseless quality. Jefferson was like a volcano with bowels of fire and a crater which spilled over in the night. He smouldered and rumbled, a natural timidity preventing the splendour of fireworks. But he was deadly.

He and Madison met often during these holidays, and an object of their growing confidence was James Monroe, the new Senator from Virginia. Monroe was a fighter, and hatred of Hamilton was his religion. Moreover, he disapproved with violence of every measure of the new government, and everybody connected with it, from Washington down, Jefferson excepted; Randolph he held to be a trimmer, and overlooked the fact that although he himself had opposed the Constitution with all his words, he was one of the first to take office under it. Jefferson needed but this younger man's incentive to disapprove more profoundly not only assumption, but Hamilton's design to establish a National Bank. That was the most criminal evidence of an ultimate dash for a throne which the Secretary of the Treasury, whose place in the Cabinet should have been second to his own, but who was the very head and front of the Administration, had yet betrayed. And as for the triumphal progress of Washington through the States in the previous autumn, and again before leaving for Mount Vernon upon the close of the last Congress, a king could have done no more. The new Republic was tottering on its rotten foundations, and Jefferson and his able lieutenants vowed themselves to the rescue. Madison was the anti-government leader in the House, Monroe would abet him in the Senate, and Jefferson would undertake the fight in the Cabinet. It cannot be said that he liked the prospect, for he read his fellow-beings too well to mistake the mettle of Hamilton. He was a peaceable soul, except when in his study with pen in hand, but stem this monarchical tide he would, and bury Hamilton under the dam.

"We are three to one," he said reassuringly to his coadjutors. "He is brilliant. I do not deny it. But against a triple power—"

"He is worth any three men I ever knew," said Madison, drearily. "We shall have to work harder than he will."

Jefferson lifted his pen, and squinted thoughtfully at its point. Monroe, who was the youngest of the trio, laughed aloud.

And these were the forces of which Hamilton felt the shock shortly after the convening of Congress.

XXIII

On the 13th of December Hamilton sent to the House of Representatives his second Report on Public Credit—no longer a nomen of bitter sarcasm—and the Report in favour of a National Bank. Congress was once more on edge. Since his first Great Report, it had considered and wrangled over his successive Reports on State Debits and Credits, West Point, Public Lands, Estimates, and Renewal of Certificates; and it had lived through the hot summer on the prospect of the excitement which the bold and creative Secretary would surely provide. Even his enemies loved Hamilton in their way, for life was torpid when he rested on his labours.

The anti-Federalists, had they needed an additional incentive for the coming battle, a condition to rouse all their strength and mettle, found it in the rapidly increasing prosperity of the country, which had raised Hamilton to a height of popularity from which it would be an historic triumph to drag him down. He was, indeed, almost at the zenith of a reputation which few men have achieved. From end to end of the Union his name was on every lip, sometimes coupled with a hiss, but oftener with every expression of honour and admiration that the language could furnish. Even in the South he had his followers, and in the North and East it was hardly worth a man's nose to abuse him. He was a magician, who could make the fortunes of any man quick enough to seize his opportunities, and the saviour of the national honour and fortunes. His fame obscured that of Washington, and abroad he was by far the most interesting and significant figure in the young country. No wonder the anti-Federalists trembled for the future, and with all the vigour of hardened muscles fought his scheme for allying the moneyed classes with the Government.

Hamilton made no secret of his design so closely to attach the wealthy men of the country to the central Government that they must stand or fall with it, coming to its rescue in every crisis; and time has vindicated his far-sighted policy. But when the National Bank was in the preliminary stages of its journey, certain of its hosts in Congress saw but another horrid menace to the liberties of the people, another step toward the final establishment of a monarchy after the British pattern. The old arguments of subservience to British institutions in the matter of funding, and other successful pets of the Secretary, were dragged forth and wrangled over, in connection with this new and doubly pernicious measure of a National Bank.

Hamilton recommended that a number of subscribers should be incorporated into a bank, to be known as the Bank of the United States; the capital to be ten million dollars; the number of shares twenty-five thousand; the par value of each share four hundred dollars; the Government to become a subscriber to the amount of two millions, and to require in return a loan of an equal sum, payable in ten yearly instalments of two hundred thousand dollars each. The rest of the capital stock would be open to the public, to be paid for, one-quarter in gold and silver, and three-quarters in the six or three per cent certificates of the national debt. The life of the bank was to end in 1811. As an inducement for prompt subscriptions a pledge would be given that for twenty years to come Congress would incorporate no other.

It is odd reading for us, with a bank in every street, not only those old diatribes in Congress against banks of all sorts, but Hamilton's elaborate arguments in favour of banks in general, the benefits and conveniences they confer upon individuals as well as nations. But in those days there were but three banks in the Union, and each had been established against violent opposition, Hamilton, in particular, having carried the Bank of New York through by unremitting personal effort. The average man preferred his stocking. Representatives from backwoods districts were used to such circulating mediums as military warrants, guard certificates, horses, cattle, cow-bells, land, and whiskey. They looked askance at a bank as a sort of whirlpool into which wealth would disappear, and bolt out at the bottom into the pockets of a few individuals who understood what was beyond the average intellect. But by far the most disquieting objection brought forward against this plan of the Secretary's was its alleged unconstitutionality.

Monroe, although a new man, and speaking seldom, exerted a systematic opposition in the Senate, and Madison, in the House, argued, with lucidity and persistence, that the Constitution had no power to grant a charter to any such institution as the Secretary proposed. Others argued that the success of this new scheme would infringe upon the rights of the States, and still others thundered the everlasting accusations of monarchical design. Nevertheless, the bill for granting the required charter passed both Houses by a handsome majority. The

312

able Federalists had contemptuously dissected the arguments against it with greater skill than even Madison could command; and confidence in Hamilton, by this time, practically was a religion. The bill was sent to Washington to sign or veto, and the anti-Federalists, disconcerted and alarmed by their signal defeat in Congress, rested their final hope on Jefferson.

The President, according to law, had but ten days in which to sign or veto a bill: if he hesitated but a moment beyond the constitutional limit, the bill became a law without his signature. It may safely be said that these ten days were the most miserable of Washington's life so far, although they were but the forerunner of many to come.

By this time the Cabinet had acquired the habit of assembling for conference about a council table in the President's house. Washington sat at the head of the table, with Hamilton on his left, and Jefferson on his right. Knox, who would have frowned upon the Almighty had he contradicted Hamilton, sat beside his Captain. Randolph sat opposite, his principles with Jefferson, but his intellect so given to hair-splitting, that in critical moments this passion to weigh every side of a proposition in turn frequently resulted in the wrench of a concession by Hamilton, while Jefferson fumed. As time went on, Washington fell into the habit of extending his long arms upon the table in front of him, and clasping his imposing hands in the manner of a rampart.

Jefferson began a tentative showing of his colours while the bill was fighting its stormy way through Congress, and Hamilton was a brief while perceiving his drift and appreciating his implacable enmity. The first time that Jefferson encountered the lightning in Hamilton's eye, the quivering of his nostril, as he half rose from his chair under the sudden recognition of what he was to expect, his legs slid forward limply, and he turned his head toward the door. Washington suppressed a smile, but it was long before he smiled again, Hamilton would have no hints and innuendoes; he forced his enemy to show his hand. But although he wrung from Jefferson his opposition to the Bank and to every scheme the Secretary of the Treasury had proposed, he could not drag him into the open. Jefferson was deprecating, politely determined to serve the country in his own way, lost in admiration of this opponent's intellect, but forced to admit his mistakes—the mistakes of a too ardent mind. The more bitter and caustic the sarcasms that leaped from Hamilton's tongue, the more suave he grew, for placidity was his only weapon of self-preservation; a war of words with Hamilton, and he would be made ridiculous in the presence of his colleagues and Washington. Occasionally the volcano flared through his pale eyes, and betrayed such hate and resentment that Washington elevated his hands an inch. The President sat like a stoic, with a tornado on one side of him and a growling Vesuvius on the other, and exhibited an impartiality, in spite of the fact that Jefferson daily betrayed his hostility to the Administration, which revealed but another of his superhuman attributes. But there is a psychological manifestation of mental bias, no matter what the control, and some men are sensitive enough to feel it. Jefferson was quite aware that Washington loved Hamilton and believed in him thoroughly, and he felt the concealed desire to side openly with the Secretary to whom, practically, had been given the reins of government. Washington, rather than show open favouritism, even to Hamilton, to whom he felt the profoundest gratitude, would have resigned his high office; but the desire was in his head, and Jefferson felt it. The campaign open, he kept up a nagging siege upon Washington's convictions in favour of his aggressive Secretary's measures, finding constant excuses to be alone with the President. Hamilton, on the other hand, dismissed the subject when left alone with Washington, unless responding to a demand. He frequently remained to the midday meal with the family, and was as gay and lively as if Jefferson, Madison, and Monroe were in the limbo to which he gladly would have consigned them. His nature was mercurial in one, at least, of its essences, and a sudden let-down, followed by congenial company, restored his equilibrium at once. But Washington watched the development of the blackness and violence of his deeper passions with uneasiness and regret, finally with alarm.

Hamilton, in truth, was roused to his dregs. The sneaking retreat of Madison from his standard and affections, the rancorous enmity of Monroe, with whom he had fought side by side and been well with whenever they had been thrown together in the bitter winters of inaction; the slow, cool, determined, deadly opposition of Jefferson, whom he recognized as a giant in intellect and despised as a man with that hot contempt for the foe who will not strip and fight in the open, which whips a passionate nature to the point of fury, had converted Hamilton into a colossus of hate which, as Madison had intimated, far surpassed the best endeavours of the powerful trio. He hated harder, for he had more to hate with,—stronger and deeper passions, ampler resources in his intellect, and an energy of temperament which Jefferson and Madison, recruited by Monroe, could not outweigh. He saw that he was in for the battle of his life, and that its finish might be deferred for years; for he made no such mistake as to underrate the strength and resources of this triple enemy; he knew that it would last until one or the other were worn out. Hamilton had no thought of defeat; he never contemplated it for a moment; his faith in himself and in the wisdom of his measures was absolute; what he looked forward to with the deepest irritation was the persistent opposition, the clogging of his wheels of progress, the constant personal attacks which might weaken him with the country before his multitudinous objects should be accomplished. He suggested resource after resource to his faithful and brilliant disciples in Congress, and he determined to force Jefferson to leave the Cabinet.

"If he only would take himself out of that room with a defiant admission that he intended to head the opposite party and fight me to the death!" he exclaimed to Mrs. Croix, one day. "What right has he to sit there at Washington's hand, a member of his Cabinet, ostensibly in its first place, and at war with every measure of the Administration? He cannot oppose me without involving the President, under whom he holds office, and if he had a grain of decent feeling he would resign rather than occupy such an anomalous position."

"He intends to force you to resign."

"You don't mean to say that he is coming here?" asked Hamilton, in disgust. "Who next?"

"Mr. Jefferson succumbed quite three weeks ago," said Mrs. Croix, gaily. "He amuses me, and I am instilling the conviction that no human being can force you to do anything you don't want to do, and that the sooner he retreats gracefully the better."

Hamilton shrugged his shoulders and made no answer. He had ceased remonstrance long since. If it pleased her to think she was fighting the battles he was forced to fight with undiminished vigour himself, he should be the last to interfere with her amusement. She was a born intrigante, and would have been miserable freckling her complexion in the open sunlight. He was too grateful to her at this time to risk a quarrel, or to condemn her for any of her violations of masculine standards. It was to her he poured out his wrath, after an encounter with Jefferson which had roused him too viciously for reaction at Washington's board or at his own. His wife he spared in every way. Not only was her delicate health taxed to the utmost with social duties which could not be avoided, the management of her household affairs, and an absorbing and frequently ailing family, but he would have controlled himself had he burst, before he would have terrified her with a glimpse of passions of whose existence she had not a suspicion. To her and his family he was ever the most amiable and indulgent of men, giving them every spare moment he could command, and as delighted as a schoolboy with a holiday, when he could spend an hour in the nursery, an evening with his wife, or take a ramble through the woods with his boys. He took a deep pride in his son Philip, directed his studies and habits, and was as pleased with every evidence of his progress as had he seen Madison riding a rail in a coat of tar and feathers. He coddled and petted the entire family, particularly his little daughter Angelica, and they adored him, and knew naught of his depths.

But Mrs. Croix knew them. In her management of Hamilton she made few mistakes, passionately as she loved him. It was in her secluded presence he stormed himself cool, was indignantly sympathized with first, then advised, then soothed. He was made to understand that the more he revealed the black and implacable deeps of his nature, the more was he worshipped, the more keen the response from other and not dissimilar deeps. His wife was necessary to him in many ways, his Egeria in many more. Although he would have sacrificed the last to the first, had it come to an issue, he would have felt as if one-half of him had been cruelly divorced. Few women understand this dual nature in men, and few are the men who do not. It has been known to exist in those who make no pretensions to genius, and in Hamilton was as natural as the versatility of his intellect. When with one he locked the other in the recesses of his mind as successfully as when at college he had accomplished herculean feats of mental accumulation by keeping but one thing before his thought at a time. What he wanted he would have, so long as his family were in no way affected; and had it not been for Mrs. Croix at this time, it might have been worse for Betsey. She cooled his fevers; her counsel was always sound. And her rooms and herself were beautiful. She had her way of banishing the world by drawing her soft blue curtains and lighting her many candles. Had she been a fool, Hamilton would have tired of her in a month; as it was, he often thought of her as the most confidential and dispensing of his friends, and no more.

During the preceding two years of their acquaintance there had been many quarrels, caused by furious bursts of temper on the part of the lady, when Hamilton forgot her for a month or more. There were times when she was the solitary woman of Earth, and others when she might have reigned on Mars. He was very busy, and he had countless interests to absorb time and thought. He never pretended to more than a romantic passion for her, and deep as was her own infatuation, it was sometimes close to hate; for she was a woman whose vanity was as strong as her passions. At this time, however, he felt a frequent need of her, and she made the most of the opportunity.

XXIV

Meanwhile, Washington, deeply disturbed by the arguments in the press and Congress against the constitutionality of the National Bank, had privately asked for the written opinions of Jefferson and Randolph, and for a form of veto from Madison. They were so promptly forthcoming that they might have been biding demand. Washington read them carefully, then, too worried and impatient for formalities, carried them himself to Hamilton's house.

"For God's sake read them at once and tell me what they amount to," he said, throwing the bundle of papers on the table. "Of course you must prepare me an answer in writing, but I want your opinion at once. I will wait."

Long years after, when Betsey was an old woman, someone asked her if she remembered any incidents in connection with the establishment of the great Bank. She replied, "Yes, I remember it all distinctly. One day General Washington called at the house, looking terribly worried. He shut himself up in the study with my husband for hours, and they talked nearly all the time. When he went away he looked much more cheerful. That night my husband did not go to bed at all, but sat up writing; and the next day we had a Bank."

Hamilton's answer, both verbally and in a more elaborate form, was so able and sound a refutation of every point advanced by the enemy that Washington hesitated no longer and signed the bill during the last moments remaining to him. Years later, when the same question was raised again, Chief Justice Marshall, the most brilliant ornament, by common consent, the Supreme Court of the United States has had, admitted that he could add nothing to Hamilton's argument. It must, also, have convinced Madison; for while President of the United States, and his opportunity for displaying the consistencies of his intellect, unrivalled, he signed the charter of the Second National Bank. Monroe, whose party was in power, and able to defeat any obnoxious measure of the Federalists, advocated; the second Bank as heartily as he had cursed the first. His defence of his conduct was a mixture of insolent frankness and verbiage. He said: "As to the constitutional objection, it formed no serious obstacle. In voting against the Bank in the first instance, I was governed essentially by policy. The construction I gave to the Constitution I considered a strict one. In the latter instance it was more liberal but, according to my judgement, justified by its powers." If anyone can tell what he meant, doubtless his own shade would be grateful.

Hamilton's second Report on the Public Credit had beer buffeted about quite as mercilessly as the Report in favour of a bank. The customs officers had, during the past year collected $1,900,000, which sufficed to pay two-thirds of the annual expenses of the Government. There was still a deficit of $826,000, and to meet future contingencies of a similar nature, the Secretary of the Treasury urged the passage of an Excise Bill.

Even his enemies admired his courage, for no measure could be more unpopular, raise more widespread wrath. It was regarded as a deliberate attempt to deprive man of his most cherished vice; and every argument was brought forth in opposition, from the historic relation of whiskey to health and happiness, to the menace of adopting another British measure. The bill passed; but it was a different matter to enforce it, as many an excise officer reflected, uncheerfully, whilst riding a rail. On the 28th of January Hamilton sent in his Report in favour of the establishment of a mint, with details so minute that he left the framers of the necessary bill little excuse for delay; but it had the same adventurous and agitated experience of its predecessors, and only limped through, in an amended form, after the wildest outburst of democratic fanaticism which any of the measures of Hamilton had induced. The proposition to stamp the coins with the head of the President was conclusive of an immediate design to place a crown upon the head of Washington. Doubtless the leaders of the Federal party, under the able tuition of their despot, had their titles ready, their mine laid. Jefferson, in the Cabinet, protested with such solemn persistence against so dangerous a precedent, and Hamilton perforated him with such arrows of ridicule, that Washington exploded with wrath, and demanded to know if neither never intended to yield a point to the other.

During this session of Congress, Hamilton also sent in Reports on Trade with India and China, and on the Dutch Loan. He was fortunate in being able to forget his enemies for days and even weeks at a time, when his existence was so purely impersonal that every capacity of his mind, save the working, slept soundly. By now, he had his department in perfect running order; and his successors have accepted his legacy, with its infinitude of detail, its unvarying practicality, with gratitude and trifling alterations. When Jefferson disposed himself in the Chair of State, in 1801, he appointed Albert Gallatin—the ablest financier, after Hamilton, the country has produced—Secretary of the Treasury, and begged him to sweep the department clean of the corruption amidst which Hamilton had sat and spun his devilish schemes. Gallatin, after a thorough and conscientious search for political microbes, informed his Chief that in no respect could the department be improved, that there was not a trace of crime, past or present. Jefferson was disconcerted; but, as a matter of fact, his administrations were passed complacently amidst Hamilton legacies and institutions. Jefferson's hour had come. He could undo all that he had denounced in his rival as monarchical, aristocratical, pernicious to the life of Democracy. But the administrations of Jefferson, Madison, and Monroe, ran from first to last on those Federal wheels which are still in use, protected within and without by Federal institutions. But their architect was sent to his grave soon after the rise of his arch-enemy to power, was beyond humiliation or party triumph; it would be folly to war with a spirit, and greater not to let well enough alone. But that is a far cry. Meanwhile the Bank was being rushed through, and its establishment was anticipated with the keenest interest, and followed by a season of crazy speculation, dissatisfaction, and vituperation. But this Hamilton had expected, and he used his pen constantly to point out the criminal folly and inevitable consequences of speculation.

XXV

Congress adjourned while the excitement was at its height. Washington went to Mount Vernon, the Cabinet scattered, and there was an interval of peace. Philadelphia in summer was always unhealthy, and liable to an outbreak of fever at any moment. Hamilton sent his family to the Schuyler estate at Saratoga. Mrs. Croix had gone as early as May to the New England coast; for even her magnificent constitution had felt the strain of that exciting session, and Philadelphia was not too invigorating in winter. Hamilton remained alone in his home, glad of the abundant leisure which the empty city afforded to catch up with the arrears of his work, to design methods for financial relief against the time to apply them, and to prepare his Report on Manufactures, a paper destined to become as celebrated and almost as widespread in its influence as the great Report on Public Credit. It required days and nights of thinking, research, correspondence, comparison, and writing; and how in the midst of all this mass of business, this keen anxiety regarding the whirlwind of speculation—which was involving some of the leading men in the country, and threatening the young Government with a new disaster; how, while sitting up half the night with his finger on the public pulse, waiting for the right moment to apply his remedies, he managed to entangle himself in a personal difficulty, would be an inscrutable mystery, were any man but Alexander Hamilton in question.

I shall not enter into the details of the Reynolds affair. No intrigue was ever less interesting. Nor should I make even a passing allusion to it, were it not for its political ultimates. A couple of blackmailers laid a trap for the Secretary of the Treasury, and he walked into it, as the wisest of men have done before and since, when the woman has been sufficiently attractive at the right moment. This woman was common and sordid, but she was young and handsome, and her affectation of violent attachment, if ungrammatical, was plausible enough to convince any man accustomed to easy conquest; and the most astute of men, provided his passions be strong enough, can be fooled by any woman at once designing and seductive. Ardent susceptibility was in the very

320

essence of Hamilton, with Scotland and France in his blood, the West Indies the mould of his youthful being, and the stormy inheritance of his parents.

But although Hamilton might succumb to a woman of Mrs. Reynold's type, she could not hold him. After liberally relieving the alleged pecuniary distress of this charmer, and weary of her society, he did his best to get rid of her. She protested. So did he. It was then that he was made aware of the plot The woman's husband appeared, and announced that only a thousand dollars would heal his wounded honour, and that if it were not immediately forthcoming, he would write to Mrs. Hamilton.

Hamilton was furious. His first impulse was to tell the man to do his worst, for anything in the nature of coercion stripped him for the fray at once. But an hour of reflection cooled his blood. No one was to blame but himself. If he had permitted himself to be made a fool of, it was but just that he should take the consequences, and not cruelly wound the woman he loved the better for his vagaries. Moreover, such a scandal would seriously affect the high office he filled, might indeed force him to resignation; not only thwarting his great ambitions, but depriving the country of services which no other man had the ability or the will to render. And a few moments forecast of the triumph of his enemies, not only over himself but possibly over his party, in case of his downfall, was sufficient in itself to force him to terms. Few are the momentous occasions in which men are governed by a single motive. Hamilton's ambitions were welded into the future happiness and glory of the country he had so ardently adopted. And if love of power was his ruling passion, it certainly was directed to the loftiest of ends. To desire to create a nation out of the resources of a vast understanding, controlled by wisdom and honour, is an ambition which should be dignified with a higher name. Small and purely personal ambitions were unknown to Hamilton, his gifts were given him for the elevation of the human race; but he would rather have reigned in hell than have sunk to insignificance on earth. As he remarked once to Kitty Livingston, the complexity of man so far exceeds that of the average woman, complexity being purely a matter of brain and having no roots whatever in sex, that it were a waste of valuable time to analyze its ramifications, and the crossings and entanglements of its threads. Hamilton paid the money, yielded further to the extent of several hundred dollars, then the people disappeared, and he hoped that he had heard the last of them. Fortunately his habits were methodical, the result of his mercantile training on St. Croix, and he preserved the correspondence.

XXVI

Hamilton looked forward to the next Congressional term with no delusions. He polished his armour until it was fit to blind his adversaries, tested the temper of every weapon, sharpened every blade, arranged them for immediate availment. In spite of the absorbing and disconcerting interests of the summer, he had followed in thought the mental processes of his enemies, kept a sharp eye out for their new methods of aggression. Themselves had had no more intimate knowledge of their astonishment, humiliation, and impotent fury at the successive victories of the invulnerable Secretary of the Treasury, than had Hamilton himself. He knew that they had confidently hoped to beat him by their combined strength and unremitting industry, and by the growing power of their party, before the finish of the preceding term. The Federalists no longer had their former majority in Congress upon all questions, for many of the men who, under that title, had been devoted adherents of the Constitution, were become alarmed at the constant talk of the monarchical tendencies of the Government, of the centralizing aristocratic measures of the Secretary of the Treasury, at the "unrepublican" formalities and elegance of Washington's "Court," at his triumphal progresses through the country, and at the enormous one-man power as exhibited in the person of Hamilton. Upon these minds Jefferson, Madison, and Monroe had worked with unremitting subtlety. It was not so much that the early Federalists wished to see Hamilton dragged from his lofty position, for they admired him, and were willing to acknowledge his services to the country; but that the idea grew within them that he must be properly checked, lest they suddenly find themselves subjects again. They realized that they had been running to him for advice upon every matter, great and insignificant, since the new Congress began its sittings, and that they had adopted the greater part of his counsels without question; they believed that Hamilton was becoming the Congress as he already was the Administration; and overlooked the fact that legislative authority as against executive had no such powerful supporter as the Secretary of the Treasury. But it was not an era when men reasoned as exhaustively as they might have done. They were terrified by bogies, and the blood rarely was out of their heads. "Monarchism must be checked," and Hamilton for some months past had watched the rapid welding of the old anti-Federalists and the timid Federalists into what was shortly to be known, for a time, as the Republican party. That Jefferson had been at work all summer, as during the previous term, with his subtle, insinuating, and convincing pen, he well knew, and for what the examples of such men as Jefferson and Madison counted—taking their stand on the high ground of stemming the menace to personal liberties. The Republican party was to be stronger far than the old anti-Federal, for it was to be a direct and constant appeal to the controlling passion of man, vanity; and Hamilton believed that did it obtain the reins of power too early in the history of the Nation, confusion, if not anarchy, would result: not only was it too soon to try new experiments, diametrically opposed to those now in operation, but, under the tutelage of Jefferson, the party was in favour of vesting more power in the masses. Hamilton had no belief in entrusting power to any man or body of men that had not brains, education, and a developed reasoning capacity. He was a Republican but not a Democrat. He recognized, long before the rival party saw their mistake in nomenclature, that this Jefferson school marked the degeneracy of republicanism into democracy. Knowing how absurd and unfounded was all the hysterical talk about monarchism, and that time would vindicate the first Administration and its party as Republican in its very essence, he watched with deep, and often with impersonal, uneasiness the growth of a party which would denationalize the government, scatter its forces, and interpret the Constitution in a fashion not intended by the most protesting of its framers. Hamilton had in an extraordinary degree the faculty which Spencer calls representativeness; but there were some things he could not foresee, and one was that when the Republicans insinuated themselves to power they would rest on their laurels, let play the inherent conservatism of man, and gladly accept the goods the Federal party had provided them. The three men who wrote and harangued and intrigued against Hamilton for years, were to govern as had they been the humblest of Hamiltonians. But this their great antagonist was in unblest ignorance of, for he, too, reasoned in the heat and height and thick of the fray; and he made himself ready to dispute every inch of the ground, checkmate every move, force Jefferson into retirement, and invigorate and encourage his own ranks. The majority in both Houses was still Federal, if diminished, and he determined that it should remain so.

As early as October his watching eye caught the first flash in the sunlight of a new blade in the enemies' armoury. One Freneau had come to town. He had some reputation as a writer of squibs and verses, and Hamilton knew him to be a political hireling utterly without principle. When, therefore, he heard incidentally that this man had lately been in correspondence and conference with the Virginian junta, and particularly that he had been "persuaded by his old friend Madison to settle in Philadelphia," had received an appointment as translating clerk in the Department of State, and purposed to start a newspaper called the *National Gazette* in opposition to Fenno's Administration organ, *The United States Gazette*, he knew what he was to expect. Fenno's paper was devoted to the Administration, and to the Secretary of the Treasury in particular; it was the medium through which Hamilton addressed most of his messages to the people. Naturally it was of little use to his enemies; and that Jefferson and his aides had realized the value of an organ of attack, he divined very quickly. He stated his suspicions to Washington immediately upon the President's arrival, and warned him to expect personal assault and abuse.

"There is now every evidence of a strong and admirably organized cabal," he added. "And to pull us down they will not stop at abuse of even you, if failure haunts them. I shall get the most of it, perhaps all. I hope so, for I am used to it."

He laughed, and quite as light-heartedly as ever; but Washington looked at him with uneasiness.

"You are a terrible fighter, Hamilton," he said. "I have never seen or dreamed of your equal. Why not merely oppose to them a massive resistance? Why be continually on the warpath? They give you a tentative scratch, and you reply with a blow under the jaw, from which they rise with a sullener determination to ruin you, than ever. When you are alone with your pen and the needs of the country, you might have the wisdom of a thousand years in your brain, and I doubt if at such times you remember your name; you are one of the greatest, wisest, coolest statesmen of any age; but the moment you come forth to the open, you are not so much a political leader as a warlike Scot at the head of his clan, and readier by far to make a dash into the neighbouring fastness than to wait for an attack. Are you and Jefferson going to fight straight through this session?—for if you are, I shall no longer yearn so much for the repose of Mount Vernon as for the silences of the tomb."

Washington spoke lightly, as he often did when they were alone, and he had returned from Virginia refreshed; but Hamilton answered contritely:—

"We both behaved abominably last year, and it was shocking that you should bear the brunt of it. I'll do my best to control myself in the Cabinet—although that man rouses all the devil in me; but not to fight at the head of my party. Oh! Can the leopard change his spots? I fear I shall die with my back against the wall, sir, and my boots on." "I haven't the slightest doubt of it. But be careful of giving too free and constant a play to your passions and your capacity for rancour, or your character will deteriorate. Tell me," he added abruptly, narrowing his eyes and fixing Hamilton with a prolonged scrutiny, "do you not feel its effects already?"

By this time the early, half-unwilling, half-magnetized affection which the boy in Hamilton had yielded to his Chief had given place to a consistent admiration for the exalted character, the wisdom, justice, and self-control of the President of the United States, and to a devoted attachment. The bond between the two men grew closer every day, and only the end of all things severed it. Hamilton, therefore, replied as frankly as if Washington had asked his opinion on the temper of the country, instead of probing the sacred recesses of his spirit:—

"There have been times when I have sat down and stared into myself with horror; when I have felt as if sitting in the ruins of my nature. I have caught myself up again and again, realizing where I was drifting. I have let a fiend loose within me, and I have turned upon it at times with a disgust so bitter and a terror so over-mastering that the mildness which has resulted has made me feel indifferent and even amiable to mine enemies. Whether this intimate knowledge of myself will save me, God knows; but when some maddening provocation comes, after reaction has run its course, I rage more hotly than ever, and only a sense of personal dignity keeps me from using my fists. I am two-thirds passion, and I am afraid that in the end it will consume me. I live

325

so intensely, in my best and my worst! I would give all I possess for your moderation and balance."

"No, you would not," said Washington. "War is the breath of your nostrils, and peace would kill you. Not that the poise I have acquired brings me much peace in these days."

Hamilton, who had spoken dejectedly, but with the deep relief which every mortal feels in a moment of open and safe confession, sprang to his feet, and stood on the hearth rug, his eyes sparkling with humour. "Confess, sir," he cried gaily. "You do not like Jefferson any better than I do. Fancy him opposite to you day after day, stinging you with honeyed shafts and opposing you with obstacle after obstacle, while leering with hypocrisy. Put yourself in my place for an instant, and blame me if you can."

"Oh," said Washington, with a deep growl of disgust, "o-h-h!" But he would not discuss his Secretary of State, even with Hamilton.

XXVII

The bombardment from Freneau's *Gazette* opened at once. It began with a general assault upon the Administration, denouncing every prominent member in turn as a monarchist or an aristocrat, and every measure as subversive of the liberties of the country. Vice-President Adams received a heavy broadside, his "Discourses on Davila," with their animadversions upon the French Revolution in particular and Democracy in general, being regarded as a heinous offence against the spirit of his country, and detrimental to the political morals of the American youth. But although the *Gazette* kept up its pretence of being an anti-Administration organ, publishing in the interests of a deluded people, it soon settled down to abuse of Hamilton.

That a large number of the articles were from Jefferson's damning pen few of the Republican leader's friends denied with any warmth, and the natural deductions of history would have settled the question, had not Freneau himself confessed the truth in his old age. What Jefferson did not write, he or Madison inspired, and Freneau had a lively pen of his own. They had promising material in General St. Clair's recent and disastrous defeat by the Indians, which, by a triumph of literary ingenuity, was ascribed to the ease and abundance with which the Secretary of the Treasury had caused money to circulate. But a far stronger weapon for their malignant use was the ruinous speculation which had maddened the country since the opening of the Bank of the United States. It was not enough that the Bank was a monarchical institution, a machine for the corruption of the Government, a club of grasping and moneyed aristocrats, but it had been purposely designed for the benefit of the few—the "corrupt squadron," namely, the Secretary and his friends—at the expense of the many. The subsequent failure for $3,000,000 of one of these friends, William Duer, gave them no pause, for his ruin precipitated a panic, and but added distinction to his patron's villany.

For a time Hamilton held his peace. He had enough to do, steering the financial bark through the agitated waters of speculation, without wasting time on personal recrimination. Even when, before the failure, he was accused of being in secret partnership with Duer, he did not pause for vindication, but exerted himself to alleviate the general distress. He initiated the practice, followed by Secretaries of the Treasury at the present moment, of buying Government loan certificates in different financial centres throughout the country, thus easing the money market, raising the price of the certificates, and strengthening the public credit. He used the sinking-fund for this purpose.

There was comparative peace in the Cabinet, an armed truce being, perhaps, a more accurate description of an uneasy psychological condition. Hamilton had made up his mind not only to spare Washington further annoyance, if possible, but to maintain a dignity which he was keenly conscious of having relinquished in the past. The two antagonists greeted each other politely when they met for the first time in the Council Chamber, although they had crossed the street several times previously to avoid meeting; and if Jefferson discoursed unctiously and at length, whenever the opportunity offered, upon the lamentable consequences of a lamentable measure, and indulged in melancholy prognostications of a general ruin, in which the Government would disappear and be forgotten, Hamilton replied for a time with but an occasional sarcasm, and a change of subject. One day, however, a long-desired opportunity presented itself, and he did not neglect it. He was well aware that Jefferson had complained to Virginia that he had been made to hold a candle to the wily Secretary of the Treasury in the matter of assumption, in other words, that his guileless understanding, absorbed in matters of State, had been duped into a bargain of which Virginia did not approve, despite the concession to the Potomac.

About two months after Congress opened, Washington, as his Cabinet seated itself, was detained in his room with a slight indisposition, but sent word that he would appear presently. For a time, Randolph and Knox talked feverishly about the Indian troubles, while Hamilton looked over some notes, and Jefferson watched his antagonist covertly, as if anticipating a sudden spring across the table. Hamilton was not in a good humour. He was accustomed to abuse in Congress, and that it was again in full tide concerned him little, for he was sure of ultimate victories in both Houses; and words which were powerless to result in a defeat for himself, or his party, he treated with the scorn which impotence deserved. But it was another matter to have his private character assailed day after day in the press, to watch a subtle pen insinuate into the public mind that a woman imperilled her reputation in receiving him, and that he was speculating in secret with the reckless friend whom he had warned over and over, and begged to desist. Freneau sent him three copies of the *Gazette* daily, lest he miss something, and he had that morning left Betsey in tears. Fenno was fighting the Secretary's battles valiantly; but there was only one pen in America which could cope with Jefferson's, and that was Hamilton's own. But aside from his accumulating cares, it was a strife to which he did not care to descend. To-day, however, he needed but a match, and Jefferson, who experienced a fearful fascination in provoking him, applied it.

"I hear that Duer is on the verge of failure," he remarked sadly.

"Yes," said Hamilton; "he is."

"I hold it to be a great misfortune that he has been connected with the Administration in any way."

"His connection was quite distinct from your department. I alone was responsible for his appointment as my assistant. There is no necessity for you to shed any hypocritical tears."

"What concerns the honour of the Administration naturally concerns the Secretary of State."

"There is no question of honour. If Duer fails, he will fail honourably, and the Administration, with which he is no longer

328

connected, will in no way be involved."

"Of those facts of course I am sure, but I fear the reflections in the press."

"Keep your own pen worthily employed, and the Administration will take care of itself."

"I do not understand you, sir," said Jefferson, with great dignity.

"I am quite ready to be explicit. Keep your pen out of Freneau's blackguard sheet, while you are sitting at Washington's right hand, at all events—"

Jefferson had elevated both hands. "I call Heaven to witness," he cried, "this black aspersion upon my character is, has been, entirely a production of the imagination of my enemies. I have never written nor inspired a line in Mr. Freneau's paper."

Hamilton laughed and returned to his notes.

"You do not believe me, sir?" demanded Jefferson, the blood boiling slowly to his large face.

"No," said Hamilton; "I do not."

Jefferson brought his mighty fist down upon the table with a bang." Sir!" he exclaimed, his husky voice unpleasantly strained, "I have stood enough from you. Are you aware that you have called me a liar, sir? I have suffered at your hands since the day I set foot in this country. I left the peace and retirement that I love, to come forth in response to a demand upon my duty, a demand I have ever heeded, and what has been my reward? The very first act I was tricked into committing was a crime against my country—"

"Were you in your dotage, sir?" thundered Hamilton, springing to his feet, and bringing his own hand down with such violence that the lead in his cuff dented his wrist. "Was your understanding enfeebled with age, that you could not comprehend the exhaustive explanation I made of the crisis in this country's affairs? Did I not give you twenty-four hours in which to think it over? What were you doing—muddling your brains with French wines?—that you could not reason clearly when relieved of my baleful fascination? Were you not protected on the following day by two men, who were more your friends than mine? I proposed a straightforward bargain, which you understood as well then as you do now. You realized to the full what the interests of the country demanded, and in a rare moment of disinterested patriotism you agreed to a compromise in which you saw no detriment to yourself. What you did not anticipate was the irritation of your particular State, and the annoyance to your vanity of permitting a younger man to have his way. Now let me hear no more of this holding a candle, and the tricking of an open mind by a wily one, unless you are willing to acknowledge that your brain was too weak to grasp a simple proposition; in which case you had better resign from public office."

"I know that is what you are trying to force me to do," gasped Jefferson, almost speechless between rage and physical fear; for Hamilton's eyes were flashing, his body curved as if he meditated immediate personal violence. "But I'll not do it, sir, any more than I or anyone else will be deluded by the speciousness of your language. You are an upstart. You have no State affinities, you despise them for a very good reason—you come from God knows where—I do not even know the name of the place. You are playing a game. You care nothing for the country you were not born in. Unless you can be king, you would treat it as your toy."

"For your absurd personalities I care nothing," said Hamilton, reseating himself. "They are but the ebullitions of an impotence that would ruin and cannot. But take heed what you write, for in injuring the Secretary of the Treasury you injure the prosperity of the country; and if you push me too far, I'll expose you and make you infamous. Here comes the President. For God's sake bottle your spite for the present."

The two men did not exchange a remark during the rest of the sitting, but Jefferson boiled slowly and steadily; Hamilton's words had raised welts under which he would writhe for some time to come. When the Cabinet adjourned he remained, and followed Washington into the library, under cover of a chat about seeds and bulbs, a topic of absorbing interest to both. When their legs were extended before the fire, Jefferson said, as abruptly as if the idea had but just presented itself:—

"Mr. President, we are both Virginians, and had cut our wisdom teeth—not that for a moment I class myself with you, sir—while young Hamilton was still in diapers."

"Children do not wear diapers in the West Indies," interrupted Washington, in his gravest accents. "I spent some months on the Island of Barbadoes, in the year seventeen hundred and fifty-one."

"Was he born In the West Indies? I had never heard. But, if I may continue, I have therefore summoned up my courage to speak to you on a subject close to my heart—for no subject can be so close as the welfare of a country to which we have devoted our lives."

He paused a moment, prepared with an answer, did the President haughtily warn him not to transgress the bounds of etiquette; but Washington was staring at the fire, apparently recalling the scenery of the Tropics.

Jefferson continued: "In the length and breadth of this Union there is not a man, not even the most ardent Republican, who has not implicit faith in the flawless quality of your patriotism and in your personal wisdom; but, and possibly unknown to you, sir, the extreme and high-handed measures, coupled with the haughty personal arrogance, of our Secretary of the Treasury have inspired a widespread belief, which is permeating even his personal friends, that he entertains subtle and insidious monarchical designs, is plotting to convert our little Republic into a kingdom. Personally, I do not believe this—"

"I should hope not. You have always seemed to me to be a man of singular wisdom and good sense. Therefore I feel sure that you are as heartily sick of all this absurd talk about monarchism as I am. There is not a word of truth in Mr. Hamilton's 'monarchical designs'; it is impossible that you should not know this as well as I do. You must also be as well aware that he has rendered services to this country which will be felt as long as it remains united. It is doubtful if anyone else could have rendered these same services, for, to my knowledge at least, we have no man in the country who combines financial genius with an unexampled boldness and audacity. He has emphatically been the man for the hour, abruptly transferred from his remote birthplace, it has seemed to me, by a special intervention of Providence; free of all local prejudices, which have been, and will continue to be, the curse of this country, and with a mettle unacted upon by years of doubt and hesitation. I do no other man in public life an injustice in my warm admiration of Mr. Hamilton's genius and absolute disinterestedness. Each has his place, and is doing his part bravely and according to his lights, many of them rendering historic services which Mr. Hamilton's will not overshadow. His are equally indisputable. This unfortunate result of establishing a National Bank was doubtless inevitable, and will quickly disappear. That the Bank is a monarchical device, you, of all men, are too wise to believe for a moment. Leave that for such sensational scoundrels as the editors of this new *Gazette* and of other papers. I regret that there is a personal antipathy between you and Mr. Hamilton, but I have not the least doubt that you believe in his integrity as firmly as I do."

Jefferson was scowling heavily. "I am not so sure that I do, sir," he said; inconsistent often in his calmest tempers, passion dissipated his power of consecutive thought. "When Mr. Hamilton and I were on friendly terms—before he took to annoying me with a daily exhibition of personal rancour, from which I have been entirely free—he has often at my own table avowed his admiration of the British Constitution, deprecated the weakness of our own admirable instrument, tacitly admitted his regret that we are a republic and not a kingdom. I have his very words in my diary. He is committed out of his own mouth. I not only believe but know him to be a lover of absolute monarchy, and that he has no faith that this country can continue to exist in its present shape. It is for that reason I hold him to be a traitor to the country with which he is merely amusing himself."

"Sir," said Washington, turning to Jefferson an immobile face, in which the eyes were beginning to glitter, "is a man to be judged by his private fancies or by his public acts? I know nothing of Mr. Hamilton's secret desires. Neither, I fancy, do you. We do know that he has resigned a brilliant and profitable practice at the bar to guide this unfortunate country out of bankruptcy and dishonour into prosperity and every promise of a great and honourable future. Pray let the matter rest there for the present. If Mr. Hamilton be really a liar and a charlatan, rest assured he will betray himself before any great harm is done. Every man is his own worst enemy. I was deeply interested in what you were saying when we entered this room. Where did you say you purchased those lily bulbs? My garden is sadly behind yours, I fear. I certainly shall enter upon an amiable rivalry with you next summer."

And Jefferson knew better than to persist.

XXVIII

On January 28th Hamilton sent to Congress his Report on Manufactures, and how anybody survived the fray which ensued can only be explained by the cast-iron muscles forged in the ancestral arena.

332

Hamilton had no abstract or personal theories regarding tariff, and would have been the first to denounce the criminal selfishness which distinguishes Protection to-day. The situation was peculiar, and required the application of strictly business methods to a threatening and immediate emergency. Great Britain was oppressing the country commercially by every method her council could devise. Defensive legislation was imperative. Moreover, if the country was to compete with the nations of the world and grow in independent wealth, particularly if it would provide internal resources against another war, it must manufacture extensively, and its manufactures must be protected. Such, in brief, was the argument of one of the ablest State papers in any country, for whose exhaustive details, the result of two years of study and comparison, of research into the commercial conditions of every State in Europe, there is no space here. The battle was purely political, for the measure was popular with the country from the first. It was opposed by the planters, with Jefferson, Madison, and Monroe in the lead. They argued that the measure would burden the people at large; that the country was too remunerative not to be able to take care of itself; that progress should be natural and not artificial; that the measure was unconstitutional; above all, as the reader need hardly be told, that no proposition had yet been advanced by the monarchical Secretary of the Treasury so "paternal," so conclusive of his ultimate designs. "To let the thirteen States, bound together in a great indissoluble union, concur in erecting one great system, superior to the control of transatlantic force and influence, and able to dictate the connection between the old and the new world," was but another subtle device to consolidate the States for sudden and utter subversion when Hamilton had screwed the last point into his crown. That in the Twentieth Century the United States would be an object of uneasiness daily approaching to terror in the eyes of Great Britain and Europe, as a result of this Report, even Hamilton himself did not foresee, much less the planters; nor that it would carry through the War of 1812 without financial distress. Above all, did no one anticipate that the three Virginians, in their successive incumbencies of the Executive Chair, would pursue the policy of protection in unhesitating obedience to the voice of the people. The first result of this Report was the great manufacturing interests of Paterson, New Jersey, which celebrated their centennial a few years ago. Paterson was Hamilton's personal selection, and it still throbs with something of his own energy.

Meanwhile he was being elected an honorary member of colleges and societies of arts and letters, and persecuted by portrait painters and sculptors. Every honour, public and private, was thrust upon him, and each new victory was attended by a public banquet and a burst of popular applause. He was apparently invulnerable, confounding his opponents and enemies without effort. Never had there been such a conquering hero; even the Virginian trio began to wonder uneasily if he were but mortal, if he were not under some mighty and invisible protection. As for the Federalists, they waxed in enthusiasm and devotion. His career was at its zenith. No man in the United States was—nor has been since—so loved and so hated, both in public and in private life. Even Washington's career had not been more triumphant, and hardly so remarkable; for he was an American born, had always had a larger measure of popular approval, and never had discovered the faculty of raising such bitter and powerful enemies. Nor had he won an extraordinary reputation until he was long past Hamilton's present age. Certainly he had never exhibited such unhuman precocity.

But although Hamilton had, by this time, extancy to suffice any man, and was hunted to his very lair by society, he had no thought of resting on his labours. He by no means regarded himself as a demi-god, nor the country as able to take care of itself. He prepared, and sent to Congress in rapid succession, his Reports on Estimates for Receipts and Expenditures for 1791-92, on Loans, on Duties, on Spirits, on Additional Supplies for 1792, on Remission of Duties, and on the Public Debt.

Nor did his labours for the year confine itself to reports. On August 4th, his patience with the scurrilities of Freneau's *Gazette* came to an end, and he published in Fenno's journal the first of a series of papers that Jefferson, in the hush of Monticello, read with the sensations of those forefathers who sat on a pan of live coals for the amusement of Indian warriors. Hamilton was thorough or nothing. He had held himself in as long as could be expected of any mortal less perfected in his self-government than George Washington: but when, finally, he was not only stung to fury by the constant and systematic calumnies of Jefferson's slanting art, but fearful for the permanence of his measures, in the gradual unsettling of the public mind, he took off his coat; and

Jefferson knew that the first engagement of the final battle had begun in earnest, that the finish would be the retirement of one or other from the Cabinet.

Hamilton began by mathematically demonstrating that Freneau was the tool of Jefferson, imported and suborned for the purpose of depressing the national authority, and exposed the absurdity of the denials of both. When he had finished dealing with this proposition, its day for being a subject of animated debate was over. He then laid before the public certain facts in the career of Jefferson with which they were unacquainted: that he had first discountenanced the adoption of the Constitution, and then advised the ratification of nine of the States and the refusal of four until amendments were secured,—a proceeding which infallibly would have led to civil war; that he had advocated the transfer of the debt due to France to a company of Hollanders in these words: "If there is a *danger* of the public debt *not being punctual*, I submit whether it may not be better, that *the discontents which would then arise* should be *transferred* from a *court* of whose *good-will we have so much need* to the *breasts* of a *private company*"—an obviously dishonourable suggestion, particularly as the company in view was a set of speculators. It was natural enough, however, in a man whose kink for repudiation in general led him to promulgate the theory that one generation cannot bind another for the payment of a debt. Hamilton, having disposed of Jefferson's attempts, under the signature of Aristides, to wriggle out of both these accusations, discoursed upon the disloyal fact that the Secretary of State was the declared opponent of every important measure which had been devised by the Government, and proceeded to lash him for his hypocrisy in sitting daily at the right hand of the President while privately slandering him; of exercising all the arts of an intriguing mind, ripened by a long course of European diplomacy, to undermine an Administration whose solidity was the only guaranty for the continued prosperity and honour of the country. Hamilton reminded the people, with a pen too pointed to fail of conviction, of the increase of wealth and happiness which had ensued every measure opposed by the Secretary of State, and drew a warning picture of what must result were these measures reversed by a party without any convictions beyond the determination to compass the downfall of the party in power. He bade them choose, and passed on to a refutation of the several accusations hurled at the Administration, and at himself in particular.

He wrote sometimes with temperance and self-restraint, at others with stinging contempt and scorn. Jefferson replied with elaborate denials, solemn protests of disinterested virtue, and counter accusations. Hamilton was back at him before the print was dry, and the battle raged with such unseemly violence, that Washington wrote an indignant letter to each, demanding that they put aside their personal rancours and act together for the common good of the country. The replies of the two men were characteristic. Hamilton wrote a frank and manly letter, barely alluding to Jefferson, and asserting that honour and policy exacted his charges and refutations. He would make no promise to discontinue his papers, for he had no intention of laying down his pen until Jefferson was routed from the controversial field, and the public satisfied of the truth. Jefferson's letter was pious and sad. It breathed a fervent disinterestedness, and provided as many poisoned arrows for his rival as its ample space permitted. It was a guinea beaten out into an acre of gold leaf and steeped in corrosive sublimate.

But during that summer of 1792 Hamilton had little time for personal explosions except in brief. The Presidential elections approached, and the greater part of his time was given to party management and counsel. Washington's renomination and election were assured. The only obstacle encountered had been Washington himself, but his yearning for peace had again retired before duty. The parties were arrayed in a desperate struggle for the Vice-Presidency, the issue to determine the vindication or the condemnation of the measures of Hamilton. Adams himself was unpopular in the anti-Federalist ranks, on account of his aristocratic tastes and his opposition to the French Revolution; but the time was propitious for a tremendous trial of strength with the omnipotent Secretary of the Treasury, and any candidate of his would have been opposed as bitterly.

Jefferson and Burr were each suggested for the office, but Hamilton brought down his heavy hand on both of them promptly, and the fight settled into a bitter struggle between Adams and Clinton. The latter's strength in the State of New York was still very great, and he was as hardy a fighter as ever. But his political past was studded with vulnerable points, and the Federalists spared him not.

It is impossible, whatever one's predilections, not to admire Clinton for his superb fighting qualities. He was indomitable, and in ability and resourcefulness second only to Hamilton himself, in party management far superior; for he had greater patience, a tenderer and more intimate concern for his meaner followers, and less trust in his own unaided efforts and the right of his cause. Hamilton by no means was blind to the pettier side of human nature, but he despised it; instead of truckling and manipulating, he would scatter it before him or grind it to pulp. There is no possible doubt that if Hamilton had happened into a country at war with itself, but with strong monarchical proclivities, he would have seized the crown and made one of the wisest and kindest of autocrats. His lines cast in a land alight from end to end with republican fires, he accepted the situation with his inherent philosophy, burned with a patriotism as steady as Washington's own, but ruled it in his own way, forced upon it measures in whose wisdom he implicitly believed, and which, in every instance, time has vindicated. But his instinct was that of the amiable despot, and he had no conciliation in him.

His opponents saw only the despot, for time had not given them range of vision. Therefore, Jefferson, Madison, Monroe, Clinton, and his other formidable enemies have a large measure of excuse for their conduct, especially as they were seldom unstung by mortifying defeat. It is doubtful if the first three, at least, ever admitted to themselves or each other that they hated Hamilton, and were determined for purely personal reasons to pull him down. Every man knows how easy it is to persuade himself that he is entirely in the right, his opponent, or even he who differs from him, entirely in the wrong. The Virginian trio had by this, at all events, talked themselves into the belief that Hamilton was a menace to the permanence of the Union, and that it was their pious duty to relegate him to the shades of private life. That in public life he would infallibly interfere with their contemplated twenty-four years Chair Trust may have been by the way. They were all men with a consciousness of public benefits to their credit, and some disinterested patriotism. If their ignoble side is constantly in evidence in their dealings with Hamilton, it by no means follows that two, at least, of our most distinguished Presidents—Monroe was a mere imitationist—had no other. Had that been the case, they would have failed as miserably as Burr, despite their talents, for the public is not a fool. But that their faults were ignoble, rather than passionate, their biographers have never pretended to deny. In many instances no apology is attempted. On the other hand, the most exhaustive research among the records of friends and enemies has failed to bring to light any evidence of mean and contemptible traits in Hamilton. No one will deny his faults, his mistakes; but they were the mistakes and faults of passion in every instance; of a great nature, capable of the extremest violence, of the deadliest hate and maddest blows, but fighting always in the open; in great crises unhesitatingly sacrificing his personal desires or hatreds to the public good. Even his detractors—those who count in letters—have admitted that his nature and his methods were too high-handed for grovelling and deceit, that the mettle of his courage was unsurpassed. Jefferson and Madison had the spirit of the mongrel in comparison; Monroe was a fighter, but cowardly and spiteful. In point of mettle alone, Adams and Clinton were Hamilton's most worthy opponents.

Burr had not shown his hand as yet. He was at war with Clinton himself, and an active and coruscating member of the Senate. But Hamilton, by this, knew him thoroughly. He read his lack of Public spirit in every successive act of his life, recognized an ambition which would not hesitate to sacrifice his best friend and the country he was using, and a subtlety and cunning which would, with his lack of principle and property, make him the most dangerous man in America should he contrive to grasp the reins of power. Therefore he checkmated his every move, careless of whether he made another powerful enemy or not.

Hamilton attempted no delusions with himself. He knew that he hated Jefferson with a violence which threatened at times to submerge all the good in him, horrified him when he sat down and looked into himself. On the other hand, he knew himself to be justified in thwarting and humiliating him, for the present policy of the country must be preserved at any cost. But he was too clear and practised an analyst to fail to separate his public from his personal rancour. He would drive Jefferson from public office for the public good, but he would experience the keenest personal pleasure in so doing. Such was Hamilton. Could a genius like his be allied in one ego with a character like Washington's, we should have a being for which the world has never dared to hope in its most Biblical moments. But genius must ever be imperfect. Life is not long enough nor slow enough for both brain and character to grow side by side to superhuman proportions.

XXIX

The following political year was a lively one for Hamilton, perhaps the liveliest of his career. As it approached, those interested in public affairs had many subjects for constant and excited discussion: the possible Vice-President, whose election was to determine the future status of the Secretary of State, and cement or weaken the centralized powers of the Administration; the battle in the two *Gazettes*, with the laurels to Hamilton, beyond all controversy, and humiliation for Jefferson and Madison; the growing strength of the "Republican" party under Madison's open and Jefferson's literary leadership; the probable policy of the Administration toward the French Revolution, with Jefferson hot with rank Democracy, and Hamilton hotter with contempt for the ferocity of the Revolutionists; the next move of the Virginians did Hamilton win the Vice-Presidency for the Administration party; and the various policies of the Secretary of the Treasury and their results. At coffee-houses, at public and private receptions, and in Mrs. Croix's drawing-room, hardly another subject was broached.

"A fool could understand politics in these days," said Betsey, one evening in December, with a sigh. "Not a word does one hear of clothes, gossip, husbands, or babies. Mrs. Washington told me the day after she returned that she had deliberately thought of nothing but butter and patchwork during the entire recess, that her poor brain might be able to stand the strain of the winter. Shall you have to work harder than ever?"

"I do not know," replied Hamilton, and at that moment he did not. He was correcting a French exercise of his son's, and feeling domestic and happy. Jefferson and he had made no pretence at formal amiability this season; they did not speak at all, but communicated on paper when the business of their respective departments required an interchange of opinion. He had vanquished his enemy in print, made him ridiculous in the eyes of all who read the *Gazettes*. Moreover, Washington, disturbed during the summer by the constant nagging of Jefferson and his agents, respecting the "monarchical schemes" and "corrupt practices" of the Secretary of the Treasury, had formulated the accusations and sent them to Hamilton for refutation. The vindication, written without passion, as cold, clear, consistent, and logical, as if dealing with an abstract proposition, had convinced, and finally, all to whom it was shown; with the exception of Jefferson, who had no intention of being convinced. Hamilton was conscious that there was no vulnerable point in his public armour. Of his private he was not so sure; Reynolds was in jail, for attempting, in company with one Clingman, to suborn a witness to commit perjury, and had appealed to him for aid. He had ignored him, determined to submit to no further blackmail, be the consequences what they might. But he was the last man to anticipate trouble, and on the whole he was in the best of humours as the Christmas holidays approached, with his boys home from their school on Staten Island, his little girl growing lovelier and more accomplished, and his wife always charming and pretty; in their rare hours of uninterrupted companionship, piquant and diverting. He had gone out with her constantly since Congress assembled, and had enjoyed the recreations of society after his summer of hard work and angry passions. Everywhere he had a triumphal progress; men and women jostled each other about him, eager for a word, a smile, making him talk at length, whether he would or not. The confidence in him was stronger than ever, but his enemies were the most powerful, collectively and individually, that had ever arrayed against a public man: Jefferson, Madison, and Monroe, with the South behind them; the Livingstons and the Clinton faction in New York; Burr, with his smiling subterranean industry; the growing menace of the Republican party. Pamphlets were circulating in the States warning voters against all who supported the Secretary of the Treasury. It was one man against odds of appalling strength and resource; for by common consent both of friends and enemies Hamilton was the Federal party. Did he fall, it must go; all blows were aimed at him alone. Could any one man stand for ever an impregnable fortress before such a battery? Many vowed that he would, for "he was more than human," but others, as firm in their admiration, shrugged their shoulders. The enemy were infuriated at the loss of the Vice-Presidency, for again Hamilton had been vindicated and Adams reflected. What would be their next move?

Betsey knew that her husband had enemies, but the fact gave her little concern; she believed Hamilton to be a match for the allied forces of darkness. She noticed when his hair was unpowdered that it was turning gray and had quite lost its boyish brightness; here and there work and care had drawn a line. But he was handsomer, if anything, and of the scars on his spirit she knew nothing. In the peace and pleasant distractions of his home his mercurial spirits leaped high above his anxieties and enmities, and he was as gay and happy, as interested in the manifold small interests of his family, as were he a private man of fortune, without an ambition, an enemy, or a care. When most absorbed or irritated he never victimized his household by moods or tempers, not only because they were at his mercy, but because his nature spontaneously gave as it received; his friends had his best always, his enemies the very worst of which his intense passionate nature was capable. Naturally his family adored him and studied his happiness.

Betsey continued her somewhat rambling remarks, "The only variety is the French Revolution."

"By the way, Washington has had a distressing letter from Madame Lafayette. She begs him to receive her boy—George Washington—and keep him until the trouble is over. The Chief fears that in the present temper of the public his reception of Lafayette's son would be given an embarrassing significance, and yet it is impossible to refuse such a request,—with Lafayette in an Austrian dungeon, his wife in daily danger of prison or guillotine, and this boy, his only son, with no one but a tutor to protect him. I offered at once to receive the child into my family—subject, of course, to your approval. Should you object? It would add to your cares—"

"I have no cares, sir. I shall be delighted; and he can talk French with the children."

"I shall send him to Staten Island with Philip and Alex. Washington will make him a liberal allowance for school and clothing. I confess I am anxious to receive him, more than anxious to show that my old friendship is undiminished. I fear to open every packet from Europe, lest I hear of Lafayette's death. Fortunately, Morris was able to render some assistance to Madame Lafayette. Morris is a source of sufficient worry himself, for he is much too independent and bold for a foreign envoy in the thick of mob rule, mad with blood."

"I hate to think of old friends in trouble," said Betsey, removing a tear. "Poor Kitty Duer! I had another letter from her to-day. It is pitiful to think of her and the poor little children, with nothing but what Lady

Sterling, who has so little, and Lady Mary can give them. Is there no way of getting Colonel Duer out of Debtor's prison?"

"I've moved heaven and earth, but certain of his creditors are inexorable. Still, I hope to have him out and on his feet before long. You are not to worry about other people this evening, for I am particularly happy. Philip is really remarkable, and I believe that Angelica is going to turn out a musical genius. What a delight it is to have one person in the world to whom one can brag about one's offspring without apology."

"Why, of course they are the most remarkable children in the world—all five of them," said Betsey, placidly.

Edward Stevens came in and threw himself on the sofa. "What a relief to come into this scene of domestic tranquillity, after the row outside!" he exclaimed. "All the world is in the streets; that is to say, all the daft American world that sympathizes with that bloody horror in France. The news that the allied armies have been beaten and the Duke of Brunswick was in full retreat when the packets sailed, has apparently driven them frantic with joy. They are yelling 'Ça ira,' bonfires are flaring everywhere, and bells ringing. All of the men are drunk, and some of the women. And yet the statesman who must grapple with this portentous problem is gossiping with his wife, and looking as if he had not a care in the world. Thank Heaven!"

"I can do nothing to-night," said Hamilton, smiling. "I have had too much experience as a practical philosopher not to be happy while I can."

"You have the gift of eternal youth. What shall you do in this French matter, Alexander the Great? All the world is waiting to know. I should worry about you if I had time in this reeking town, where it is a wonder any man has health in him. Oh, for the cane-fields of St. Croix! But tell me, what is the policy to be—strict neutrality? Of course the President will agree with you; but fancy Jefferson, on his other side, burning with approval for the very excesses of the Revolution, since they typify democracy exultant. And of course he is burrowing in the dark to increase his Republican party and inspire it with his fanatical enthusiasm for those inhuman wretches in France. I believe he would plunge us into a war to-morrow."

"No, he is an unwarlike creature. He would like to trim, keep this country from being actually bespattered with blood, but coax the Administration to give the Revolutionists money and moral support. He will do nothing of the sort, however. The policy of this remote country is absolute, uncompromising, neutrality. Let Europe keep her hands off this continent, and we will let her have her own way across the water. The United States is the nucleus of a great nation that will spread indefinitely, and any further Europeanizing of our continent would be a menace which we can best avoid by observing from the beginning a strictly defensive policy. To weaken it by an aggressive inroad into European politics would be the folly of schoolboys not fit to conduct a nation. We must have the Floridas and Louisiana as soon as possible. I have been urging the matter upon Washington's attention for three years. Spain is a constant source of annoyance, and the sooner we get her off the continent the better—and before Great Britain sends her. We need the Mississippi for navigation and must possess the territories that are the key to it. How idiotic, therefore, to antagonize any old-world power!"

"You *are* long-headed!" exclaimed Stevens. "Good heavens! Listen to that! The very lungs of Philadelphia are bellowing. Our people must be mad to see in this hideous French Revolution any resemblance to their own dignified and orderly struggle for freedom."

"It is so easy to drive men mad," said Hamilton, contemptuously. "Particularly when they are in constant and bitter opposition to the party in power, and possess a leader as subtle and venomous as Thomas Jefferson—'Thomas,' as he signed a letter to Washington the other day. You may imagine the disgust of the Chief."

"Not another word of politics this night!" exclaimed Mrs. Hamilton. "I have not uttered a word for just twenty-five minutes. Alexander, go and brew a beaker of negus."

XXX

The next morning Hamilton was sitting in his office when the cards of James Monroe, F.A. Muhlenberg, and A. Venable were brought in.

"What on earth can they want?" he thought. "Monroe? We have not bowed for a year. Two days ago he turned into a muddy lane and splashed himself to his waist, that he might avoid meeting me."

His first impulse was to excuse himself, on the plea of the pressing nature of his work; but curiosity triumphed, and he told his page to admit the men.

Muhlenberg was again Speaker of the House; Venable was a Representative from Virginia. Hamilton was not friendly with either, but nodded when they passed him. He greeted them amiably as they entered to-day, and exchanged a frigid bow with Monroe. The Senator from Virginia took a chair in the rear of the others, stretched his long legs in front of him, and folded his arms defiantly. He looked not unlike a greyhound, his preference for drab clothing enhancing the general effect of a pointed and narrow leanness.

There was a moment of extreme awkwardness. Muhlenberg and Venable hitched their chairs about. Monroe grinned spasmodically, and rubbed his nose with his upper lip.

"Well, gentlemen," said Hamilton, rapping his fingers on the table. "What can I do for you?" He scented gun-powder at once.

"I am to be the spokesman in this delicate matter, I believe," said Muhlenberg, who looked red and miserable, "and I will, with your permission, proceed to my unpleasant task with as little delay as possible."

"Pray do," replied Hamilton. "The daily assaults of my enemies for several years have endowed me with a fortitude which doubtless will carry me through this interview in a creditable manner."

"I assure you, sir, that I do not come as an enemy, but as a friend. It is owing to my appeal that the matter was not laid directly before the President."

"The President?" Hamilton half rose, then seated himself again. His eyes were glittering dangerously. Muhlenberg blundered on, his own gaze roving. The Federal term of endearment for Hamilton, "The Little Lion," clanged suddenly in his mind, a warning bell.

"I regret to say that we have discovered an improper connection between yourself and one Reynolds." He produced a bundle of letters and handed them to Hamilton. "These are not in your handwriting, sir, but I am informed that you wrote them."

Hamilton glanced at them hastily, and the angry blood raced through his arteries.

"These letters were written by me," he said. "I disguised my handwriting for purposes of my own. What is the meaning of this unwarrantable intrusion into a man's private affairs? Explain yourself at once."

"That is what we have come for, sir. Unfortunately we cannot regard it as a private affair, but one which concerns the whole nation."

"The whole nation!" thundered Hamilton. "What has the nation to do with an affair of this sort? Why cannot you tell the truth and say that you gloat in having discovered this wretched affair,—a common enough episode in the lives of all of you,—in having another tid-bit for Freneau? Why did you not take it to him at once? What do you mean by coming here personally to take me to task?"

"I think there is some misapprehension, sir," said Muhlenberg. "It would be quite impossible for any one present to have misconducted himself in the manner in which the holder of those letters, Mr. Reynolds, accuses you of having done. And surely the whole country is intimately concerned in the honesty—or the dishonesty—of the Secretary of the Treasury."

The words were out, and Muhlenberg sat with his mouth open for a moment, as if to reinhale the air which was escaping too quickly for calm speech. Then he set his shoulders and braced himself to meet the Secretary's eyes. Hamilton was staring at him, with no trace of passion in his face. His eyes looked like steel; his whole face had hardened into a mask. He had realized in a flash that he was in the meshes of a plot, and forced the heat from his brain. "Explain," he said. "I am listening."

"As you are aware, sir, this James Clingman, who has been arrested with Reynolds, was a clerk in my employ. You will also recall that when he applied to me to get him out, I, in company with Colonel Burr, waited on you and asked your assistance. You said that you would do all that was consistent, but we did not hear from you further. Clingman refunded the money, or certificates, which they had improperly obtained from the Treasury, the action was withdrawn, and he was discharged to-day. While the matter was pending I had several conversations with Clingman, and he frequently dropped hints to the effect that Reynolds had it in his power materially to injure the Secretary of the Treasury, as he knew of several very improper transactions of his. At first I paid no attention to these hints, but when he went so far as to assert that Reynolds had it in his power to hang the Secretary of the Treasury, that the latter was deeply concerned in speculation with Duer, and had frequently advanced him—Reynolds, I mean—money with which to speculate, then I conceived it my duty to take some sort of action, and yesterday communicated with Mr. Monroe and Mr. Venable. They went at once to call on Reynolds—whom I privately believe to be a rascal, sir—and he asserted that he was kept in prison by your connivance, as you feared him; and promised to put us in possession of the entire facts this morning. When we returned at the hour appointed, he had absconded, having received his discharge. We then went to his house and saw his wife, who asserted, after some circumlocution, that you had been concerned in speculations with her husband, that at your request she had burnt most of the letters you had written to herself and her husband, and that all were in a disguised hand—like these few which she had preserved. You will admit that it is a very serious charge, sir, and that we should have been justified in going directly to the President. But we thought that in case there might be an explanation—"

"Oh, there is an explanation," said Hamilton, with a sneer. "You shall have it at my pleasure. I see that these notes implicate me to the extent of eleven hundred dollars. Strange, that a rapacious Secretary of the Treasury, handling millions, and speculating wildly with a friend of large resources, should have descended to such small play as this. More especially strange that he should have deliberately placed himself in the power of such a rascal as this Reynolds—who seems to impress every one he meets with his blackguardism—and communicated with him freely on paper; you will have observed that I acknowledged these notes without hesitation. What a clumsy knave you must think me. I resent the imputation. Perhaps you have noticed that in one of these notes I state that on my honour I cannot accommodate him with the three hundred dollars he demands, because it is quite out of my power to furnish it. Odd, that a thieving Secretary, engaged in riotous speculation, could not lay his hand on three hundred dollars, especially if it were necessary to close this rascal's mouth. I doubt, gentlemen, if you will be able to convince the country that I am a fool. Nevertheless, I recognize that this accusation must be met by controverting proof; and if you will do me the honour to call at my house to-night at nine o'clock, I shall, in the presence of the Comptroller of the Treasury, furnish these proofs."

He rose, and the others pushed back their chairs and departed hastily. Muhlenberg's red face wore a look of relief, but Monroe scowled. Neither had failed to be impressed by the Secretary's manner, and the Speaker of the House, ashamed of his part in the business, would gladly have listened to an immediate vindication.

Hamilton sat motionless for some moments, the blood returning to his face, for he was seething with fury and disgust.

"The hounds!" he said aloud, then again and again. He was alone, and he never had conquered his youthful habit of muttering to himself. "I can see Monroe leaping, not walking, to the jail, the moment he learned of a chance to incriminate me. The heels at the end of those long legs must have beaten the powder from his queue. And this is what a man is to expect so long as he remains in public life—if he succeeds. He resigns a large income, reduces his family almost to poverty, works himself half to death, rescues the country from contempt, launches it upon the sea of prosperity; and his public rewards are more than counterbalanced by the persecutions of his enemies. I have been on the defensive from the moment I entered public life. Scarcely a week but I have been obliged to parry some poisoned arrow or pluck it out and cauterize. The dreams of my youth! They never soared so high as my present attainment, but neither did they include this constant struggle with the vilest manifestations of which the human nature is capable." He brought his fist down on the table. "I am a match for all of them," he exclaimed. "But their arrows rankle, for I am human. They have poisoned every hour of victory."

He caught up his hat and went out into the air. The solace of Mrs. Croix in his blacker moods occurred to him; and he walked down Chestnut Street as rapidly as he could, in the crowd, lifting his hat now and again to cool his head in the frosty air. It was a brilliant winter's day; drifts of snow hid the dead animals and the garbage in the streets; and all the world was out for Christmas shopping. As it was one of the seasons for display, everybody was in his best. The women wore bright-coloured taffetas or velvets, over hoops flattened before and behind, muskmelon bonnets or towering hats. They whisked their gowns about, that their satin petticoats be not overlooked. The men wore the cocked hat, heavily laced, and a long coat, usually of light-coloured cloth, with a diminutive cape, the silver buttons engraved with initials or crest. Their small clothes were very short, but heavy striped stockings protected their legs; on their feet were pointed shoes, with immense silver buckles. Hamilton was dressed with his usual exquisite care, his cuffs carefully leaded. But his appearance interested him little to-day. For the moment, however, he forgot his private annoyance in the portent on every side of him. Few of the seekers after gifts had entered the shops. They blocked the pavements, even the street, talking excitedly of the news of the day before. Fully half the throng sported the tri-coloured cockade, the air hissed with "Citizen," "Citess," or rang with a volley of "Ça ira! Ça ira!"

Hamilton set his teeth. "It *is* the next nightmare," he thought. "The Cabinet is quiet at present—Jefferson, mortified and beaten, is coaxing back his courage for a final spring. When the time comes to determine our attitude there will be Hell, nothing less." But his nostrils quivered. He might rebel at poisoned arrows, but he revelled in the fight that involved the triumph of a policy.

His mind was abstracted, the blood was still in his brain as he entered Mrs. Croix's drawing-room. For a moment he had a confused idea that he had blundered into a shop. The chairs, the sofas, the floor, were covered with garments and stuffs of every hue. Hats and bonnets were perched on every point. Never had he seen so much gorgeous raiment in one space before. There were brocades, taffetas, satins, lutestrings, laces, feathers, fans, underwear like mist. While he was staring about him in bewilderment, Mrs. Croix came running in from her bedroom. Her hair was down and tangled, her dressing sacque half off, her face flushed, her eyes sparkling. She looked half wanton, half like a giddy girl darting about among her first trunks.

"Hamilton!" she cried. "Hamilton!" She flew at him much as his children did when excited. "Look! Look! Look! Is this not magnificent? This is the happiest day of my life!"

"Indeed? Are you about to set up a shop?"

"A shop? I am about to deck myself once more in the raiment that I love. Have I not drooped in weeds long enough, sir? I am going to be beautiful again! I am going to wear all those lovely things—all! all! And I am going to Lady Washington's to-morrow night. Mrs. Knox will take me. But I vow I do not care half so much for that as for my beautiful things. They arrived by the London packet yesterday, but have only now been delivered. I ordered them long since, and hardly could control my impatience till they came. I am so happy! I feel like a bird that has been plucked for years."

Hamilton looked at her in amazement, and despair. More than once he had caught a glimpse of the frivolous side of her nature, but that it could spread and control her he never had imagined. Her intelligence, her passions, her inherited and accumulated wisdom, were crowded into some submerged cell. There was nothing in her at the present moment for him, and he turned on his heel without a word and left the house. She rapped sharply on the window as he passed, but he did not look up. He was filled with that unreasoning anger peculiar to man when woman for once has failed to respond. He consigned her and her clothes to the devil, and looked at his watch. It was ten minutes to one. His dinner hour was two o'clock. He would go home to his wife, where he should have gone in the first place. She never had failed him, or if she had he could not recall the occasion. Her little dark face rose before him, innocent and adorable. He could not tell her of the cause of his annoyance,—it suddenly occurred to him that the less of that matter confided to Mrs. Croix the better,—but then he never worried her with his troubles. He would merely go and bask in her presence for an hour, confess to a headache, and receive her sweet ministrations.

As he entered his own house, and, relieved of his coat and hat by the waiting black, ran up the stair, he thought he heard a soft babble of voices. Knowing that his wife would, if he desired it, dismiss at once any company she might have, he knocked confidently at her door and entered. For a moment he felt inclined to rub his eyes, and wondered if he were the victim of delirium. The bed was covered with bandboxes, the sofa with new frocks. Betsey was sitting before the mirror, trying on a cap, and her sisters, Peggy and Cornelia, were clapping their hands. Angelica was perched on the back of a chair, her eyes twice their natural size, Hamilton attempted instant retreat, but Betsey saw his reflection in the mirror.

"You?" she cried. "What a surprise and pleasure. Come here, sir, at once."

Meanwhile his two sisters-in-law, whose expected visit he had quite forgotten, ran forward and kissed him effusively. With the desire in his heart to rend the Universe in twain he went forward and smiled down into his wife's eager face.

"Angelica has sent me so many things!" she exclaimed. Her face was flushed, her eyes sparkling. She looked sixteen. "And this cap is the most bewitching of all. You came just at the right moment; it is quite singular. Read—".

She thrust a letter from Mrs. Church into his hand, and he read where his wife pointed. "Someone who loves you will tell you if it is becoming or not." And on the following page. "Kiss my saucy Brother for me. I call him my Brother with an air of pride. And tell him, *Il est l'homme le plus aimable du monde.*"

"It is charming," said Hamilton, pinching his wife's chin. "It is like a frame. You never looked half so sweet."

Betsey cooed with delight. Hamilton, having done his duty, was about to retire in good order, when he met his little daughter's eyes. They had dismissed the wonderful cap and were fixed on him with an expression that gave him a sudden thrill. It was not the first time he had seen in Angelica so strong a resemblance to his mother that he half believed some fragment of Rachael Levine had come back to him. Her eyes were dark, but she had a mane of reddish fair hair, and a skin as white as porcelain, a long sensitive nose, and a full mobile mouth. She had none of his mother's vitality and dash, however. She was delicate and rather shrinking, and he knew that Rachael at her age must have been a marvel of mental and physical energy. It was only occasionally, when he turned suddenly and caught Angelica staring at him, that he experienced the odd sensation of meeting his mother's eyes, informed, moreover, with an expression of penetrating comprehension—an expression he recalled without effort. The child idolized him. She sat outside his study while he wrote, crawling in between the legs of anyone who opened the door? to sit at his feet; or, if he dismissed her, in another part of the room until he left it. She watched for his daily returns, and usually greeted him from the banister post. Amiable, intelligent, pretty, affectionate, and already putting forth the tender leaves of a great gift, her father thought her quite perfect, and they had long conversations whenever he was at leisure in his home. She demanded a great deal of petting, and he was always ready to humour her, the more as she was the only girl, and the one quiet member of his little family—although she had been known to use her fists upon occasion. Her prettiness and intelligence delighted him, her affection was one of the deepest pleasures of his life, and he was thankful for the return to him of his mother's beautiful and singular features. To-day the resemblance was so striking that he contracted his eyelids. Angelica straightened herself, gave a spring, and alighted on his chest.

"Take me downstairs and talk to me," she commanded. "'Tis nearly an hour to dinner."

Hamilton swung her to his shoulder, and went downstairs. On the way he laughed out loud. The past half-hour tossed itself into the foreground of his mind, clad in the skirts of high comedy. Tragedy fled. The burden in his breast went with it. Far be it from him to cherish a grudge against the sex that so often reduced the trials of public life to insignificance. Women were delicious irresponsible beings; man was an ingrate to take their shortcomings seriously.

"Why do you laugh?" asked his daughter, whose arm nearly strangled him.

"You were very angry when you came into mamma's room."

"Indeed?" said Hamilton, nettled. "Was I not smiling?"

"Yes, sir; but you often smile when you would like to run the carving-knife into somebody."

They had reached the library. Hamilton sat the child on the edge of his table and took a chair closely facing her. "What do you mean, you little witch?" he demanded. "I am always happy when I am at home."

"Almost always. Sometimes you are very angry, and sometimes you are sad. Why do you pretend? Why don't you tell us?"

"Well," said Hamilton, with some confusion. "I love you all very much, you see, and you do make me happy—why should I worry you?"

"I should feel better if you told me—right out. It gives me a pain here."

She laid her hand to her head, and Hamilton stared at her in deepening perplexity. Another child—anything feminine, at least— would have indicated her heart as the citadel of sorrow. "Why there?" he asked. "Do you mean a pain?"

"Yes, a pain, but not so bad as when I am in Albany or Saratoga and you are here. Then I worry all the time."

"Do you mean that you are ever unhappy?"

"I am unhappy whenever you are, or I am afraid that you are. I know that you are very big and the cleverest man in the world, and that I am too little to do you any good, and I don't know why I worry when I am away." "But, my dear child, what in Heaven's name do you mean? Have you ever spoken to your mother of this?"

Angelica shook her head. Her eyes grew larger and wiser. "No; I

351

should only worry Betsey, and she is always happy. She is not clever like you and me."

Hamilton rose abruptly and walked to the window. When he had composed his features he returned. "You must not criticise your mother in that way, my dear. She is a very clever little woman, indeed."

Angelica nodded. "If she were clever, you would not say 'little.' Nobody says that you are a very clever little man. When I'm big, I'll not be called little, either. I love our dear Queen Bess, but I'm *all yours*. Why were you so angry to-day?"

"I couldn't possibly tell you," replied her father, turning cold. "You must not ask too many questions; but I am very grateful for your sympathy. You are my dear little girl, and you make me love you more and more, daily."

"And will you tell me whenever you are not feeling like what you are making the rest believe?"

"If it will make you any happier, I will whisper it into your pink little ear. But I think I should be a very bad father to make you unhappy."

"I told you, sir, that I am more unhappy when I imagine things. It is just like a knife," and again she pointed to her head.

Hamilton turned pale. "You are too young to have headaches," he said. "Perhaps you have been studying too hard. I am so ambitious for my children; but the boys have taken to books as they have to kites and fisticuffs. I should have remembered that girls—" His memory gave up the stories of his mother's precocity. But this child, who was so startlingly like the dead woman, was far less fitted to carry such burdens. So sensitive an intelligence in so frail a body might suddenly flame too high and fall to ashes. He resolved to place her in classes of other little girls at once, and to keep her in the fields as much as possible. None knew better than he how close the highly strung unresting brain could press to madness. He had acquired a superhuman control over his. If this girl's brain had come out of his own, it must be closely watched. She had not inherited his high light spirits, but the melancholy which had lain at the foundations of his mother's nature; she would require the most persistent guarding. He took her face between his hands and kissed it many times.

"Very well," he said, "we will have our little secrets. I will tell you when I am disturbed, and you will sit close beside me with your doll until I feel better. But remember, I expect as much confidence in return. You will never have a care nor a terror nor an annoyance that you will not confide it to me directly."

She nodded. "I'm always telling you things to myself. And I won't cry any more in the night, when I think you have felt badly and could not tell anyone. It will all go away if you talk to me about it," she added confidently.

Hamilton swung her to his shoulder again and started for the dining room.

"The child is uncanny," he thought. "Can there be anything in that old theory that tormented and erring souls come back to make their last expiation in children? That means early death!" He dismissed the thought promptly.

XXXI

After dinner he called on Oliver Wolcott, the Comptroller, one of his closest friends, and related the scene of the morning, adding the explanation. Wolcott was a Puritan, and did not approve of the marital digressions of his friends. But in this case the offence was so much less than the accusation that he listened with frequent ejaculations of content. He agreed at once to call at Hamilton's house at eight o'clock, look over the papers, and read them aloud when the trio arrived.

"And may the devil damn them," he added. "It will be one of the keenest pleasures of my life to confound them. The unpatriotic villains! They know that in disgracing you they would discredit the United States, and in their hearts they know that your measures are the only wheels for this country to run on; but to their party spite they would sacrifice everything. I'll be there."

And when the men called that night at nine o'clock, he read them the correspondence from beginning to end—Reynold's letters, and those of the woman. More than once Muhlenberg begged him to desist, but he was merciless. When he had finished, Hamilton explained that he had disguised his handwriting lest the man forge or make other use of it.

The three rose as soon as the ordeal was over. "It is no use for me to attempt to express my regret or my humiliation," said Muhlenberg, "I shall be ashamed of this as long as I live."

"I feel like an ass and a spy," exclaimed Venable. "I heartily beg your pardon, sir."

"Your mistake was justifiable. Are you satisfied?"

"More than satisfied."

Hamilton turned to Monroe.

"I made a mistake," said the Senator from Virginia. "I beg your pardon."

"And I shall hear no more of this?"

He received the solemn promise of each, then let them go. But he locked the letters carefully in their drawer again.

"Are you going to keep those things?" asked Wolcott. "It must have made you sick to listen to them."

"It did. Perhaps I shall keep them for penance, perhaps because I do not trust Monroe."

XXXII

Hamilton was not long kept in ignorance of the next tactics of his enemies. They made their deadliest assault soon after Christmas. Immediately upon the assembling of Congress it was suggested that the Secretary of the Treasury be asked to furnish a plan for reducing the public debt. Madison arose and fired the first gun. What Congress wanted was not a plan, but a statement of the national finances. The Federalists replied that the information would come in due course, and that the House was in duty bound to ask the Secretary to furnish a scheme. The Republicans, led by Madison, protested that already too much power had been invested in the Secretary of the Treasury, that it had exceeded constitutional limits. Moreover, he overwhelmed them with volumes, deliberately calculated to confuse their understandings. One Giles, who did the dirty work of the party, announced that the Secretary was not fit to make plans, and added the numerous and familiar denunciations. But the Republicans were outvoted, and the suggestions were called for. Hamilton furnished them immediately. His plan to reduce the debt was met by so strenuous an opposition from the Republicans that it was defeated, and by the party which had been most persistent in their detestation of the obnoxious burden. Rather than add to the laurels of Hamilton, they would shoulder it with equanimity. But this defeat was but an incident. The Secretary of the Treasury, as the result of a series of resolutions, was bidden to lay before Congress an account of the moneys borrowed at Antwerp and Amsterdam; the President to furnish a statement of the loans made by his authority, their terms, what use had been made of them, how large was the balance; the chiefs of departments to make a return of the persons employed and their salaries. Hamilton, by this time, was fully alive to the fact that he was about to be subjected to fresh persecution, and the agility of his enemies could not keep pace with his. He furnished the House with an itemized list—which it took the Committee days to plod through—of his bookkeepers, clerks, porters, and charwomen, and the varying emoluments they had received since the Department was organized, three years and a half before. He further informed them that the net yield of the foreign loan was eighteen millions six hundred and seventy-eight thousand florins, that the loans were six in number, that three bore five per cent interest, two four and a half, and one four per cent The enemy was disconcerted but not discouraged. Five fresh resolutions were moved almost immediately. Impartial historians have agreed that Jefferson suggested these shameful resolutions, and that Madison drew them up. Giles brought them forward. In a vociferous speech he asserted that no man could understand the Secretary's report, that his methods and processes were clothed in a suspicious obscurity. It was his painful duty to move the adoption of the following resolutions: That copies of the papers authorizing the foreign loans should be made; that the names of the persons to whom and by whom the French debt had been paid be sent to Congress; that a statement of the balances between the United States and the Bank be made; that an account of the sinking-fund be rendered, how much money had come into it and where from, how much had been used for the purchase of the debt and where the rest was deposited. The fifth demanded an account of the unexpended revenue at the close of the preceding year. Giles charged that a serious discrepancy existed between the report of the Secretary and the books of the Bank—not less than a million and a half. It had been the purpose of Jefferson and Madison to bring forward the resolutions with an air of comparative innocence. But the vanity of Giles carried him away, and his speech informed Congress, and very shortly the country, that the honesty of the Secretary of the Treasury had been impeached, and that he was called upon to vindicate himself.

In crises Hamilton never lost his temper. The greater the provocation, as the greater the danger, the colder and more impersonal he became. Nor was it in his direct impatient nature to seek to delay an evil moment any more than it was to protect himself behind what the American of to-day calls "bluff." In this, the severest trial of his public career, he did not hesitate a moment for irritation or protest. He called upon his Department to assist him, and with them he worked day and night, gathering, arranging, elaborating all the information demanded by Congress. When he was not directing his subordinates, he was shut up in his library preparing his statements and replies. His meals were taken to him; his family did not see him for weeks, except as he passed them on his way to or from the front door. He sent in report after report to Congress with a celerity that shattered his health, but kept his enemies on the jump, and worked them half to death. The mass of manuscript he sent would have furnished a modest bookstore, and the subjects and accounts with which he was so familiar drove Madison and others, too opposed to finance to master the maze of it, close upon the borders of frenzy. It had been their uncommunicated policy to carry the matter over to the next session, but Hamilton was determined to have done with them by adjournment.

And in the midst of this tremendous pressure arrived George Washington
Lafayette.

It was on the first Saturday of his retirement into the deep obscurity of his library, with orders that no one knock under penalty of driving him from the house, that Hamilton, opening the door suddenly with intent to make a dash for his office, nearly fell over Angelica. She was standing just in front of the door, and her face was haggard.

"How long have you been here?" demanded her father.

"Three hours, sir."

"Three! Have you stood all that time?"

Angelica nodded. She was determined not to cry, but she was wise enough not to tax the muscles of her throat.

Hamilton hesitated. If the child fidgeted, she would distract his attention, great as were his powers of concentration; but another searching of her eyes decided him.

"Very well," he said. "Go in, but mind you imagine that you are a mouse, or you will have to leave."

When he returned, she was sitting in a low chair by his desk, almost rigid. She had neither doll nor book. "This will never do," he thought. "What on earth shall I do with the child?" His eye fell upon the chaos of his manuscript. He gathered it up and threw it on the sofa. "There," he said, "arrange that according to the numbers, and come here every five minutes for more."

And Angelica spent two hours of every day in the library, useful and happy.

One day Hamilton was obliged to attend a Cabinet meeting, and to spend several hours at his office just after. Returning home in the early winter dusk, he saw two small white faces pressed against the hall window. One of them was Angelica's, the other he had never seen. As he entered, his daughter fell upon him.

"This is George Washington Lafayette," she announced breathlessly. "He came to-day, and he doesn't speak any English, and he won't go near Betsey or anyone but me, and he won't eat, and I know he's miserable and wretched, only he won't cry. His tutor's ill at the Inn."

The little Frenchman had retired to the drawing-room. Angelica darted after him and dragged him forward into the light. He was small for his age, but his features had the bold curious outline of his father's. He carried himself with dignity, but it was plain that he was terrified and unhappy. Hamilton gave him a warm embrace, and asked him several questions in French. The boy brightened at once, answered rapidly and intelligently, and took firm possession of his new friend's hand.

"I am more happy now," he announced. "I don't like the other people here, except this little girl, because they do not speak French, but you are a Frenchman, and I shall love you, as my father said I should— long ago! I will stay with you day and night."

"Oh, you will?" exclaimed Hamilton. "I am going to send you to school with my boys."

"Oh, not yet, sir! not yet!" cried the boy, shrilly. "I have seen so many strangers on that dreadful ship, and in France—we hid here, there—moving all the time. I wish to live with you and be your little boy."

"And so you shall, but I am uncommonly busy."

"He is a very quiet little boy," interposed Angelica, who was three years his junior. "He would not move if he sat in your room, and I will take him for a walk every day. He will die if he has to sit in a room by himself all day."

"I shall sleep with you, sir, I hope?" asked young Lafayette, eagerly. "I have thought all day of the dark of to-night. I have seen such terrible things, sir!"

"Good Heaven!" thought Hamilton, "is it not enough to be dry nurse to a nation?" But he could not refuse, and during the few hours he snatched for sleep he was half strangled. By day the boy sat quietly in a corner of the library, and studied the text-books his guardian bought him. Betsey did all she could to win him, but he had no faith in people who could not speak his language. Angelica, like all of Hamilton's children, knew something of French, and he liked her and accepted her motherly attentions; but Hamilton he adored. The moment his absorbed friend made for the front door he was after him, and Hamilton let him run at his heels, lest he get neither air nor exercise. He had no time at present to take him to call on his august godfather, and, in truth, he dreaded the prospect. Washington knew nothing of children, and his diminutive namesake would probably be terrified into spasms.

XXXIII

The three long and exhaustive reports, accounting honourably for every penny entrusted to the Secretary of the Treasury, and justifying every payment, measure, and investment, had gone to the Congress. Nine days later Giles brought forward nine resolutions of censure against the Secretary of the Treasury. But by this time Congress had made up its mind, and many of the Republicans were disgusted and humiliated. The Federalists were triumphant, and amused themselves with Giles, drawing him on, to confound him with ridicule and proof of the absurdity of his charges. Madison, desperate, lost his head and the respect of many of his colleagues, by asserting hysterically that the House was impotent to change the truth of the accusations, and that in the tribunal of public opinion the Secretary would be condemned. But Hamilton was triumphantly vindicated by Congress and the Nation at large. His house was in a state of siege for weeks from people of all parts of the country, come to congratulate him; his desk obliterated by letters he had no time to read. The Federals were jubilant. Their pride in

Hamilton was so great that a proclamation from above would not have disturbed their faith, and they were merciless to the discomfited enemy. In truth, the Virginian trio and their close adherents were mortified and confounded. In their hearts they had not believed Hamilton guilty of dishonesty, but they had been confident that his affairs were in chaos, that large sums must have escaped, not conceiving that any mortal could at the same time create gigantic schemes, and be as methodical as a department clerk in every detail of his great office.

Although Hamilton had commanded his brain to dwell exclusively upon the vindication and its means, the deeps below were bitter and hot. When the work was over, and exhausted in body and mind he went about his duties mechanically, or attempted to find distraction in his family, he felt as if the abundant humanity in him were curdled; and he longed for a war, that he might go out and kill somebody. It was small compensation that the Virginian ring were grinding their teeth, and shivering under daily shafts of humiliation and ridicule. So terrible was the position in which they had placed him, so immeasurably had they added to the sum of his contempt for human kind, that individually they occupied, for a time, but a corner of his thought.

His only solace during this trial had been Washington; he had been too busy and too frozen for Mrs. Croix. But that closest of his friends, although forced by his high office to a position of stern neutrality, did all he could in private to convince Hamilton of his unaltered affection and regard. As soon as the vindication was complete he fell into the habit of finishing his daily walk with an hour in Hamilton's library. But if his visits were a pleasure to his Secretary, they were wretchedness unleavened for two other members of the family. The President never failed to ask for Angelica and George Washington Lafayette; and upon their prompt but unwilling advent he would solemnly place one on either knee, where they remained for perhaps half an hour in awe-stricken misery. They had orders to show no distress, and they behaved admirably; but although young Lafayette was rapidly learning English, the fact did not lessen his fear of this enormous man, who spoke so kindly, and looked as if he could have silenced the Terror with the awful majesty of his presence. Angelica, being an independent little American, was less overwhelmed, but she was often on the verge of hysterics. It was the short session of Congress, and in March, George, with scalding but dignified tears, accompanied his godfather to Mount Vernon, whence he wrote Hamilton a daily letter of lament, until habit tempered his awe; from that point he passed with Gallic bounds into an ardent affection for the great man, who, if of an unearthly dignity, was always kind, and, when relieved of the cares of State, uniformly genial.

The respite in Philadelphia was brief. In April came the first news of the beheading of the French king; and the same tardy packets brought word that France was at war with England and Spain. Hamilton sent the news, express haste, to Washington, and dismissed every consideration from his brain but the terrible crisis forced upon the United States, and the proper measures to save her from shipwreck. In the early stages of the French Revolution he had predicted the developments with such accuracy to Henry Walter Livingston that the new Secretary of Legation, upon his arrival in Paris, told Gouverneur Morris—United States minister since 1792—that to his astonishment he found nothing to surprise him. Therefore the prophet had long been determined upon the policy the United States should pursue when this crisis shot out of the eastern horizon; he had now but to formulate it in such a manner that every point could be grasped at once by the Cabinet, and acted upon. When Washington arrived in Philadelphia and summoned his advisers, Hamilton presented twelve questions for discussion, the most pressing of which were: Shall a proclamation issue for the purpose of preventing interferences of the citizens of the United States in the war between France and Great Britain, etc.? Shall it contain a declaration of neutrality? Shall a minister from this Republic of France be received? Jefferson was in a far less enviable position than Hamilton. He neither wished for war, nor dared he machinate for it; but with all his democratic soul he loved the cause which was convulsing the world from its ferocious centre in France. Had Jefferson come of stout yeoman stock, like John Adams, or of a long line of patrician ancestors, like Hamilton, and, to a lesser degree, like Washington, he might, judging from certain of his tastes, and his love of power, have become, or been, as aristocratic in habit and spirit as were most men of his wealth, position, and importance in the young country. But the two extremes met in his blood. The plebeianism of his father showed itself in the ungainly shell, in the indifference to personal cleanliness, and in the mongrel spirit which drove him to acts of physical cowardice for which his apologists blush. But his mother had belonged to the aristocracy of Virginia, and this knowledge induced a sullen resentment that he should be so unlike her kind, so different in appearance from the courtly men of his State. Little was wanting to accelerate his natural desire to level his country to a plane upon which with his gifts he easily could loom as a being of superior mould; but when a British sovereign publicly turned his back upon him, and the English court, delighted with its cue, treated him with an unbearable insolence, nothing more was needed to start the torrent of his hate against all who stood for aristocracy. Democracy rampant on all sides of him, during his sojourn in France, found in him not only an ardent sympathizer, but a passionate advocate. He quite overlooked the fact that he failed to persuade the country of his enthusiasm to accord the United States fair commercial treatment: it embodied and demonstrated his ideal of liberty, equality, fraternity, and he was its most devoted friend, unresting until he had insinuated his own admiration into the minds of his followers in America, and made Jacobinism a party issue.

To turn his back upon France, therefore, to help her neither in money nor moral support, was a policy he had no intention to pursue, could he avoid it; but knowing his weakness in the Cabinet, he suggested an extra session of Congress. It would then be an easy matter to throw the responsibility upon his followers in both Houses, while he stood to the country as working consistently and harmoniously in his great office.

But Hamilton, who understood him thoroughly, would listen to no proposition which would involve weeks of delay, inflame further the public mind, and give Jefferson an opportunity to make political capital. Moreover, he would have no such confession of weakness go out from the Administration. He prevailed, and in that first meeting Jefferson was forced to consent also to the immediate issue of a proclamation to the people. He argued with such fervour, however, against the use of the word "neutrality," declaring that the Executive had no constitutional authority so far to commit the people, that Washington, to humour him, omitted the word, while declaring authoritatively for the substance. It was also agreed that Genet, the new Minister from France, sent by the Revolutionists to succeed M. Ternant, should be received. The first meeting closed tranquilly, for both Hamilton and Jefferson had tacitly

361

admitted that it was no time for personal recrimination.

But the Cabinet met daily, and other subjects, notably Hamilton's contention that their treaties made with a proper French government no longer existed, came up for elaborate discussion; Hamilton had an exhaustive report prepared on each of them. The two Secretaries, who hated each other as two men hardly have hated before or since, and who realized that they had met for their final engagement in official life, soon dismissed any pretence at concord, and wrangled habitually—with cutting sarcasm or crushing force on Hamilton's part, with mild but deadly venom on Jefferson's; until he too was maddened by a jagged dart which momentarily routed his tender regard for his person. Jefferson wrenched one victory from the Cabinet despite Hamilton's determined opposition: Genet's reception should be absolute. But on all other important points the Secretary of the Treasury scored, and stone by stone built up the great policy of neutrality which prevailed until the year 1898; impressed into the Government the "Doctrine"—he had formulated it in "The Federalist"—which was to immortalize the name of a man who created nothing. Hamilton, with all the energy and obstinacy of his nature, was resolved that the United States should not have so much as a set-back for the sake of a country whose excesses filled him with horror, much less run the risk of being sucked into the whirlpool of Europe; and he watched every move Jefferson made, lest his secret sympathies commit the country. When, after a triumphal procession through miles of thoughtless enthusiasts, who remembered only the services of France, forgot that their friends had been confined entirely to the royalty and aristocracy that the mob was murdering, and were intoxicated by the extreme democracy of the famous Secretary of State, Genet arrived in Philadelphia, inflated and bumptious, his brain half crazed by the nervous excitement of the past two years, and was received with frigid politeness by Washington, Hamilton was not long discovering that Jefferson was in secret sympathy and intercourse with this dangerous fire-brand. The news had preceded and followed the new minister that he had been distributing blank commissions to all who would fit out privateers to prey upon British commerce, opening headquarters for the enlistment of American sailors into the French service, and constituting French consuls courts of admiralty for the trial and condemnation of prizes brought in by French privateers.

As soon as he arrived in Philadelphia he demanded of Hamilton the arrears of the French debt, which the Secretary had refused to pay until there was a stable government in France to receive it. Hamilton laughed, locked the doors of the Treasury, and put the key in his pocket. To Genet's excited volubility and pertinacity he paid as little attention as to Jefferson's arguments. Moreover, he reversed all Citizen Genet's performances in the South; and in course of time, even the captured British ships, to the wrath and disgust of Jefferson, were returned to their owners.

Freneau's *Gazette* supported the Secretary of State with the desperation of an expiring cause; in this great final battle, were Jefferson driven from the Cabinet, his faithful organ must scurry to the limbo of its kind. It assailed the Administration for ingratitude and meanness, then turned its attention almost exclusively to the Secretary of the Treasury. It accused him of abstracting the moneys due to France, of plundering the industrious farmer with the Excise Law, destroying the morals of the people by Custom House duties; resurrected the old discrimination cry and asserted vehemently that he, and he alone, had robbed the poor soldiers. It raked every accusation, past and present, from its pigeon holes. Jefferson, on the other hand, was held up as a model of the disinterested statesman, combining virtues before which those falsely attributed to Washington paled and expired; and as the only man fit to fill the Executive Chair. Genet accepted all this as gospel, fortunately, perhaps, for the country; for his own excesses and impudence, his final threat to appeal from the President to the people, ruined him with the cooling heads of the Republican party, and finally lost him even the support of Jefferson.

Meanwhile, after stormy meetings of the Cabinet, Hamilton, in the peace of his library, with Angelica sorting his pages,—until she went to the North,—had written a series of papers defending the proclamation. They were so able and convincing, so demonstrative of the treasonable efforts of the enemy to undermine the influence of the Administration, so cool and so brilliant an exposition of the rights and powers of the Executive, that on July 7th Jefferson wrote to Madison: "For God's sake, my dear sir, take up your pen. Select the most striking heresies, and cut him to pieces in the face of the public."

Madison hastened to obey his chief in a series of papers which tickled the literary nerve, but failed to convince. That the laurels were to Hamilton was another bitter pill which Jefferson was forced to swallow. Nevertheless, Hamilton, despite his victories, felt anything but amiable. He was so exhausted that he was on the verge of a collapse, and triumphs were drab under the daily harassment of Jefferson, Genet, and Freneau. Matters came to a climax one day in August, shortly before the outbreak of yellow fever.

XXXIV

Hamilton laid down a copy of Freneau's *Gazette*, whose editorial columns were devoted, as usual, to persuading the people of the United States that they were miserable, and that they owed their misery to the Secretary of the Treasury. It also contained a shameful assault upon the President. As he lifted another paper from the pile on his library table, his eyes fell on the following address to himself:—

O votary of despotism! O abettor of Carthaginian faith! Blush! Can you for a moment suppose that the hearts of the yeomanry of America are becoming chilled and insensible to the feelings of insulted humanity like your own? Can you think that gratitude, the most endearing disposition of the human heart, is to be argued away by your dry sophistry? Do you suppose the people of the United States prudently thumb over Vattel and Pufendorf to ascertain the sum and substance of their obligations to their generous brethren, the French? No! no! Each individual will lay his hand on his heart and find the amount there. He will find that manly glow, both of gratitude and love, which animated his breast when assisted by this generous people in establishing his own liberty and shaking off the yoke of British despotism!

In the *Aurora* he was denounced as the foe of France and the friend of Great Britain and Spain, the high priest of tyranny, the bitterest enemy of the immortal French trio, Liberté, Egalité, Fraternité; the subtle and Machiavellian adviser of Washington, who, relieved of this pernicious influence, would acknowledge the debts of gratitude and follow the will of the American people.

"Are they mad?" he thought, flinging the entire pile into the wastebasket. "Or are they merely so eager for power and our ruin that they are indifferent to the fact that the Administration, and the foundations upon which it stands, never has needed the support of the people more than now? Can only the party in power afford to be patriotic? What a spectacle is this, that I, an alien born, am wearing out my life and sacrificing my character, to save from themselves a people who pant for my ruin! Has the game been worth the candle? Debt, my family crowded into a house not half large enough to hold them, my health almost gone, my reputation, in spite of repeated vindications, undermined by daily assault—for the fools of the world believe what they are told, and I cannot compromise my dignity by replying to such attacks as these; above all, a sickening and constant disgust for life and human nature! *Is* the game worth the candle? Had I remained at the bar, I should have given my family abundance by now; with only the kind and quantity of enemies that stimulate. It is only politics that rouse the hellish depths in the human heart. It is true that I have saved the country, made it prosperous, happy, and honoured. But what guaranty have I that this state will last beyond the administration of Washington? With the Republicans in power the whole edifice may be swept away, the country in a worse plight than before, and the author of its brief prosperity forgotten with his works. I shall have lived in vain, and leave my sons to be educated, my family to be supported, by my father-in-law."

He was in no mood to see the reverse side of the picture; and indeed his cares were so many and overwhelming at this time that it is little wonder he believed he had lost for ever the gay buoyancy of his spirits. In addition to the predominating trials, financial matters were demanding all the leisure he should have given to rest, heavy failures in England having seriously affected the money concerns of the United States; and the rebellions in the West against the Excise Law were sounding a new alarm. Moreover, his constant efforts to obtain Duer's release were unavailing; he could get no word of Lafayette; and the last packet had brought a rumour of the murder of Gouverneur Morris by the mob. Altogether, he may be excused for forgetting that he was still the most dazzling figure in America, in the full tide of actual success, and an object of terrified hatred to a powerful ring who could reach their zenith over his political corpse, and by no other means whatever.

He picked up his hat, and went forth reluctantly to a Cabinet meeting. It was early, and he saw Washington for a few moments alone in the library. The President was in a no more cheerful or amiable frame of mind than himself. His responsibilities in this terrible crisis wore on his spirits and temper; and the daily fear that his Secretaries would come to blows,—for Jefferson was in the worst humour of the quintette,—to say nothing of the assaults of the press, made him openly regret the hour he was persuaded into the Executive Chair. But his entire absence of party spirit, despite his secret sympathy with every measure of Hamilton's, his attitude of stern neutrality, never emerged more triumphantly from any trial of his public career; nor did he ever exhibit the magnanimity of his character more strikingly than in his undisturbed affection for Hamilton, while daily twitted with being the tool of his "scheming and ambitious Secretary."

Hamilton saw a copy of Freneau's *Gazette* in the waste-basket, but by common consent they ignored the subjects which would be unavoidable in a few moments, and spoke of the stifling heat, of the unhealthy state of Philadelphia, the menace of the San Domingo refugees pouring into the city, of the piles of putrid coffee and hides on the wharves at the foot of Mulberry Street, and of the carcasses of rotting hogs and horses which lay everywhere.

"Thank Heaven, we can get our women and children out of it," said the President. "And unless we can finish this business in another week, I shall take the Government to the country. I suppose we are entitled to escape with our lives, if they leave us nothing else."

They entered the Council Chamber and found the others in their accustomed seats. Jefferson's brow was corrugated, his weak and mincing mouth pressed out of shape. He had just finished reading the last of Hamilton's "No Jacobin" papers, published that morning, in which Genet's abominable breaches of decorum, violation of treaties, and deliberate insults to the Executive—and through him to the American people—had been set forth in so clear pointed and dispassionate a manner, that no thinking Republican who read could fail to be convinced of the falseness of his position in supporting this impudent and ridiculous Frenchman. Furthermore, the Secretary of State had been forced, through the exigencies of his position, to sign despatch after despatch, letter after letter, in violation of his private sympathies. He was feeling not only as angry as a cornered bull, but extremely virtuous. He hated what he firmly believed to be the cold and selfish policy of the Administration, as he hated every other policy it had executed; and the knowledge that he had sacrificed his personal feelings to save his country from discord, made him feel a far better man than the Secretary of the Treasury, who had a diabolical talent for getting his own way. He had some reason to be pleased with his conduct, and with his share in contributing to a series of measures which later on won for the Cabinet at that crucial period the encomiums of history; and when time had abated the fevers, Hamilton would have been the first to acknowledge that Jefferson not only was the brake which the Administration needed at that time, but that, owing to his popularity with the French and the masses of the United States, he reduced the danger of a popular uprising.

As Hamilton took his seat this morning, however, the blood was in his head, and he and Jefferson exchanged a glance of sullen hate which made Washington extend his long arms at once. All went well until the President, with a premonitory sigh, introduced the dynamic name, Genet. Hamilton forgot his debility, and was all mind, alert and energetic. Jefferson, who had come to hate Genet as an intolerable nuisance, would have been the first at another moment to counsel the demand for recall which he knew was now inevitable, but he was in too bad a humour to-day to concur in any measure agreeable to Hamilton.

The latter had replied promptly to Washington's remark that the time had come to take definite action with regard to the light-headed Frenchman, who continued to fit out and despatch privateers, and was convulsing the country generally.

"Pray send him home, bag and baggage, sir. He is not entitled to the dignity or consideration of the usual formalities. Moreover, he is the trigger of the United States so long as he remains at liberty in it. I estimate that there is a new Jacobin club formed daily. At any moment he may do something which will drive these fools, under their red caps and cockades, mad with admiration."

Jefferson brought his brows down to the root of his nose. "'Fools' is not the word for an honest enthusiasm for liberty, sir. I regret the present excitement—its manifestations at this moment—as much as anyone—"

"Indeed? I am amazed. Who, then, is responsible for them?"

"Not I, sir."

"Oh, let us have no more hypocrisy, at all events," said Hamilton, contemptuously. He had his wrath under control, but he suddenly

367

determined to force the climax. "If you had employed your secret pen to better purpose, or not employed it at all, there would not be a Jacobin club in the country; this ridiculous Frenchman, unencouraged by your private sympathy, by your assurances of my inability to withhold the residue of the debt, would have calmed down long since. I accuse you here, deliberately and publicly, instead of writing private letters to the public, both because I have not your commanding talent for patient and devious ways, and because I wish you to declare, unequivocally, whether or not you purpose to continue this policy of obstruction. Time presses. We must act at once with regard to this Frenchman. Reserve subterfuge for some more opportune time, and let us know what you intend to do."

Jefferson looked with appeal at Washington, who usually interposed when his Secretaries arrived at personalities. But Washington, although his face was as immobile as stone, was so sick with anger and disgust over the whole situation, at what appeared to be the loss of the popular faith in himself, and the ridicule and abuse which had filled the columns of Freneau's paper that morning, that it was a relief to him to hear Hamilton explode.

"I repudiate every word you have said, sir," growled Jefferson. "More I will not say. As to Citizen Genet, with whom I have never had a word of private intercourse—" Here, even Washington lifted his head, and Hamilton laughed outright. Jefferson continued, determined upon martyrdom rather than rouse the terrible passions opposite: "As to Citizen Genet, if the Cabinet agree that it is best he leave this country. I shall demand that his recall be requested in the regular manner, in accordance with every principle of international courtesy. He may be imprudent, intoxicated with the glorious wine of liberty, but he is a Frenchman, a distinguished citizen of the great country that came so nobly to our rescue, and I protest against the base ingratitude which would fling insults in the teeth of an unfortunate people."

Hamilton threw back his head impatiently, and drummed with his fingers on the table. "The primary motive of France for the assistance she gave us was, obviously, to enfeeble a hated and powerful rival. A second motive was to extend her relations of commerce in the new world, and to acquire additional security for her possessions there, by forming a connection with this country when detached from Great Britain. To ascribe to her any other motives, to suppose that she was actuated by friendship toward us, is to be ignorant of the springs of action which invariably regulate the cabinets of princes. A despotic court aid a popular revolution through sympathy with its principles! For the matter of that, if you insist upon American statesmen being sentimental fools, the class that assisted us has been murdered by the rabble, which I refuse to recognize as France. And if it be your object to reduce this country to a similar position that you may climb over maddened brains to power—"

"Hear!" roared Jefferson, justly indignant. "I? Never a man loved peace as I do. My life has been hell since you have forced me into daily conflict, when, God knows, I perish with desire for the peace of my homely life in Virginia. Power! I scorn it, sir. I leave that to restless upstarts like yourself—"

He stopped, choking. Hamilton laughed contemptuously. "You are at work with your pen day and night, strengthening your misnamed party, and preparing the way by which you can lift yourself to a position where you can undo all that the party you hate, because it is composed of gentlemen, has accomplished for the honour and prosperity of your country. You are perfectly well aware that Genet was sent here to stir up a civil war, and embroil us with Europe at the same time, and you have secretly sympathized with and encouraged him. I cannot make up my mind whether you are a villain, or merely the victim of a sublimated and paradoxical imagination. But in either case, I wish to be placed on record as asserting that you are the worst enemy the United States is cursed with to-day."

This was too much for Jefferson, who had convinced himself that he was a high-minded and self-sacrificing statesman, stooping to devious ways for the common good. He forgot his physical fear, and shouted, pounding the table with his fist:—

"How dare you, sir? How dare you? It is you who are ruining, corrupting, and dishonouring this unhappy country, with your Banks, your devilish methods to cement the aristocracy, your abominable Excise Law—"

"Oh, but you have counteracted that so effectively! I was coming to that point. I conceived a measure by which to meet an imperative financial demand, and you, by your agents, by your secret machinations, have been the author of insurrection after insurrection, of the most flagrant breaches of the laws of your country. You have cost innumerable men, engaged in the pursuit of plain duty, their self-respect, and in several cases their lives. Another hideous problem is approaching—one, I am persuaded, that can be solved by arms and bloodshed alone; and to your pen, to your deliberate unsettling of men's minds, to the hatred you have inspired for the lawful government of this country, to you, and to you alone—"

"It's a lie! a lie!" shouted Jefferson. "You are speaking to an honourable man, sir! one who occupies a position in this country both by birth and breeding that you would give your soul—you adventurer!—to possess. Go back to your Islands! You have no place here among men of honourable birth. It's monstrous that this country should be ruled by a foreign bastard—!"

For a moment, every one present had a confused idea that a tornado was in the room. Then two doors were wrenched open, Jefferson fled down the street, with Randolph, bearing his hat, in pursuit; Knox was holding Hamilton firmly in his arms; and Washington, who had risen some moments since, and stood staring in grim disgust, awaiting the end, was divided between a desire to laugh, and to give way to a burst of fury himself.

Hamilton had made no attempt to struggle when Knox caught him, but he now withdrew from the relaxing arms, and the Secretary of War left the room hastily. Hamilton, to Washington's astonishment, flung himself into a chair, and dropped his head on his arms. In a moment, he began to sob convulsively. A malignant fever was breeding in his depressed system; the blood still surged in his head. He had a despairing sense that his character was in ruins; he was humiliated to his depths; he despised himself so bitterly that he forgot the existence of Jefferson.

The humour and anger died out of Washington. He went forward hastily and locked the door. Then he stooped over Hamilton, and pressed him closely in his arms.

"My dear boy!" he said huskily. "My dear boy!"

XXXV

That was the last of Hamilton's battles in the Cabinet. Jefferson resigned; although, in order that the Administration might, until the crisis was past, preserve an unbroken front to the country, he reluctantly consented to withhold his resignation until the assembling of Congress. He retired to Monticello, however; and apologized to the Secretary of the Treasury.

Hamilton, almost immediately, was taken down with yellow fever, which broke out suddenly and raged with a fearful violence. To the ordinary odours of carcasses and garbage, were added those of vinegar, tar, nitre, garlic, and gunpowder. Every disinfectant America had ever heard of was given a trial, and every man who possessed a shot-gun fired it all day and all night. The bells tolled incessantly. The din and the smells were hideous, the death carts rattled from dawn till dawn; many were left unburied in their houses for a week; hundreds died daily; and the city confessed itself helpless, although it cleaned the streets. Hamilton had a very light attack, but Dr. Stevens dropped in frequently to see him; he privately thought him of more importance than all Philadelphia.

Lying there and thinking of many things, too grateful for the rest to chafe at the imprisonment, and striving for peace with himself, Hamilton one day conceived the idea of immersing yellow-fever patients in ice-water. Microbes were undiscovered, but Hamilton, perhaps with a flashing glimpse of the truth, reasoned that if cold weather invariably routed the disease, a freezing of the infected blood should produce the same result. He succeeded in convincing Stevens, with the issue that when the scourge was over, the young West Indian doctor had so many cures to his credit, where all other physicians had failed, that the City Council presented him with a silver tankard, gratefully inscribed, and filled with golden coins. Hamilton's fecund brain, scattering its creations, made more than one reputation.

Meanwhile, he awoke one day to find Mrs. Croix sitting beside his bed. She had left town in June, and usually did not return until late in September. She wore a white frock and a blue sash, and looked like an angel about to do penance.

"I have come back to take care of the sick, including yourself," she announced, "I was born to be a nurse, and I felt that my place was here. I have come to see you first, and I shall call daily, but otherwise I am in Dr. Stevens's hands."

Hamilton stared at her. He was not surprised, for she was kind hearted in her erratic imperious fashion, and much beloved by the poor;

nor was she afraid of anything under heaven. But she was the last person he had wished to see; she was for his triumphant hours, or his furious, not for helpless invalidism. He had longed consistently for his wife, and written to her by every packet-boat, lest she suspect his illness and return to the plague-stricken city. He was filled with a sudden resentment that any other woman should presume to fill her chair. To forget her under overwhelming provocation he had reconciled to his conscience with little difficulty, for his extenuations were many, and puritanism had not yet invaded the national character; but to permit another woman to ministrate to him when ill, he felt to be an unpardonable breach of his Eliza's rights, and his loyalty rebelled. So, although he treated Mrs. Croix with politeness while she remained, he gave orders to Dr. Stevens to keep her away upon any pretext he chose. "I am too nervous to be bothered with women," he added; and Stevens obeyed without comment.

Hamilton's convalescence was cheered by two facts: the revival of his spirits and equilibrium, and frequent assurances from his wife that for the first time in five years she was entirely well. She wrote that she had regained all her old colour, "spring," vivacity, and plumpness, and felt quite ten years younger. Hamilton was delighted; for her courage had so far exceeded her strength that he had often feared a collapse. Although she detested the sight of a pen, she was so elated with her recovered health that she wrote to him weekly. Suddenly, and without explanation, the letters stopped. Still, he was quite unprepared for what was to follow, and on the first of October, his health improved by a short sojourn in the country, he went to the wharf to meet the packet-boat which invariably brought his family; his pockets full of sweets, and not a misgiving in his mind.

As he stood on the wharf, watching the boat towed slowly to dock, his four oldest children suddenly appeared, waving their hats and shouting like young Indians. James, who was as broad as he was long, and was wedged firmly between Angelica and Philip lest he turn over, swelled a chorus which excited much amusement among by-standers. To Hamilton's surprise his wife did not occupy her usual place behind that enthusiastic group, but as the boat touched the pier, and all four precipitated themselves upon him at once,—the three oldest about his neck, and James upon his pockets,—he forgot her for the moment in the delight of seeing and embracing his children after three months of separation. He emerged from that wild greeting, dishevelled and breathless, only to disappear once more within six long arms and a circle of sunburned faces. Hamilton received from his children an almost frantic affection; indeed, few people merely liked him; it was either hate or a love which far transcended the bounds of such affection as the average mortal commands. The passion he inspired in his children cost one his life, another her reason, and left its indelible mark on a third; but for what they gave, they received an overflowing measure in return; no man was ever more passionately attached to his brood, nor took a greater delight in its society.

Suddenly, through the web of Angelica's flying locks, he saw that his wife had appeared on deck and was about to land. He disentangled himself hastily and went forward to greet her. In a flash he noted that she was prettier than ever, and that she was affected by something far more extraordinary than an increase of health. She threw back her head, and her black eyes flashed with anger as he approached with the assurance of thirteen years of connubial ownership; but she greeted him politely and took his arm. No explanation was possible there; and he escorted her and the children to the coach as quickly as possible. Philip, Angelica, and Alexander were sensible at once of the chasm yawning between the seats; they redoubled their attentions to their father, and regarded their mother with reproving and defiant eyes. Poor Betsey, conscious that she was entirely in the right, felt bitter and humiliated, and sought to find comfort in the indifference of James, who was engaged with a cornucopia and blind to the infelicity of his parents.

When they reached the house, Hamilton dismissed the children and opened the door of his library.

"Will you come in?" he said peremptorily.

Mrs. Hamilton entered, and sat down on a high-backed chair. She was very small, her little pigeon toes were several inches above the floor; but no judge on his bench ever looked so stern and so inexorable.

"Now," said Hamilton, who was cold from head to foot, for he had an awful misgiving, "let us have an explanation at once. This is our first serious misunderstanding, and you well know that I shall be in misery until it is over—"

"I have not the least intention of keeping you in suspense," interrupted Betsey, sarcastically. "I am too thankful that you did not happen to come to Saratoga when *I* was prostrated with misery. I have gone through everything,—every stage of wretchedness that the human heart is capable of,—but now, thank Heaven, I am filled with only a just indignation. Read that!"

She produced a letter from her reticule and flipped it at him. Even before he opened it he recognized the familiar handwriting, the profuse capitals, of Mrs. Reynolds. Fortunately, he made no comment, for the contents were utterly different from his quick anticipation. It contained a minute and circumstantial account of his visits during the past year to Mrs. Croix, with many other details, which, by spying and bribing, no doubt, she had managed to gather. Failing one revenge, the woman had resorted to another, and fearing that it might be lost among the abundant and surfeiting lies of the public press, she had aimed at what he held most dear. The letter was so minute and circumstantial that it would have convinced almost any woman.

There was but one thing for Hamilton to do, and he lied with his unsurpassable eloquence. When he paused tentatively, his wife remarked:—

"Alexander, you are a very great man, but you are a wretchedly poor liar. As Mr. Washington would say, your sincerity is one of the most valuable of your gifts, and without it you could not convince a child. As if this were not enough, only yesterday, on the boat, I overheard two of your intimate friends discussing this intrigue as a matter of course. There was not a word of censure or criticism; they were merely wondering when you would add to your enemies; for as this woman was desperately in love with you, she was bound to hate you as violently when you tired of her. I think men are horrors!" she burst out passionately. "When, unable to bear this terrible affliction any longer, and unwilling to worry my poor mother, I took that letter and my grief to my father—what do you suppose he said? After he had tried to convince me that the story was a base fabrication, and that an anonymous communication should be destroyed unread—as if any woman living would not read an anonymous letter!—he said, crossly, that women did not understand men and never made allowances for them; and he went on to make as many excuses for you as if he were defending himself; and then wound up by saying that he did not believe a word of it, and that the letter was written by someone you had flouted. But it seemed to me in those awful days that I was awake for the first time, that for the first time I understood you—and your horrid sex, in general—I do! I do!"

She looked so adorable with her flashing eyes, the hot colour in her cheek, and the new personality she exhibited, that Hamilton would have foregone a triumph over his enemies to kiss her. But he dared not make a false move, and he was terribly perplexed.

"I can only reiterate," he said, "that this letter is a lie from beginning to end. It is written by a woman, who, with her husband, has blackmailed me and jeopardized my reputation. I treated them as they deserved, and this is their next move. As for Mrs. Croix, I repeat, she is a most estimable person, whose brilliant wit and talent for politics draw all public men about her. There is hardly one among them who might not be victimized by a similar attack. I doubt if I have called half as often as many others. As for the friends whom you heard discussing my visits—you know the love of the human mind for scandal. Please be reasonable. You have made me the most wretched man on earth, I shall be unfit for public duty or anything else if you continue to treat me in this brutal manner. I hardly know you. No woman was ever more loved by her husband or received more devotion."

Betsey almost relented, he looked so miserable. But she replied firmly: "There is one condition I have a right to make. If you agree to it, I will consider if I can bring myself to believe your denial and your protestations. It is that you never enter Mrs. Croix's house again, nor see her willingly."

Hamilton knew what the promise would mean, but his mind worked with the rapidity of lightning in great crises, and never erred. He replied promptly:

"I will see her once, and once only—to give her a decent reason for not calling again—that I understand I am compromising her good name, or something of the sort. I have accepted too much hospitality at her hands to drop her brusquely, without a word of explanation."

"You can write her a letter. You can merely send polite excuses when she invites you. You are very busy. You have every excuse. Gradually, she will think no more about you—if it be true that she is nothing to you. You have your choice, sir! Either your promise, or I return by the next packet to Albany."

But Hamilton, always considerate of women, and despising the weakness and brutality which permits a man to slink out of an amour, would not retreat, and Betsey finally settled herself in her chair, and said, with unmistakable determination:—

"Very well, go now. I shall not move from this room—this chair—until you return."

Hamilton caught his hat and left the house. Although he was possessed by the one absorbing desire to win back his wife, who had never been so dear as to-day, when for the first time she had placed him at arm's length and given him a thorough fright, still his brain, accustomed to see all sides of every question at once, and far into the future, spoke plainly of the hour when he would regret the loss of Mrs. Croix. He might forget her for weeks at a time, but he always reawakened to a sense of her being with a glowing impression that the world was more alive and fair. The secret romance had been very dear and pleasant. The end was come, however, and he was eager to pass it.

His eye was attracted to a chemist's window, and entering the shop hastily, he purchased a bottle of smelling salts. The act reminded him of Mrs. Mitchell, and that he had not heard from her for several months. He resolved to write that night, and permitted his mind to wander to the green Island which was almost lost among his memories. The respite was brief, however.

To his relief he found Mrs. Croix in her intellectual habit. The lady, who was reading in the door of her boudoir above the garden steps, exclaimed, without formal greeting:—

"I am transported, sir. Such descriptions never were written before. Listen!"

Hamilton, who hated descriptions of scenery at any time, and was in his most direct and imperative temper, stood the infliction but a moment, then asked her attention. She closed the book over her finger and smiled charmingly.

"Forgive me for boring you," she said graciously. "But you know my passion for letters; and if truth must be told, I am a little piqued. I have not laid eyes on you for a fortnight. Not but that I am used to your lapses of memory by this time," she added, with a sigh.

Hamilton went straight to the point. He told her the exact reason for the necessary breach, omitting nothing but the episode of Mrs. Reynolds; one cause of reproach was as much as a man could be expected to furnish an angry woman.

For Mrs. Croix was very angry. At first she had pressed her hand against her heart as if about to faint, and Hamilton had hastily extracted the salts; but the next moment she was on her feet, towering and expanding like an avenging queen about to order in her slaves with scimitars and chargers.

"Do you mean," she cried, "that I am flouted, flung aside like an old cravat? I? With half the men in America in love with me? Good God, sir! I have known from the beginning that you would tire, but I thought to be on the watch and save my pride. How dare you come like this? Why could you not give me warning? It is an outrage. I would rather you had killed me."

"I am sorry I have blundered," said Hamilton, humbly. "But how in Heaven's name can a man know how a woman will take anything? I had such respect for your great intelligence that I thought it due you to treat you as I would a man—"

"A man?" exclaimed Mrs. Croix. "Treat me like a man! Of all the supremely silly things I ever heard one of your sex say, that is the silliest. I am not a man, and you know it."

Hamilton hastened to assure her that she was deliberately averting her intelligence from his true meaning. "You have never doubted my sincerity for a moment," he added. "You surely know what it will cost me never to see you again. There is but one cause under heaven that could have brought me to you with this decision. You may believe in my regret—to use a plain word—when you reflect upon all that you have been to me."

He was desperately afraid that her anger would dissolve in tears, and he be placed in a position from which he was not sure of emerging with a clear conscience,—and he dared take home nothing less. But Mrs. Croix, however she might feel on the morrow, was too outraged in her pride and vanity to be susceptible either to grief or the passion of love. She stormed up and down the room in increasing fury, her eyes flashing blue lightning, her strong hands smashing whatever costly offering they encountered. "Wives! Wives! Wives!" she screamed. "The little fools! What are wives for but to keep house and bring up babies? They are a class apart. I have suffered enough from their impertinent interference. Am I not a woman apart? Will you assert that there is a 'wife' in America who can hold her own with me for a moment in anything? Was I not created to reveal to men—and only the ablest, for I waste no time on fools—the very sublimation of my sex—a companionship they will find in no silly little fool, stupid with domesticity? Am I to submit, then, to be baulked by a sex I despise—and in the greatest passion that ever possessed a woman?" She stopped and laughed, bringing her lashes together and moving forward her beautiful lips. "What a fool I am!" she said. "You will come back when the humour seizes you. I had forgot that your family returned to-day. You are in your most domestic mood—and I have been inflicted with that before. But there will come an hour when neither your wife nor any other mortal power will keep you away from me. Is it not true?"

Hamilton had turned pale; his ready imagination had responded with a presentiment of many desperate struggles. He rose, and took her hand forcibly.

"No," he said. "I shall not return. Believe me, that is the hardest sentence I have ever pronounced upon myself. And forgive me if I have been rude and inconsiderate. It was the result of the desire to have the agony over as quickly as possible. I should have found the anticipation unbearable, and I do not believe it would have been more soothing to you. There is no reason why your pride should be wounded, for this is not the result of satiety on my part, but of an imperative necessity. Shake hands with me."

She wrenched her hand free and, seizing a vase, flung it into a mirror. Hamilton retreated.

XXXVI

He had been gone just thirty-five minutes, Betsey received him with stern approval and announced that she had implicit faith in his promise to avoid Mrs. Croix in the future. But it was quite evident that his punishment was unfinished, and with due humility and some humour he bided her pleasure. Between the two women he had a lively month. Mrs. Croix wrote him a letter a day. At first it was evident that she had taken herself in hand, that her pen was guided by her marvellous intelligence. She apologized charmingly for her exhibition of temper, and for any reflection she might have made upon the most estimable of women, who (with a sigh) had the happiness to be the wife of Alexander Hamilton. She ignored his ultimatum and asked him to come at once, and talk the matter over calmly. Hamilton replied with the graceful playfulness of which he was master, but left no doubt of his continuity of purpose. After the interchange of several letters of this complexion, in which Mrs. Croix was quite conscious of revealing the ample resources of her wit, spirit, and tact, she broke down and went through every circumstance of a despairing woman fighting to recover the supreme happiness of her life. At times she was humble, she prostrated herself at his feet. Again she raved with all the violence of her nature. Her pride, and it was very great, was submerged under the terrible agony of her heart. Even passion was forgotten, and she was sincere for the moment when she vowed that she had no wish beyond his mere presence.

Hamilton was horribly distressed. He would rather she had turned upon him at once with all her tigerish capacity for hate. But he had given his word to his wife, and that was the end of it. He answered every letter, but his gallantry and kindness were pitch and oil, and it was with profound relief that he watched the gradual stiffening of her pride, the dull resentment, even although he knew it meant that an enemy, subtle, resourceful, and venomous, was in the process of making. In her final letter she gave him warning—and a last opportunity. But of this he took no notice.

Meanwhile, Betsey had led him a dance. Naturally bright, but heretofore too sheltered and happy, too undisturbed in her trust, she had done little thinking, little analysis, felt nothing but amusement for the half-comprehended vagaries of men. But jealousy and suffering give a woman, in a week, a fill of knowledge and cunning that will serve her a lifetime. Betsey developed both coquetry and subtlety. She knew that if she obtained command of the situation now, she should hold it to the end, and she was determined that this crisis should result in a close and permanent union. If she finally believed his denial, she was much too shrewd to give him the satisfaction of regaining his former mastery of her mind; but she ceased to speak of it. Meanwhile, he was devoting his energies to winning her again, and he had never found life so interesting. She radiated a new bewitchment, and he had always thought her the most adorable woman on the planet. He divined a good many of her mental processes; but if he was a trifle amused, he was deeply respectful. She was sufficiently uncertain in this new character to torment him unbearably, and when she occasionally betrayed that she was interested and fascinated, he was transported. When she finally succumbed, he was more in love than he had ever been in his life.

XXXVII

The next seven years of Hamilton's life must be reviewed very rapidly. Interesting as they might be made, space diminishes, and after all they were but the precursor of the last great battle of the giants.

In the spring of 1794 the Virginian ring rallied for their final assault in Congress. Their spokesman this time was a worthless man, named Fraunces, and he brought forth a charge against the Secretary of the Treasury of unfaithfulness in office. Hamilton promptly demanded another investigation. The result may be found in the following letters from eminent Federals in Virginia. The first is from Colonel Carrington, dated Richmond, July 9th.

I do not write this letter as congratulatory upon the final issue of the Inquiry into the Treasury Department, as I never conceived you exposed to receive injury therefrom. I write to express my most sincere wishes that you will not suffer the illiberality with which you have been treated to deprive the public of your services, at least until the storm which hangs over us, and is to be dreaded, not less from our own follies and vices than the malignance and intrigues of foreigners, blows over. It is true you have been abused, but it has been and still is, the fate of him who was supposed out of the reach of all slander. It is indeed the lot, in some degree, of every man amongst us who has the sense or fortitude to speak and act rationally, and such men must continue so to speak and act if we are saved from anarchy.

On July 20th, Thomas Corbin wrote to Hamilton deploring the political conditions in Virginia created by Thomas Jefferson, in which these significant passages occur:—

Calumny and misrepresentation are the only weapons made use of by the faction of Virginia. By a dexterous management of these they have brought into popular disrepute, and even into popular odium, some of the wisest and best characters in the United States.

War is waged by this faction against every candidate who possesses the union of requisites. Independent fortune, independent principles, talents, and integrity are denounced as badges of aristocracy; but if you add to these good manners and a decent appearance, his political death is decreed without the benefit of a hearing. In short, with a few exceptions everything that appertains to the character of a gentleman is ostracized. That yourself and Mr. Jay should be no favorites in Virginia, is not to be wondered at. But all those whose good opinion is worth your acceptance entertain for you both the same veneration and esteem, and hear the aspersions of your enemies with the same indignation that I do; who, after the closest examination, and the purest conviction can conscientiously subscribe myself etc.

In the autumn the whiskey disturbances in western Pennsylvania assumed such serious proportions that Hamilton insisted upon recourse to arms. With his usual precision he had calculated the numbers of the insurgents, and the amount of troops necessary to overwhelm them. Washington issued requisitions for fifteen thousand men, and set out with the troops, his first intention being to command in person. Hamilton accompanied him, and upon the President's return to Philadelphia, assumed the general superintendence of the army, whose commander, Henry Lee, was one of his devoted adherents. Many motives have been ascribed to Hamilton for this exceptional proceeding, and Washington was bitterly assailed for "not being able to move without his favourite Secretary at his elbow," and for giving additional conspicuousness to a man whose power already was a "menace to Republican liberties." Randolph, then the nominal Secretary of State, but quite aware that while Hamilton remained in the Cabinet he was but a figurehead, was so wroth, that later, in his futile "Vindication," following what practically was his expulsion from the Cabinet, he animadverted bitterly upon a favour which no one but Hamilton would have presumed to ask. Fauchet, the successor of Genet, in the intercepted letter to his government, which brought about the fall of Randolph, convicting him of corruption and treachery, has this to say:—

The army marched; the President made known that he was going to command it; Hamilton, as I have understood, requested to follow him; the President dared not refuse him. It does not require much, penetration to divine the object of this journey. In the President it was wise, it might also be his duty. But in Mr. Hamilton it was a consequence of the profound policy which directs all his steps; a measure dictated by a perfect knowledge of the human heart. Was it not interesting for him, for his party, tottering under the weight of events without and accusations within, to proclaim an intimacy more perfect than ever with the President, whose very name is a sufficient shield against the most formidable attacks? Now, what more evident mark could the President give of his intimacy than by suffering Mr. Hamilton, whose name, even, is understood in the west as that of a public enemy, to go and place himself at the head of the army which went, if I may use the expression, to cause his system to triumph against the opposition of the people? The presence of Mr. Hamilton with the army must attach it more than ever to his party.

There were depths in Hamilton's mind which no wise mortal will ever attempt to plumb. It is safe to say he did nothing without one eye on a far-reaching policy; and aside from the pleasure of being in the saddle once more, riding over the wild Alleghanies in keen October weather, after four years of the stenches and climatic miseries of Philadelphia, aside from his fear of Governor Miffin's treachery, and his lack of implicit confidence in Lee's judgement, it is quite likely that he had some underlying motive relative to the advantage of his party, which had been weakened by the incessant assaults upon himself. By going with the army he not only demonstrated the perfect confidence reposed in him by Washington, and his determination that his laws should be enforced, but he gave emphasis to his belief that the resistance to the Excise Law had been deliberately instigated by the Republicans under the leadership of his avowed enemies. In this connection the following extract from Fauchet's letter is highly interesting, intimate as he was with the Republican leaders.

Such therefore were the parts of the public grievance, upon which the western people most insisted. Now, these complaints were systematizing by the conversations of influential men, who retired into those wild countries, and who from principle, or from a series of particular heart-burnings, animated discontents already too near to effervescence. At last the local explosion is effected. The western people calculated on being supported by some distinguished characters in the east, and even imagined they had in the bosom of the government some abettors, who might share in their grievance or their principle.

The rioters, sobered by the organized force and its formidable numbers, surrendered without bloodshed.

In January of the following year Hamilton resigned from the Cabinet. The pressing need of his services was over, and he had many reasons for retiring from office: his health was seriously impaired, he had a growing family of boys to educate; he expected his father by every ship from the Windward Islands, to spend his last years in the home to which his son had so often invited him; Mrs. Mitchell was now a widow and almost penniless; and his disgust of office was so uncompromising that no consideration short of an imperative public duty would have induced him to continue. But his principal reason, as he wrote to Mrs. Church, was that he wished to indulge his domestic happiness more freely. Washington let him go with the less reluctance because he promised immediate response to any demand the President might make upon him. He went with his wife, Angelica, and the younger children to Albany and the Saratoga estate, where he remained until the first of June, endeavouring to regain his health in the forest and on the river. Young Lafayette lived with him until his return to France, in 1798.

Upon Hamilton's return to New York he immediately engaged in practice, which he supplemented by coaching students; but he continued to be Washington's chief adviser, and the correspondence was continuous upon every problem which confronted the harassed President. Indeed, when one reads its bulk, one wonders if the Cabinet did anything but execute Hamilton's suggestions. Randolph kicked his heels in impotent wrath, and his successor's correspondence with Hamilton was almost as voluminous as Washington's. So was Wolcott's, who hardly cancelled a bond without his former chief's advice; William Smith, the auditor-general, was scarcely less insistent for orders. Hamilton wrote at length to all of them, as well as to the numerous members of Congress who wanted advice, or an interpretation of some Constitutional provision hitherto on the shelf. What time he had for his practice and students would remain a mystery, were it not for the manifest price he paid in the vigours of all but will and brain.

During the summer of 1794 Talleyrand visited the United States. He brought a package from Mrs. Church to Mrs. Hamilton, and a cordial letter from the same important source to the statesman whom he ranked higher than any man of his time. "He improves upon acquaintance," wrote Mrs. Church to her sister; "I regret that you do not speak French." But her sister's husband spoke French better than any man in America, and after the resignation from the Cabinet, Talleyrand spent most of his time in the little red brick house at 26 Broadway, where Hamilton was working to recover his lost position at the bar. "I have seen the eighth wonder of the world," wrote the Frenchman, one morning, after a ramble in the small hours, which had taken him past the light in Hamilton's study, "I have seen the man who has made the fortune of a nation, toiling all night to supply his family with bread." The men found great delight in each other's society. Hamilton was the most accomplished and versatile man in America, the most brilliant of conversationists, the most genial of companions, and hospitable of hosts. Talleyrand epitomized Europe to him; and the French statesman had met no one in his crowded life who knew it better. If he gave to Hamilton the concentrated essence of all that ardent brain had read and dreamed of, of all that fate had decreed he never should see in the mass, Talleyrand placed on record his tribute to Hamilton's unmortal powers of divination, and loved and regretted him to the close of his life.

Different as the men were in character, they had two points in common,—a passionate patriotism, and the memory of high ideals. Public life had disposed of Talleyrand's ideals, and Hamilton, after an education in the weakness and wickedness of human nature which left nothing to be desired, would have been equally destitute, had it not been for his temperamental gaiety and buoyant philosophy. There were times when these deserted him, and he brooded in rayless depths, but his Celtic inheritance and the vastness of his intellect saved him from despair until the end. Talleyrand was by no means an uncheerful soul; but his genius, remarkable as it was, flowed between narrower lines, and was unwatered by that humanity which was Hamilton's in such volume. Both men had that faculty of seeing things exactly as they are, which the shallow call cynicism; and those lost conversations appeal to the imagination of the searcher after truth.

Jay's treaty was the most formidable question with which Hamilton was called upon to deal before the retirement of Washington to private life, and it gave him little less trouble than if he had remained in the Cabinet.

It had been his idea to send a special envoy to England to remonstrate with the British Government for her abominable oppressions and accumulating outrages, decide if possible upon a treaty with her which would soothe the excitement in the United States,—as wild in the spring of 1794 as the Jacobin fever,—and avert war. It was the desire of Washington and the eminent Federalists that this mission be undertaken by Hamilton, for he had an especial faculty for getting what he wanted: however obstinate he might be, his diplomacy was of the first order when he chose to use it. But he believed that, having suggested the mission, he could not with propriety accept it, and that his services could be given more effectively in the Cabinet. Moreover, the violent opposition which the proposal immediately raised among the Republicans, notably Randolph and Monroe,—the latter so far transcending etiquette as to write to Washington, denouncing his Secretary of the Treasury,—made it probable that his enemies would defeat his confirmation in the Senate. He suggested the name of Chief Justice Jay; and after the usual bitter preliminaries, that exalted but not very forcible personage sailed for England in the latter part of April, 1794. Negotiations were very slow, for Britain still felt for us a deep and sullen resentment, nourished by our Jacobin enthusiasms. In January, however, news came that the treaty was concluded; and Hamilton, supposing that the matter was settled, resigned from the Cabinet. It has been asserted that when he read this famous instrument, he characterized it as "an old woman's treaty," and it is very probable that he did. Nevertheless, when, after a stormy passage through the Senate, it was launched upon the country, and, systematically manipulated by the practised arts of Jacobinism, carried the United States almost to the verge of civil war, Hamilton accepted the treaty as the best obtainable, and infinitely preferable to further troubles. He took up his pen, having previously been stoned while attempting to speak in its defence, and in a series of papers signed "Catullus," wrote as even he had not done since the days of "The Federalist." Their effect was felt at once; and as they continued to issue, and Hamilton's sway over the public mind, his genius for moulding opinion, became with each more manifest, Jefferson, terrified and furious, wrote to Madison:—

Hamilton is really a Colossus to the anti-Republican party. Without numbers he is a host in himself. They have got themselves into a defile where they might be finished; but too much security on the Republican part will give time to his talents and indefatigableness to extricate them. We have had only middling performances to oppose him. In truth when he comes forward there is no one but yourself can meet him.... For God's sake take up your pen and give a fundamental reply to "Curtius" and "Camillus."

But Madison had had enough of pen encounter with Hamilton. "He who puts himself on paper with Hamilton is lost," Burr had said; and Madison agreed with him, and entered the lists no more. The excitement gradually subsided. It left ugly scars behind it, but once more Hamilton had saved his party, and perhaps the Union. In connection with the much disputed authorship of the Farewell Address I will merely quote a statement, heretofore unpublished, made by Mrs. Hamilton, in the year 1840.

Desiring that my children shall be fully acquainted with the services rendered by their father to our country, and the assistance rendered by him to General Washington during his administrations, for the one great object, the independence and stability of the government of the United States, there is one thing in addition to the numerous proofs which I leave them, and which I feel myself in duty bound to state: which is that a short time previous to General Washington's retiring from the Presidency, in the year 1796, General Hamilton suggested to him the idea of delivering a farewell address to the people on his withdrawal from public life, with which idea General Washington was well pleased, and in his answer to General Hamilton's suggestion, gave him the heads of the subject on which he would wish to remark, with a request that Mr. Hamilton would prepare a draft for him. Mr. Hamilton did so, and the address was written principally at such times as his office was seldom frequented by his clients and visitors, and during the absence of his students to avoid interruption; at which times he was in the habit of calling me to sit with him, that he might read to me as he wrote, in order, as he said, to discover how it sounded upon the ear, and making the remark, "My dear Eliza, you must be to me what old Molière's nurse was to him."

The whole or nearly all the "address" was read to me by him, as he wrote it, and the greater part if not all was written in my presence. The original was forwarded to General Washington, who approved of it with the exception of one paragraph; of, I think, from four to five lines, which, if I mistake not, was on the subject of the public schools; which was stricken out. It was afterward returned to Mr. Hamilton who made the desired alteration, and was afterward delivered to General Washington, and published in that form, and has since been known as "General Washington's Farewell Address." Shortly after the publication of the address, my husband and myself were walking in Broadway when an old soldier accosted him with the request of him to purchase General Washington's farewell address, which he did, and turning to me said, "That man does not know he has asked me to purchase my own work."

The whole circumstances are at this moment so perfectly in my mind that I can call to mind his bringing General Washington's letter to me, who returned the address, and remarked on the only alteration which he (General Washington) had requested to be made.

New York, Aug. 7th, 1840.

ELIZABETH HAMILTON. JAMES A. WASHINGTON. JA.R. MACDONALD.

In 1797 Hamilton was forced by treachery and the malignancy of Jacobinism into the most painful and mortifying act of his public career. He had been hailed by certain enthusiastic Federalists as the legitimate successor of Washington. It was a noble ambition, and there is no doubt that Hamilton would have cherished it, had he been less of a philosopher, less in the habit of regarding a desire for the impossible as a waste of time. Not only were older men in the direct line of promotion, but he knew that as the author of the Excise Law he was hated by one section of the Commonwealth, and that as the parent of the manufacturing interest, to say nothing of the Assumption measure, he had incurred the antagonism of the entire South. Lest these causes for disqualification be obscured by the brilliancy of his reputation, Jefferson's unresting and ramifying art had indelibly impressed the public mind with the monarchical-aristocratical tendencies and designs of the former Secretary of the Treasury, and of his hatred for a beloved cause overseas. Hamilton had given an absolute negative to every suggestion to use his name; but one at least had found its way into print, and so terrified the enemy that they determined upon one more powerful blow at his good name. Monroe had a fresh cause for hatred in his humiliating recall from France, which he ascribed to the influence of Hamilton. No doubt the trio were well satisfied for a time with their carefully considered scheme. The pamphlet published in 1797, called "The History of the United States for 1796," and edited by a disreputable man named Callender, was the concentrated essence of Jacobinical fury and vindictiveness against Alexander Hamilton. It surpassed any attack yet made on him, while cleverly pretending to be an arraignment of the entire Federalist party; shrieking so loudly at times against Washington, Adams, and Jay, that the casual reader would overlook the sole purport of the pamphlet. "It is ungenerous to triumph over the ruins of declining fame," magnanimously finished its attack upon Washington. "Upon this account not a word more shall be said!"

It omitted a recital of the two Congressional attacks upon Hamilton's financial integrity, as to refrain from all mention of the vindications would have been impossible; but it raked up everything else for which it had space, sought to prove him a liar by his defence of the Jay treaty in the Camillus papers, and made him insult Washington in language so un-Hamiltonian that to-day it excites pity for the desperation of the Virginians. When it finally arrived at the pith and marrow of the assault, however, it was with quite an innocent air. This was a carefully concocted version of the Reynolds affair. Callender had obtained possession of the papers which Monroe, Muhlenberg, and Venable had prepared to submit to the President, before hearing Hamilton's explanation. He asserted that this explanation was a lie, and that the Secretary of the Treasury had not only speculated with the public funds, but that he had made thirty thousand pounds by the purchase of army certificates. It was also alleged that Hamilton ordered his name withdrawn as a Presidential candidate, in consequence of a threat that otherwise these same papers would be published.

It is a curious instance of the fatuity of contemporaries, that Hamilton's enemies reckoned upon a sullen silence, in the face of damning assault, from the greatest fighter of his time. Indubitably, they argued that he would think it best to pass the matter over; no man could be expected to give to the public the full explanation. But they reckoned with an insufficient knowledge of this host, as they had done many a time before. Hamilton had no desire to hold office again, but he was still the great leader of a great party, as determined as ever that at no cost should there be a stain on his public honour. He consulted with his closest friends, among them his wife. As the sin was now five years old—and the woman a derelict—Mrs. Hamilton found it easier to forgive than an unconfessed liaison with the most remarkable woman of her time. Although she anticipated the mortification of the exposure quite as keenly as her husband, she cherished his good name no less tenderly, and without hesitation counselled him to give the facts to the public. This he did in a pamphlet which expounded the workings of the "Jacobin Scandal Club," told the unpleasant story without reserve, and went relentlessly into the details of the part played in it by Monroe, Muhlenberg, and Venable. He forced affidavits from those bewildered gentlemen, the entire correspondence was published, and the pamphlet itself was a masterpiece of biting sarcasm and convincing statement. It made a tremendous sensation, but even his enemies admired his courage. The question of his financial probity was settled for all time, although the missile, failing in one direction, quivered in the horrified brains of many puritanical voters. Mrs. Reynolds, now living with Clingman, made no denial, and it is doubtful if even she would have echoed the one animadversion of the discomfited enemy,—that Hamilton had given the name of a mistress to the public. It is a weak and dangerous sentimentalism which would protect a woman of commerce against the good name of any man. The financial settlement makes her a party in a contract, nothing more, and acquits the payer of all further responsibility. She has no good name to protect; she has asked for nothing but money; she is a public character, whom to shield would be a thankless task. When this Reynolds woman added the abomination of blackmail to her trade, and further attempted the ruin of the man who had shown her nothing but generosity and consideration, it need hardly be added that Hamilton would have been a sentimental fool to have hesitated on any ground but detestation of a public scandal.

He never traced the betrayal of a secret which all concerned had promised to keep inviolate, but he had his suspicions. Mrs. Croix, now living in a large house on the Bowling Green, was the animated and resourceful centre of Jacobinism. She wore a red cap to the theatre and a tri-coloured cockade on the street. Her *salon* was the headquarters of the Republican leaders, and many a plot was hatched in her inspiring presence. The Virginian Junta were far too clever to put themselves in the power of a drunkard like Callender, but they were constantly in collusion with Mrs. Croix. They knew that she feared nothing under heaven, and that she had devoted herself to Hamilton's ruin. Callender drew upon her for virus whenever his own supply ran down, and would have hailed the Reynolds concoction, even had it gone to him naked and begging. Hamilton saw the shadow of a fair hand throughout the entire pamphlet, and, indeed, could have traced many an envenomed shaft, since 1793, to a source which once had threatened to cloy him with its sweetness.

Meanwhile John Adams had been elected President of the United States, and Thomas Jefferson, Vice-President. Hamilton had made no secret of the fact that he should prefer to see Thomas Pinckney succeed Washington, for he contemplated the possibility of Adams in the Executive Chair, with distrust and uneasiness. In spite of that eminent statesman's intrepidity, integrity, and loyal Federalism, he was, in Hamilton's opinion, too suspicious, jealous of influence, and hot headed, to be a safe leader in approaching storms. With Pinckney as a brilliant and popular figurehead, Hamilton well knew that his own hand would remain on the helm. With the irascible old gentleman from Massachusetts in the Chair, his continued predominance was by no means certain. Washington once said of Hamilton that he undoubtedly was ambitious, but that his ambition was of that laudable kind which prompts a man to excel in whatever he takes in hand; adding that his judgement was intuitively great. The truth was that Hamilton regarded the United States as his child. He had made her wealthy and respected, he foresaw a future importance for her equal to that of any state in Europe. "I anticipate," he wrote to Rufus King, "that this country will, ere long, assume an attitude correspondent with its great destinies— majestic, efficient, and operative of great things. A noble career lies before it." The first of the "Imperialists," he had striven for years to awaken the Government to the importance of obtaining possession of Louisiana and the Floridas, and he also had his eye on South America. Naturally, he wanted no interruption; the moment the security of the country was threatened, he was as alert and anxious as if his nursery were menaced with an Indian invasion. Without conceit or vanity no man ever was more conscious of his great powers; moreover, no American had made such sacrifices as he. Washington and almost all the leading men possessed independent fortunes. Hamilton had manifested his ability from the first to equal the income of the wealthiest, did he give his unbroken services to the pursuit of his profession. But he had lived for years upon a pittance, frequently driven to borrow small sums from his friends, that he might devote his energies entirely to his country. And no man ever gave more generously or with less thought of reward; although he would have been the last to deny his enjoyment of power. For a born leader of men to care little whether he had a few trusted friends or an army at his back, would merely indicate a weak spot in his brain.

It was quite natural, therefore, that he thought upon John Adams's idiosyncrasies with considerable disquiet. Nevertheless, with the high priest of Jacobinism in the field, his first object was to secure the office for the Federalist party. The race was too close for serious consideration of any other ultimate. He counselled every Federalist to cast his vote for Adams and Pinckney; better a tie, with the victory to Adams, than Thomas Jefferson at the head of the Nation. Of course there was a hope that Pinckney might carry the South. But the Adams enthusiasts dreaded this very issue, and threw away their votes for the Vice-Presidency. Pinckney's followers in the South pursued the same policy. The consequence was that Adams won by three votes only. Again his pride was bruised, and again he attributed his mortification to Hamilton. If he had disliked him before, his dislike in a constant state of irritation through the ascendency and fame of the younger man, he hated him now with a bitterness which formed a dangerous link between himself and the Republican leaders. The time came when he was ready to humiliate his country and ruin his own chance of reelection, to dethrone his rival from another proud eminence and check his upward course. Another source of bitterness was Hamilton's continued leadership of the Federalist party, when himself, as President, was entitled to that distinction. But that party was Hamilton's; he had created, developed it, been its Captain through all its triumphant course. Even had he been content to resign his commission,—which he did not contemplate for a moment,—the great majority of the Federalists would have forced it into his hand again. Adams declared war. Hamilton, always ready for a fight, when no immediate act of statesmanship was involved, took up the gauntlet. Adams might resist his influence, but the Cabinet was his, and so were some of the most influential members of Congress, including Theodore Sedgwick of Massachusetts, the president pro tem. of the Senate. It was some time before Adams realized the full extent of this influence; but when he did discover that his Secretary of State, Timothy Pickering, his Secretary of the Treasury, Oliver Wolcott, and his Secretary of War, James M'Henry, were in the habit of consulting Hamilton upon every possible question before giving the President their valuable opinions, and that upon one occasion, at least, a letter of Hamilton's had been incorporated by the Secretary of War into a Presidential Message, he was like to die of apoplexy. He wrote, in his wrath:—

Hamilton is commander-in-chief of the Senate, of the House of Representatives, of the heads of departments, of General Washington, and last, and least, if you will, of the President of the United States!

But the President's advisers were free to seek advice without the Cabinet if they chose, and Washington had encouraged them to go to Hamilton. Hamilton was at liberty to give it, and Adams could find no evidence that he had counselled rebellion against himself; nor that he had used his great influence for any purpose but the honour of the country.

And never had the country needed his services more. When Adams, grim and obstinate, stepped forward as head of the Nation, he found himself confronted with the menace of France. In retaliation for Genet's disgrace, the Revolutionists had demanded the recall of Gouverneur Morris, whose barely disguised contempt, and protection of more than one royalist, had brought him perilously near to the guillotine. Burr had desired the vacant mission, and his pretensions were urged by Monroe and Madison. Washington recognized this as a device of the Opposition to embarrass him, and he had the lowest opinion of Burr's rectitude and integrity. Pressure and wrath produced no effect, but he offered to appoint Monroe. It might be wise to send a Jacobin, and the President hoped that ambition would preserve this one from compromising the country. He made the mistake of not weighing Monroe's mental capacity more studiously. The least said of the wild gallop into diplomacy of our fifth President the better. He was recalled, and Charles Cotesworth Pinckney sent in his place. The French, who had found Monroe entirely to their taste, refused to receive the distinguished lawyer and soldier. To escape indignity he was forced to retire to Holland. The new Republic violated her treaties with increasing insolence, and Bonaparte was thundering on his triumphant course. France was mocking the world, and in no humour to listen to the indignant protests of a young and distant nation. To dismember her by fanning the spirit of Jacobinism, and, at the ripe moment,—when internal warfare had sufficiently weakened her,—reduce her to a French colony, was a plot of which Hamilton, Rufus King, then minister to England, and other astute statesmen more than suspected her. But although Hamilton abhorred France and was outraged at her attitude, the spirit of moderation which had regulated all his acts in public life suffered no fluctuation, and he immediately counselled the sending of a commission to make a final attempt before recourse to arms. War, if inevitable, but peace with honour if possible; it was not fair to disturb the prosperity of the young country except as a last resort. For once he and Adams were agreed. Hamilton suggested Jefferson or Madison as a sop to the Revolutionists, with two Federalists to keep him in order. But the President would have his own commissioners or none. He despatched Marshall and Gerry and ordered C.C. Pinckney to join them. Talleyrand refused them official reception, and sent to them, in secret, nameless minions—known officially, later on, as X.Y.Z.—who made shameful proposals, largely consisting of inordinate demand for tribute. Marshall and Pinckney threw up the commission in disgust. The Opposition in Congress demanded the correspondence; and Adams, with his grimmest smile, sent it to the Senate. It was a terrible blow to the Jacobins, not only the manner in which France had prejudiced her interests in this country; some of the disclosures were extremely painful to ponder upon. "Perhaps," one of the backstairs ambassadors had remarked, "you believe that, in returning and exposing to your countrymen the unreasonableness of the demands of this Government, you will unite them in resistance to those demands. You are mistaken. You ought to know that the diplomatic skill of France, and the means she possesses in your country, are sufficient to enable her, with *the French party in America*, to throw the blame, which will attend the rupture, on the Federalists, as you term yourselves, but the British party, as France terms you; and you may assure yourselves this will be done."

Jefferson retired to weep alone. Several of the faction resigned from Congress. Hamilton published his pamphlets, "The Stand," "France," and "The Answer," and the whole country burst into a roar of vengeance, echoing Pinckney's parting shot: "Millions for defence, not a cent for tribute!" "Hail Columbia" was composed, and inflamed the popular excitement. Federalist clubs paraded, wearing a black cockade, and one street riot followed another. Brockholst Livingston had his nose pulled, and killed his man. With the exception of the extreme Jacobins, who never swerved from their devotion to France and the principles she had promulgated with the guillotine, the country was for war to a man, and the President inundated with letters and memorials of encouragement. The immediate result was the augmentation of the Federalist party, and the decline of Jacobinism.

For a long while past, Hamilton had been urging naval and military preparations. A bold front, he thought, would be more effective than diplomacy; and the sequel proved his wisdom. When the crisis came a bill for a Provisional Army was passed at once, another for the increase of the Navy, and liberal appropriations were made. The proposed alliance with Great Britain, Hamilton effectually opposed, for he was almost as exasperated with England as with France; in her fear that the French party in the United States would triumph and declare war upon her, she had renewed her depredations upon our commerce.

Few believed that Washington would serve again, and the Nation turned naturally to Hamilton as its General-in-chief. He had manifestly been born to extricate them from difficulties. Even the Presidential faction put their pride in their pockets, and agreed that he was the one man in the country of matchless resource and military genius; they passed over the veterans of the war without controversy. But there was one man who never put his pride in his pocket, and that was John Adams. Rather than present to Alexander Hamilton another opportunity for distinction and power, he would himself cull fresh laurels for George Washington; the supply of his old rival was now so abundant that new ones would add nothing. Hamilton already had written to Washington as peremptorily as only he dared, urging that he must come forth once more and without hesitation. Washington replied that he would as cheerfully go to the tombs of his ancestors, but admitted the obligation, and asked Hamilton would he serve with him? Hamilton answered that he would on condition that he be second in command to himself; he would make no further sacrifice for an inconsiderable reward. When Washington, therefore, received Adams's invitation, he made his acceptance conditional upon being given the power to appoint his generals next in rank. Adams, meanwhile, without waiting for his answer, had sent his name to the Senate, and it had been confirmed as a matter of course. Washington was irritated, but persisted in his condition, and sent in the names of Alexander Hamilton for Inspector-General, with the rank of Major-General, C.C. Pinckney and Knox for Major-Generals, and a list of Brigadiers and Adjutant-Generals. Adams, fuming, sent the names to the Senate, and they were confirmed in the order in which Washington had written them; but when they came back, jealousy and temper mastered him, and he committed the intemperate act which tolled the death-knell of the Federalist party: he ordered the commissions made out with Hamilton's name third on the list. Knox and Pinckney, he declared, were entitled to precedence; and so the order should stand or not at all. He had not anticipated an outcry, and when it arose, angry and determined, he was startled but unshaken. The leading men in Congress waited upon him; he received a new deluge of letters, and the most pointed of them was from John Jay. Hamilton alone held his peace. He saw the terrible mistake Adams had made, and dreaded the result. He wrote to Washington that he should be governed entirely by his wishes, that he should not embarrass him in any manner, and that it never should be said of himself that his ambition or interest had stood in the way of the public welfare. But when Adams stood with his head down, like an angry bull, and it was plain to be seen that his astonishing attitude was prompted by personal hatred alone, when the Cabinet and all the eminent men in the Nation, with the exception of the Republican leaders, faced him with an equally determined front, there was nothing for Hamilton to do but to stand his ground; and he stood it. Washington put an end to the unfortunate controversy. He gave Adams his choice between submission or the selection of another General-in-chief. Adams submitted, but Hamilton had in him an enemy no less malignant than Thomas Jefferson himself. Adams had roused the deep implacability of Hamilton's nature. All hope of even an armed truce for party advantage between the two great Federalists was over. Hamilton had one cause for resentment which alone would have made him ardently desire retaliation: General Knox, who had loved him devotedly for twenty years, was bitterly alienated, and the breach was never healed.

Hamilton made his headquarters in New York, where he could, after a fashion, attend to his law practice,—he was now the leading counsel at the bar,—but he entered upon his new duties with all his old spirit and passionate energy. Although France might be discomfited by the readiness and resource of the United States, the imposing front erected by a universal indignation, there were reasons which made the reverse possible; and Hamilton thrilled with all the military ardours of his youth at the prospect of realizing those half-forgotten ambitions. He had, in those days, sacrificed his burning desire for action and glory to a sense of duty which had ruled him through life like a tyrannical deity. Was he to reap the reward at this late hour? finish his life, perhaps, as he had planned to begin it? Once more he felt a boundless gratitude for the best friend a mortal ever made. Washington passed Hamilton over the heads of those superior in military rank, because he knew that he alone was equal to the great task for which himself was too old and infirm; but Hamilton never doubted that he did it with a deep sense of satisfied justice and of gratitude.

Never had Hamilton's conspicuous talent for detail, unlimited capacity for work, genius for creating something out of nothing, marshalled for more active service than now. He withheld his personal supervision from nothing; planning forts, preparing codes of tactics, organizing a commissariat department, drafting bills for Congress, advising M'Henry upon every point which puzzled that unfinished statesman, were but a few of the exercises demanded of the organizer of an army from raw material. The legislation upon one of his bills finally matured a pet project of many years, the Military Academy at West Point. Philip Church, the oldest son of Angelica Schuyler, was his aide; John Church, after a brilliant career as a member of Parliament, having returned to American citizenship, his wife to as powerful a position as she had held in London.

It is hardly necessary to inform any one who has followed the fortunes of Hamilton as far as this that he purposed to command an army of aggression as well as defence. A war with France unrolled infinite possibilities. Louisiana and the Floridas should be seized as soon

396

as war was declared, and he lent a kindly ear to Miranda, who was for overthrowing the inhuman rule of Spain in South America. "To arrest the progress of the revolutionary doctrines France was then propagating in those regions, and to unite the American hemisphere in one great society of common interests and common principles against the corruption, the vices, the new theories of Europe," was an alluring prospect to a man who had given the broadest possible interpretation to the Constitution, and whose every conception had borne the stamp of an imperialistic boldness and amplitude.

But these last of his dreams ended in national humiliation. This time he had sacrificed his private interests, his vital forces, for worse than nothing. One enemy worked his own ruin, and Louisiana was to add to the laurels of Jefferson.

Talleyrand, astonished and irritated by these warlike preparations and the enthusiasm of the infant country, wisely determined to withdraw with grace while there was yet time. He sent a circuitous hint to President Adams that an envoy from the United States would be received with proper respect. For months Adams had been tormented with the vision of Hamilton borne on the shoulders of a triumphant army straight to the Presidential chair. His Cabinet were bitterly and uncompromisingly for war; Hamilton had with difficulty restrained them in the past. Adams, without giving them an inkling of his intention, sent to the Senate the name of William Vans Murray, minister resident at The Hague, to confirm as envoy extraordinary to France.

For a moment the country was stupefied, so firm and uncompromising had been the President's attitude hitherto. Then it arose in wrath, and his popularity was gone for ever. As for the Federalist party, it divided into two hostile factions, and neither had ever faced the Republicans more bitterly. A third of the party supported the President; the rest were for defeating him in the Senate, and humiliating him in every possible way, as he had humiliated the country by kissing the contemptuous hand of France the moment it was half extended.

Hamilton was furious. He had been in mighty tempers in his life, but this undignified and mortifying act of the President strained his statesmanship to the utmost. It stood the strain, however; he warned the Federalist leaders that the step taken was beyond recall and known to all the world. There was nothing to do but to support the President. He still had an opportunity for revenge while openly protecting the honour of the Nation. Did Murray, a man of insufficient calibre and prestige, go alone, he must fail; Adams would be disgraced; war inevitable, with glory, and greater glory, for himself. But when circumstances commanded his statesmanship, he ceased to be an individual; personal resentments slumbered. He insisted that Murray be but one of a commission, and Adams, now cooled and as disquieted as that indomitable spirit could be, saw the wisdom of the advice; Oliver Ellsworth and General Davie, conspicuous and influential men, were despatched. Once more Hamilton had saved his party from immediate wreck; but the strength which it had gathered during the war fever was dissipated by the hostile camps into which it was divided, and by the matchless opportunity which, in its brief period of numerical strength, it had given to Thomas Jefferson.

The Federalist party had ruled the country by virtue of the preponderance of intellect and educated talents in its ranks, and the masterly leadership of Alexander Hamilton. The Republican party numbered few men of first-rate talents, but the upper grade of the Federalist was set thick with distinguished patriots, all of them leaders, but all deferring without question to the genius of their Captain. For years the harmonious workings of their system, allied to the aggregate ability of their personnel, and the watchful eye and resourceful mind of Hamilton, the silent but sympathetic figure of Washington in the background, had enabled them to win every hard-fought battle in spite of the often superior numbers of the Opposition. That Jefferson was able in the face of this victorious and discouraging army to form a great party out of the rag-tag and bobtail element, animating his policy of decentralization into a virile and indelible Americanism, proved him to be a man of genius. History shows us few men so contemptible in character, so low in tone; and no man has given his biographers so difficult a task. But those who despise him most who oppose the most determined front to the ultimates of his work, must acknowledge that formational quality in his often dubious intellect which ranks him a man of genius.

His party was threatened with disorganization when the shameful conduct of the France he adored united the country in a demand for vengeance, and in admiration for the uncompromising attitude of the

Government. Not until the Federalists, carried away by the rapid recruiting to their ranks, passed the Alien and Sedition laws, did Jefferson find ammunition for his next campaign. As one reads those Resolutions to-day, one wonders at the indiscretion of men who had kept the blood out of their heads during so many precarious years. Three-quarters of a century later the Chinese Exclusion Act became a law with insignificant protest; the mistake of the Federalists lay in ignoring the fears and raging jealousies of their time. If Hamilton realized at once that Jefferson would be quick to seize upon their apparent unconstitutionality and convert it into political capital, he seems to have stood alone, although his protests resulted in the modification of both bills.

Let us not establish a tyranny! [he wrote to Wolcott]. Energy is a very different thing from violence. If we make no false step we shall be essentially united; but if we push things to an extreme, we shall then give to faction body and solidity.

In their modified form they were sufficiently menacing to democratic ideals, and Jefferson could have asked for nothing better. He immediately drafted his famous Kentucky Resolutions, and the obedient Madison did a like service for Virginia. The Resolutions of Madison, although containing all the seeds of nullification and secession, are tame indeed compared with the performance of a man who, enveloped in the friendly mists of anonymity, was as aggressive and valiant as Hamilton on the warpath. These Resolutions protested against the unconstitutionality of the Federal Government in exiling foreigners, and curbing the liberty of the press, in arrogating to itself the rights of the States, and assuming the prerogatives of an absolute monarchy. If Jefferson did not advise nullification, he informed the States of their inalienable rights, and counselled them to resist the centralizing tendency of the Federal Government before it was too late. Even in the somewhat modified form in which these Resolutions passed the Kentucky legislature, and although rejected by the States to which they were despatched, they created a sensation and accomplished their primary object. The war excitement had threatened to shove the Alien and Sedition laws beyond the range of the public observation. The Kentucky and Virginia Resolutions roused the country, and sent the Republicans scampering back to their watchful shepherd. It is one of the master-strokes of political history, and Jefferson culled the fruits and suffered none of the odium. That these historic Resolutions contained the fecundating germs of the Civil War, is by the way.

Such was the situation on the eve of 1800, the eve of a Presidential election, and of the death struggle of the two great parties.

It was in December of this year of 1799 that Hamilton bent under the most crushing blow that life had dealt him. He was standing on the street talking to Sedgwick, when a mounted courier dashed by, crying that Washington was dead. The street was crowded, but Hamilton broke down and wept bitterly. "America has lost her saviour," he said; "I, a father."

BOOK V

THE LAST BATTLE OF THE GIANTS AND THE END

—∽—

I

The sunlight moved along the table and danced on Hamilton's papers, flecking them and slanting into his eyes. He went to the window to draw the shade, and stood laughing, forgetting the grave anxieties which animated his pen this morning. In the garden without, his son Alexander and young Philip Schuyler, his wife's orphan nephew, who lived with him, were pounding each other vigorously, while Philip, Angelica, Theodosia Burr, and Gouverneur Morris sat on the fence and applauded.

"What a blessed provision for letting off steam," he thought, with some envy. "I would I had Burr in front of my fists this moment. I suppose he is nothing but the dupe of Jefferson, but he is a terrible menace, all the same."

The girls saw him, and leaping from the fence ran to the house, followed more leisurely by Morris.

"You are loitering," exclaimed Angelica, triumphantly, as she entered the room without ceremony, followed by Theodosia. "And when you loiter you belong to me."

She had grown tall, and was extremely thin and nervous, moving incessantly. But her face, whether stormy, dreamy, or animated with the pleasure of the moment, was very beautiful. Theodosia Burr was a handsome intellectual girl, with a massive repose; and the two were much in harmony.

"If I snatch a moment to breathe," Hamilton was beginning, when he suddenly caught two right hands and spread them open.

"What on earth does this mean?" he demanded. The little paws of the two most fastidious girls he knew were dyed with ink. Both blushed vividly, but Angelica flung back her head with her father's own action.

"We are writing a novel," she said.

"You are doing what?" gasped Hamilton.

"Yes, sir. All the girls in New York are. Why shouldn't we? I guess we inherit brains enough."

"All the girls in New York are writing novels!" exclaimed Hamilton. "Is this the next result of Jacobinism and unbridled liberty, the next development of the new Americanism as expounded by Thomas Jefferson? Good God! What next?"

"You have the prophetic eye," said Morris, who was seated on the edge of the table, grinning sardonically. (He was bald now, and looked more wicked than ever.) "What of woman in the future?"

"She has given me sufficient occupation in the present," replied Hamilton, drily. "Heaven preserve me from the terrors of anticipation." "Well, finish your novel. If you confine your pens to those subjects of which you know nothing, you will enjoy yourselves; and happiness should be sought in all legitimate channels. But as a favour to me, keep your hands clean."

The girls retired with some hauteur, and Morris said impatiently:—

"I thought I had left that sort of thing behind me in France, where Madame de Staël drove me mad. I return to find all the prettiest women running to lectures on subjects which they never can understand, and scarifying the men's nerves with pedantic allusions. I always believed that our women were the brightest on the planet, but that they should ever have the bad taste to become intellectual—well, I have known but one woman who could do it successfully, and that is Mrs. Croix. What has she to do with this sudden activity of Burr's? Is he handling French money?"

"Are you convinced that she is a French spy?"

"I believe it so firmly that her sudden departure would reconcile me to the Alien law. Where has Burr found the money for this campaign? He is bankrupt; he hasn't a friend among the leaders; I don't believe the Manhattan Bank, for all that he is the father of it, will let him handle a cent, and Jefferson distrusts and despises him. Still, it is just possible that Jefferson is using him, knowing that the result of the Presidential election will turn on New York, and that after himself Burr is the best politician in the country. I doubt if he would trust him with a cent of his own money, but he may have an understanding with the Aspasia of Bowling Green. Certainly she must have the full confidence of France by this time, and she is the cleverest Jacobin in the country."

"I wish that dark system could be extirpated, root and branch," said Hamilton. "I have been too occupied these past two years to watch her, or Burr either, for that matter. Organizing an army, and working for your bread in spare moments, gives your enemies a clear field for operations. I have had enough to do, watching Adams. Burr has stolen a march that certainly does credit to his cunning. That is the most marvellous faculty I know. He is barely on speaking terms with a leader—Jefferson, Clinton, the Livingstons, all turned their backs upon him long since, as a man neither to be trusted nor used. The fraud by which he obtained the charter of the Manhattan Bank has alienated so many of his followers that his entire ticket was beaten at the last elections. Now he will have himself returned for the Assembly from Orange, he is manipulating the lower orders of New York as if they were so much wax, using their secrets, wiping the babies' noses, and hanging upon the words of every carpenter who wants to talk: and has actually got Clinton—who has treated him like a dog for years—to let him use his name as a possible candidate for the Legislature. Doubtless he may thank Mrs. Croix for that conquest. But his whole work is marvellous, and I suppose it would be well if we had a man on our side who would stoop to the same dirty work. I should as soon invite a strumpet to my house. But I am fearful for the result. With this Legislature we should be safe. But Burr has converted hundreds, if not thousands, to a party for which he cares as much as he does for the Federal. If he succeeds, and the next Legislature is Republican, Jefferson will be the third President of the Unites States, and then, God knows what. Not immediate disunion, possibly, for Jefferson is cunning enough to mislead France for his own purposes; nor can he fail to see that Jacobinism is on the wane—but a vast harvest of democracy, of disintegration, and denationalization, which will work the same disaster in the end. If Burr could be taught that he is being made a tool of, he might desist, for he would work for no party without hope of reward. He may ruin us and gain nothing."

"It is a great pity we have not a few less statesmen in our party and a few more politicians. When we began life, only great services were needed; and the Opposition, being engaged in the same battle of ideas, fought us with a merely inferior variety of our own weapons. But the greatest of our work is over, and the day of the politician has dawned. Unfortunately, the party of this damned lag-bellied Virginian has the monopoly. Burr is the natural result and the proudest sample of the French Revolution and its spawn. But your personal influence is tremendous. Who can say how many infuscated minds you will illumine when it comes to speech-making. Don't set your brow in gloom."

"I have not the slightest intention of despairing. The deep and never ceasing methods of the Jacobin Scandal Club have weakened my influence with the masses, however; no doubt of that. Its policy is to iterate and reiterate, pay no attention to denials, but drop the same poison daily until denial is forgotten and men's minds are so accustomed to the detraction, belittling, or accusation, that they accept it as they accept the facts of existence. Jefferson has pursued this policy with my reputation for ten years. During the last eight he has been ably abetted by Mrs. Croix, his other personal agents, and those of France. Now they have enlisted Burr, and there is no better man for their work in the country."

"They know that if you go, the party follows. That is their policy, and may they spend the long evening of time in Hell. But I believe you will be more than a match for them yet; although this is by far the most serious move the enemy has made." "I wish to Heaven I had persisted in the Great Convention until I carried my point in regard to having the electors chosen by the people in districts. Then I should snap my fingers at Burr in this campaign, for he is an indifferent speaker, and political manipulation would count for very little. With C.C. Pinckney in the chair for eight years, I should feel that the country was planted on reasonably sure foundations. It must be Adams and Pinckney, of course, but with proper harmony Pinckney will carry the day. Rather Jefferson in the chair than Adams—an open army that we can fight with a united front, than a Federal dividing the ranks, and forcing us to uphold him for the honour of the party—to say nothing of being responsible for him."

"Jefferson is the less of several evils—Burr, for instance."

"Oh, Burr!" exclaimed Hamilton. "I should be in my dotage if Burr became President of the United States. Personally, I have nothing against him, and he is one of the most agreeable and accomplished of men. Theodosia half lives here. Perhaps no man ever hated another as I hate Jefferson, nor had such cause. He has embittered my life and ruined my health; he has made me feel like a lost soul more than once. But better Jefferson a thousand times than Burr. God knows I hate democracy and fear it, but Jefferson is timid and cautious, and has some principles and patriotism; moreover, a desire for fame. Burr has neither patriotism nor a principle, nor the least regard for his good name. He is bankrupt, profligate—he has been living in the greatest extravagance at Richmond Hill, and his makings at the bar, although large, are far exceeded by his expenses; there is always a story afloat about some dark transaction of his, and never disproved: he challenged Church for talking openly about the story that the Holland Land Company had, for legislative services rendered, cancelled a bond against him for twenty thousand dollars; but the world doubts Burr's bluster as it doubts his word. At present he is in a desperate way because Alexander Baring, in behalf of a friend, I.I. Augustine, is pressing for payment on a bond given to secure the price of land bought by Burr and Greenleaf, and he has been offering worthless land claims in settlement, and resorting to every artifice to avert a crisis. Baring wanted me to take the case, but of course I wouldn't touch it. I sent him to Rinnan. The man is literally at the end of his tether. It is a coup or extinction—failure means flight or debtor's prison. Furthermore, he is a conspirator by nature, and there is no man in the country with such extravagant tastes, who is so unscrupulous as to the means of gratifying them. He is half mad for power and wealth. The reins of state in his hands, and he would stop at nothing which might give him control of the United States Treasury. To be President of the United States would mean nothing to him except as a highway to empire, to unlimited power and plunder. We have been threatened with many disasters since we began our career, but with no such menace as Burr. But unless I die between now and eighteen hundred and one, Burr will lose the great game, although he may give victory to the Republican party."

"I am not surprised at your estimate and revelations," said Morris, "for I have heard much the same from others since my return. It was this certainty that he is bankrupt that led me to believe he was handling French money in this election—and he is flinging it right and left in a manner that must gratify his aspiring soul. Considering his lack of fortune and family influence, he has done wonders in the way of elevating himself. This makes it the more remarkable that with his great cleverness he should not have done better—"

"He is not clever; that is the point. He is cunning. His is wholly the brain of the conspirator. Were he clever, he would, like Thomas Jefferson, fool himself and the world into the belief that he is honest. Intellect and statesmanship he holds in contempt. He would elevate himself by the Catiline system, by the simple method of proclaiming himself emperor, and appropriating the moneybags of the country. There is not one act of statesmanship to his credit. To him alone, of all prominent Americans, the country is indebted for nothing. The other night at a dinner, by the way, he toasted first the French Revolution, then Bonaparte. It is more than possible that you are right, for France, whether Directory or Consulate, is not likely to change her policy regarding this country. Nothing would please either Talleyrand or Bonaparte better than to inflame us into a civil war, then swoop down upon us, under the pretence of coming to the rescue. Burr would be just the man to play into their hands, although with no such intention. Jefferson is quite clever enough to foil them, if he found that more to his interest. Well, neither is elected yet. Let us hope for the best. Go and ask Angelica to play for you. I have letters to write to leaders all over the State."

II

Burr was the author of municipal corruption in New York, the noble grandsire of Tammany Hall. While Hamilton was too absorbed to watch him, he had divided New York, now a city of sixty thousand inhabitants, into districts and sections. Under his systematic management the name of every resident was enrolled, and his politics ascertained. Then Burr and his committees or sub-committees laid siege to the individual. Insignificant men were given place, and young fire-eaters, furious with Adams, were swept in. Hundreds of doubtful men were dined and wined at Richmond Hill, flattered, fascinated, conquered. Burr knew the private history, the income, of every man he purposed to convert, and made dexterous use of his information. He terrified some with his knowledge, fawned upon others, exempted the stingy from contributions provided he would work, and the lazy from work provided he would pay. It is even asserted that he blackmailed the women who had trusted him on paper, and forced them to wring votes from their men. He drafted a catalogue of names for the electoral

Legislature, calculated to impose the hesitant, who were not permitted to observe that he smarted and snarled under many a kick. Strong names were essential if the Republicans were to wrest New York from the Federals after twelve years of unbroken rule, but strong men had long since ceased to have aught to do with Burr; although Jefferson, as Hamilton suspected, had recently extended his politic paw. But in spite of snubs, curt dismissals, and reiterated intimations that his exertions were wasting, Burr did at last, by dint of flattery, working upon the weak points of the men he thoroughly understood, convincing them that victory lay in his hands and no other,—some of them that he was working in harmony with Jefferson,—induce Clinton, Brockholst Livingston, General Gates,—each representing a different faction,—and nine other men of little less importance, to compose the city ticket. All manner of Republicans were pleased, and many discontented Federalists. Burr, knowing that his own election in New York was hopeless, was a candidate for the Assembly in the obscure county of Orange; and the Legislature which would elect the next President was threatened with a Republican majority, which alarmed the Federalist party from one end of the Union to the other.

Hamilton had never been more alert. The moment he was awake to the danger his mind closed to every other demand upon it, and he flung himself into the thick of the fight. He would have none of Burr's methods, but he spoke daily, upon every least occasion, and was ready to consult at all hours with the distracted leaders of his party. Morris, Troup, Fish, and other Federalists, accustomed to handling the masses, also spoke repeatedly. But Adams had given the party a terrible blow, scattering many of its voters far and wide. They felt that the country had been humiliated, that it was unsafe in the hands of a man who was too obstinate to be advised, and too jealous to control his personal hatreds for the good of the Union; the portent of tyranny in the Alien and Sedition laws had terrified many, and the promises of the Republicans were very alluring. The prospect of a greater equality, of a universal plebeianism, turned the heads of the shopkeepers, mechanics, and labouring men, who had voted hitherto with the Federalist party through admiration of its leaders and their great achievements. In vain Hamilton reminded them of all they owed to the Federalists: the Constitution, the prosperity, the *peace*. He was in the ironical position of defending John Adams. They had made up their minds before they went to hear him speak, and they went because to hear him was a pleasure they never missed. Upon one occasion a man rushed from the room, crying, "Let me out! Let me out! That man will make me believe anything." Frequently Hamilton and Burr spoke on the same platform, and they were so polite to each other that the audience opened their mouths and wondered at the curious ways of the aristocracy. It was a period of great excitement. Men knocked each other down daily, noses were pulled,—a favourite insult of our ancestors,—and more than one duel was fought in the woods of Weehawken.

The elections began early on the 29th of April and finished at sunset on May 2d. Hamilton and Burr constantly addressed large assemblages. On the first day Hamilton rode up to the poll in his district to vote, and was immediately surrounded by a vociferating crowd. Scurrilous handbills were thrust in his face, and his terrified horse reared before a hundred threatening fists. A big carter forced his way to its side and begged Hamilton to leave, assuring him there was danger of personal violence, and that the men were particularly incensed at his aristocratic manner of approaching the polls.

"Thank you," said Hamilton, "but I have as good a right to vote as any man, and I shall do it in the mode most agreeable to myself."

"Very well, General," said the carter. "I differ with you in politics, but I'll stick by you as long as there is a drop of blood in my body."

Hamilton turned to him with that illumination of feature which was not the least of his gifts, then to the mob with the same smile, and lifted his hat above a profound bow. "I never turned my back upon my enemy," he said, "I certainly shall not flee from those who have always been my friends."

The crowd burst into an electrified roar. "Three cheers for General Hamilton!" cried the carter, promptly, and they responded as one man. Then they lifted him from his horse and bore him on their shoulders to the poll. He deposited his ballot, and after addressing them to the sound of incessant cheering, was permitted to ride away. The incident both amused and disgusted him, but he needed no further illustrations of the instability of the common mind.

The Republicans won. On the night of the 2d it was known that the Federalists had lost the city by a Republican majority of four hundred and ninety votes.

A few weeks before, when uncertainties were thickest, Hamilton had written to William Smith, who was departing for Constantinople: "... You see I am in a humour to laugh. What can we do better in *this best of all possible worlds*? Should you ever be shut up in the seven towers, or get the plague, if you are a true philosopher you will consider this only as a laughing matter."

He laughed—though not with the gaiety of his youth—as he walked home to-night through the drunken yelling crowds of William Street, more than one fist thrust in his face. His son Philip was with him, and his cousin, Robert Hamilton of Grange, who had come over two years before to enlist under the command of the American relative of whom his family were vastly proud. A berth had been found for him in the navy, as better suited to his talents, and he spent his leisure at 26 Broadway. Both the younger men looked crestfallen and anxious. Philip, who resembled his father so closely that Morris called him "his heir indubitate," looked, at the moment, the older of the two. Ill health had routed the robust appearance of Hamilton's early maturity, and his slender form, which had lost none of its activity or command, his thin face, mobile, piercing, fiery, as ever, made him appear many years younger than his age.

"Why do you laugh, sir?" asked Philip, as they turned into Wall Street,

"I feel as if the end of the world had come."

"That is the time to laugh, my dear boy. When you see the world you have educated scampering off through space, the retreat led by the greatest rascal in the country, your humour, if you have any, is bound to respond. Moreover, there is always something humorous in one's downfall, and a certain relief. The worst is over."

"But, Cousin Alexander," said Robert Hamilton, "surely this is not ultimate defeat for you? You will not give up the fight after the first engagement—you!"

"Oh, no! not I!" cried Hamilton. "I shall fight on until I have made Thomas Jefferson President of the United States. Should I not laugh? Was any man ever in so ironical a situation before? I shall move heaven and America to put Pinckney in the chair, and I shall fail; and to save the United States from Burr I shall turn over the country I have made to my

409

bitterest enemy."

"That would not be my way of doing, sir," said Robert. "I'd fight the rival chieftain to his death. Perhaps this Burr is not so real a Catiline as you think him. Nobody has a good word for him, but I mean he may not have the courage for so dangerous an act as usurpation."

"Courage is just the one estimable if misdirected quality possessed by Burr, and, whetted by his desperate plight, no length would daunt him. A year or two ago he hinted to me that I had thrown away my opportunities. Pressed, he admitted that I was a fool not to have changed the government when I could. When I reminded him that I could only have done such a thing by turning traitor, he replied, 'Les grands âmes se soucient peu des petits moraux.' It was not worth while to reason with a man who had neither little morals nor great ones, so I merely replied that from the genius and situation of the country the thing was impracticable; and he answered, 'That depends on the estimate we form of the human passions, and of the means of influencing them.' Burr would neither regard a scheme of usurpation as visionary,—he is sanguine and visionary to a degree that will be his ruin,—nor be restrained by any reluctance to occupy an infamous place in history."

They had reached his doorstep in the Broadway. The house was lighted. Through the open windows of the drawing-room poured a musical torrent. Angelica, although but sixteen, shook life and soul from the cold keys of the piano, and was already ambitious to win fame as a composer. To-night she was playing extemporaneously, and Hamilton caught his breath. In the music was the thunder of the hurricane he so often had described to his children, the piercing rattle of the giant castinets [sic], the roar and crash of artillery, the screaming of the trees, the furious rush of the rain. Robert Hamilton thought it was a battlepiece, but involuntarily he lifted his hat. As the wonderful music finished with the distant roar of the storm's last revolutions, Hamilton turned to his cousin with the cynicism gone from his face and his eyes sparkling with pride and happiness.

"What do I care for Burr?" he exclaimed. "Or for Jefferson? Has any man ever had a home, a family, like mine? Let them do their worst. Beyond that door they cannot go."

"Burr can put a bullet into you, sir," said Robert Hamilton, soberly. "And he is just the man to do it. Jefferson is too great a coward. For

God's sake be warned in time."

Hamilton laughed and ran up the stoop. His wife was in the drawing-room with Angelica, who was white and excited after the fever of composition. Mrs. Hamilton, too, was pale, for she had heard the news. But mettle had been bred in her, and her spirits never dropped before public misfortune. She had altered little in the last seven years. In spite of her seven children her figure was as slim as in her girlhood, her hair was as black, her skin retained its old union of amber and claret. The lingering girlishness in her face had departed after a memorable occasion, but her prettiness had gained in intellect and character; piquant and roguish, at times, as it still was. It was seven years since she had applied her clever brain to politics and public affairs generally—finance excepting—and with such unwearied persistence that Hamilton had never had another excuse to seek companionship elsewhere. Moreover, she had returned to her former care of his papers, she encouraged him to read to her whatever he wrote, and was necessary to him in all ways. She loved him to the point of idolatry, but she kept her eye on him, nevertheless, and he wandered no more. When he could not accompany her to Saratoga in summer, she sent the children with one of her sisters, and remained with him, no matter what the temperature, or the age of a baby. But she made herself so charming that if he suspected the surveillance he was indifferent, and grateful for her companionship and the intelligent quality of her sympathy. Elizabeth Hamilton never was a brilliant woman, but she became a remarkably strong-minded and sensible one. Femininely she was always adorable. Although relieved of the heavier social duties since the resignation from the Cabinet, Hamilton's fame and the popularity of both forced them into a prominent position in New York society. They entertained constantly at dinner, and during the past seven years many distinguished men besides Talleyrand had sat at their hospitable board: Louis Philippe d'Orleans,—supported for several years by Gouverneur Morris,—the Duc de Montpensier, the Duke of Kent, John Singleton Copley, subsequently, so eminent as jurist and statesman, Kosciusko, Count Niemcewicz, the novelist, poet, dramatist, and historian, were but a few. All travellers of distinction brought letters to Hamilton, for, not excepting Washington, he was to Europeans the most prosilient of Americans. If there had been little decrease of hard work during these years, there had been social and domestic pleasures, and Hamilton could live in the one or the other with equal thoroughness. He was very proud of his wife's youthful appearance, and to-night he reproached her for losing so many hours of rest.

"Could anyone sleep in this racket?" she demanded, lightly. "You must be worn out. Come into the dining room and have supper."

And they all enjoyed their excellent meal of hot oysters, and dismissed politics until the morrow.

III

But if Hamilton consigned politics to oblivion at midnight and slept for the few hours demanded by outraged nature, he plunged from the crystal of his bath into their reeking blackness early in the morning. He had laughed the night before, but he was in the worst of tempers as he shut his study door behind him. For the first time in his life he was on a battle-ground with no sensation of joy in the coming fight. The business was too ugly and the prospect was almost certain defeat. Were the first battle lost, he knew that a sharper engagement would immediately succeed: his political foresight anticipated the tie, and he alone had a consummate knowledge of the character of Burr. That the Republicans would offer Burr the office of Vice-President was as positive as that Jefferson would be their first and unanimous choice. Clinton and Chancellor Livingston might be more distinguished men than the little politician, but the first was in open opposition to Jefferson, and the second was deaf. Burr's conquest of New York entitled him to reward, and he would accept it and intrigue with every resource of his cunning and address for the larger number of votes, regardless of the will of the people. If the result were a tie, the Federals would incline to anybody rather than Jefferson, and Hamilton would be obliged to throw into the scale his great influence as leader of his party for the benefit of the man he would gladly have attached to a fork and set to toast above the coals of Hell. He had no score to settle with Burr, but to permit him to become President of the United States would be a crime for which the leader of the Federalist party would be held responsible. When the inevitable moment came he should hand over the structure he had created to the man who had desired to rend it from gable to foundation; both because it was the will of the people and because Jefferson was the safer man of the two.

So far his statesmanship triumphed, as it had done in every crisis which he had been called upon to manipulate, and as it would in many more. But for once, and as regarded the first battle, it failed him, and he made no attempt to invoke it. This was the blackest period of his inner life, and there were times when he never expected to emerge from its depths. The threatened loss of the magnificent power he had wielded, the hatreds that possessed and overwhelmed him, the seeming futility of almost a lifetime of labour, sacrifices without end and prodigal dispensing of great gifts, the constant insults of his enemies, and the public ingratitude, had saturated his spirit with a raging bitterness and roused the deadliest passions of his nature. The marah he had passed through while a member of the Cabinet was shallow compared to the depths in which he almost strangled to-day. Not only was this the final accumulation, but the inspiring and sustaining affection, the circumscribing bulwark, of Washington was gone from him. "He was an Aegis very essential to me," he had said sadly, and he felt his loss more every day that he lived.

He knew there was just one chance to save the Presidency to the Federalist party. Did he employ the magic of his pen to recreate the popularity of John Adams, it was more than possible that thousands would gladly permit the leader they had followed for years to persuade them they had judged too hastily the man of whom they had expected too much. But by this time there was one man Hamilton hated more implacably than Jefferson, and that was John Adams. Besides the thorough disapproval of the Administration of Adams, which, as a statesman, he shared with all the eminent Federals in the country, his personal counts with this enemy piled to heaven. Adams had severed the party he had created, endeavoured to humiliate him before the country, refused, after Washington's death, to elevate him to his rightful position as General-in-chief of the army he had organized, alienated from him one of the best of his friends, and primarily was answerable for the crushing defeat of yesterday. With one of the Pinckneys at the helm, Hamilton could have defied Jefferson and kept the Democrats out of power; but the man next in eminence to himself in his own party had given his supremacy its death-blow, and it is little wonder if his depths resembled boiling pitch, if the heights of his character had disappeared

413

from his vision. He was, above all things, intensely human, with all good and all evil in him; and although he conquered himself at no very remote period, he felt, at the present moment, like Lucifer whirling through space.

Troup, now a retired judge of the U.S. District Court of New York, and a man of some fortune, ready as of old to be Hamilton's faithful lieutenant, entered and looked with sympathy and more apprehension at his Chief.

"I've not come to bemoan this bad business," he said, sitting down at a desk and taking up his pen. "What next? It looks hopeless, but of course you'll no more cease from effort than one of your Scotch ancestors would have laid down his arms if a rival chieftain had appeared on the warpath with the world at his back. Is it Adams and C.C.P. to the death?"

"It is Pinckney; Adams only in so far as he is useful. He still has his following in the New England States. The leaders in those States, first and second, must be persuaded to work unanimously for Adams and Pinckney, with the distinct understanding that in other States votes for Adams will be thrown away. This, after I have persuaded them of Adams's absolute unfitness for office. If we carry and it comes to a tie, there is no doubt to whom the House will give the election."

Troup whistled. "This is politics!" he said. "I never believed you'd go down to your neck. I wish you'd throw the whole thing over, and retire to private life."

"I shall retire soon enough," said Hamilton, grimly. "But Adams will go first."

Troup knew that it was useless to remonstrate further. He had followed this Captain to the bitter end too often. Underneath the immense sanity of Hamilton's mind was a curious warp of obstinacy, born of implacability and developed far beyond the normal bounds of determination. When this almost perverted faculty was in possession of the brain, Hamilton would pursue his object, did every guardian in his genius, from foresight to acuteness, rise in warning. His present policy if a failure might be the death of the Federalist party, but the flashing presentiment of that historic disaster did not deter him for a moment.

"It is the time for politics," Hamilton continued. "Statesmanship goes begging. I shall be entirely frank about it, for that matter. There will

414

be no underhand scheming, Adams is welcome to know every step I take. The correspondence must begin at once. I'll make out a list for you. I shall begin with Wolcott."

IV

When the tidings of the New York election reached Philadelphia, the Federals of the House met in alarmed and hurried conference. In their desperation they agreed to ask Hamilton to appeal to the Governor of New York, John Jay, to reconvene the existing legislature that it might enact a law authorizing in that State the choice of Presidential electors in districts. Why they did not send a memorial to Jay themselves, instead of placing Hamilton in a position to incur the full odium of such a suggestion, can only be explained by the facts that during the entire span of the party's existence, their leader had cheerfully assumed the responsibility in every emergency or crisis, and that if the distinguished formalist in the Executive Mansion of New York had a weak spot in him, it was for Hamilton.

When Hamilton read this portentous letter, he flushed deeply and then turned white. The expedient had not occurred to him, but it was too near of kin to his disapproval of a provision which had delivered the State into the hands of an industrious rascal, not to strike an immediate response; especially in his present frame of mind. He was alone with his wife at the moment, and he handed her the letter. She read it twice, then laid it on the table. "It savours very much of fraud, to me," she said. "Why do politics so often go to the head?"

"Sometimes one sort rises as an antidote to another. There comes a time in human affairs when one is forced into a position of choosing between two evils; a time when the scruples of delicacy and propriety, as relative to a common course of things, ought to yield to the extraordinary nature of the crisis."

"Right is right, and wrong is wrong," said Betsey, with her Dutch sturdiness. "This measure—were it adopted by Mr. Jay—would merely mean that the party in power was taking an unconstitutional advantage of its situation to nullify the victories gained by the other."

"The victories you speak of were won by fraud and every unworthy device. I am not arguing that, such being the case, we are justified in turning their weapons upon them, but that for the good of the country

415

the enemy should be suppressed before they are able to accomplish its demoralization, if not its ruin. The triumph of Jefferson and Jacobinism, the flourishing of Democracy upon the ruins of Federalism, too long a taste of power by the States rights fanatics, means, with the weak spots in our Constitution, civil war. Burr has sowed the seeds of municipal corruption, which, if the sower be rewarded by the second office in the gift of the people, will spread all over the Union. That many in the ranks of Democracy are in the pay of France, and design the overthrow of the Government, there is not a shadow of doubt. If Jefferson should die in office, or a tie, in spite of all I could do, should give the Presidency to Burr, there is nothing that man's desperate temper would not drive him to accomplish during the time remaining to him—for he will never be the first choice of the Democrats. Therefore, I shall propose this measure to Jay in the course of the next two or three days, unless upon mature deliberation I alter my present opinion that the grave crisis in national affairs justifies it, or I conceive something better."

"You will violate your higher principles," said his wife, who had matured in a previous era. "And it will be a terrible weapon for your enemies."

"I have now reached that happy point where I am entirely indifferent to the broadsides of my enemies; and I believe that if I conclude to take this step, my conscience—and history—will justify me." "If you succeed," said Betsey, shrewdly. "But Mr. Jay is very rigid, and he lacks your imagination, your terrible gift of seeing the future in a flash."

"It is quite true that I have little hope of persuading Jay; as little as I have of endowing him with the gift of foresight. But, if I think best, I shall make the attempt, and whatever the consequences, I shall not regret it."

Betsey said no more. She knew the exact amount of remonstrance Hamilton would stand, and she never exceeded it. When his fighting armour was on, no human being could influence him beyond a certain point, and she was too wise to risk her happiness. Although he was too careful of her to let her suspect the hideous conflicts which raged in his soul, she was fully aware of his bitter obstinacy, and that he was the best hater in the country. She had many gloomy forebodings, for she anticipated the terrible strain on what was left of his constitution.

There was one person who, through her inherited intuitions, understood Hamilton, and that was Angelica. He had kept her at arm's length, great as the temptation to have a sympathetic confidant had been, particularly after he had withdrawn from the intimate companionship of Washington; she was so highly wrought and sensitive, so prone to hysteria, that he had never yielded for a moment, even when she turned her head slowly toward him and stared at him with eyes that read his very soul. On the evening after the elections he had played and sung with her for an hour, then talked for another with Philip, who was the most promising student of Columbia College, a youth of fine endowments and elevated character. He was the pride and delight of Hamilton, who could throttle both apprehensions and demons while discussing his son's future, and listening to his college trials and triumphs. Upon this particular evening Angelica had suddenly burst into tears and left the room. The next morning Hamilton sent her to Saratoga; and, much as he loved her, it was with profound relief that he arranged her comfortably on the deck of the packet-boat.

On the 7th he wrote to the Governor; but, as he had feared, Jay would take no such audacious leap out of his straight and narrow way. The letter was published in the *Aurora* before it reached Albany, and Hamilton had reason to believe that Burr had a spy in the post-office.

Hamilton executed the orders for disbanding the army, then made a tour of several of the New England States, holding conferences and speaking continually. He found the first-class leaders at one with him as to the danger of entrusting the Executive office to Adams a second time, and favourably inclined to Pinckney. But the second-rate men of influence were still enthusiastic for the President, and extolling him for saving the country from war. Hamilton listened to them with no attempt to conceal his impatience. He pointed out that if Talleyrand had made up his mind that it was best to avoid a war, he would have made a second and regular overture, which could have been accepted without humiliation to the country, and the severance of the Federalist party.

As if Adams had not done enough to rouse the deadly wrath of Hamilton, he announced right and left that the Federalist defeat in New York had been planned by his arch enemy, with the sole purpose of driving himself from office; that there was a British faction in the country and that Hamilton was its chief. He drove Pickering and

M'Henry from his Cabinet with contumely, as the only immediate retaliation he could think of, and Wolcott would have followed, had there been anyone to take his place. Franklin once said of Adams that he was always honest, sometimes great, and often mad. Probably so large an amount of truth has never again been condensed into an epigram. If Adams had not become inflamed with the ambition that has ruined the lives and characters of so many Americans, he would have come down to posterity as a great man, with a record of services to his country which would have scattered his few mistakes into the unswept corners of oblivion. But autocratic, irritable, and jealous, all the infirmities of his temper as brittle with years as the blood-vessels of his brain, the most exacting office in the civilized world taxed him too heavily. It is interesting to speculate upon what he might have been in this final trial of his public career, had Hamilton died as he took the helm of State. If Hamilton's enemies very nearly ruined his own character, there is no denying that he exerted an almost malign influence upon them. To those he loved or who appealed to the highest in him he gave not only strength, but an abundance of sweetness and light, illuminating mind and spirit, and inspiring an affection that was both unselfish and uplifting. But his enemies hated him so frantically that their characters measurably deteriorated; to ruin or even disconcert him they stooped and intrigued and lied; they were betrayed into public acts which lowered them in their own eyes and in those of all students of history. Other hatreds were healthy and stimulating by comparison; but there is no doubt that Adams, Jefferson, and Madison fell far lower than they would have done had Hamilton never shot into the American heavens, holding their fields at his pleasure, and paling the fires of large and ambitious stars.

The political excitement in the country by this time surpassed every previous convulsion to such an extent that no man prominent in the contest could appear on the street without insult. Although he never knew it, Hamilton, every time he left the house, was shadowed by his son Philip, Robert Hamilton, Troup, John Church, or Philip Church. For the Democratic ammunition and public fury alike were centred on Hamilton. Adams came in for his share, but the Democrats regarded his doom as sealed, and Hamilton, as ever, the Colossus to be destroyed. The windows of the bookshops were filled with pamphlets, lampoons, and cartoons. The changes were rung on the aristocratical temper and the monarchical designs of the leader of the Federalists, until Hamilton was sick of the sight of himself with his nose in the air and a crown on his head, his train borne by Jay, Cabot, Sedgwick, and Bayard. The people were warned in every issue of the *Aurora, Chronicle,* and other industrious sheets, that Hamilton was intriguing to drive the Democratic States to secession, that he might annihilate them at once with his army and his navy. The Reynolds affair was retold once a week, with degrading variations, and there was no doubt that spies were nosing the ground in every direction to obtain evidence of another scandal to vary the monotony. Mrs. Croix, being Queen of the Jacobins, was safe, so press and pamphlet indulged in wild generalities of debauchery and rapine. It must be confessed that Jefferson fared no better in the Federalist sheets. He was a huge and hideous spider, spinning in a web full of seduced citizens; he meditated a resort to arms, did he lose the election. As to his private vices, they saddled him with an entire harem, and a black one at that.

When Hamilton heard that Adams had asserted that he was the chief of a British faction, he wrote to the President, demanding an explanation; and his note had that brief and frigid courtesy which indicated that he was in his most dangerous temper. Adams ignored it. Hamilton waited a reasonable time, then wrote again; but Adams was now too infuriated to care whether or not he committed the unpardonable error of insulting the most distinguished man in the country. He was in a humour to insult the shade of Washington, and he delighted in every opportunity to wreak vengeance on Hamilton, and would have died by his hand rather than placate him.

Then Hamilton took the step he had meditated for some time past, one which had received the cordial sanction of Wolcott, and the uneasy and grudging acquiescence of Cabot, Ames, Carroll of Carrollton, Bayard, and a few other devoted but conservative supporters. He wrote, for the benefit of the second-class leaders, who must be persuaded to cast their votes for Pinckney, to vindicate Pickering and M'Henry, and—it would be foolish to ignore it—to gratify his deep personal hatred, the pamphlet called "The Public Conduct and Character of John Adams, Esq., President of the United States." His temper did not flash in it for a second. It was written in his most concise and pointed, his most lucid and classic, manner; and nothing so damning ever flowed from mortal brain. He set forth all Adams's virtues and services with judicial impartiality. There they were for all to read. Let no man forget them. Then he counterbalanced and overbalanced them by the weaknesses, jealousies, and other temperamental defects which had arisen in evidence with the beginnings of the President's public career. He drilled holes in poor Adams's intellect which proved its unsoundness and its unfitness for public duty, and he lashed him without mercy for his public mistakes and for his treatment of his Secretaries and himself. It was a life history on ivory, and a masterpiece; and there is no friend of Hamilton's who would not sacrifice the memory of one of his greatest victories for the privilege of unwriting it.

This was one of his creations that he did not read to his wife, but Troup was permitted a glance at the manuscript. He dropped it to the floor, and his face turned white. "Do you intend to publish this thing?" he demanded. "And with your name signed in full?"

"I intend to print it. I had every intention of scattering it broadcast, but I have yielded to the dissuasions of men whose opinions I am bound to respect, and it will go only to them and to the second-class leaders as yet unconvinced. To their entreaties that I would not sign my name I have not listened, because such a work, if anonymous, would be both cowardly and futile. The point is to let those for whom it is intended know that a person in authority is talking; and anonymous performances are legitimate only when published and unmistakable, when given in that form as a concession to the fashion of the age."

Troup groaned. "And if it falls into the enemy's hands?"

"In that case, what a hideous opportunity it would enclose, were it unsigned."

"Oh, sign it!" said Troup, wildly. He set his heel on the manuscript, and looked tentatively at Hamilton. He knew the meaning of the expression he encountered, and removed his heel. It was months since he had seen the gay sparkle in Hamilton's eyes, humour and sweetness curving his mouth. When Hamilton's mouth was not as hard as iron, it relaxed to cynicism or contempt. He was so thin that the prominence of the long line from ear to chin and of the high hard nose, with its almost rigid nostrils, would have made him look more old Roman coin than man, had it not been for eyes like molten steel. "Politics and ambition!"

thought Troup. "What might not the world be without them?"

"Let us change the subject," he said. "I hear that Mrs. Croix makes a convert an hour from Federalism to Democracy. That is the estimate. And a small and select band know that she does it in the hope of hastening your ruin. I must say, Hamilton, that as far as women are concerned, you are punished far beyond your deserts. There is hardly a man in public life who has not done as much, or worse, but the world is remarkably uninterested, and the press finds any other news more thrilling. The Reynolds woman is probably responsible for many remorseful twinges in the breasts of eminent patriots, but your name alone is given to the public. As for Mrs. Croix, I don't suppose that any mere mortal has ever resisted her, but if any other man has regretted it, history is silent. What do you suppose is the reason?"

Hamilton would not discuss Mrs. Croix, but he had long since ceased to waste breath in denial. He made no reply.

"Do you know my theory?" said Troup, turning upon him suddenly. "It is this. You are so greatly endowed that more is expected of you than of other men. You were fashioned to make history; to give birth, not for your own personal good, but for the highest good of a nation, to the greatest achievement of which the human mind is capable. Therefore, when you trip and stumble like any fool among us, when you act like a mere mortal with no gigantic will and intellect to lift him to the heights and keep him there, some power in the unseen universe is infuriated, and you pay the price with compound interest. It will be the same with that thing on the floor. If you could be sure that it would never fall into the hands of a Jacobin, even then it would be a mistake to print it, for it is mainly prompted by hatred, and as such is unworthy of you. But if it finds its way to the public, your punishment will be even in excess of your fault. For God's sake think it over."

Hamilton made no reply, and in a moment Troup rose. "Very well," he said, "have your own way and be happy. I'll stand by you if the citadel falls."

Hamilton's eyes softened, and he shook Troup's hands heartily. But as soon as he was alone, he sent the manuscript to the printer.

V

M.L. Davis, the authentic biographer of Burr, tells this interesting

421

anecdote concerning the Adams pamphlet:—'

Colonel Burr ascertained the contents of this pamphlet, and that it was in the press. The immediate publication, he knew, must distract the Federal party, and thus promote the Republican cause in those States where the elections had not taken place. Arrangements were accordingly made for a copy as soon as the printing of it was completed; and when obtained, John Swartwout, Robert Swartwout, and Matthew L. Davis, by appointment met Colonel Burr at his house. The pamphlet was read, and extracts made for the press. They were immediately published.

When Hamilton read the voluminous extracts in the marked copies of the Democratic papers which he found on the table in his chambers in Garden Street, his first sensation was relief; subterranean methods were little to his liking. He was deeply uneasy, however, when he reflected upon the inevitable consequences to his party, and wondered that his imagination for once had failed him. Everyone who has written with sufficient power to incite antagonism, knows the apprehensive effect of extracts lifted maliciously from a carefully wrought whole. Hamilton felt like a criminal until he plunged into the day's work, when he had no time for an accounting with his conscience. He was in court all day, and after the five o'clock dinner at home, returned to his office and worked on an important brief until eight. Then he paid a short call on a client, and was returning home through Pearl Street, when he saw Troup bearing down upon him. This old comrade's face was haggard and set, and his eyes were almost wild. Hamilton smiled grimly. That expression had stamped the Federal visage since morning.

Troup reached Hamilton in three strides, and seizing him by the arm, pointed to the upper story of Fraunces' Tavern. "Alec," he said hoarsely, "do you remember the vow you made in that room twenty-five years ago? You have kept it until to-day. There is not an instance in your previous career where you have sacrificed the country to yourself. No man in history ever made greater sacrifices, and no man has had a greater reward in the love and loyalty of the best men in a nation. And now, to gratify the worst of your passions, you have betrayed your country into the hands of the basest politicians in it. Moreover, all your enemies could not drag you down, and no man in history has ever been assailed by greater phalanxes than you have been. It took you—

yourself—to work your own ruin, to pull your party down on top of you, and send the country we have all worked so hard for to the devil. I love you better than anyone on earth, and I'll stick to you till the bitter end, but I'd have this say if you never spoke to me again."

Hamilton dropped his eyes from the light in the familiar room of Fraunces' Tavern, but the abyss he seemed to see at his feet was not the one yawning before his friend's excited imagination. He did not answer for a moment, and then he almost took away what was left of Troup's breath.

"You are quite right," he said. "And what I have most to be thankful for in life, is that I have never attracted that refuse of mankind who fawn and flatter; or have dismissed them in short order," he added, with his usual regard for facts. "Come and breakfast with me to-morrow. Good night."

He walked home quickly, told the servant at the door that he was not to be disturbed, and locked himself in his study. He lit one candle, then threw himself into his revolving chair, and thought until the lines in his face deepened to the bone, and only his eyes looked alive. He wasted no further regrets on the political consequences of his act. What was done, was done. Nor did he anticipate any such wholesale disaster as had distracted the Federalists since the morning issues. He knew the force of habit and the tenacity of men's minds. His followers would be aghast, harshly critical for a day, then make every excuse that ingenuity could suggest, unite in his defence, and follow his lead with redoubled loyalty. His foresight had long since leaped to the end of this conflict, for the Democratic hordes had been augmenting for years; his own party was hopelessly divided and undermined by systematic slander. To fight was second nature, no matter how hopeless the battle; but in those moments of almost terrifying prescience so common to him, he realized the inevitableness of the end, as history does to-day. His only chance had been to placate Adams and recreate his enemy's popularity.

The day never came when he was able to say that he might have done this at the only time when such action would have counted. He had been inexorable until the pamphlet was flung to the public; and then, although he was hardly conscious of it at the moment, he was immediately dispossessed of the intensity of his bitterness toward Adams. The revenge had been so terrible, so abrupt, that his hatred seemed disseminating in the stolen leaves fluttering through the city. Therefore his mind was free for the appalling thought which took possession of it as Troup poured out his diatribe; and this thought was, that he was no longer conscious of any greatness in him. Through all the conflicts, trials, and formidable obstacles of previous years he had been sustained by his consciousness of superlative gifts combined with loftiness of purpose. Had not his greatness been dinned into his ears, he would have been as familiar with it. But he seemed to himself to have shrivelled, his very soul might have been in ashes—incremated in the flames of his passions. He had triumphed over every one of his enemies in turn. Historically he was justified, and had he accomplished the same end impersonally, they would have been the only sufferers, and in the just degree. But he had boiled them in the vitriol of his nature; he had scarred them and warped them and destroyed their self-respect. Had these raging passions been fed with other vitalities? Had they ravaged his soul to nourish his demons? Was that his punishment,—an instance of the inexorable law of give and take?

He recalled the white heat of patriotism with which he had written the revolutionary papers of his boyhood, the numberless pamphlets which had finally roused the States to meet in convention and give the wretched country a Constitutional Government, *"The Federalist"*; which had spurred him to the great creative acts that must immortalize him in history. He contrasted that patriotic fire with the spirit in which he had written the Adams pamphlet. The fire had gone out, and the precipitation was gall and worm-wood. Even the spirit in which he had first attacked Jefferson in print was righteous indignation by comparison.

Had he hated his soul to cinders? Had the bitterness and the implacability he had encouraged for so many years bitten their acids through and through the lofty ideals which once had been the larger part of himself? Had the angel in him fallen to the bottom of the pit in that frightful nethermost region of his, for his cynical brain to mock, until that, too, was in its grave? He thought of the high degree of self-government, almost the perfection, that Washington had attained,—one of the most passionate men that had ever lived. Did that great Chieftain stand alone in the history of souls? He thought of Laurens, with his early despair that self-conquest seemed impossible. Would he have

424

conquered, had he lived? What would he or Washington think, were they present to-night? Would they hate him, or would their love be proof against even this abasement? He passionately wished they were there, whether they came to revile or console. Isolated and terror-stricken, he felt as if thrust for ever from the world of living men.

His mind had been turned in, every faculty bent introspectively, but for some moments past his consciousness had vibrated mechanically to an external influence. It flew open suddenly, as he realized that someone was watching him, and he wheeled his chair opposite the dusk in the lower end of the room. For a moment it, seemed to him that every function in him ceased and was enveloped in ice. A face rested lightly on the farther end of the long table, the fair hair floating on either side of it, the eyes fixed upon him with an expression that flashed him back to St. Croix and the last weeks of his mother's life. He fancied in that moment that he could even discern the earthen hue of the skin. When he realized that it was Angelica, he was hardly less startled, but he found his voice.

"When did you return?" he asked, in as calm a tone as he could command.

"And why did you hide in here?"

"I came down with Grandpa, who made up his mind in a minute. And I came in here to be sure to have a little talk with you alone. I was going to surprise you as soon as you lit the candle, and then your face frightened me. It is worse now."

Her voice was hardly audible, and she did not move. Hamilton went down and lifted her to her feet, then supported her to a chair opposite his own. He made no search for an excuse, for he would not have dared to offer it to this girl, whose spiritual recesses he suddenly determined to probe. Between her and the dead woman there was a similarity that was something more than superficially atavistic. His practical brain refused to speculate even upon the doctrine of metempsychosis. He was like his mother in many ways. That unique and powerful personality had stamped his brain cells when he was wholly hers. He recalled that his own soul had echoed faintly with memories in his youth. What wonder that he had given this inheritance to the most sensitively constituted of his children, whose musical genius, the least sane of all gifts, put her in touch with the greater mysteries of the

Universe? That nebulous memories moved like ghosts in her soul he did not doubt, nor that at such moments she was tormented with vague maternal pangs. He conquered his first impulse to confess himself to her; doubtless she needed more help than he. She was staring at him in mingled terror and agony.

"Why do you suffer so when I suffer?" he asked gently; then bluntly, "do you yearn over me as if I were your child, and in peril?"

"Yes," she answered, without betraying any surprise; "that is it. I have a terrible feeling of responsibility and helplessness, of understanding and knowing nothing. I feel sometimes as if I had done you a great wrong, for which I suffer when you are in trouble, and I am no more use to you than John or little Eliza. If you would tell me. If you would let me share it with you. You remember I begged as a child. You have made believe to tell me secrets many times, but you have told me nothing. My imagination has nearly shattered me."

"Do you wish to know?" he asked. "Are you strong enough to see me as I see myself to-night? I warn you it will be a glimpse into Hell."

"I don't care what it is," she answered, "so long as it is the reality, and you let me know you as I do underneath my blindness and ignorance."

Then he told her. He talked to her as he would have talked to the dead had she risen, although without losing his sense of her identity for a moment, or the consciousness of the danger of the experiment. He showed her what few mortals have seen, a naked soul with its scars, its stains, and its ravages from flame and convulsion. He need not have apprehended a disastrous result. She was compounded of his essences, and her age was that indeterminate mixture of everlasting youth and anticipated wisdom which is the glory and the curse of genius. She listened intently, the expression of torment displaced by normal if profound sympathy. He had begun with the passions inspired by Jefferson; he finished with the climax of deterioration in the revenge he had taken on Adams, and the abyss of despair into which it had plunged him. He drew a long breath of relief, and regarded his little judge with some defiance. She nodded.

"I feel old and wise," she said, "and at the same time much younger, because I no longer shrink from a load on my mind I cannot understand. And you—it has all gone." She darted at the candle and held it to his face. "You look twenty years younger than when you sat there and thought. I believed you were dying of old age."

"I feel better," he admitted, "But nothing can obliterate the scars. And although I shall always be young at intervals, remember that I have crowded three lifetimes into one, and that I must pay the penalty spiritually and physically, although mentally I believe I shall hold my own until the end." He leaned forward on a sudden impulse and took both her hands. "I make you a vow," he said, "and I have never broken even a promise—or only one," he added, remembering Troup's accusation. "I will drive the bitterness out of myself and I will hate no more. My public acts shall be unaccompanied by personal bitterness henceforth. Not a vengeance that I have accomplished has been worth the hideous experience of to-night, and so long as I live I shall have no cause to repeat it."

"If you ever broke that vow," said Angelica, "I should either die or go crazy, for you would sink and never rise again."

VI

As Hamilton had anticipated, the Jacobin press shouted and laughed itself hoarse, vowed that it never could have concocted so effective a bit of campaign literature, and that the ursine roars of Adams could be heard from Dan to Beersheba. Burr, as yet undetected, almost danced as he walked. The windows were filled with parodies of the pamphlet, entitled, "The Last Speech and Dying Words of Alexander Hamilton," "Hamilton's Last Letter and His Amorous Vindication," "A Free Examination of the Morals, Political and Literary Characters of John Adams and Alexander Hamilton." One cartoon displayed the sinking ship *Administration*, with the Federal rats scuttling out of her, and Hamilton standing alone on the deck; another, "The Little Lion" sitting, dejected and forlorn, outside the barred gates of "Hamiltonopolis." The deep, silent laughter of Jefferson shook the continent.

The Federalist leaders were furious and aghast. But they recovered, and when the time came, every Federalist delegate to the Electoral College, with one exception, voted precisely as Hamilton had counselled. South Carolina deserted Pinckney because he would not desert Adams, but she would have pursued that policy had the pamphlet never been written; and whether it affected the defeat of the Federalists in Pennsylvania and other States is doubtful. The publication in August of Adams's letter to Tench Coxe, written in 1792, when he was bitterly disappointed at Washington's refusal to send him as minister to England, and asserting that the appointment of Pinckney was due to British influence, thus casting opprobrium upon the integrity of Washington, had done as much as Hamilton's pamphlet, if not more, to damn him finally with the Federalists. Hamilton's chief punishment for his thunderbolt was in his conscience, and his leadership of his party was not questioned for a moment. He expected a paternal rebuke from General Schuyler, but that old warrior, severe always with the delinquencies of his own children, had found few faults in his favourite son-in-law; and he took a greater pride in his career than he had taken in his own. Now that gout and failing sight had forced him from public life, he found his chief enjoyment in Hamilton's society. General Schuyler survived the death of several of his children and of his wife, but Hamilton's death killed him. Assuredly, life dealt generously with our hero in the matter of fathers, despite or because of an early oversight. James Hamilton had never made the long and dangerous journey to the North, and he had died on St. Vincent, in 1799, but what filial regret his son might have dutifully experienced was swept away on the current of the overwhelming grief for Washington. And as for mothers, charming elder sisters, and big brothers, eager to fight his battles, no man was ever so blest. In December Hamilton received the following letter from William Vans Murray:—

Paris, Oct. 9th, 1800.

Dear Sir: I was extremely flattered by the confidence which your letter by Mr. Colbert proved you have in my disposition to follow your wishes. A letter from you is no affair of ceremony. It is an obligation on any man who flatters himself with the hope of your personal esteem. Mr. Colbert gave it to me yesterday. I immediately, in particular, addressed a letter to Bonaparte, and made use of your name, which I was sure would be pleasing to him. To-day I dined with him. The Secretary of State assured me that he received it kindly, and I can hope something good from him. If any come it will be your work. I never before spoke or wrote to Bonaparte on any affair other than public business. It will be very pleasing to you if we succeed, that your silent agency works good to the unhappy and meritorious at such a distance. I know nothing better belonging to reputation.

Poor Adams!

General Davie arrived by the next ship, bringing with him a convention concluded with France on the 30th of October. He also brought a letter to Hamilton from one of the commission, with a copy of the document and a journal of the proceedings of the negotiators. The writer was Oliver Ellsworth, Chief Justice of the United States Supreme Court. Adams might occupy the chair of State, but to the Federals Hamilton was President in all but name.

Sedgwick and Gouverneur Morris, now a member of the Senate, not knowing of the communication, wrote immediately to Hamilton, acquainting him with the contents of the treaty.

It contains no stipulation for satisfaction of the injuries we have received [Sedgwick wrote in wrath]. It makes the treaty of '78 a subject for future negotiation. It engages that we shall return, in the condition they now are, all our captures. It makes neutral bottoms a protection to their cargoes, and it contains a stipulation directly in violation of the 25th article of our treaty with Great Britain. Such are the blessed effects of our mission! These are the ripened fruits of this independent Administration! Our friends in the Senate are not enough recovered from their astonishment to begin to reflect on the course they shall pursue.

This treaty was a far more deadly weapon in Hamilton's hands than the entire arsenal he had manipulated in his pamphlet, for campaign literature is often pickled and retired with the salt of its readers. But did this mission fail, did Adams lose his only chance of justification for sending the commission at all, did the Senate refuse to ratify, and war break out, or honourable terms of peace be left to the next President, then Adams's Administration must be stamped in history as a failure, and he himself retire from office covered with ignominy. But had Hamilton not recovered his balance and trimmed to their old steady duty the wicks of those lamps whose brilliance had dimmed in a stormy hour, his statesmanship would have controlled him in such a crisis as this. He knew that the rejection of the treaty would shatter the Federal party and cause national schisms and discords; that, if left over to a Jacobin administration, the result would be still worse for the United States. It was a poor thing, but no doubt the best that could have been extracted from triumphant France; nor was it as bad in some respects as the irritated Senate would have it. Such as it was, it must be ratified, peace placed to the credit of the Federalists, and the act of the man they had made President justified. Hamilton was obliged to write a great many letters on the subject, for the Federalists found it a bitter pill to swallow; but he prevailed and they swallowed it.

Meanwhile, the Electoral College had met. Adams had received sixty-five votes, Pinckney sixty-four, Jefferson and Burr seventy-three each. That threw the decision upon the House of Representatives, for Burr refused to recognize the will of the people, and withdraw in favour of the man whom the Democratic hemisphere of American politics had unanimously elected. Burr had already lost caste with the party by his attempts to secure more votes than the leaders were willing to give him, and had alarmed Jefferson into strenuous and diplomatic effort, the while he piously folded his visible hands or discoursed upon the bones of the mammoth. When Burr, therefore, permitted the election to go to the House, he was flung out of the Democratic party neck and crop, and Jefferson treated him like a dog until he killed Hamilton, when he gave a banquet in his honour. Burr's only chance for election lay with the Federalists, who would rather have seen horns and a tail in the Executive Chair than Thomas Jefferson. Hamilton had anticipated their hesitation and disposition to bargain with Burr, and he bombarded them with letters from the moment the Electoral College announced the result, until the House decided the question on the 17th of February. He analyzed Burr for the benefit of the anxious members until the dark and poisonous little man must have haunted their dreams at night. Whether they approached Burr or not will never be known; but they were finally convinced that to bargain with a man as unfigurable as water would be throwing away time which had far better be employed in extracting pledges from Jefferson.

One of Hamilton's letters to Gouverneur Morris, who wielded much influence in the House, is typical of many.

... Another subject. *Jefferson or Burr?* The former beyond a doubt. The latter in my judgement has no principle, public or private; could be bound by no agreement; will listen to no monitor but his ambition; and for this purpose will use the worst portion of the community as a ladder to climb to permanent power, and an instrument to crush the better part. He is bankrupt beyond redemption, except by the resources that grow out of war and disorder; or by a sale to a foreign power, or by great peculation. War with Great Britain would be the immediate instrument. He is sanguine enough to hope everything, daring enough to attempt everything, wicked enough to scruple nothing. From the elevation of such a man may heaven preserve the country.

Let our situation be improved to obtain from Jefferson assurances on certain points: the maintenance of the present system, especially on the cardinal articles of public credit—a navy, neutrality. Make any discreet use you may think fit of this letter.

He was deeply alarmed at the tendency of the excited House, which sat in continuous session from the 11th to the 17th, members sleeping on the floor and sick men brought thither on cots, one with his wife in attendance. The South was threatening civil war, and Burr's subsequent career justified his alarm and his warnings; but in spite of his great influence he won his case with his followers by a very small margin. They were under no delusions regarding the character of Burr, their letters to Hamilton abound in strictures almost as severe as his own, but their argument was that he was the less of two evils, that every move he made could be sharply watched. It is quite true that he would have had Federalists and Democrats in both Houses to frustrate him; but it does not seem to have occurred to the former that impeachment would have been inevitable, and Jefferson President but a year or two later than the will of the people decreed. But it was a time of terrible excitement, and for the matter of that their brains must have been a trifle clouded by the unvarying excitement of their lives. Bayard of Delaware, with whom Hamilton had fought over point by point, winning one or more with each letter, changed his vote on the last ballot from Burr to a blank. Hamilton's friends knew that Burr would kill him sooner or later, for the ambitious man had lost his one chance of the great office; but Hamilton chose to see only the humour of the present he had made Thomas Jefferson. That sensible politician had tacitly agreed to the terms suggested by the Federalists, when they debated the possibility of accepting him, and Hamilton knew that he was far too clever to break

431

his word at once. What Hamilton hoped for was what came to pass: Jefferson found the machinery of his new possession more to his taste than he could have imagined while sitting out in the cold, and he let it alone.

VII

Hamilton was now free to devote himself to the practice of law, with but an occasional interruption. It hardly need be stated that he kept a sharp eye on Jefferson, but for the sake of the country he supported him when he could do so consistently with his principles. More than once the President found in him an invaluable ally; and as often, perhaps, he writhed as on a hot gridiron. Hamilton came forth in the pamphlet upon extreme occasions only, but he was still the first political philosopher and writer of his time, and the Federalists would have demanded his pen upon these occasions had he been disposed to retire it. Although out of the active field of politics, he kept the best of the demoralized Federalists together, warning them constantly that the day might come when they would be called upon to reorganize a disintegrated union, and responding to the demands of his followers in Congress for advice. In local politics he continued to make himself felt in spite of the fattening ranks of Democracy. His most powerful instrument was the *New York Evening Post*, which he founded for the purpose of keeping the Federalist cause alive, and holding the enemy in check. He selected an able man as editor, William Coleman of Massachusetts, but he directed the policy of the paper, dictating many of the editorials in the late hours of night. This journal took its position at once as the most respectable and brilliant in the country.

He also founded the Society for the Manumission of Slaves, securing as honorary member the name of Lafayette—now a nobleman at large once more. But all these duties weighed lightly. For the first time in his life he felt himself at liberty to devote himself almost wholly to his practice, and it was not long before he was making fifteen thousand dollars a year. It was an immense income to make in that time, and he could have doubled it had he been less erratic in the matter of fees. Upon one occasion he was sent eight thousand dollars for winning a suit, and returned seven. He invariably placed his own valuation upon a case, and frequently refused large fees that would have been paid with gratitude. If a case interested him and the man who asked his services were poorer than himself, he would accept nothing. If he were convinced that a man was in the wrong, he would not take his case at any price. He was delighted to be able to shower benefits upon his little family, and he would have ceased to be Alexander Hamilton had he been content to occupy a second place at the bar, or in any other pursuit which engaged his faculties; but for money itself, he had only contempt. Perhaps that is the reason why he is so out of tune with the present day, and unknown to the average American.

Washington, after the retirement of John Jay, had offered Hamilton the office of Chief Justice of the United States; but Hamilton felt that the bar was more suited to his activities than the bench, and declined the gift. His legal career was as brilliant and successful as his political, but although none is more familiar to ambitious lawyers, and his position as the highest authority on constitutional law has never been rivalled, his achievements of greater value to the Nation have reduced it in history to the position of an incident. There is little space left, and somewhat of his personal life still to tell, but no story of Hamilton would be complete without at least a glimpse of this particular shuttle in the tireless loom of his brain. Such glimpses have by no one been so sharply given as by his great contemporary, Chancellor Kent.

He never made any argument in court [Kent relates] without displaying his habits of thinking, resorting at once to some well-founded principle of law, and drawing his deductions logically from his premises. Law was always treated by him as a science, founded on established principles.... He rose at once to the loftiest heights of professional eminence, by his profound penetration, his power of analysis, the comprehensive grasp and strength of his understanding, and the firmness, frankness and integrity of his character.... His manners were affable, gentle and kind; and he appeared to be frank, liberal and courteous in all his professional intercourse. [Referring to a particular case the Chancellor continues.] Hamilton by means of his fine melodious voice, and dignified deportment, his reasoning powers and persuasive address, soared far above all competition. His preeminence was at once and universally conceded.... Hamilton returned to private life and to the practice of the law in '95. He was cordially welcomed and cheered on his return, by his fellow citizens. Between this year and 1798, he took his station as the leading counsel at the bar. He was employed in every important and every commercial case. He was a very great favourite with the merchants of New York and he most justly deserved to be, for he had shown himself to be one of the most enlightened, intrepid and persevering friends to the commercial prosperity of this country. Insurance questions, both upon the law and fact, constituted a large portion of the litigated business in the courts, and much of the intense study and discussion at the bar. Hamilton had an overwhelming share of this business.... His mighty mind would at times bear down all opposition by its comprehensive grasp and the strength of his reasoning powers. He taught us all how to probe deeply into the hidden recesses of the science, and to follow up principles to their far distant sources. He ransacked cases and precedents to their very foundations; and we learned from him to carry our inquiries into the commercial codes of the nations of the European continent; and in a special manner to illustrate the law of Insurance by the secure judgement of Emerigon and the luminous commentaries of Valin.... My judicial station in 1798 brought Hamilton before me in a new relation.... I was called to listen with lively interest and high admiration to the rapid exercise of his reasoning powers, the intensity and sagacity with which he pursued his investigations, his piercing criticisms, his masterly analysis, and the energy and fervour of his appeals to the judgement and conscience of the tribunal which he addressed. [In regard to the celebrated case of Croswell vs. the People, in the course of which Hamilton reversed the law of libel, declaring the British interpretation to be inconsistent with the genius of the American people, Kent remarks.] I have always considered General Hamilton's argument in this cause as the greatest forensic effort he ever made. He had come prepared to discuss the points of law with a perfect mastery of the subject. He believed that the rights and liberties of the people were essentially concerned.... There was an unusual solemnity and earnestness on his part in this discussion. He was at times highly impassioned and pathetic. His whole soul was enlisted in the cause, and in contending for the rights of the Jury and a free Press, he considered that he was establishing the surest refuge against oppression.... He never before in my hearing made any effort in which he commanded higher reverence for his principles, nor equal admiration of the power and pathos of his eloquence.... I have very little doubt that if

General Hamilton had lived twenty years longer, he would have rivalled Socrates or Bacon, or any other of the sages of ancient or modern times, in researches after truth and in benevolence to mankind. The active and profound statesman, the learned and eloquent lawyer, would probably have disappeared in a great degree before the character of the sage and philosopher, instructing mankind by his wisdom, and elevating the country by his example.

[Ambrose Spencer, Attorney General of the State,—afterward Chief Justice,—who did not love him, having received the benefit of Hamilton's scathing sarcasm more than once, has this to say.] Alexander Hamilton was the greatest man this country ever produced. I knew him well. I was in situations to observe and study him. He argued cases before me while I sat as judge on the bench. Webster has done the same. In power of reasoning, Hamilton was the equal of Webster; and more than this can be said of no man. In creative power, Hamilton was infinitely Webster's superior, and in this respect he was endowed as God endows the most gifted of our race. If we call Shakspeare a genius or creator, because he evoked plays and character from the great chaos of thought, Hamilton merits the same appellation; for it was he, more than any other man, who thought out the Constitution of the United States and the details of the Government of the Union; and out of the chaos that existed after the Revolution, raised a fabric, every part of which is instinct with his thought. I can truly say that hundreds of politicians and statesmen of the day get both the web and woof of their thoughts from Hamilton's brains. He, more than any man, did the thinking of the time.

His fooling was as inimitable as his use of passion and logic, and on one occasion he treated Gouverneur Morris, who was his opposing counsel, to such a prolonged attack of raillery that his momentary rival sat with the perspiration pouring from his brow, and was acid for some time after. During his earlier years of practice, while listening to Chancellor Livingston summing up a case in which eloquence was made to disguise the poverty of the cause, Hamilton scribbled on the margin of his brief: "Recipe for obtaining good title for ejectment: two or three void patents, several *ex parte* surveys, one or two acts of usurpation acquiesced in for the time but afterwards proved such. Mix well with half a dozen scriptural allusions, some ghosts, fairies, elves, hobgoblins, and a *quantum suff.* of eloquence." Hamilton also originated the practice of preparing "Points," now in general use.

VIII

Hamilton, after the conclusion of the great libel case in the spring of 1804, returned from Albany to New York to receive honours almost as great, if less vociferous, than those which had hailed him after the momentous Convention of 1788. Banquets were given in his honour, the bar extolled him, and the large body of his personal friends were triumphant at this new proof of his fecundity and his power over the minds of men. They were deeply disturbed on another point, however, and several days after his arrival, Troup rode out to The Grange, Hamilton's country-seat, to remonstrate.

Hamilton, several years since, had bought a large tract of wooded land on Harlem Heights and built him a house on the ridge. It commanded a view of the city, the Hudson, and the Sound. The house was spacious and strong, built to withstand the winds of the Atlantic, and to shelter commodiously not only his family, but his many guests. The garden and the woods were the one hobby of his life, and with his own hands he had planted thirteen gum trees to commemorate the thirteen original States of the Union. Fortunately his deepest sorrow was not associated with this estate; Philip had fallen before the house was finished. This brilliant youth, who had left Columbia with flying honours, had brooded over the constant attacks upon his father,—still the Colossus in the path of the Democrats, to be destroyed before they could feel secure in their new possessions,—until he had deliberately insulted the most recent offender, received his challenge, and been shot to death close to the spot where Hamilton was to fall a few years later. That was in the autumn of 1801. Hamilton's strong brain and buoyant temperament had delivered him from the intolerable suffering of that heaviest of his afflictions, and the severe and unremitting work of his life gave him little time to brood. If he rarely lost consciousness of his bereavement, the sharpness passed, and he was even grateful at times that his son, whose gifts would have urged him into public life, was spared the crucifying rewards of patriotism.

As Troup rode up the avenue and glanced from right to left into the heavy shades of the forest, with its boulders and ravines, its streams and mosses and ferns, then to the brilliant mass of colour at the end of the avenue, out of which rose the stately house, he sighed heavily.

"May the devil get the lot of them!" he said.

It was Saturday, and he found Hamilton on his back under a tree, the last number of the *Moniteur* close to his hand, his wife and Angelica looking down upon him from a rustic seat. Both the women were in mourning, and Betsey's piquant charming face was aging; her sister Peggy and her mother had followed her son.

Hamilton had never recovered his health, and he paid for the prolonged strains upon his delicate system with a languor to which at times he was forced to yield. To-day, although he greeted the welcome visitor gaily, he did not rise, and Troup sat down on the ground with his back to the tree. As he looked very solemn, Mrs. Hamilton and Angelica inferred they were not wanted, and retired.

"Well?" said Hamilton, laughing. "What is it? What have I done now?"

"Put another nail into your coffin, we are all afraid. The story of the paper you read before the Federalist Conference in Albany is common talk; and if Burr is defeated, it will be owing to your influence, whether you hold yourself aloof from this election or not. Why do you jeopardize your life? I'd rather give him his plum and choke him with it—"

"What?" cried Hamilton, erect and alert. "Permit Burr to become Governor of New York? Do you realize that the New England States are talking of secession, that even the Democrats of the North are disgusted and alarmed at the influence and arrogance of Virginia? Burr has a certain prestige in New England on account of his father and Jonathan Edwards, and his agents have been promoting discussion of this ancestry for some time past. Do the Federalists of New York endorse him, this prestige will have received its fine finish; and New Englanders have winked his vices out of sight because Jefferson's treatment of him makes him almost virtuous in their eyes. The moment he is Governor he will foment the unrest of New England until it secedes, and then, being the first officer of the leading State of the North, he will claim a higher office that will end in sovereignty. He fancies himself another Bonaparte, he who is utterly devoid of even that desire for fame, and that magnificence, which would make the Corsican a great man without his genius. That he is in communication with his idol, I happen to know, for he has been seen in secret conversation with fresh Jacobin spies. Now is the time to crush Burr once for all. Jefferson has intrigued the

Livingstons and Clinton away from him again; the party he patched together out of hating factions is in a state of incohesion. If the Federals—"

"That is just it," interrupted Troup; "the man is desperate. So are his followers, his 'little band.' They were sick and gasping after Burr's failure to receive one vote in the Republican caucus for even the Vice-Presidency, and they know that the Louisiana Purchase has made Jefferson invincible with the Democrats—or the Republicans, as Jefferson still persists in calling them. They know that Burr's chance for the Presidency has gone for ever. So New York is their only hope. Secession and empire or not, their hope, like his, is in the spoils of office; they are lean and desperate. If you balk them—"

"What a spectacle is this!" cried Hamilton, gaily. He threw himself back on the grass, and clasped his hands behind his head. "Troup, of all men, reproaching me for keeping a vow he once was ready to annihilate me for having broken. That offence was insignificant to the crime of supinely permitting our Catiline to accomplish his designs."

"If I could agree with you, I should be the last to counsel indifference; no, not if your life were the forfeit. But I never believed in Burr's talent for conspiracy. He is too sanguine and visionary. He desires power, office, and emolument—rewards for his henchmen before they desert him; but I believe he'd go—or get—no farther, and the country is strong enough to stand a quack or two; while, if we lose you—"

"You will live to see every prophecy I have made in regard to Burr fulfilled. I will not, because so long as I am alive he shall not even attempt to split the Union, to whose accomplishment and maintenance I pledged every faculty and my last vital spark. Sanguine and visionary he may be, but he is also cunning and quick, and there is a condition ready to his hand at the present moment. Jefferson is bad enough, Heaven knows. He has retained our machinery, but I sometimes fancy I can hear the crumbling of the foundations; the demoralizing and the disintegrating process began even sooner than I expected. He is appealing to the meanest passion of mankind, vanity; and the United States, which we tried to make the ideal Republic, is galloping toward the most mischievous of all establishments, Democracy. Every cowherd hopes to be President. What is the meaning of civilization, pray, if the educated, enlightened, broad-minded, are not to rule? Is man permitted to advance, progress, embellish his understanding, for his own selfish benefit, or for the benefit of mankind? And how can his superiority avail his fellows unless he be permitted to occupy the high offices of responsibility? God knows, he is not happy in his power; he is, indeed, a sacrifice to the mass. But so it was intended. He is the only sufferer, and mankind is happier."

"Jefferson and Burr both have a consummate knowledge of the limited understanding; they know how to tickle it with painted straws and bait it with lies. Bonaparte is not a greater autocrat than Jefferson, but our tyrant fools the world with his dirty old clothes and his familiarities. But I am not to be diverted. I want to keep you for my old age. I believe that you have done your part. It has been a magnificent part; there is no greater in history. Your friends are satisfied. So should you be. I want you to give up politics before it is too late. I fear more than one evil, and it has kept me awake many nights. Burr is not the only one who wishes you under ground. His 'little band' is composed of men who are worse than himself without one of his talents. Any one of them is capable of stabbing you in the dark. The Virginia Junta know that the Federalist party will exist as long as you do, and that some external menace might cohere and augment it again under your leadership. At every Federalist banquet last Fourth you were toasted as the greatest man in America; and I know this undiminished enthusiasm—as well as the influence of the *Evening Post*—alarms them deeply. They are neither great enough nor bad enough to murder you, nor even to employ someone to do it; but more than one needy rascal knows that he has only to call you out and kill you according to the code, to be rewarded with an office as soon as decency permits. There is another menace. I suppose you have heard that Mrs. Croix married a Frenchman named Stephen Jumel while you were in Albany?"

"Yes!" exclaimed Hamilton, with interest; "who is he?"

"A Parisian diamond merchant and banker, a personal friend of Bonaparte. The belief is that he came over here as a special emissary of the Consulate. Of course he brought a letter to that other illustrious agent, and to the amazement of everybody he married her. They must handle thousands of French money between them. France would be something more than glad to hear of your elimination from this complicated American problem; particularly, if you demonstrate your power by crushing this last hope of Burr's. I doubt if Burr would call you out with no stronger motive than a desire for personal revenge. He is no fool, and he knows that if he kills you, he had better put a bullet through his own brain at once. He is a sanguine man, but not so sanguine as not to know that if he compassed your death, he would be hounded into exile. But he is in a more desperate way financially than ever. He can borrow no more, and his debtors are clamouring. If he is defeated in this election, and the Jumels are sharp enough to take advantage of his fury and despair,—I think she has been watching her chance for years; and the talk is, she is anxious, for her own reasons, to get rid of Burr, besides,—I believe that a large enough sum would tempt Burr to call you out—"

"He certainly is hard up," interrupted Hamilton, "for he rang my front door bell at five o'clock this morning, and when I let him in he went on like a madman and begged me to let him have several thousands, or Richmond Hill would be sold over his head."

"And you gave them to him, I suppose? How much have you lent him altogether? I know from Washington Morton that Burr borrowed six hundred dollars of you through him."

"I lent him the six hundred, partly because his desperate plight appeals to me—I believe him to be the unhappiest wretch in America— and more because I don't want Europe laughing at the spectacle of a Vice-President of the United States in Debtor's prison. Of course I can't lend him this last sum myself, but I have promised to raise it for him."

"Well, I argue with you no more about throwing away money. Did you listen to what I said about Madame Jumel?"

"With the deepest interest. It was most ingenious, and does honour to your imagination." Troup, with an angry exclamation, sprang to his feet. Hamilton deftly caught him by the ankle and his great form sprawled on the grass. He arose in wrath.

"You are no older than one of your own young ones!" he began; then recovered, and resumed his seat. "This is the latest story I have heard of you," he continued: "Some man from New England came here recently with a letter to you. When he returned to his rural home he was asked if he had seen the great man. 'I don't know about the *great*' he replied; 'but he was as playful as a kitten.'"

Hamilton laughed heartily. "Well, let me frolic while I may," he said. "I shall die by Burr's hand, no doubt of that. Whether he kills me for revenge or money, that is my destiny, and I have known it for years. And it does not matter in the least, my dear Bob. I have not three years of life left in me."

IX

Burr was defeated by a majority of seven thousand votes; and New England, which had hoped, with the help of a man who was at war with all the powerful families of New York,—Schuylers, Livingstons, and Clintons at the head of them,—to break down the oligarchy of which it had been jealous for nearly a century, deserted the politician promptly. Incidentally, Hamilton had quenched its best hope of secession, for the elected Governor of New York, Judge Lewis, was a member of the Livingston family. Burr was in a desperate plight. Debtor's prison and disgrace yawned before him; his only followers left were a handful of disappointed politicians, and these deserted him daily. But although his hatred of Hamilton, by now, was a foaming beast within him, he was wary and coolheaded, and history knows no better than he did that if he killed the man who was still the most brilliant figure in America, as well as the idol of the best men in it, cunning, and skill, and mastery of every political art would avail him nothing in the future; every avenue but that frequented by the avowed adventurer would be closed to him. Moreover, he must have known that Hamilton's life was almost over, that in a very few years he could intrigue undisturbed. Nor could he have felt a keen interest in presenting to Jefferson so welcome a gift as his own political corpse. But desperate for money, crushed to the earth, his hatred for Hamilton cursing and raging afresh, the only conspicuous enemy who might be bought with gold of the man who was still a bristling rampart in the path of successful Jacobinism, he was in a situation to fall an easy victim to greater plotters than himself. His act, did he challenge Hamilton, would be ascribed to revenge, and the towering figures in the background of the tragedy would pass unnoticed by the horrified spectators in front.

On June 18th William Van Ness, Burr's intimate friend, waited upon Hamilton with a studiously impertinent note, demanding an acknowledgment or denial of the essence of certain newspaper paragraphs, which stated that the leader of the Federalists had, upon various occasions, expressed his low opinion of the New York politician, and in no measured terms. Hamilton replied, pointing out the impossibility of either acknowledging or denying an accusation so vague, and analyzed at length the weakness of Burr's position in endeavouring to pick a quarrel out of such raw material. He said, in conclusion:—

I stand ready to avow or disavow promptly and explicitly any precise or definite opinion which I may be charged with having declared of any gentleman. More than this cannot fitly be expected from me; and especially, it cannot reasonably be expected that I shall enter into an explanation upon a basis so vague as that which you have adopted. I trust on more reflection you will see the matter in the same light with me. If not I can only regret the circumstance and must abide the consequences.

Hamilton foresaw the inevitable end, and commenced putting his affairs in order at once; but, for both personal and abstract reasons, holding the practice of duelling in abhorrence, he was determined to give Burr any chance to retreat, consistent with his own self-respect. Burr replied in a manner both venomous and insulting, and Hamilton called upon Colonel Pendleton, General Greene's aide during the Revolution, and asked him to act as his second. On the 23d he received a note from Van Ness, inquiring when and where it would be most convenient for him to receive a communication, and the correspondence thereafter was conducted by the seconds.

It was Sunday, and Hamilton was at The Grange, when the note from Van Ness arrived. He was swinging in a hammock, and he put the missive in his pocket, shrugged his shoulders, and lifted himself on his elbow. His entire family, with the exception of his wife and Angelica, were shouting in the woods. The baby, a sturdy youngster of two, named for the brother who had died shortly before his birth, emerged in a state of fury. He had eighty-two years of vitality in him, and he roared like a young bull. Hamilton's children inherited the tough fibre and the longevity of the Schuylers. Of the seven who survived him all lived to old age, and several were close to being centenarians.

Angelica was busy in her aviary, close by. She was now twenty, and one of the most beautiful girls in the country, but successive deaths had kept her in seclusion; and the world in which her parents were such familiar figures was to remember nothing of her but her tragedy. Betsey, still as slim as her daughter, ran from the house at the familiar roar, and Gouverneur Morris came dashing through the woods with a half-dozen guests, self-invited for dinner. It was an animated day, and Hamilton was the life of the company. He had no time for thought until night. His wife retired early, with a headache; the boys had subsided even earlier. At ten o'clock Angelica went to the piano, and Hamilton threw himself into a long chair on the terrace and clasped his hands behind his head.

"So," he thought, "the end has come. My work is over, I suppose. Personally, I am of no account. All I would have demanded, by way of reward for services faithfully executed, was the health to make a decent living and ten or fifteen years of peaceful and uninterrupted intimacy with my family. For fame, or public honours, or brilliant successes of any sort, I have ceased to care. Nothing would tempt me to touch the reins of public life again unless in the event of a revolution. I believe I have crushed that possibility with this election; otherwise, I doubt if my knell would have sounded. On the bare possibility that such is not the case, and that my usefulness may not be neutralized by public doubt of my courage, I must accept this challenge, whether or not I have sufficient moral courage to refuse it. I believe I have; but that is neither here nor there, and I shall fall. Should I survive, the sole reason would be danger ahead. For the last two years I have felt myself moving steadily deathward. By this abrupt exit I but anticipate the inevitable a year or two, and doubtless it seems to the destiny that controls my affairs as the swiftest way to dispose of Burr, and awaken the country to the other dangers that menace it. To the last I am but a tool. No man was ever so little his own master, so thrust upon a planet for the accomplishment of public and impersonal ends alone. I have been permitted a certain amount of domestic felicity as my strength was best conserved thereby, my mind free to concentrate upon public duties. I was endowed with the gift of fascination, that men should follow me without question, and this country be served with immediate effectiveness, I have received deep and profound satisfaction from both these concessions, but it would not matter in the least if I had not. They were inevitable with the equipment for the part I had to play. I have had an astonishing and conquering career against the mightiest obstacles, and I may as a further concession, be permitted an enduring place in history; but that, also, is by the way. I conquered, not to gratify my love of power and to win immortal fame, but that I might accomplish the part for which I was whirled here from an almost inaccessible island fifteen hundred miles away—to play my part in the creation of this American empire. It has been a great part, creatively the greatest part. The proof that no native-born American could have played it lies in the fact that he did not. The greatest of her men have abetted me; not one has sought to push me aside and do my work. My only enemies have been those who would pull my structure down; the most ambitious and individual men in the Union, of the higher sort, are my willing followers. To win them I never plotted, nor did I ever seek to dazzle and blind them. Part of my equipment was the power to convince them without effort of my superior usefulness; there was no time to lose. I am nothing but a genius, encased in such human form as would best serve its purpose; an atom of the vast creative Being beyond the Universe, loaned for an infinitesimal part of time to the excrescence calling itself The United States of North America, on the dot called Earth. Now the part is played, and I am to be withdrawn. That my human heart is torn with insupportable anguish, matters not at all. I leave that behind."

Hamilton had been bred in the orthodox religion of his time, and its picturesqueness, including its ultimates of heaven and hell, had taken firm hold of his ardent imagination. But in his cosmic moments the formulations of this planet played no part.

"I have not even a mother-country," he thought. "I am a parent, not a child. My patriotism has been that of a tigress for her young, not of a man for his fatherland. God knows I am willing, and always have been, to die for this country, which is so much my own, but why—why—need I have been made so human? Could I not have understood men as well? Could I not have performed my various part without loving my wife and children, my friends, with the deepest tenderness and passion of which the human heart is capable? Then I would go without a pang, for I am tired, and death would be a relief. But, since all humanity was forced into me, why should not I, now that I have faithfully done my part, be permitted a few years of happiness by my hearthstone?"

He raised his hands as if to shut out the cold high stars. He had had few bitter moments since the night, four years before, when he had deliberately exorcised bitterness and hate; and that mellowness had come to him which came to his great rivals in their old age. But to-night he let the deeps rise. He ached with human wants, and he was bidden to work out his last act of service to the country for whose sole use he had been sent to Earth.

He dropped his hands and stared at the worlds above. "Must I go on?" he thought. "Is that it? Does other work await me elsewhere? Has the Almighty detached from himself a few creative egos, who go from world to world and do their part; removed the day their usefulness is over, that they shall not dissipate their energy, nor live until men regard with slighting wonder the work of the useless old creature in their midst, withdraw from it their first reverence? I go in the fulness of my maturity and the high tide of respect and affection; I go in the dramatic manner of my advent, and my work will be a sacred thing;—even my enemies will not dare to pull it down until such time as they are calm enough to see it as it is; and then the desire will have passed. Doubtless all things are best and right.... Maturity? I feel as old as time and as young as laughter."

He sat up suddenly and bent his head. Millions of tiny bells were ringing through the forest. So low, so golden, so remote they sounded, that they might have hung in the stars above or in the deeps of the earth. He listened so intently for a moment that life seemed suspended, and he saw neither the cool dark forest nor the silver ripple of the Hudson, but a torn and desolate land, and a gravestone at his feet. Then he passed his hand over his forehead with a long breath, and went softly into the drawing-room.

Angelica sat at the piano, with her head thrown back, her long fair hair hanging to the floor. Her dark eyes were blank, but her fingers shook from the keys the music of a Tropic night. It was a music that Hamilton had not sent a thought after since the day he landed in America, thirty-one years ago. It had come to her, with other memories, by direct inheritance.

He went to the dining room hastily and poured out a glass of wine. When he returned, Angelica, as he expected, was half lying in a chair, white and limp.

"Drink this," he said, in the bright peremptory manner to which his children were accustomed. "I think you are not strong enough yet to indulge in composition. You have grown too fast, and creation needs a great deal of physical vigour. Now run to bed, and forget that you can play a note."

Angelica sipped the wine obediently, and bade him good night. As she toiled up the stairs she prayed for the physical strength that would permit her to become the great musician of her ambitious dreams. Her prayer was answered; the great strength came to her, and her music was the wonder of those who listened; but they were very few.

Hamilton went into his library, prepared to write until morning. Bitterness and cosmic curiosity had vanished; he was the practical man, with a mass of affairs to arrange during the few days that were left to him. But he did no work that night. The door-knocker pounded loudly. The servants had gone to bed. He took a lamp, and unchained and unlocked the front door, wondering what the summons meant, for visitors in that lonely spot were rare after nightfall. A woman stood in the heavy shade of the porch, and behind her was a carriage. She wore a long thin pelisse; and the hood was drawn over her face. Nevertheless, she hesitated but a moment. She lifted her head with a motion of haughty defiance that Hamilton well remembered, and stepped forward.

"It is I, Hamilton," she said. "I have come to have a few words with you alone, and I shall not leave until—"

"Come in, by all means," said Hamilton, politely. "You were imprudent to choose such a dark night, for the roads are dangerous. When you return I will send a servant ahead of you with a lantern."

He led the way to the library and closed the door behind them. Madame Jumel threw off her cloak, and stood before him in the magnificence of cloth of gold and many diamonds. Her neck blazed, and the glittering tower of her hair was a jewel garden. She was one of the women for whom splendour of attire was conceived, and had always looked her best when in full regalia. To-night she was the most superb creature that man had ever seen or dreamed of. Even her great eyes looked like jewels, deep and burning as that blue jewel of the West Indies, the Caribbean Sea; but her lips and cheeks were like soft pink roses. Hamilton had seen her many times since the day of parting, for she went constantly to the theatre, and had been invited to the larger receptions until her reckless Jacobinism had put the final touch to the disapproval of Federal dames; but he had never seen her in such beauty as she was to-night. Eleven years had perfected this beauty, taken from it nothing. He sighed, and the past rose for a moment; but it seemed a century behind him.

"Will you not sit down?" he asked. "Can I fetch you a glass of wine? I remember you never liked it, but perhaps, after so long a drive—"

"I do not wish any wine," said Madame Jumel, shortly. She was nonplussed by this matter-of-fact acceptance of a situation which she had intended should be intensely dramatic. She was not yet gone, however.

"No one ever could get the best of you, Hamilton," she exclaimed. "I have come here to-night—how terribly delicate you look," she faltered, with a sudden pallor. "I have not seen you for so long—"

"My health does not give me the least concern," said Hamilton, hurriedly, wondering if he could lay his hand on a bottle of smelling-salts without awaking his wife. "Pray go on. To what am I indebted for the honour of this visit?"

Madame Jumel rose and swept up and down the long room twice. "Can there be anything in that tale of royal blood?" thought Hamilton. "Or in that other tale of equally distinguished parentage?"

She had paused with her back to him, facing one of the bookcases.

"Classics, classics, classics!" she exclaimed, in a voice which grew steadier as she proceeded. "That was the only taste we did not share. Don Quixote in Spanish, Dante and Alfieri in Italian; and all the German brutes. Ah! Voltaire! Rousseau! What superb editions! No one can bind but the French. And the dear old *Moniteur*—all bound for posterity, which will never look at it."

She returned and stood before him, and she was quite composed.

"I came to tell you," she said, "that when you die, it will be by the hand of my deputy. I tell you because I am determined that your last earthly thought shall be of me."

"*Cherchez la femme—toujours!* Why are you doing this?" he asked curiously. "You no longer love me, and your hate should have worn out long since."

"Neither my hate nor my love has ceased for a second. I married Jumel for these jewels, for the courts of Europe, for a position in this country which the mighty Schuylers cannot take from me again. But I would fly with you to-morrow, and live with you in a hole under ground. I came to make no such proposal, however; I know that you would

447

sacrifice even your family to your honour, and everything else in life to them. For years I waited, hoping that you would suddenly come back to me, hating you and injuring you in every way my Jacobinism could devise, but ready to wipe your shoes with my hair the moment you appeared. Now the hard work of your life is over. You look forward to years of happiness with your family on this beautiful estate, while I am married to a silly old Frenchman—who, however, has brought me my final means of revenge. I know you well. You would rather be alive now than at any time of your life. Well, you shall go. And I would pray, if that were my habit, that into these last days you may condense all the agonies of parting from those you love that I have ached and raged through in these eleven long years."

"God knows I have bitterly regretted that you should suffer for my passions. And, if it is any satisfaction to you, I go unwillingly, and the parting will be very bitter."

She drew a sharp breath, and flung her head about. "One cannot triumph over you!" she cried. "Why was I such a fool as to come here to-night? My imagination would have served me better."

"Is it French money?" asked Hamilton.

"Yes, but I alone am responsible. We handle immense sums, and its disposal is left to our discretion. This will be distasteful neither to France nor Virginia,—I suppose I may have Louisiana, if I want it!—but I am no man's agent in this matter."

"You are magnificent! It is quite like you to disdain to share your terrible responsibility. I can lighten it a little. I shall not shoot Burr."

"I should rather you did. Still, it does not matter. He will be disposed of, and I shall lead the hue and cry."

"You are young to be so brutal. Will your conscience never torment you?"

"I have too much brain to submit to conscience, and you know it. I shall suffer the torments of the damned, but not from conscience. But I would rather suffer with you out of the world than in it. I have stood that as long as a mere mortal can stand anything. Revenge is not my only motive. Either you or I must go, and as I have now found the means of boundless distraction, I live. I have been on the point of killing myself and you more than once. But my power to injure you gave me an exquisite satisfaction; and then, I always hoped. Now the time for the

448

period has come." Her chin sank to her neck, and she stared at him until her eyes filled. "Do you love them so much more than you ever loved me?" she asked wistfully.

Hamilton turned away his head. "Yes," he said.

She drew a long shivering breath. "Ah!" she said. "You are a frail shadow of yourself. You have no passion in you. And yet, even as you are, I would fling these jewels into the river, and live with you until you died in my arms. You may think me a monster, if you like, but you shall die knowing that your wife does not love you as I do."

Hamilton leaned forward and dried her tears. "Say that you forgive me," she said; for audacity was ever a part of genius.

"Yes," he said grimly, "I forgive you. You and Bonaparte are the two magnificent products of the French Revolution. I am sorry you are not more of a philosopher, but, so far as I alone am concerned, I regret nothing."

"Oh, men!" she exclaimed, with scorn. "They are always philosophers when they are no longer in love with a woman. But you will give me your last conscious moment?"

"No," he said deliberately, "I shall not."

She sprang to her feet. "You will! Thank you for saying that, though! I was about to grovel at your feet. Take me to my coach! What a fool I was to come here!" She seized her pelisse, and wound it about her as she ran down the hall. Hamilton followed, insisting that she give him time to awaken a servant. But she would not heed. She flung herself into her coach, and called to the driver to gallop his horses, unless he wished to lose his place on the morrow. Hamilton stood on the porch, listening to the wild flight down the rough hill through the forest But it was unbroken, so long as he could hear anything, and he laughed suddenly and entered the house.

"The high farce of tragedy," he thought. "Probably a mosquito will settle on Burr's nose as he fires, and my life be spared."

X

The challenge was delivered on Wednesday. Hamilton refused to withdraw his services from his clients in the midst of the Circuit Court, and July 11th, a fortnight later, was appointed for the meeting. When Hamilton was not busy with the important interests confided to him by his clients, he arranged his own affairs, and drew up a document for publication, in the event of his death, in which he stated that he had criticised Burr freely for years, but added that he bore him no ill-will, that his opposition had been for public reasons only, that his impressions of Burr were entertained with sincerity, and had been uttered with motives and for purposes which appeared to himself commendable. He announced his intention to throw away his fire, and gave this reason for yielding to a custom which he had held in avowed abhorrence: "The ability to be in future useful, whether in resisting mischief or effecting good, in those crises of our public affairs which seem likely to happen, would probably be inseparable from a conformity with public prejudice in this particular."

Burr spent several hours of each day in pistol practice, using the cherry trees of Richmond Hill as targets. Thurlow Weed, in his "Autobiography," has told of Burr's testament, written on the night before the duel. Having neither money nor lands, but an infinitude of debts, to bequeath his daughter, he left her a bundle of compromising letters from women. The writers moved in circles where virtue was held in esteem, and several were of the world of fashion. They had, with the instinct of self-defence, which animates women even in that stage where they idealize the man, omitted to sign their names. Burr supplied the omission in every case and added the present address. That Hamilton would throw away his fire was a possibility remote from the best effort of Burr's imagination, and although he knew that no one could fire more quickly than himself, he was not the man to go to the ground unprepared for emergencies: if his daughter, now Mrs. Alston, would obey his hint and blackmail, she might realize a pretty fortune. That Theodosia Burr, even with the incentive of poverty, would have sunk to such ignominy, no one who knows the open history of her short life will believe; but the father, whose idol she was, insulted her and stained her memory, too depraved and warped to understand nobility in anyone, least of all in one of his own blood. In the study of lost souls Burr has appealed to many analysts, and by no one has been made so attractive as by Harriet Beecher Stowe; who, knowing naught by experience of men of the world, either idealized them as interesting villains or transformed them into beasts. In Burr she saw the fallen angel, and bedewed him with many Christian tears. But I doubt if Burr, the inner and real Burr, had far to fall. His visible divergence from first conditions was as striking as, no doubt, it was natural. As the grandson of Jonathan Edwards, the son of the Reverend Aaron Burr, and reared by relatives of that same morbid, hideous, unhuman school of early New England theology, it only needed a wayward nature in addition to brain and spirit to send him flying on his own tangent as soon as he was old enough to think. After that his congenital selfishness did the rest. For a time he climbed the hill of prizes very steadily, taking, once in a way, a flight, swift as an arrow: in addition to great ability at the bar, and a cunning which rose to the dignity of a talent, he was handsome, magnetic, well-bred, and polished, studied women with the precision of a vivisectionist, assumed emotions and impulses he could not feel with such dexterity that even men yielded to his fascination until they plumbed him; had in fact many of the fleeting kindly instincts to which every mortal is subject who is made of flesh and blood, or comes of a stock that has been bred to certain ideals. Every wretch has a modicum of good in him, and in spite of the preponderance of evil in Burr, had he been born under kindly Southern skies with a gold spoon in his mouth, if, when ambitions developed, he had had but to stretch out his hand to pluck the prizes of life, instead of exercising the basest talents of his brain to overreach more fortunate men, why it is possible that his nature might not have hardened into a glacier: its visible third dazzling and symmetrical, its deadly bulk skulking below the surface of the waters which divided the two parts of him from his victims; might have died in the chaste reclusion of an ancestral four-poster, beneficiaries at his side. But that immalleable mind lacked the strong fibre of logic and foresight—which is all that moral force amounts to—that lifts a man triumphant above his worst temptations; and he paid the bitter and hideous penalty in a poverty, loneliness, and living death that would have moved the theologians of his blood to the uneasy suspicion that punishment is of this earth, a logical sequence of foolish and short-sighted acts. Both men and women are allowed a great latitude in this world; they have little to complain of. It is only when the brain fails in its part, or the character is gradually undermined by lying and dishonour, that the inevitable sequence is some act which arouses the indignation of society or jerks down the iron fist of the law. When Burr took to the slope he slid with few haltings. In his long life of plottings and failures, from his sympathy with the Conway Cabal to his desperate old age, there were no depths of blackguardism that he did not touch. Whether Madame Jumel spoke the truth or not to Hamilton on that night of their last interview, it was entirely in keeping with his life and character that he should kill for hire.

On the Fourth of July, the Society of the Cincinnati gave its annual dinner. This society, then the most distinguished in the Union, and membered by men who had fought in the War of Independence, had, upon the death of Washington, their first President, elected Hamilton to the vacant office. He presided at this banquet, and never had appeared nor felt happier. Not only did that peculiar exaltation which precedes certain death possess him, as it possesses all men of mettle and brain in a like condition, but the philosophy which had been born in him and ruled his imagination through life had shrugged its shoulders and accepted the inevitable. Hamilton knew that his death warrant had been signed above, and he no longer experienced a regret, although he had often felt depressed and martyred when obliged to go to the courts of Albany and leave his family behind him. He had lost interest in his body; his spirit, ever, by far, the strongest and the dominant part of him, seemed already struggling for its freedom, arrogant and blithe as it approached its final triumph. There is nothing in all life so selfish as death; and the colossal ego which genius breeds or is bred out of, isolated Hamilton even more completely than imminent death isolates most men. The while he gave every moment he could spare to planning the future comfort and welfare of his family, he felt as if he had already bade them farewell, and wondered when and how he should meet them again.

At this gathering he was so gay and sportive that he infected the great company, and it was the most hilarious banquet in the society's history. The old warriors sighed, and wondered at his eternal youth. When he sprang upon the table and sang his old camp-song, "The Drum," he looked the boy they remembered at Valley Forge and Morristown. There was only one member of the company who was unelectrified by the gay abandon of the evening, and his sombre appearance was so marked in contrast that it was widely commented on afterward. Burr frequently leaned forward and stared at Hamilton in amazement. As the hilarity waxed, his taciturnity deepened, and he finally withdrew.

The secret was well kept. Few knew of the projected meeting, and none suspected it, although Burr's pistol practice aroused some curiosity. He had been a principal in a number of duels, and killed no one. But he was known to have more than one bitter score to pay, for this last campaign had exceeded every other in heat and fury. So many duels had studded it, and so many more impended, that the thinking men of the community were roused to a deep disapproval of the custom. The excitement and horror over the sacrifice of Hamilton, full-blew this sentiment.

On Saturday, Hamilton gave a dinner at the Grange, and a guest was one of Washington's first aides, Colonel Trumbull. As he was leaving, Hamilton took him aside and said, with an emphasis which impressed Trumbull even at the moment: "You are going to Boston. You will see the principal men there. Tell them from me, as my request, for God's sake to cease these conversations and threatings about a separation of the Union. It must hang together as long as it can be made to. If this Union were to be broken, it would break my heart."

The following day preceded the duel. Hamilton attended an entertainment given by Oliver Wolcott, whose fortunes he had made, raising the capital of a business that could be presided over by no one so well as a former Secretary of the Treasury. It was a large reception, and he met many of his old friends. Lady Kitty Duer, widowed, but pleasantly circumstanced, was there, and Kitty Livingston, once more bearing her old name in a second marriage. Bitter as the feeling between her house and Hamilton still was, she had declared long since that she would not cut him again; and although they never met in private, they often retired to a secluded corner at gatherings and talked for an hour. His first reason for attending this reception was to shake her hand as they parted. Madame Jumel was there, paling the loveliness of even the young daughters of Mrs. Jay and Lady Kitty Duer. Those who did not mob about Hamilton surrounded her, and although her cheek was without colour, she looked serene and scornful.

After the reception Hamilton spent an hour with Troup. This oldest of his friends, and Angelica, were the only people whose suspicion he feared. Troup was quite capable of wringing Burr's neck, and his daughter of taking some other desperate measure. But it was long now since he had given Angelica reason for anxiety, and she had ceased to watch him; and to-day, Troup, whom he had avoided hitherto, was treated to such a flow of spirits that he not only suspected nothing, but allowed himself to hope that Hamilton's health was mending. Hamilton dared not even hold his hand longer than usual at parting, although he longed to embrace him.

That night, in the late seclusion of his library, Hamilton wrote two letters to his wife, in one of which he recommended Mrs. Mitchell to her care; then the following to Sedgwick, still a close friend, and probably the most influential man in New England:—

NEW YORK, July 10th, 1804.

MY DEAR SIR: I have received two letters from you since we last saw each other—that of the latest date being the twenty-fourth of May. I have had on hand for some time a long letter to you, explaining my view of the course and tendency of our politics, and my intentions as to my own future conduct. But my plan embraced so large a range, that, owing to much avocation, some indifferent health, and a growing distaste for politics, the letter is still considerably short of being finished. I write this now to satisfy you that want of regard for you has not been the cause of my silence.

I will here express but one sentiment, which is, that DISMEMBERMENT of our EMPIRE will be a clear sacrifice of great positive advantages, without any counterbalancing good; administering no relief to our real disease, which is DEMOCRACY; the poison of which, by a subdivision, will only be the more concentrated in each part, and consequently the more virulent. King is on his way to Boston where you may chance to see him and hear from himself his sentiments. God bless you.

A.H.

As he folded and sealed the letter he suddenly realized that the act was the final touch to the order of his earthly affairs, and he lifted his hand as though to see if it were still alive. "To-morrow night!" he thought. "Well, now that the hour has come, I go willingly enough. I have been permitted to live my life; why should I murmur? There has been sufficient crowded into my forty-seven years to cover a century. I have been permitted to play a great part in history, to patch together a nation out of broken limbs and inform it with a brain. It is right that I should regard myself in this final hour as a statesman and nothing more, and that I should go without protest, now that I have no more to do. I can only be deeply and profoundly thankful that out of three millions of Americans I was selected, that I have conquered in spite of all obstacles, and remained until I have nothing more to give. It is entirely right and fitting that I should die as I have lived, in the service of this country. Only a sacrifice can bring these distracted States to reason and eliminate the man most dangerous to their peace. If I have been chosen for this great part, I should be unworthy indeed if I rebelled."

XI

Hamilton crossed the river to Weehawken at seven the next morning. He was accompanied by Pendleton, and his surgeon, Dr. Hosack. It was already very hot. The river and the woods of the Jersey palisades were dim under a sultry blue haze. There was a swell on the river, and Pendleton was very sick. Hamilton held his head with some humour, then pointed out the great beauty of the Hudson and its high rugged banks, to distract the unhappy second's mind.

"The majesty of this river," he said, "its suggestion of a vast wild country almost unknown to the older civilizations, and yet peopled with the unembodied spirits of a new and mighty race, quicked my unborn patriotism, unconsciously nourished it until its delivery in Boston."

"It would have curdled mine," said Pendleton. "Who knows—if you had been of a bilious temperament, the face of our history might wear a pug nose and a weak chin."

Hamilton laughed. "It never could have done that while Washington's profile was stamped on the popular fancy. But lesser causes than seasickness have determined a man's career. Perhaps to my immunity I owe the fact that I am not a book-worm on St. Croix. If I had even once felt as you did just now, my dear Pendleton, I should never have set sail for America."

"Thank God!" said Pendleton. They were beaching. A moment later he and Hamilton had climbed to the ledge where Burr and Van Ness awaited them. It was the core of a thick grove, secluded from the opposite shore and from the high summit of the great palisade.

455

Hamilton and Burr nodded pleasantly. The men were dressed in the silken finery of their time, and looked like a pleasuring quartette in that green and lovely spot. Through leafy windows they saw the blue Hudson, the spires and manor-houses, the young city, on the Island. The image of Philip rose to Hamilton, but he commanded it aside.

Pendleton had the choice of position and was to give the word. He had brought with him John Church's pistols, now in their fourth duel. Their first adventure caused the flight of Church to America. Since then, they had been used in his duel with Burr and by Philip Hamilton.

He handed one of the pistols to Hamilton, and asked him if he should set the hair-spring.

"No, not this time," said Hamilton.

Pendleton gave the word. Burr raised his arm, deliberately took aim, and fired, Hamilton lifted himself mechanically to the tips of his feet, turned sideways, and fell on his face. His pistol went off, and Pendleton's eye involuntarily followed the direction of the ball, which severed a leaf in its flight. Often afterward he spoke of the impression the cloven leaf made on him, a second of distraction at which he caught eagerly before he bent over Hamilton. Hosack scrambled up the bank, and Burr, covered with an umbrella by Van Ness, hastily withdrew.

Hamilton was half sitting, encircled by Pendleton's arm, when the surgeon reached the spot. His face was gray. He muttered, "This is a mortal wound," then lost consciousness. Hosack ascertained, after a slight examination, that the ball was in a vital part, and for a few moments he thought that Hamilton was dead; he did not breathe, nor was any motion of heart or pulse perceptible. With Pendleton's assistance, Hosack carried him down the bank and placed him in the barge. William Bayard had offered his house in case of disaster, and the boat was propelled over to the foot of Grand Street as rapidly as possible. Before reaching the shore the surgeon succeeded in reviving Hamilton, who suddenly opened his eyes.

"My vision is indistinct," he said. In a moment it grew stronger, and his eye fell on the case of pistols. His own was lying on the top. "Take care of that pistol," he said. "It is undischarged and still cocked. Pendleton knows that I did not intend to fire at him." He closed his eyes, and said nothing further except to enquire the state of his pulse, and to remark that his lower extremities had lost all feeling. As the boat reached the pier, he directed that his wife and children be sent for at once, and that hope be given them. Bayard was standing on the shore in a state of violent agitation. It was in these pleasant grounds of his that the great banquet had been given to Hamilton after the Federalists had celebrated their leader's victory at Poughkeepsie, and he had been his friend and supporter during the sixteen years that had followed.

Hamilton was placed in bed on the lower floor of Bayard's house; and, in spite of the laudanum that was liberally administered, his sufferings were almost intolerable. His children were not admitted to the room for some time, but his wife could not be kept from him. She knew nothing of the duel, but she saw that he was dying; and the suddenness and horror, the end of her earthly happiness, drove her frantic. She shrieked and raved until Hamilton was obliged to rouse himself and attempt to calm her. The children were huddled in the next room, and when the pain subsided for a time, they were brought in. Hamilton's eyes were closed. When he was told that his children were beside his bed, he did not open them at once. In those moments he forgot everything but the agony of parting. Finally, he lifted his heavy eyelids. The children stood there, the younger clinging to the older, shivering and staring in terror. Hamilton gave them one look, then closed his eyes and did not open them again for several moments. As the children were led from the room, one of the boys fainted.

Through Hamilton's heavy brain an idea forced itself, and finally took possession. Angelica had not stood in that little group. He opened his eyes, half expecting that which he saw—Angelica leaning over the foot-board, her face gray and shrunken, her eyes full of astonishment and horror.

"Are you going to die—to die?" she asked him.

"Yes," said Hamilton. He was too exhausted to console or counsel submission.

"To die!" she repeated. "To die!" She reiterated the words until her voice died away in a mumble. Hamilton was insensible for the moment to the physical torments which were sending out their criers again, and watched her changed face with an apprehension, which, mercifully, his mind was too confused by pain and laudanum to formulate. Angelica suddenly gripped the foot-board with such force that the bed shook; her eyes expanded with horror only, and she cowered as if a whip cracked above her neck. Then she straightened herself, laughed aloud, and ran out of the room. Hamilton, at the moment, was in the throes of an excruciating spasm, and was spared this final agony in his harsh and untimely death. Angelica was hurried from the house to a private asylum. She lived to be seventy-eight, but she never recovered her reason.

Meanwhile, the grounds without were crowded with the friends of the dying man,—many of them old soldiers,—who stood through the night awaiting the end. Business in New York was entirely suspended. The populace had arisen in fury at the first announcement on the bulletin boards, and Burr was in hiding lest he be torn to pieces.

Hamilton slept little, and talked to his wife whenever he succeeded in calming her. Her mental sufferings nearly deprived her of health and reason; but she lived a half a century longer, attaining the great age of ninety-seven. It was a sheltered and placid old age, warm with much devotion; her mind remained firm until the end. Did the time come when she thought of Hamilton as one of the buried children of her youth?

Troup, Fish, Wolcott, Gouverneur Morris, Rufus King, Bayard, Matthew Clarkson, some twenty of Hamilton's old friends, were admitted to the death room for a moment. He could not speak, but he smiled faintly. Then his eyes wandered to the space behind them. He fancied he saw the shadowy forms of the many friends who had preceded him: Laurens, Tilghman, Harrison, Greene, André, Sterling, Duane, Duer, Steuben,—Washington. They looked at him as affectionately as the living, but without tears or the rigid features of extremest grief. It is a terrible expression to see on the faces of men long intimate with life, and Hamilton closed his eyes, withdrawing his last glance from Morris and Troup.

Of whom did Hamilton think in those final moments? Not of Eliza Croix, we may be sure. Her hold had been too superficial. Perhaps not even of Elizabeth Schuyler, although he had loved her long and deeply. What more probable than that his last hour was filled with a profound consciousness of the isolation in which his soul had passed its mortal tarrying? Surrounded, worshipped, counting more intimate friends sincerely loved than any man of his time, gay, convivial, too active for many hours of introspection, no mortal could ever have stood more utterly alone than Hamilton. Whether or not the soul is given a sentient immortality we have no means of discovering, but the most commonplace being is aware of that ego which has its separate existence in his brain, and is like to no other ego on earth; and those who think realize its inability to mingle with another. Hamilton, with his unmortal gifts, his unsounded depths, must have felt this isolation in all its tragic completeness. There may have been moments when the soul of Washington or Laurens brushed his own. Assuredly no woman companioned it for a fraction of a second. Whatever his last thoughts, no man has met his end with more composure.

He died at two o'clock in the afternoon.

XII

The humour and vivacity which had seldom been absent from Hamilton's face in life withdrew its very impress with his spirit. His features had something more than the noble repose, the baffling peace, of death; they looked as if they had been cast long ago with the heads of the Caesars. Gouverneur Morris, staring at him through blistered eyeballs as he lay in his coffin, recalled the history of the House of Hamilton, of its direct and unbroken descent—through the fortunate, and famed, and crowned of the centuries—from the Great Constantine, from "The Macedonian," founder of a dynasty of Roman Emperors, and from the first of the Russian monarchs. Throughout that history great spirits had appeared from time to time, hewed the foundations of an epoch, and disappeared. What long-withdrawn creators had met in this exceptionally begotten brain? Did those great makers of empire, whose very granite tombs were dust, return to earth when their immortal energies were invoked to create a soul for a nation in embryo? Morris reviewed the dead man's almost unhuman gift for inspiring confidence, exerted from the moment he first showed his boyish face to the multitude; for triumphing to his many goals as if jagged ramparts had been grass under his feet. He had been the brain of the American army in his boyhood; he had conceived an empire in his young twenties; he had poured his genius into a sickly infant, and set it, a young giant, on its legs, when he was long under twoscore. Almost all things had come to him by intuition, for he had lived in advance of much knowledge.

He communicated these thoughts to Troup, who left the room with

459

him, his head bent, his arms hanging listlessly. "He might have come in some less human form," added Morris, bitterly. "This is the worst time of *my* life. I am not ashamed to say I've cried my eyes out."

"I have cried my heart out," said Troup.

The funeral took place from the house of John Church, in Robinson Street, near the upper Park. Express messengers had dashed out from New York the moment Hamilton breathed his last, and every city tolled its bells as it received the news. People flocked into the streets, weeping and indignant to the point of fury. Washington's death had been followed by sadness and grief, but was unaccompanied by anger, and a loud desire for vengeance. Moreover, Hamilton was still a young man. Few knew of his feeble health; and that dauntless resourceful figure dwelt in the high light of the public imagination, ever ready to deliver the young country in its many times of peril. His death was lamented as a national calamity.

On the day of the funeral, New York was black. Every place of business was closed. The world was in the windows, on the housetops, on the pavements of the streets through which the cortège was to pass: Robinson, Beekman, Peal, and Broadway to Trinity Church. Those who were to walk in the funeral procession waited, the Sixth Regiment, with the colours and music of the several corps, paraded, in Robinson Street, until the standard of the Cincinnati, shrouded in crêpe, was waved before the open door of Mr. Church's house. The regiment immediately halted and rested on its reversed arms, until the bier had been carried from the house to the centre of the street, when the procession immediately formed. This was the order of it:—

> The Military Corps
> The Society of the Cincinnati
> Clergy of all Denominations
> The Body of Hamilton
> The General's Horse
> The Family
> Physicians
> The Judges of the Supreme Court (in deep mourning)
> Mr. Gouverneur Morris in his carriage
> Gentlemen of the Bar and students at law (in deep mourning)
> Governor and Lieutenant-Governor of the State

Mayor and Corporation of the City

Members of Congress and Civil Officers of the United States

The Minister, Consuls, and Residents of Foreign Powers

The Officers of the Army and Navy of the United States

Military and Naval Officers of the Foreign Powers

Militia Officers of States

Presidents, Directors, and Officers of the respective Banks

Chamber of Commerce and Merchants

Marine Society, Wardens of the Port, and Masters and Officers
of the Harbour

The President, Professors, and students of Columbia College

The different Societies

The Citizens in general, including the partisans of Burr

On the coffin were Hamilton's hat and sword. His boots and spurs were reversed across his horse. The fine gray charger, caparisoned in mourning, was led by two black servants, dressed in white, their turbans trimmed with black.

The military escorted him in single file, with trailing arms, the band playing "The Dead March in Saul," minute guns from the Artillery in the Park answered by the British and French warships in the harbour. But for the solemn music, its still more solemn accompaniment, the tolling of muffled bells, and the heavy tramp of many feet, there was no sound; even women of an hysterical habit either controlled themselves or were too impressed to give way to superficial emotion. When the procession after its long march reached Trinity Church the military formed in two columns, extending from the gate to the corners of Wall Street, and the bier was deposited before the entrance. Morris, surrounded by Hamilton's boys, stood over it, and delivered the most impassioned address which had ever leapt from that brilliant but erratic mind. It was brief, both because he hardly was able to control himself, and because he feared to incite the people to violence, but it was profoundly moving. "He never lost sight of your interests!" he reiterated; "I declare to you before that God in whose presence we are now so especially assembled, that in his most private and confidential conversations, his sole subject of discussion was your freedom and happiness. Although he was compelled to abandon public life, never for a moment did he abandon the public service. He never lost sight of your

461

interests. For himself he feared nothing; but he feared that bad men might, by false professions, acquire your confidence and abuse it to your ruin. He was ambitious only of glory, but he was deeply solicitous for you."

The troops formed an extensive hollow square in the churchyard, and terminated the solemnities with three volleys over the coffin in its grave. The immense throng, white, still aghast, and unreconciled, dispersed. The bells tolled until sundown. The city and the people wore mourning for a month, the bar for six weeks. In due time the leading men of the parish decided upon the monument which should mark to future generations the cold and narrow home of him who had been so warm in life, loving as few men had loved, exulted in the wide greatness of the empire he had created.

It bears this inscription:

TO THE MEMORY OF
ALEXANDER HAMILTON
THE CORPORATION OF TRINITY HAVE ERECTED THIS
MONUMENT IN TESTIMONY OF THEIR RESPECT FOR THE
PATRIOT OF INCORRUPTIBLE INTEGRITY THE SOLDIER OF
APPROVED VALOUR THE STATESMAN OF CONSUMMATE WISDOM
WHOSE TALENTS AND VIRTUES WILL BE ADMIRED BY GRATEFUL
POSTERITY LONG AFTER THIS MARBLE SHALL
HAVE MOULDERED TO DUST
HE DIED JULY 12TH 1804, AGED 47

The End

www.ingramcontent.com/pod-product-compliance
Lightning Source LLC
Chambersburg PA
CBHW021209090426
42740CB00006B/171